THE EUROPEAN UNION SERIES

General Editors: Neill Nugent, William E. Paterson, Vincent Wright

The European Union series is designed to provide an authoritative library on the European Union, ranging from general introductory texts to definitive assessments of key institutions and actors, policies and policy processes, and the role of member states.

Books in the series are written by leading scholars in their fields and reflect the most up-to-date research and debate. Particular attention is paid to accessibility and clear presentation for a wide audience of students, practitioners and interested general readers. The series consists of four major strands:

- General textbooks
- The major institutions and actors
- The main areas of policy
- The member states and the Union

The series editors are **Neill Nugent**, Professor of Politics and Jean Monnet Professor of European Integration, Manchester Metropolitan University, and **William E. Paterson**, Director of the Institute of German Studies, University of Birmingham.

Their co-editor until his death in July 1999, **Vincent Wright**, was a Fellow of Nuffield College, Oxford University. He played an immensely valuable role in the founding and development of *The European Union Series* and is greatly missed.

Feedback on the series and book proposals are always welcome and should be sent to Steven Kennedy, Palgrave Macmillan, Houndmills, Basingstoke, Hampshire RG21 6XS, UK, or by e-mail to s.kennedy@palgrave.com

---

General textbooks

Published

Desmond Dinan **Encyclopedia of the European Union**
[Rights: Europe only]

Desmond Dinan **Europe Recast: a History of European Union**
[Rights: Europe only]

Desmond Dinan **Ever Closer Union: An Introduction to European Integration (2nd edn)**
[Rights: World excluding North and South America, Philippines and Japan]

Simon Hix **The Political System of the European Union**

John McCormick **Understanding the European Union: A Concise Introduction (2nd edn)**

Brent F. Nelsen and Alexander Stubb **The European Union: Readings on the Theory and Practice of European Integration (3rd edn)**
[Rights: Europe only]

Neill Nugent (ed.) **European Union Enlargement**

Neill Nugent **The Government and Politics of the European Union (5th edn)**
[Rights: World excluding USA and dependencies and Canada]

John Peterson and Elizabeth Bomberg **Decision-making in the European Union**

Ben Rosamond **Theories of European Integration**

Forthcoming

Laurie Buonanno and Neill Nugent **Policies and Policy Processes of the European Union**

Mette Eilstrup Sangiovanni (ed.) **Debates on European Integration: A Reader**

Andrew Scott **The Political Economy of the European Union**

Philippa Sherrington **Understanding European Union Governance**

Series Standing Order (outside North America only)
ISBN 0–333–71695–7 hardback
ISBN 0–333–69352–3 paperback
Full details from www.palgrave.com

European Union Enlargement

Edited by

Neill Nugent

palgrave
macmillan

Published 2004 by
PALGRAVE MACMILLAN
Houndmills, Basingstoke, Hampshire RG21 6XS and
175 Fifth Avenue, New York, N.Y. 10010
Companies and representatives throughout the world

PALGRAVE MACMILLAN is the global academic imprint of the Palgrave
Macmillan division of St. Martin's Press, LLC and of Palgrave Macmillan Ltd.
Macmillan® is a registered trademark in the United States, United Kingdom
and other countries. Palgrave is a registered trademark in the European
Union and other countries.

ISBN 1–4039–1352–8 hardback
ISBN 1–4039–1353–6 paperback

This book is printed on paper suitable for recycling and made from fully
managed and sustained forest sources.

A catalogue record for this book is available from the British Library.

A catalog record for this book is available from the Library of Congress.

10   9   8   7   6   5   4   3   2   1
13   12   11   10   09   08   07   06   05   04

Printed and bound in Great Britain by
Creative Print & Design (Wales), Ebbw Vale

Contents

List of Figures, Tables and Boxes

Figures

Tables

Boxes

Preface

This book has its origins in Prague in January 2002. The original reason for my planning to be in Prague was to accompany students to EuroSim – the annual simulation of a European Union issue, which has been held for some years under the auspices of the Transatlantic Consortium for European Union Studies and Simulations (TACEUSS). However, some time before the Prague simulation it was agreed with TACEUSS colleagues that, in parallel with EuroSim, I would convene a small research workshop. The workshop would be attended by TACEUSS faculty and would be on the same subject as EuroSim 2002 – the enlargement of the European Union.

Enlargement has been the most important issue facing the European Union since at least the mid-1990s. From having been a West European organization that had enlarged only gradually and in stages – from the original six member states, to nine, 10, 12, and then 15 – the Union found itself faced in the mid-1990s with 13 applications. Three of these applications – from Cyprus, Malta and Turkey – were from the south of the continent and had been on the table for some years, whilst the other 10 were new and were from former communist countries in Central and Eastern Europe. The Union thus had to deal from the mid-1990s with both an unprecedented number and variety of countries seeking membership.

With the exception of Turkey, by 1997 the Union had accepted all of the applications in principle. This resulted in accession negotiations being opened with six of the applicants in 1998, and with the remaining six in 2000. At the December 2002 European Council meeting it was decided that the negotiations had been completed with 10 of the 12 and that they could join the Union in May 2004. It was also decided that the two countries with which negotiations had not been completed – Bulgaria and Romania – would probably be able to join in 2007, and furthermore that negotiations would be opened with Turkey in 2005 if it continued on its path of democratization and liberalization.

Enlargement is thus of immense importance for the European Union. Moreover, it is an issue that will continue to dominate deliberations in and about the Union for many years to come. It will do so for at least three reasons. First, there will be many 'settling in' problems associated with the 2004 enlargement. Second, even after the 2004 'big bang' enlargement and the projected 'mini enlargement' of 2007, the Turkish application will raise numerous and unprecedented challenges and will take many years before coming to fruition. And third, there are still more countries that either wish to join the accession queue, including several in South Eastern Europe, or may consider joining it at some future date, including Norway and Switzerland.

This importance of the subject of enlargement, coupled with the considerable interest in and knowledge of the subject that was displayed by the twenty or so faculty who attended the Prague workshop, led me to propose a book on the subject to Palgrave Macmillan. I was, of course, aware that other books on enlargement already existed, but there seemed to be space for a book that would be new in at least two ways. First, it would be completed when the outcomes of the key Copenhagen summit and the various ratifications of the Treaty of Accession were known. Second, whereas other books on enlargement have focused primarily, and often exclusively, on the implications of enlargement for the applicants, this book would focus on the implications of enlargement for the Union.

The 2002 workshop was small-scale, but nonetheless eight of the 20 who were present have contributed to this book – Michael Ambrosi, Laurie Buonanno, Michele Chang, Ann Deakin, Janet Mather, John Occihipinti, Eleanor Zeff and myself. The other chapters have been written by people who were approached because I was aware they had a relevant knowledge and expertize. I am most grateful to all the contributors for their chapters.

I am grateful also to William Paterson, my co-editor of Palgrave Macmillan's *European Union Series*. He provided valuable advice in the early stages of the book's development and acted as the discussant on a panel at the 2003 Nashville conference of the European Union Studies Association where drafts of four of the book's chapters were presented – those by Chang, Mather, Occhipinti and Zeff.

As always, I am indebted to Steven Kennedy of Palgrave Macmillan for providing constant encouragement and insightful advice.

Events associated with enlargement are, of course, constantly unfolding. Updating information on key events, which will supplement this book, will be provided on the Palgrave Macmillan European Union webpage at www.palgrave.com/politics/eu

NEILL NUGENT

List of Abbreviations

ACP	African, Caribbean and Pacific Countries
AFSJ	Area of Freedom, Security and Justice
AKP	Justice and Development Party (of Turkey)
CAP	Common Agricultural Policy
CCP	Common Commercial Policy
CCT	Common Customs Tariff
CEEC	Central and Eastern European Country
CEPOL	European Police College
CET	Common External Tariff
CFP	Common Fisheries Policy
CFSP	Common Foreign and Security Policy
CIS	Customs Information System
CMEA	Council of Mutual Economic Assistance
COPS	Political and Security Committee
CoR	Committee of the Regions
COREPER	Committee of Permanent Representatives
CSCE	Conference on Security and Cooperation in Europe
CSF	Community Support Framework
DG	Directorate General
EAGGF	European Agricultural Guidance and Guarantee Fund
EBRD	European Bank for Reconstruction and Development
EC	European Community
ECB	European Central Bank
ECOFIN	Council of Economic and Finance Ministers
ECSC	European Coal and Steel Community
EDC	European Defence Community
EDF	European Development Fund
EEA	European Economic Area
EEB	European Environmental Bureau
EEC	European Economic Community
EFTA	European Free Trade Association
EIB	European Investment Bank
EMS	European Monetary System
EMU	European Monetary Union
EP	European Parliament
EPC	European Political Cooperation
ERDF	European Regional Development Fund
ERM	Exchange Rate Mechanism
ERRF	European Rapid Reaction Force
ESC	Economic and Social Committee

ESCB	European System of Central Banks
ESDI	European Security Defence Identity
ESF	European Social Fund
ESDP	European Security and Defence Policy
EU	European Union
EUMC	European Union Military Committee
Euratom	European Atomic Energy Community
EUR-OP	Office for Official Publications of the European Communities
FDI	foreign direct investment
FRY	Former Republic of Yugoslavia
FTA	Free Trade Area
G7/8	Group of Seven/Eight
GATT	General Agreement on Tariffs and Trade
GDP	gross domestic product
GDR	German Democratic Republic
GNI	gross national income
GNP	gross national product
GSP	Generalized System of Preferences
IGC	Intergovernmental Conference
IMF	International Monetary Fund
IMP	Integrated Mediterranean Programme
IPR	intellectual property rights
ISPA	Instrument for Structural Policies for Pre-Accession
JHA	Justice and Home Affairs
LI	liberal intergovernmentalism
MEP	Member of the European Parliament
MFN	most favoured nation
MLG	multi-level governance
NATO	North Atlantic Treaty Organization
NCB	National Central Bank
NGO	non-governmental organization
NPAA	National Programme for the Adoption of the *Acquis*
NTB	non-tariff barrier (to trade)
ODA	official development assistance
OECD	Organisation for Economic Co-operation and Development
OJ	*Official Journal of the European Communities*
OLAF	European Anti-Fraud Office
OMC	open method of coordination
OSCE	Organisation for Security and Co-operation in Europe
PDB	Preliminary Draft Budget
PES	Party of European Socialists
PHARE	Programme of Community Aid for Central and Eastern European Countries

PTA	preferential trade arrangement
QMV	qualified majority vote/voting
R & TD	Research and Technological Development
RTA	regional trade arrangement
SAPARD	Standard Accession Programme
SCA	Special Committee on Agriculture
SEA	Single European Act
SEM	Single European Market
SGP	Stability and Growth Pact
SIS	Schengen Information System
SME	small and medium sized enterprise
TACIS	Programme for Technical Assistance to the Independent States of the Former Soviet Union and Mongolia
TEC	Treaty Establishing the European Community
TEU	Treaty on European Union
UK	United Kingdom
UN	United Nations
USA	United States of America
VAT	value added tax
WEU	Western European Union
WTO	World Trade Organization

Notes on the Contributors

Gerhard Michael Ambrosi is Jean Monnet Professor of Economics at the University of Trier, Germany.

Clive Archer is Research Professor in Politics at Manchester Metropolitan University.

Nickos Baltas is Professor of Economics and Jean Monnet Professor of European Economics at the Athens University of Economics and Business and also President of the Hellenic University Association for European Studies.

Michael Baun is Professor of International Relations at Valdosta State University, Georgia.

Laurie Buonanno is Associate Professor of Political Science at the State University of New York, College at Fredonia.

Maurizio Carbone is a PhD candidate at the University of Pittsburgh and *intra muros* consultant at the European Commission, DG Development.

Michele Chang is Assistant Professor in Political Science at Colgate University.

Ann Deakin is Associate Professor in Geosciences at the State University of New York, College at Fredonia.

Heather Grabbe is Deputy Director of the Centre for European Reform, London, and a Non-Stipendary Junior Research Fellow of Wolfson College, Oxford University.

Adrian van den Hoven is an adviser in the external relations department of the Union of Industrial and Employers' Confederations of Europe (UNICE) in Brussels.

Janet Mather is Senior Lecturer in Politics at Manchester Metropolitan University.

Lee Miles is Senior Lecturer in Politics, Research Director and Deputy Head of the Department of Politics and International Studies at the University of Hull.

Neill Nugent is Professor of Politics and Jean Monnet Professor of European Integration at Manchester Metropolitan University.

John D. Occhipinti is Associate Professor of Political Science, Canisius College in Buffalo.

David Phinnemore is Senior Lecturer in European Integration in the School of Politics and International Studies, Queen's University Belfast.

Eleanor E. Zeff is Assistant Professor of Politics and International Relations at Drake University in Des Moines, Iowa.

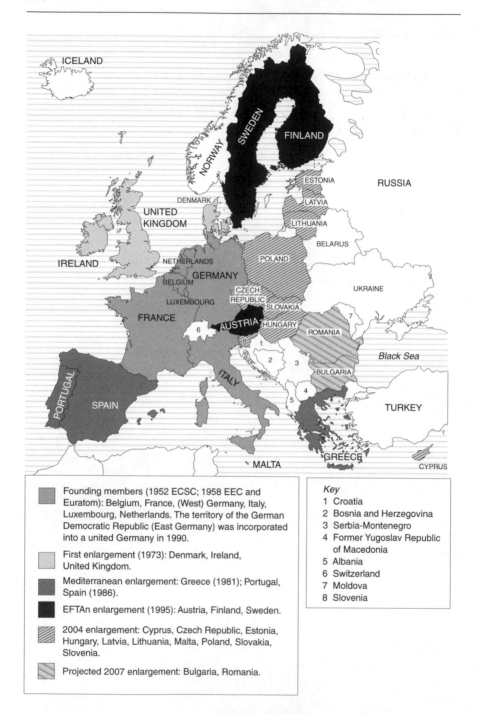

Founding members (1952 ECSC; 1958 EEC and Euratom): Belgium, France, (West) Germany, Italy, Luxembourg, Netherlands. The territory of the German Democratic Republic (East Germany) was incorporated into a united Germany in 1990.

First enlargement (1973): Denmark, Ireland, United Kingdom.

Mediterranean enlargement: Greece (1981); Portugal, Spain (1986).

EFTAn enlargement (1995): Austria, Finland, Sweden.

2004 enlargement: Cyprus, Czech Republic, Estonia, Hungary, Latvia, Lithuania, Malta, Poland, Slovakia, Slovenia.

Projected 2007 enlargement: Bulgaria, Romania.

Key
1 Croatia
2 Bosnia and Herzegovina
3 Serbia-Montenegro
4 Former Yugoslav Republic of Macedonia
5 Albania
6 Switzerland
7 Moldova
8 Slovenia

Map of the European Union and Neighbouring European States

Chapter 1

The EU and the 10 + 2 Enlargement Round: Opportunities and Challenges

NEILL NUGENT

Introduction

Enlargement has long featured prominently and consistently on the European Community/European Union agenda. Indeed, since the Community was founded in the 1950s there seldom has been a time when at least one, and usually more than one, of the following circumstances has not applied: membership applications have been known to be pending; Community/Union institutions and member states have been considering whether applications are acceptable in principle; accession negotiations have been in progress; and new members have been in the course of being accommodated and settling in. Enlargement is thus best viewed not as series of discrete events but rather as an ongoing process.

As an ongoing process, it is thus the case that although enlargement has dominated the EU agenda in recent years it is hardly in itself a new phenomenon. What is new, however, is the scale of the enlargement process that has been underway since, in the mid-1990s, 10 Central Eastern European countries (CEECs) applied for EU membership and so joined Cyprus, Malta, and Turkey, which already had membership applications on the table. The 10 CEECs were Bulgaria, the Czech Republic, Hungary, Estonia, Latvia, Lithuania, Poland, Slovakia, Slovenia and Romania. In December 2002, the leaders of the existing EU member states decided that Cyprus, Malta and all of the CEECs apart from Bulgaria and Romania had met the EU's membership conditions and could become EU members on 1 May 2004. The leaders also decided that Bulgaria and Romania could join in 2007, provided that by that time they meet the membership conditions. As for Turkey – the only one of the applicants with which accession negotiations had not been opened – a very strong indication was given that as long as it continued with its internal reform programme the leaders would authorise the opening of accession negotiations at their December 2004 meeting.

1

Because of its dominance by CEECs, the enlargement round that began in the mid-1990s is often referred to as the Eastern enlargement. However, although this designation has the merit of being short and snappy, it often results in the two Mediterranean islands of Cyprus and Malta being overlooked. The term most used in this book is, therefore, the 10 + 2 enlargement round.

The 10 + 2 round is quite momentous. It is so partly because of the sheer number of applicants involved. The largest number of applicants the EU has faced in any single enlargement round before is four, in the enlargement rounds of the early 1970s and early-to-mid-1990s. In the 10 + 2 round that number has been 12, or 13 if Turkey is included. It is momentous also because of the opportunities and challenges it offers to the EU. These opportunities and challenges constitute the main focus of this book. The focus, in other words, is not on individual states involved in the 10 + 2 round – be they pre-enlargement members or new members – but rather is on enlargement and the EU itself.

The chapters of the book fall into three broad groups. The early chapters – from 1 to 5 – examine the contextual and historical background of the 10 + 2 round. Chapters 6 to 17 consider the impact of the round on key social, political, economic and external dimensions and features of the EU. And chapters 18 and 19 take an overview, by analyzing in Chapter 18 the usefulness of integration theory in helping to explain the enlargement process and by considering in Chapter 19 the overall implications of the 10 + 2 round for the EU.

This opening chapter has two main parts. The first part examines why the EU has been willing to enlarge, and in so doing stresses the opportunities offered by enlargement. The second part analyses the challenges enlargement has posed to the EU

Why Has the EU Been Willing to Enlarge?

By the time of the 1995 enlargement – when Austria, Finland and Sweden joined – the EU was already a well established and, on most counts, highly successful organization. States that in previous times had been, at best, deeply suspicious of each other and, at worst, had engaged in hostilities against each other were, within the EU, not only working closely together but were integrating in a wide range of political and economic activities. A true security community existed between the member states, with all being well-established liberal democracies and with differences between them arising primarily over 'bread-and-butter' matters rather than deriving from deep ideological or territorial questions. Such differences as did exist were being resolved for the most part through give-and-take bargaining by national officials and politicians working in a mixture of supranational and intergovernmental decision-making contexts.

As well as providing a framework for steady and understanding political relationships between its member states, the EU was also successful in economic terms. By the early 1990s the Single European Market (SEM) had been largely achieved, all member states were conducting at least 60 per cent of their trade with the rest of the EU, and growth and prosperity were rising at levels that probably would not have been attained if the EU did not exist.

The accession of Austria, Finland and Sweden was not seen as posing any significant threat to this success of the EU. All were model liberal democratic states with well functioning market economies and per capita incomes significantly above the EU average. Unlike the Mediterranean states that joined the European Community (EC) in the 1980s, they would be net contributors to the EU budget. Throughout the period of their accession process, the general perception was that the three states that joined in 1995 would be welcome additions to the EU and would strengthen the organization in important respects.

Such perceptions have been by no means as universally held in respect of enlarging the EU beyond its 1995 boundaries. Increasing the size of the EU to approaching 30 member states, and in time perhaps more, has been seen as being highly problematical. The main reason for this is that the 10 + 2 states and Turkey are not 'ordinary' applicants, like those countries which joined the EU in the 1995 round. Rather, collectively, and in some cases individually, they have posed major difficulties and challenges for the EU. The nature of these difficulties and challenges are set out later in this chapter and in subsequent chapters, but at their heart have been two sets of concerns. On the one hand have been concerns about the capacities of many of the CEECs to function, for at least some years to come, as effective and efficient Union members. On the other hand have been concerns about whether the Union has the ability to absorb new members without undermining its effectiveness and efficiency. Taken together, these concerns have given rise to considerable doubts in the pre-enlargement 15 member states of the EU (hereafter referred to as the EU-15) about the wisdom of the 10 + 2 enlargement process: might admitting the applicants not weaken the Union and even endanger its nature and threaten its achievements?

Given these concerns, why then has the EU been willing to enlarge? Broadly speaking, two types of explanation have been advanced in the academic literature, one based on a rationalist perspective and the other on a sociological/constructivist approach (for a review of theoretical debates on enlargement, see Schimmelfennig and Sedelmeier, 2002).

Rationalist explanations

For those taking a rationalist perspective, the explanation for why the EU has been willing to enlarge is to be found essentially in 'hard-headed' calculations by governments of the EU-15 states. These calculations have been focused around two main considerations: the promotion of security and economic opportunities.

The promotion of security

Since the early 1990s, most collective EU statements and individual statements by EU leaders that have covered the rationale of enlarging the EU to CEECs have been littered with references to 'peace', stability', and 'security'. For example, the Conclusions of the 1994 Essen European Council referred to the accession of CEECs as helping to ensure 'the lasting peace and stability of the European continent and neighbouring regions' (European Council, 1994b: 3). As such, enlargement has been seen as furthering EU foreign policy goals by bringing the continent together on a more stable and secure basis.

The security justification of enlargement has been not so much a 'hard' security justification – the parallel enlargement of the North Atlantic Treaty Organization (NATO) has been more responsible for the protection of Europe from military threats and for enabling Europe to deal with problems that might require a major military response. Rather, it has been concerned more with 'soft' security – that is, with creating a framework in which countries can reduce uncertainties in their relationships by setting them on a more solid footing, by working closely with one another, and thereby by building understandings and confidence. This has been seen as being both desirable in itself and as helping to provide a measure of protection from such possible security threats as the (re)fragmentation of Europe, the (re)emergence of illiberal political forces, and the rise of nationalism.

A particular theme of the security justification of enlargement has been that EU membership will help CEECs to establish themselves as solid liberal democratic political systems. The EU-15 – and especially states such as Finland, Germany and Austria, which border CEECs – have been anxious to be protected against domestic political instability in Central and Eastern Europe, for this could have considerable security implications for Western Europe. EU membership for CEECs should, it has been thought, assist CEECs to consolidate their newly based democratic systems by bringing them inside 'the democratic fold'. Moreover, it opens them up to the possibility of sanctions if there is any democratic 'slippage', for Articles 6 and 7 of the Treaty on European Union (TEU) provide for suspension of EU rights if a member state is in serious and persistent breach of the Union's founding principles of liberty, democracy, respect for human rights and fundamental freedoms, and the rule of law.

Another important aspect of the soft security justification for enlargement is that the end of the Cold War and the fluidity that has thereby followed in Central and Eastern Europe has exacerbated Europe's problems with organized crime, illegal drugs, and the unauthorized movement of peoples across borders. Since these problems are transnational in nature and require a concerted approach amongst governments to tackle them, it is argued that it is better to have CEECs inside the EU helping to solve the problems on a common basis rather than outside, where they are likely to be aggrieved and not overly helpful.

Economic opportunities

Enlargement offers opportunities for modest economic gains for the EU-15. The main reason it does so is that the size of the EU's internal market will be considerably increased, with the accession of the 10 + 2 countries increasing the EU's population by some 106 million people and the accession of Turkey increasing it by another 65 or so million. The benefits come not so much from trade liberalization in the new EU, for most tariffs and other trade barriers between the EU-15 and the new member states were removed in the early-to-mid 1990s with the consequence that bi-lateral EU-CEEC trade has since been increasing at double digit rates on an annual basis. Rather, it will come from the increased business confidence that will stem from the creation of the expanded common regulatory framework, from the increased size of the area in which similar macroeconomic and financial policies are being pursued, from the investment incentives provided by countries that have generally well-educated populations and that are on the very edge of becoming knowledge-based economies, and from the production and marketing opportunities arising from the fact that since the early 1990s the economies of the CEECs have, on average, been growing at a markedly faster rate than the average in the EU-15. It is impossible to be precise as to how much enlargement will bolster the overall economy of the EU-15 but, as many observers have noted, economic integration does customarily raise overall GDP levels by promoting trade, investment, competitiveness and economies of scale (see, for example, Grabbe, 2001: 22). Leaving aside the gains that have already accrued from the liberalization of trading conditions, a 1–2 per cent total increase in EU-15 GDP in the first few years after enlargement is a common estimate.

Enlargement undoubtedly offers proportionately more economic opportunities to the acceding states than it does to the EU-15. Because the new member states are starting from a lower economic base and because their economies are small when compared to that of the EU-15 – their total GDP amounts to only about 6 per cent of EU-15 GDP – they potentially have much more to gain. They do so both directly from increased trade and, less directly but no less significantly, from the improvements to their economic base that is offered by increased investment, technology transfer, and skills enhancement. Many predictions have been made of the likely size of the impact of enlargement on acceding states: the European Commission, for example, has estimated an annual figure of between 1.3 per cent and 2.1 per cent in the initial years of membership (European Commission, 2001d).

* * *

Of course, there have been variations between the EU-15 in respect of the extent to which, and the intensity with which, the motivations for enlargement outlined above have been felt. The EU-15 are not equally advantaged by enlargement, nor are they equally positioned in terms of the disadvantages and risks that enlargement brings. This has resulted in variations between the EU-15 in their attitudes towards the enlargement process. The EU-15 states that have tended to be the strongest advocates and supporters of enlargement have been those which:

- are geographically close to the acceding states – for they are the most likely to acquire trade and security benefits (for discussion on this, see especially Chapters 5, 10, 15 and 16)
- will not incur major budgetary losses – the accession of relatively poor member states, some of them with large agricultural sectors, has, from the very beginning of the accession process, concerned the major EU-15 beneficiaries of the Common Agricultural Policy (CAP) and the Union's Structural Funds (see Chapter 12)
- will not lose influence – as France in particular is likely to do – from the anticipated geo-political shift westwards (see Chapter 9).

The major beneficiary – and hence an arch supporter of enlargement – is Germany, primarily because of its geographical position and the economic potential that enlargement to the east offers to it. Another member state with potentially much to gain, though not so much in a structural sense, is the UK, which sees a larger and more heterogeneous EU as being likely to assist the aim that has long been a central feature of UK European policy, namely slowing down some aspects of the integration process. The member states with least to gain from CEEC accessions are those less-prosperous states on the EU's western side – Ireland, Spain and Portugal – that are not only unlikely to gain much from the larger market but are threatened with reductions in EU budgetary support.

As for attitudes towards particular applicants, from an early stage of the accession process there was more support for the early membership of countries such as Hungary and the Czech Republic, which are relatively advanced politically and economically, than for Bulgaria or Romania, which are the least advanced of the CEEC 10. Beyond this general support, some applicants came to virtually have patrons amongst the member states. For example, as is shown in Chapter 3, Germany was a very strong supporter of Poland, the Scandinavian member states promoted the three Baltic applicants, and Greece sponsored Cyprus.

Sociological/constructivist explanations

Sociologists, and more particularly constructivists, believe that the actions of political actors such as national governments cannot be wholly explained in rational, egoistical or instrumental terms. In trying to explain EU enlargement, the stances adopted by existing member states are viewed as not being driven, or at least not completely driven, by 'objective' national political and economic situations and needs. Rather, the stances are seen as being socially constructed. Taking this a stage further, constructivists see the nature and outcome of international interactions as being shaped largely by social identities, norms and values. This means that the decision of the EU to enlarge is to be explained largely in social terms.

That it must be explained in this way is seen as being necessary because although enlargement unquestionably offers opportunities for the EU-15, it also, as both this chapter and other chapters of the book show, presents them with stiff challenges and unwanted consequences. An overall cost–benefit analysis does not clearly and indisputably show that enlargement is beneficial either for the EU as a whole or for most of the EU-15 states. Certainly, if attention is focused just on the most measurable dimension of the consequences of enlargement – economic implications – a few EU-15 states will be net gainers, but for many the balance sheet will be not much affected and for a few it may even be in the red. And enlargement clearly does create risks for the EU: to its internal cohesion and functioning, to its security and borders if the new neighbours to the east and south prove to be unstable, and possibly to its legitimacy if enlargement makes for a more fractious, divided and less-effective Union. Surely, many sociologists and constructivists ask, if rational and utilitarian calculations were the sole guides to the actions of the EU-15 in respect of enlargement, countries like Spain and Ireland would have vetoed the exercise.

Interesting work in dealing with this perceived weakness in rationalist explanations has been undertaken by, amongst others, Frank Schimmelfennig (2001 and 2002). Drawing heavily, though not exclusively, on a constructivist perspective, Schimmelfennig takes as his central starting point in seeking an explanation for EU enlargement the fact that those countries that the EU has been willing to accept as members have displayed democratic values, respect for the rule of law, pluralist political and economic systems, and liberal domestic and foreign policies. What is the significance of this? In a comparative study of the EU, NATO and the Council of Europe, Schimmelfennig put it this way:

States that share the collective identity and have adopted the values and norms of an international community will also seek to become members of the organizations that represent it. The international organizations, in turn, will admit those states that have adopted the community values and norms and are therefore regarded as legitimate members . . . In sum, the extension of the regional organization will tend to be congruent with the extension of the international community on which it is based. (Schimmelfennig, 2002: 599)

On this basis, EU enlargement is, he argues, 'not *sui generis* but appears to follow the same logic as the enlargement of other Western organizations' (*ibid*: 623).

In another study, Schimmelfennig (2001) explores why, given that most existing member states had reservations about allowing CEECs to become members, enlargement still went ahead. In his view, the post-Cold War position in Europe certainly justified the EU in contracting association agreements with CEECs (that is, agreements involving a range of close political and economic ties), but not, given all the difficulties CEECs would create, admitting them to membership. The explanation why admittance was granted, he argues, is found in 'rhetorical action', which describes how actors come 'to focus on their collective identity and honor their obligations as community members' (p. 63). In the EU context, the collective identity and the obligations are seen by Schimmelfennig as involving a commitment to the integration of all liberal European states. As soon as some EU-15 states (for quite rational reasons) began to press for enlargement to CEECs, other, less enthusiastic, states became swept up in a rhetorical commitment, which led to a 'rhetorical entrapment' involving a process of virtual drift toward a policy commitment they did not at heart support: 'By argumentatively "entrapping" the opponents of a firm commitment to Eastern enlargement, they [the supporters of enlargement] brought about a collective outcome that would not have been expected given the constellation of powers and interests' (p.77).

Just as Schimmelfennig criticizes rationalist explanations for not explaining how enlargement 'drivers' managed to persuade enlargement 'brakemen', so can constructivist explanations be criticized. For example, at a theoretical level they can be accused of taking too narrow a perspective when used alone. Is it, for instance, really the case, as Schimmelfennig says when summarizing the constructivist perspective, that 'sharing a community of values and norms with outside states is both necessary and sufficient for their admission to the organization' (2001: 61)? If this is so, why, for instance, has the EU not amended the Common Fisheries Policy so as to enable Iceland to become a member state? At an empirical level, constructivists can be accused of interpreting evidence in a manner that suits their case. For example, the way in which Schimmelfennig presents the extent to which existing member states were 'drivers' and 'brakemen' on enlargement can be disputed, especially in regard to the extent to which some states were resolved that enlargement should not proceed at all. Certainly some states harboured reservations about enlargement, but all recognized that there were general advantages to be gained.

But that values have been of at least some importance in promoting the enlargement process seems indisputable. The key values, however, may have been ones not so much of liberal-democratic political rectitude but more ones of, as Sjursen (2002: 508) puts it, 'kinship-based duty'. On this basis, enlargement is to be understood, in part at least, in terms of the existence of a community-based identity 'that drives enlargement towards Eastern Europe and motivates the EU to accept its costs. It shows that the decision on enlargement is the result of an understanding of who the Europeans are and what it means to be European' (Sjursen, 2002: 508). This is not to suggest that the notion of what is European is forever fixed and cannot shift. But it is to affirm, as Sjursen puts it, 'that in order to trigger a decision to enlarge, something more than instrumental calculations and something less than a selfless concern for human rights has been at play' (Sjursen, 2002: 509).

A key concern that most certainly has been at play is that many EU decision-makers – in member states and in EU institutions – have felt a responsibility, amounting almost to a moral duty, to assist CEECs. When the CEECs rid themselves of the communist system Western Europe had so opposed for the 40 plus years of the Cold War, many EU policy practitioners were quick to argue that the EC/EU virtually had an obligation to help CEECs to realize their ambitions to become prosperous, democratic, and mainstream European states. As Sedelmeir has shown, 'The discourse of a collective EU identity, characterized by a "responsibilty" towards the CEECs, became a central aspect of EU policy' (Sedelmeir, 2000: 269). As this discourse built, so did EU states gradually and incrementally move towards a commitment to admitting CEECs to membership. The strength of the sentiments contained in the discourse – that it would be not only irresponsible and churlish but forgetful and unprincipled not to try and accommodate CEEC needs – perhaps has weakened as time has passed since the collapse of communism and the Kohl–Mitterrand generation of EU leaders has been replaced. However, the essence of the collective identity established in the early post-communist years has remained. Later EU leaders may have been less influenced by the somewhat intangible considerations of the discourse than their predecessors and have taken an increasingly calculating view of the benefits and costs of enlargement. But their commitment to the project has not seriously wavered and there can be little doubt that feelings do still persist that Western Europe 'owes' something to the CEECs for the price they paid for their years of 'occupation' and that a (re)united Europe is in itself a good thing.

The Challenge of Enlargement for the EU

The 10 + 2 enlargement round has posed and still poses many challenges for the EU. Some of these challenges arise solely from enlargement whilst others have different roots but have come to present themselves in altered, and usually more complex, guises as a result of enlargement.

It is useful and convenient to group the main challenges under six broad headings.

The identity problem

There is an extensive debate in the academic literature about whether the EU can be said to be based on a collective identity and what the implications of the existence or absence of such an identity are for the stability and effectiveness of the EU as a political system (see, for example, Smith, 1992; Howe, 1995).

It is not difficult to make out a case that no collective identity exists and that this is a key reason why the EU system so often creaks. There is, after all, much diversity amongst the peoples and governments of the EU-15 states: diversity based on language, religious background, political ideology, and, above all, national and cultural histories and interests. Does not this diversity, especially that stemming from nationhood, make it hard for EU citizens to identify with one another and with the EU polity? Insofar as any sort of collective identity can be said to exist is it based on anything more than but the loosest of generally shared attachments and values, related perhaps to notions of the desirability of democracy and individual liberty? And does this absence of a firm common identity not make it extremely difficult to construct and maintain a strong and fully effective political system?

Whether widening of the EU will dilute such identity as the EU-15 can claim to have depends largely on how strong or weak the pre-enlargement identity is perceived to be. If it is confined to little more than vague attachments to democratic values then arguably there is not much room for further weakening. But even if this is the case, widening still may be seen as a threat because it may be judged to end, or at least seriously endanger, any prospect of a genuine EU identity being forged, be it through such symbols as the flag and the anthem or through policy effectiveness. This is because the CEECs, and even more so Turkey and potential applicants in south-east Europe, are, in important respects, very different from the EU's current member states. For those who aspire to the creation of a federal Europe, this is a major concern. For those who have no such aspirations, it provides a real opportunity to slow the pace of integrationist advance.

Key identity issues arising from enlargement are explored in depth in Chapter 6.

Institutions and decision-making processes

At the 1993 Copenhagen summit EU leaders laid down three sets of conditions applicant states would have to meet if they wished to be considered for membership (see pp. 35–6). It is often forgotten that a fourth condition for enlargement was also laid down at Copenhagen, though this condition was for the EU itself:

> The Union's capacity to absorb new members, while maintaining the momentum of European integration, is also an important consideration in the general interest of both the Union and the candidate countries. (European Council, 1993: 12)

This condition generally has been taken as meaning that the EU's institutions and its decision-making systems must be adapted so as to accommodate new member states in a way that will not in itself produce a slow down in the integration process.

Regarding the adaptation of the institutions, prior to the 10 + 2 round acceding states have been accommodated simply by allocating them an appropriate number of votes and places. So, new member states have been given a voting weight in the Council, a number of Members of the European Parliament (MEPs), one Commissioner (except in the cases of the UK and Spain which, because they are large states, were allocated two), a judge in the European Court of Justice and (since the 1995 enlargement round) in the Court of First Instance, and so on. This approach has, however, not been so easy to use in the 10 + 2 enlargement round, partly because some institutions – notably the Commission and the EP – were seen as already becoming too large and partly because of the sheer number of applicants.

As for adapting decision-making systems, since the time of the Spanish and Portuguese accessions in the mid-1980s it has been recognized that bringing in new member states makes quick and efficient decision-making more difficult unless policy and law-making processes are streamlined. This perceived problem is part of a concern that widening (accepting new member states) might threaten deepening (furthering institutional and policy integration). In consequence, treaty reforms have made some provisions to avoid the possibility of decision-making deadlocks – notably by increasing the number of decisions that can be taken by qualified majority vote (QMV) in the Council of Ministers. Because of the scale of the 10 + 2 round and because also incremental reform was seen by many as having gone almost as far as it usefully could, there were calls from many quarters from the mid-1990s for there to be a thorough overhaul of the decision-making systems before any more members joined. However, in the event, the debate between the national governments in the two Intergovernmental Conferences that deliberated on the institutional and decision-making reforms that would be required by the 10 + 2 round focused primarily, as previously, on further reducing the national veto in the Council by extending QMV.

The solutions that were eventually agreed to the challenges of institutional and decision-making adaptation are outlined in Chapter 3 and examined at length in Chapter 8. The widening/deepening issue is explored in Chapters 4 and 5.

Internal dynamics and balances

The number and variety of states acceding in the 10 + 2 round has raised questions about how the EU's internal political dynamics and balances will be affected by enlargement. Will the EU, it is asked, not become more internally divided into groupings of member states than ever before? Divided, for example, between the economically modernized and affluent on the one hand and the economically underdeveloped and poor on the other; between core member states and periphery states; between old and new members; between eurozone and non eurozone members; and, in policy areas ranging from taxation harmonization to defence integration, between the able and/or willing and the unable and/or unwilling.

Clearly, there is some potential for increased internal differentiation. But the impact of this should not be exaggerated. One reason for this is that there have always been differences between EU member states, yet EU processes – though slow and difficult at times – have not been brought to a standstill. The fact is that internal EU dynamics have, for the most part, not rotated around fixed internal majority or minority power blocs or coalitions, but rather around viewpoints, alliances and coalitions that have shifted according to issues. In only a very few issue areas have coalitions between member states been reasonably fixed, as, for example, with re-distributional issues, where less prosperous states have usually allied with one another, and with proposals for CAP reform which have produced loose north/south and reformer/consolidator alliances.

Another reason for not exaggerating the impact of enlargement on increased differentiation is that the new member states do not constitute a homogeneous bloc, though the CEECs are sometimes portrayed as doing so. This suggests that, as in the EU-15, most alliances in the expanded EU will be essentially short-term in character, constituted in response to particular circumstances and issues. So, for example, Poland may well link up with the UK in opposing EU-wide tax harmonization measures but part company from it on external trade policy by adopting a more protectionist stance.

In sum, it can therefore be anticipated, as is shown in Chapter 9, that internal dynamics and balances will be disturbed by enlargement but probably not undermined fundamentally by it. Certainly there will be a further decline in the formerly pivotal role of the Franco–German axis. Perhaps there may be more large-state–small-state confrontations, at least on institutional issues: when all 10 + 2 states have joined the EU, 19 of the then 27 member states will have a population of less than 12 million (Archer and Nugent, 2002: 4–5). On budgetary matters and re-distributional policies, CEECs may well form alliances both amongst themselves and with poorer EU-15 states. And on CAP issues, many CEECs may band together to press for more funds to be directed towards them, but link with some EU-15 states, especially France, to resist pressures for fundamental reform of the CAP system.

The economy and related policy difficulties

Though the accession of CEECs, and perhaps in time Turkey, creates enormous potential market opportunities for EU-15 states, it also creates considerable economic difficulties. It does so for three main reasons.

First, although the accession of the 10 + 2 increases the size of both the EU's population and territory by around one-third, the size of the EU's GDP increases by only about 5 per cent (a little higher if exchange rate misalignments are factored in) and its per capita GDP drops by about 18 per cent. With the exceptions of Cyprus and Slovenia, in 2003 all applicants had a GDP per head lower than that of the EU's poorest member state, Greece. Moreover, all applicants were below the EU average, with eight (Bulgaria, Estonia, Latvia, Lithuania, Poland, Romania, Slovakia, and Turkey) at less than 50 per cent of the average and three (Bulgaria, Romania and Turkey) at less than 30 per cent (figures accessed from the EU's Eurostat Office). Overall, in 2003 the 10 + 2 states had a GDP per head of approximately 40 per cent of the EU-15 – as compared with the average of 70 per cent per head for Spain and Portugal, with which comparisons are often made, when they acceded.

Bringing less prosperous states into the EU necessarily brings with it pressures, and, many feel, obligations, for generous redistributive policies to be adopted to assist these states. In particular, enlargement has brought the size and use of the EU's cohesion policies and of the funds most associated with them – the European Regional Development Fund (ERDF), the European Social Fund (ESF), and the Cohesion Fund – that together account for over 35 per cent of the EU's budget, sharply into focus. It has done so because the need to use these funds to assist CEECs, and the fact that under unreformed rules new member states would be major beneficiaries of the funds, has been recognized from the outset of the enlargement process. However, it has also been clear from the outset that existing beneficiaries of the funds – Greece, Ireland, Portugal and Spain, in particular – would be anxious to ensure that a consequence of their supporting CEEC accessions would not be a significant reduction in the assistance they themselves were receiving from the funds. This situation combined to suggest one of three, or some combination of three, options to the EU in the pre-accession period: a significant increase in overall expenditure on structural operations; reform of the funds so that payments would be much more targeted on poorer and more needy areas; giving acceding states in the early years of their membership less favourable treatment than EU-15 states. The approach that was eventually agreed was based mainly on the third option, with payments to new member states planned to be both capped and phased.

Second, the CAP, which accounts for around 45 per cent of the EU's budget, has been a major problem, for most CEECs have relatively large, but inefficient, agricultural sectors. Whereas, as Appendix 1 shows, agriculture accounts for less than 5 per cent of EU-15 employment, it accounts in Poland, for example, for around 19 per cent and in Romania for 44 per cent. In total, enlargement to the CEECs will more than double the size of the EU's agricultural labour force, increase its agricultural area by about half, but raise its output by only about 12 per cent.

A consequence of this is that the CAP posed problems to the EU-15 that were similar to those faced in respect of cohesion spending. In essence, three policy options had to be considered: greatly increase overall CAP spending; radically overhaul the CAP so that the general level of support funding was drastically reduced and/or support was more tightly directed; be less generous to new member states than to existing states. As with cohesion spending, the solution adopted drew mainly from the third option, with CAP support for the new members to be gradually phased-in up to 2013.

The settlements on structural operations and the CAP were thus hardly favourable from the viewpoint of the new member states. The EU-15 were just not willing to countenance a significant increase to the overall size of the EU's budget to prepare the applicants for enlargement or to support them after enlargement. Nor were the existing beneficiaries of the Structural Funds and the CAP willing to forego their allocations in favour of the newcomers. At the 1999 Berlin European Council meeting, where decisions were taken on the EU's 2000–2006 financial perspective (long-term budget), less than 10 per cent was set aside for pre-accession and enlargement aid. Based on the assumption that six states would become members in 2002, a total of €67 billion was assigned for spending on the accession states (European Council, 1999a). When these figures were updated at the December 2002 Copenhagen summit, a maximum total of €40.8 billion was set aside for 2004–2006, based on the assumption that 10 states would join in May 2004 (European Council, 2002c: Annex 1). These figures covered spending under all headings – agriculture, structural operations, funds to assist with improving nuclear safety, the improvement of border control, etc. Moreover, these ceiling figures were misleadingly 'high' since: (i) they would be partly offset by the fact that the new states would also be paying into the budget – probably contributing around €15 billion between 2004–06; and (ii) the new member states probably would not be able to use all the money allocated to them because of administrative and co-financing problems (Grabbe, 2002b:1). (See also Chapters 3 and 12 for figures on the funding of enlargement.)

There are a number of reasons why the EU-15 have been cautious, not to say skimpy, in their financial allocations to support enlargement. First, at a time when they have been practising financial prudence at home – partly, for most of them, because of the restraints imposed by Economic and Monetary Union (EMU) – EU-15 states have had no wish to be 'profligate' at the EU level. Second, Germany, the EU's principal paymaster, has been reluctant to transfer more money to the EU given that it is still paying the costs of German unification. Third, the EU's budget has always been relatively small and several EU-15 states, especially those with a more cautious approach to the integration process, have not been inclined to approve an upward drift. And fourth, the Commission, aware of the factors just outlined, in its highly influential 1997 document *Agenda 2000: For a Stronger and Wider Union* (European Commission, 1997), which was prepared for the European Council, suggested that enlargement could be achieved within the budgetary ceiling that had been set in 1992 – for the EU's 1993–99 financial perspective – of 1.27 per cent of overall EU GDP.

The EU-15 therefore took the decision to give only modest pre-accession aid and to phase-in post-accession aid gradually to the new member states. Certainly the 10 + 2 states were afforded much less generous treatment than were the last group of relatively poor states to become members, the Mediterraneans in the 1980s. Thus, the new member states naturally perceive their treatment to have been unfair, which guarantees that the matter is by no means closed but will linger, and quite possibly fester, in the enlarged EU. On both CAP and cohesion spending, it can be anticipated that the new members will press for both the overall levels and the nature of the distribution of financial support to feature prominently on future EU agendas.

Third, there is still a heavy reliance in the CEECs on outdated and inefficient industries that have only been able to survive through low costs – especially cheap labour – and state support of various kinds. This situation is changing as the CEEC economies modernize and liberalize, helped in no small part by the stimulus and guidance of the accession process, but there remains far to go. There has been a concern in some EU-15 states that the low CEEC costs could be a problem, with cheap exports resulting in EU-15 products being uncompetitive, with investment being attracted from the EU-15 to the CEECs, and with mass labour flows from CEECs to the higher wage economies of Western Europe. The indications are that these worries are not justified: although some 70 per cent of CEEC exports go to the EU, imports from CEECs amount to no more than 1 per cent of EU-15 GDP; cheaper CEEC imports appear to have improved EU-15 competitiveness and certainly have benefited consumers; by transferring some investment in labour-intensive industries to CEECs, EU-15 companies should be able to ensure they stay competitive on a global scale; and most experts think labour flows are unlikely to be large scale and may even be below the levels which some Western European countries – with their low birth rates and ageing populations – will require (Barysch, 2003:2).

Of course, from the CEECs' viewpoint, it clearly will be damaging for them if their economies prove to be uncompetitive post-accession and they do not attract the inward investment they anticipate. But it could be damaging also for the wider internal market economy, with pressures placed not only on re-distributive policies but also on macroeconomic and financial policy coordination and convergence.

Other internal policy concerns

Since EU membership involves accepting all of the *acquis*, the EU and the new member states have naturally had to address a range of problems and difficulties in internal policy areas beyond those considered in the previous section. These policy areas are too numerous to be reviewed here, but many of them are considered in Chapter 3 and in other chapters. Suffice it to say at this point that the list of particularly difficult policy areas has included energy, consumer protection, research, free movement of capital, border controls and the environment.

Environment may be taken to illustrate the sort of difficulties the EU has had to confront and the sort of approaches that have been taken to deal with them. The Commission has identified three particular environmental challenges arising from enlargement:

- legal: the transposition of EU directives into the legal order of applicants;
- administrative: establishing sufficiently staffed and well-equipped administrations to perform environmental planning, permitting, and monitoring;
- financial: substantial investment in infrastructure and technology to make up for previous under-investment (European Commission, 2003f: 45).

The first of these challenges arises because there are nearly 300 EU environmental laws, many of them in the form of directives. Directives have to be transposed into national law, so the EU has had to ensure that the transpositions have occurred and have done so in an accurate and legally correct manner.

The second challenge – which has occurred in many policy areas in addition to the environment – stems from the EU being anxious to ensure that not only are EU laws transposed, but that new member states have sufficiently resourced and trained administrations and judicial systems to ensure laws are actually applied. As part of meeting this challenge, the EU has worked with the new member states on many institution-building activities, including designing management systems and seeing to the equipping and training of public officials. Despite the very considerable efforts that have been made, however, their effect has been diminished by the high turnover of personnel in the public sector in most of the CEECs. This turnover, which is explained partly by a politicization of bureaucracies but mainly by talented personnel leaving the public sector for higher-paid jobs in the private sector, inevitably makes for a lack of collective learning.

The third challenge has been the most difficult. Because of the legacy of inefficient planned economies and insensitive political systems, all of the CEECs emerged from communism with economies that were focused on productive output and paid little attention to environmental protection and management. In consequence, the CEECs have major problems with, amongst other things, air quality, water pollution, waste management, and protection of habitats. Tackling these sort of problems in advance of EU membership naturally was not 'merely' a matter of ensuring the *acquis* was incorporated into national law and that adequate implementation mechanisms were in place, as to some extent it was with policy areas such as taxation and consumer protection. This is because much of EU environmental policy and law is extremely expensive to implement, with, for example, major investment needed to bring industrial plant up to EU standards for the disposal of toxic and hazardous substances into rivers, seas, the air, and land.

But cost problems notwithstanding, progress in tackling environmental problems has been made. Not all of this progress has, it should be emphasized, been a consequence of the EU. The very act of creating a market economy has obliged CEECs to modernize, with the consequences that many old and inefficient production bases have been closed, many new – environmentally cleaner – industries have been developed, and business as a whole has had to become more energy efficient. Paralleling this, the creation of democratic political systems has obliged CEEC decision-makers to become sensitive to the environmental concerns of voters.

As for the effect of the EU in promoting the tackling of environmental problems, that has been important even since before accession processes formally began. Because they wanted to become EU members, applicants were anxious to show they were doing as much as they could to meet the environmental *acquis* as fully and as soon as possible. So, the very act of seeking membership put applicants on the road to reform. Once on this road, and especially since the accession processes got underway, much of what has been done has involved working with EU representatives and within EU frameworks.

Where it became clear during accession negotiations that an aspect of the environmental *acquis* could not be applied by the target date for EU membership, transitional arrangements involving extra time were usually negotiated. As is shown in Chapter 3, the EU was unwilling to permit as many transitional arrangement for the 10 +2 as it did for the Mediterranean applicants. However, an 'exceptional' (the Commission's word) number of such arrangements, all involving the third of the three challenges listed above (the financial challenge) and all with a specific time and scope, were negotiated in the environmental policy area. Examples of these arrangements include directives dealing with air quality, waste management, water quality, nature protection and industrial pollution and risk management (for a full list, see European Commission 2003b: 45–8).

External relations and policies

The EU is an extremely important international actor. It is so most notably in the sphere of trade, where it uses its Common Commercial Policy (CCP) and the fact that it accounts for over one-fifth of all international trade with considerable effect in global, regional, and bi-lateral trade negotiations. Beyond trade, other dimensions of EU external relations and policies cover development policy (taken together, the EU and its member states account for around 55 per cent of both international development aid and humanitarian aid), the Common Foreign and Security Policy (CFSP), and 'internal' policies such as environment and energy which have important external dimensions.

By virtue of increasing its population, geographical size, and economic output and activity, an enlarged EU should carry more weight when conducting its external relations and policies. However, the advantages deriving from increased size and weight may be counter-balanced by the fact that the EU will also be much more heterogeneous in its membership and so will find it even more difficult than it has in the past to develop united stances on the bases of shared identities and interests. The extent to which particular policy areas will be affected will vary. Taking, for example, the CCP – the EU's most comprehensive and integrated external policy – a key affect will be that the trade needs and preferences of the new member states will have to be accommodated when the Council of Ministers gives negotiating mandates to the Commission and when it considers whether the outcomes of trade negotiations should be approved. But, overall, as is shown in Chapter 15, it can be assumed that the CCP will continue broadly in its existing form. This assumption can be made for three reasons: the CCP is not an 'optional' policy but is at the heart of the EU as the basis of the customs union; there are no reasons for thinking new member states will bring insuperable trade problems with them to the Council table; and, if necessary, decisions can be made in the Council by QMV.

The CFSP, by contrast, is quite a different matter, it having been difficult enough, as is shown in Chapter 16, to develop on even just a partial basis before the 10 + 2 round. The problem has stemmed largely from differences between member states over what the CFSP should do, how it should be organized, and how it should be conducted. To be sure, a CFSP of sorts has gradually been built, on the basis of: the identification of generally defined goals, including safeguarding the common values, fundamental interests, independence and integrity of the Union, strengthening the security of the Union, and developing and consolidating democracy and the rule of law; the establishment of a number of policy instruments, including common strategies, joint actions, common positions, and various mechanisms of cooperation; and the creation of a modest security capability for crisis management situations. However, the achievements of the CFSP have been limited overall, as is exemplified by the inability of the EU to prevent or stop the hostilities in the Balkans in the 1990s.

At the heart of at least some of the differences between EU-15 states on CFSP-related matters have been relations with the US. Whilst all EU-15 have testified to the importance of the transatlantic relationship, they have differed in at least emphasis over the extent to which the EU should seek to be, and should seek to present itself as being, generally independent of the US. These differences were no more clearly demonstrated and were no sharper than during the US-led 2003 campaign to overthrow the regime of Saddam Hussein in Iraq. EU states were divided in their attitude towards the war, with the United Kingdom (the only EU member to participate actively in the campaign), Spain and Italy leading those who supported the US position, and France, Germany and Belgium being prominent amongst the states that opposed it. CEECs tend to be transatlanticists in their foreign policy orientations, and certainly were very much so during the war – a stance that so incurred the wrath of the French President, Jacques Chirac, that he informed them it would have been preferable had they remained quiet! This is not to say that CEECs do not want a distinctive European external relations voice to exist – they have, for example, supported the EU's position against the US on issues such as the Kyoto Protocol and the International Criminal Court. Moreover, it may be assumed that with membership they will become increasingly socialized into 'thinking European'. However, it does seem likely that their transatlantic leanings will tilt the balance of opinion more in the direction of ensuring that EU foreign and security policies are firmly located within the transatlantic framework, which could make for future problems.

Another CFSP problem that enlargement could exacerbate is that created by the existence in the EU of, on the one hand, a small group of large countries which are ready and able (because of their military resources) to drive foreign policy and, on the other hand, a larger group of mainly small countries that are often interested in having a significant role but are unwilling or unable to participate in a major way. As Heather Grabbe has pointed out (2002a: 5), the EU needs to find an answer to the question of how the member states can get together on foreign policy issues in numbers ranging from two to the total membership without provoking resentment because a directoire of large states is seen to be running foreign policy.

One other possible CFSP problem arising from enlargement that merits noting is that some acceding states have particular external policy interests and orientations that could create considerable difficulties in some circumstances. Cyprus is the most obvious such state, and the EU wanting to open accession negotiations with Turkey is the most obvious such circumstance.

Perhaps the greatest and most pressing external challenge of all arising from enlargement, however, is the EU's relations with its new neighbours. With enlargement, the EU's borders move to the east and the south. There are new borders with five states – Croatia, Serbia-Montenegro, Romania, Ukraine and Belarus. There are longer borders with Russia. And there is a new presence in the Eastern Mediterranean with Cyprus and in the Southern Mediterranean with Malta. Clearly it is in the EU's interests that the new neighbours are stable, secure, prosperous and democratic. At present, most of them fall down on at least the prosperity count, and some on other counts too. With most of the new neighbours the EU already has special arrangements, in the form of stabilization and association agreements with countries of the former Yugoslavia, partnership and cooperation agreements with former Soviet states, and a mixture of assorted bi-lateral agreements and multilateral agreements under the Barcelona Process with Mediterranean states. These agreements all have the promotion of trade, economic growth, and stable government at their core. The arrangements with the former Yugoslav states even have eventual EU membership as a goal. But whether the agreements go far enough is open to question. Certainly there are many who would argue that the EU needs a more coherent strategy towards, and more generous policies for, these new neighbours so as to assist them to develop economically and politically. If appropriate actions are not taken, the EU may well have neighbours that will not only (continue to) be potentially unstable and thereby pose a generalized and somewhat unclear form of threat, but also will exacerbate a host of difficult ongoing problems in such areas as illegal immigration, transnational crime, and drug trafficking. As William Wallace has put it, the EU's vulnerability to its neighbours, which is because of the background threat of disorder spilling across its borders should give its member governments a shared self-interest in promoting a mutually beneficial relationship, rather than one in which minimal concessions are dragged out of both sides. It is in the EU's strongest self-interest, therefore, to invest in stability and cooperation across its borders. The costs of defending the EU from unstable states in its neighbourhood would be much higher than those of promoting prosperity and security beyond its borders. (2003: 19)

Concluding Comments

Much public commentary on enlargement has focused on the challenges that it poses to the prosperity, stability and continued development of the EU. That such challenges exist is undeniable, but they need to be placed in the context of the many opportunities that also are offered.

The challenges should also be placed in the context of the fact that, as the former Prime Minister of the Netherlands, Wim Kok, observed in 2003 in a report on enlargement he prepared for the Commission, enlargement is taking place at a time when the EU is already facing many other challenges (Kok, 2003). Amongst these challenges are institutional functioning, improving the efficiency of the economy, creating an internal area of freedom and justice, tackling cross-border crime and illegal movements of people, and establishing the EU's place in the world. Enlargement may be an additional challenge at a difficult time, but it also, as Kok argues (p.4), offers the possibility of being a catalyst in helping to make progress in tackling some of these outstanding problems. Indeed, in some respects it has already been something of a catalyst. For example, it certainly influenced important reforms to the CAP that were agreed by EU Agriculture Ministers in June 2003 – reforms that moved the CAP system further away from direct production support. And the projected new European Constitution, which has as its main purpose simplifying the EU's institutions and operation and making them more understandable to the citizenry, has at least some of its origins in the spotlight that enlargement has thrown on how the EU functions. As for enlargement being a catalyst for future problem solving, the extension of police, judicial, and border control cooperation to so much more of the European continent offers great opportunities for dealing with a variety of internal security issues.

Chapter 2

Previous Enlargement Rounds[*]

NEILL NUGENT

This chapter considers the three enlargement rounds prior to the 10 + 2 round. The chapter shows how and why the EC-6 moved to the EU-15, outlines the impact of acceding states on the EC/EU, helps to set the 10 + 2 round in context, and serves as a base for evaluating the ways and extent to which the 10 + 2 round is unique in some respects but part of a recurring pattern in others.

The First Enlargement Round: the United Kingdom, Denmark and Ireland

Towards accession

Three factors were especially important in governing the UK's attitude towards European integration in the early post-war years. First, the UK saw itself as operating within what Winston Churchill described as three overlapping and interlocking relationships: the Empire and Commonwealth; the Atlantic Alliance and the 'special relationship' with the United States; and Western Europe. Until the early 1960s, Western Europe was seen as being the least important of these relationships. Second, successive British governments were not prepared to accept the loss of sovereignty that integration implied. There were several reasons for this, of which the most important were: Britain's long established parliamentary tradition; the record, in which there was considerable pride, of not having been invaded or controlled by foreign powers in modern times; a generally held view that cessation of sovereignty was neither desirable nor necessary since Britain was still a world power of the first rank; and a certain distaste with the idea of being dependent on the not altogether highly regarded governments and countries of 'the Continent'. Third, Britain's circumstances were such that three of the four main integrationist organizations to be proposed in the 1950s had few attractions in terms of their specific areas of concern: the restrictions

---

[*] Parts of this chapter draw on material from Nugent (2003): 23–35.

on national decision-making powers entailed in the European Coal and Steel Community (ECSC) looked very unappealing to a country whose coal and steel capacity far exceeded that of any of the six states which constituted the ECSC (Belgium, France, Germany, Italy, Luxembourg and the Netherlands); the European Defence Community (EDC) would have limited governmental manoeuvrability and options at a time when Britain's defences were already stretched by the attempt to maintain a world role; and Euratom looked as though it would involve sharing secrets with less advanced nuclear powers. Only the EEC seemed to have much to offer, but amongst the problems it carried with it was its proposed supranationalism. Attempts were made to persuade the six ECSC states that founded the EEC not to be so ambitious and to direct their attention to the construction of a West European free trade area, but with no success. As a result, and with a view to increasing its bargaining power with the six, Britain looked to other non-signatories of the EEC Treaty. This led, in January 1960, to the Stockholm Convention, which established the European Free Trade Association (EFTA). The founding members of EFTA were Austria, Denmark, Norway, Portugal, Sweden, Switzerland and the UK.

Shortly after the EEC began functioning in 1958, the attitude of the UK government began to change and membership came to be sought. The first enlargement of the Community could, in fact, have occurred much earlier than it did had President de Gaulle not opposed UK applications in 1961 and 1967. He did so for a mixture of reasons: he feared the UK would rival and attempt to thwart his desire to place France at the centre of the European stage; he believed UK membership would unsettle the developing Franco–German alliance – an alliance that was given symbolic force with the signing in 1963 of a Friendship Treaty between the two countries; he thought the UK would try to change some aspects of the Community that were of particular benefit to France, notably the emerging Common Agricultural Policy; and he was suspicious of the UK's close links with the United States, thinking they would pave the way for American penetration and domination of Europe if the UK joined the Community. So the UK was barred from Community membership until de Gaulle was replaced as French President by Georges Pompidou in 1969. A different view was then taken in Paris: the UK might serve as a useful counterweight to the increasingly strong and self-confident Germany; UK governments would lend support to France's opposition to pressures from within the Community for increased supranationalism; and France would probably gain economically by virtue of having better access to UK markets and as a result of the UK being a net contributor to the Community budget.

The reasons for the UK's changed position on Europe were a mixture of the political and the economic. Politically, it was increasingly clear that the UK was no longer a world power of the first rank. The 1956 Suez debacle underlined the decline, and the increasing tendency from 1960 for key world issues to be discussed between the US and the USSR on a purely bilateral basis further confirmed it. Paralleling this decline, the nature and status of the 'special relationship' with the US weakened and became increasingly questionable. Furthermore, the British Empire was giving way to the Commonwealth, a very loose organization that was not capable of providing the UK with much international political support.

On all the usual economic indicators, such as growth in trade, investment, gross national product and income, by the early 1960s it was apparent that the member states of the EC were outperforming the UK. For example, between 1958 and 1969 real earnings in Britain increased by about 38 per cent, whereas in the EC they increased on average by about 75 per cent. Quite simply the figures appeared to show that the Community was a success; all this at a time when the UK's pattern of trade, even when not a Community member, was turning away from the Commonwealth and towards Europe. Moreover, the growing economic strength of the EC seemed to be linked with growing political status.

Thus when Pompidou opened the EC door, the government of Edward Heath entered willingly. Negotiations opened in June 1970 and were completed less than 18 months later – a remarkably rapid process when compared to the years of negotiations to which some later applicant have been subject. That the negotiations were completed so quickly is testimony to the much more limited *acquis* of the EC at that time as compared with later years, to the political will of the six to admit the UK, and to the UK government's strategy of deferring tackling some problems – notably on UK budgetary contributions – until after membership had been secured.

The UK formally became an EC member on 1 January 1973.

*   *   *

Denmark and Ireland were not interested in joining the Communities that were founded in the 1950s. Both of their economies were heavily dependent on agriculture, so the ECSC had little to offer them. As for the EEC, there were several reasons to doubt that it would be to their benefit, the most important of which was that both countries had strong economic and historical links elsewhere: in Denmark's case with the other Scandinavian countries and with the UK; in Ireland's case with the UK. These links with the UK resulted in both of them tying their willingness to join the EC with the outcome of the UK's attempts to gain membership, so they both applied and then withdrew their applications on two occasions in the 1960s and then became members with the UK in 1973.

Like Denmark and Ireland, Norway paralleled the UK in twice seeking EC membership in the 1960s and then again in the early 1970s.

However, though, like its counterparts, the Norwegian government succeeded in negotiating terms of entry in 1972, these were then rejected by the Norwegian people in a referendum following a campaign in which suspicions about the implications for Norwegian agriculture, fishing and national sovereignty featured prominently

The impact of the 1973 entrants on the EC/EU

Since joining the Community, Britain has been, to use a much-used term coined by Stephen George, something of an awkward partner (George, 1998). This was especially so during the Conservative Party's term of office between 1979 and 1997, when Britain's relations with the other member states were frequently very difficult. They were so because the UK government subscribed to views and adopted positions that its Community partners did not, for the most part, share. There were three particular sources of difficulty. First, there was the budgetary issue, which, as was noted above, the Heath government had rather pushed aside during the accession negotiations but which was taken up by Margaret Thatcher under the banner 'we want our money back'. The problem here was that the UK – largely because it is not a major recipient from the CAP – was making excessive net contributions to the EU budget. The creation of the European Regional Development Fund (ERDF) in 1975 was largely occasioned by this UK budgetary difficulty, being designed in such a way that the UK would be a significant beneficiary. However, this did not satisfy the Conservatives who wanted to put less money into the budget and who also did not want such money as was returned to be in the form of funds that were controlled and monitored from Brussels. As a result, there were rows on the matter in the early 1980s, reaching up to the European Council, until a formula for a British 'rebate' was agreed at the 1984 Fontainebleau summit. Second, the governments led by both Thatcher and John Major took a largely minimalist view of the ideal nature of the EC/EU. They thought that in essence it should be not much more than an integrated and de-regulated internal market, with some intergovernmental cooperation tacked on in a limited number of areas where policy issues clearly crossed national boundaries. This position resulted in the UK playing a leading role and making a strong contribution to the moves from the early 1980s to complete the internal market. However, unlike the governments of other member states, the UK government did not subscribe to the view that the proper and efficient operation of this market required common economic, financial and social policies, let alone a single currency. This position linked in with the budgetary issue to make the UK the leading, and until the 1995 enlargement virtually the sole, advocate of a much tighter CAP. Third, the Conservatives were willing to support the development of intergovernmental cooperation when that seemed useful – as, for example, in aspects of foreign policy and internal security policy – but they almost invariably sought to resist supranational developments and any loss of national sovereignty.

Following the election of the Labour Party to office in 1997, the British stance in the EU became much more cooperative. This was exemplified by the willingness of the government led by Tony Blair to incorporate extensions to supranational decision-making in the Amsterdam and Nice Treaties, to provide a lead in the development of EU defence policy, and by the more positive tone displayed by British ministers towards Europe. However, in important respects, Britain has remained in the slow integration stream under Labour. This is demonstrated by the insistence that Britain be given an opt-out from certain treaty provisions that strengthen the EU's justice and home affairs policies and also by the decision to continue the policy of the Conservatives of not joining the single currency system.

*   *   *

Denmark's record since joining the Community has been not wholly dissimilar from that of the UK in that, aware of domestic scepticism about the supposed benefits of EC/EU membership, Danish governments have tended to be cautious in their approach to integration. The most dramatic manifestation of Danish concern with the integration process occurred in 1992, when in a national referendum the Danish people rejected Denmark's ratification of the Maastricht Treaty. This rejection, which was reversed in a second referendum in 1993, upset the schedule for applying the Treaty, took much wind out of the sails of those who wished to press ahead quickly with further integration, and resulted in Denmark distancing itself from certain future integrationist projects. As part of this distancing, Denmark, like the UK, did not join the single currency when it was launched in 1999, and then, in a referendum held in September 2000, the Danish people rejected a proposal to join by 53 per cent to 47 per cent.

Apart from one exceptional circumstance, Ireland has created no particular difficulties for the EC/EU since its accession. From time to time Irish governments have intimated that their support for further integration is conditional on Ireland continuing to be afforded generous treatment under the CAP and the Structural Funds, but there has been no significant resistance to developments aimed at deepening the integration process. The exceptional circumstance was the decision of the Irish people in a referendum held in June 2001 to reject ratification of the Nice Treaty: 54 per cent voted against ratification and 46 per cent voted in favour, on a very low turnout of 35 per cent. Unlike the two 'No' votes in Denmark, the Irish rejection was explained primarily not in terms of anti-EU sentiments but rather a variety of domestic political circumstances. The vote put the implementation of the Nice Treaty on hold throughout the EU. The June 2001 vote was reversed in a second referendum held in October 2002, when the Treaty was approved by 63 per cent to 37 per cent on a 48 per cent turnout.

The Mediterranean Enlargement Round: Greece, Spain and Portugal

Strictly speaking, there were two enlargements of the EC in the 1980s: in 1981 when Greece joined and in 1986 when Portugal and Spain joined. However, because of the many similarities between these three states and because of many similarities in the nature of their accession processes, it is common to group the 1981 and 1986 enlargements together under the heading of 'the Mediterranean round'. This is the approach taken here.

Towards accession

In the 1950s the Greek economy had been unsuitable for ECSC or EEC membership, being predominantly peasant-based. Additionally, Greece's history, culture and geographical position put it outside the Western European mainstream. But just as the countries that joined the Community in 1973 would have liked to have become members earlier, so was the accession of Greece delayed longer than Greek governments would have liked. The initial problem, recognized on both sides when Greece made its first approaches to Brussels soon after the EEC came into being, was the underdeveloped nature of the Greek economy. A transitional period prior to membership was deemed to be necessary and this was negotiated in the form of an Association Agreement that came into force in 1962. Full incorporation into the Community would, it was understood, follow when the Greek economy was capable of sustaining the obligations imposed by membership. However, between April 1967, when there was a military coup in Greece, and June 1974, when civilian government was re-established, the Association Agreement was virtually suspended. It might be thought that this would have further delayed full membership, but in fact it had the opposite effect. After elections in Greece in November 1974 the new government immediately made clear its wish to become a full member of the Community. The Commission issued a formal opinion that Greece was still not economically ready and proposed a pre-accession period of unlimited duration, during which economic reforms could be implemented. In response, the Greek government restated its wish for full membership, and particularly emphasized how membership could help both to underpin Greek democracy and to consolidate Greece's West European and Western Alliance bonds. The Council of Ministers was sympathetic to these arguments and rejected the Commission's proposal. Membership negotiations were opened in July 1976 and Greece entered the Community on 1 January 1981.

For many years both political and economic circumstances counted against Spanish and Portuguese membership. Politically, both countries were authoritarian dictatorships to which the democratic governments of the EC-6 did not wish to be too closely attached. Economically, both were predominantly agricultural and underdeveloped, and both pursued essentially autarkic economic policies until the end of the 1950s: factors that hardly made them suitable candidates for the ECSC, and that had the knock-on effect of excluding them from the negotiations that led to the creation of the EEC.

As with Greece, political considerations were extremely important in the relations between the two Iberian states and the Community prior to their accession. Initially, the influence was a negative one: if Spain and Portugal had not had dictatorial political systems until the mid-1970s, in all probability they would have been allowed to join the Community much sooner than they did. Not that there was anything in the EC treaties to specify that members must be liberal democracies: Article 237 of the EEC Treaty simply stated 'Any European State may apply to become a member of the Community'. The assumption was, however, that a democratic political system was a necessary qualification for entry.

So, although both Spain and Portugal requested negotiations on association with the Community as early as 1962, and Spain made it quite clear that its request was with a view to full membership at some future date, both countries were treated with caution by the Community. Eventually they were granted preferential trade agreements, but it was only with the overthrow of the Caetano regime in Portugal in 1974 and the death of the Spanish leader, General Franco, in 1975 that full membership became a real possibility. Portugal applied in March 1977 and Spain in July 1977. The ensuing negotiations were protracted and difficult, covering, amongst many problems, the threat posed to other Mediterranean countries by Spanish agriculture, the size of the Spanish fishing fleet, fears of cheap Spanish and Portuguese labour moving north, and the implications for the Structural Funds – from which both countries, but especially Spain, expected to receive considerable aid. As with the Greek negotiations, political factors helped to overcome these difficulties: the member states wished to encourage political stability in southern Europe; there was the opportunity to widen and strengthen the political and economic base of the Community; and, by helping to link southern Europe to the north, there were strategic advantages for both Western Europe and NATO. Portugal and Spain joined the EC on 1 January 1986.

The impact of the Mediterraneans on the EC/EU

If the 1973 enlargement round resulted in a tilting of the balance of the

Community to the north, the Mediterranean enlargement brought about some counterbalancing to the south. Three consequences of this were, and still are, especially important. First, the CAP has been adjusted to give greater support to southern European produce. Second, EU policy towards the Mediterranean area has been given a much higher priority than hitherto. As part of this, in 1995 the so-called Barcelona Process was launched, which includes amongst its aims the creation by 2010 of a free trade area encompassing the EU and virtually all Mediterranean Basin states. Third, since the three acceding Mediterranean states were the poorest states in the EU-12 and then EU-15, they have pressed consistently for high levels of structural and re-redistributive EU spending. Spain, in, particular, has adopted a tough negotiating position, threatening, for example, to veto the 1995 enlargement round until it was 'bought off' with the creation of the Cohesion Fund, from which it was the major beneficiary.

Since its accession, Greece has generally supported the advancement of the integration process. That said, particular Greek policies, concerns and special needs have sometimes created difficulties: the (until recently) somewhat unstable nature of the Greek economy has meant that it has sometimes had to seek special economic assistance from its partners; although it wished to join the single currency from its launch, it was the only EU member state that was unable to meet the qualifying convergence criteria for entry into the first wave; its deep-rooted hostility towards Turkey and its complicated web of friendships and hostilities with parts of the former Yugoslavia have been major obstacles in the way of EU attempts to develop united and effective policies in South-East Europe; and its special links with Cyprus led to it making threatening noises from the late 1990s about possibly vetoing EU enlargement to CEECs should Cyprus's application be blocked.

Since their accession both Spain and Portugal have broadly gone along with integrationist developments, with the former perhaps being a little more integrationist than the latter. The fear expressed in some quarters before their accession that they would come to constitute a disruptive Iberian bloc has not been realized. As would be expected, they do frequently adopt similar positions on issues of common concern, such as the CAP and the Structural Funds, but, like other member states, their preferences on specific policy matters often diverge.

The EFTAn Enlargement Round: Austria, Finland and Sweden

Towards accession

In 1992 the EC formally opened accession negotiations with Austria, Finland and Sweden, and in 1993 it opened negotiations with Norway.

These negotiations were concluded successfully in March 1994, with a view to each of the countries becoming members of the EU after the terms of accession had been ratified at national level. However, though ratification, via national referendums, did duly occur in Austria, Finland and Sweden, in Norway, for reasons that are set out below, it did not. In consequence, three rather than four countries became EU members on 1 January 1995.

Two sets of factors stimulated the four countries (and Switzerland too, of which more below) to seek membership of the EU. First, what previously had been regarded as virtually insuperable obstacles to EC membership came to be seen as less of a problem in the late 1980s and early 1990s. For Austria and Sweden (and also Switzerland) the end of the Cold War reduced the importance of their traditional attachment to neutrality. For Finland, the difficulties posed by the country's relative geographical isolation and special position in relation to the Soviet Union disappeared. Second, there were the relationships of these countries to the EC. Austria, Finland, Sweden and Norway, plus Switzerland, Iceland and the micro state of Liechtenstein, made up the membership of EFTA. When EFTA was constituted in 1960 – with Denmark, Portugal and the UK then also as members, but not, at that stage, Finland, Iceland or Liechtenstein – it had two principal objectives: the establishment of a free trade area in industrial products between the member countries, and the creation of a base for making the whole of Western Europe a free trade area for industrial goods. The first of these objectives was established in 1966 with the removal of virtually all customs duties and quantitative restrictions on trade in industrial products between EFTA countries, and the second objective was achieved in 1977 with the creation of an industrial free trade area between the EC and EFTA. Over time, however, despite relations between the EC and EFTA being friendly, and being indeed further developed via cooperation in such areas as environmental protection, scientific and technical research, and transport policy, the EFTA states increasingly came to view key aspects of the EC-EFTA relationship as unsatisfactory. One reason for their dissatisfaction was that the EC was collectively much stronger than EFTA. Another, and related, reason was that the EC was prone to present EFTA with *de facto* situations to which the EFTA countries had little option but to adjust, as, for example, when the Community laid down product specifications. This latter problem, of having to accept trading rules they had played no part in helping to formulate, became of increasing concern to EFTA countries as the EC's programme to complete the internal market by 1992 – the Single European Market (SEM) programme – gathered pace in the late 1980s and early 1990s. This concern played an important part in encouraging the EFTA countries to reconsider the attractions of EC membership. It also led the EC – concerned that a widening of its membership might threaten its own deepening – to suggest that EC-EFTA relations be strengthened by the creation of a European Economic Area (EEA) that would, in effect, extend the SEM programme to the EFTA states but would stop short of EC membership. The EEA was duly negotiated, and after a series of delays during the ratification process, occasioned by Switzerland withdrawing from the agreement (see below), came into effect in January 1994. However, by that stage it had come to be accepted by most interested parties – including the governments of the EC, which in the meantime had succeeded in moving Community deepening forward via the Maastricht Treaty – that the ambitions of the governments of Austria, Finland, Sweden and Norway would be satisfied only by full EU membership.

The negotiation of accession terms with the EFTAns (as the applicants were collectively called) was much easier and quicker than in previous negotiating rounds. This was partly because each of the applicants was already well adjusted to EU membership, being prosperous (and hence not posing potential problems for the EU budget), having already incorporated much of the Community's *acquis* into national law, and having a well-established democratic political system. It was partly also because many of the matters that normally have to be covered in accession negotiations had already been sorted out in the EEA negotiations and agreement.

The impact of the EFTAns on the EU

The impact of the EFTAn round on the EU has tended to be under-estimated by observers. This is mainly because, unlike the 1973 and Mediterranean rounds, the EFTAn round did not bring in a new big state, did not lead directly to any major new policy prioritization, and did not provide a base for new internal dissension. Nonetheless, the round has had significant consequences. Some of these consequences have been general in nature, whilst others have been more focused and specific.

One almost immediate general consequence, intensified by the fact that the EFTAns joined just as the EU was moving towards the 10 + 2 round, was to increase pressures for fundamental reform of EU institutions and processes. In a mechanical sense, the EFTAns, like their predecessors in the 1973 and Mediterranean rounds, were fitted into the institutional framework relatively easily. However, the move from 12 to 15 member states did intensify feelings that the EU was becoming too big to be able to conduct its business on the basis of a system that had been devised for a much smaller number of states. A second general consequence has been, by bringing net contributors to the budget into the Union, to expand 'the existing coalition of member stares that instinctively opposes new EU expenditure' (Peterson and Bomberg, 1998: 43).

And a third general consequence – coming out of Scandinavian political culture – has been to increase promotion of the virtues of openness, transparency and democracy in EU governance.

More focused and specific consequences have been a result of the EFTAns, like all acceding states, bringing particular policy concerns and interests to the EU table. Four instances of this have been particularly striking. First, Austria, because of its geographical position and also because of domestic electoral support for the far right, has taken a very active role in deliberations on justice and home affairs (JHA) matters, including EU asylum and immigration policy. In the 10 + 2 accession negotiations, it worked closely with Germany to ensure that the internal market principle of free movement of people would not apply immediately to the movement of people from CEECs to the EU-15. Second, Sweden has been an important contributor to the debate about EMU, and a source of some irritation amongst eurozone states in that it is one of the three EU-15 states not to have joined the single currency system. When the system was established the Swedish government chose, mainly for Eurosceptic reasons, not to participate, even though Sweden did not have an opt-out like Denmark and the UK. The Swedish government and most Swedish elites later campaigned actively in favour of entering the single currency when a referendum was held on the issue in September 2003, but 56 per cent of the 81 per cent of Swedes who voted rejected their urgings. Not only was this rejection important in itself, but it was also widely seen as damaging the prospects of the British government holding a referendum on euro membership. Third, Finland and Sweden have been active in elevating the importance of environmental and consumer protection considerations on the policy agenda. And, fourth, Finland and Sweden have played a central role in helping to develop the EU's Northern Dimension, which involves cooperation between states in the Baltic region.

The EFTAns that did not join: Norway, Switzerland and Iceland

The completion of the EFTAn round left Norway, Switzerland and Iceland as the only significant Western European states that were not members of the EU. Why have they stayed out?

As noted above, Norway re-applied for membership in 1992. It did so partly for the reasons set out earlier in relation to the unsatisfactory nature of EC-EFTA decision-making relations, partly because the government felt that Norway could not afford to ignore the applications of its neighbours and be the only Scandinavian country not to become an EU member, and partly because there were grounds (although by no means overwhelming grounds) for believing that the long-standing public opposition to membership was no longer as strong as it had been. Accession terms were quickly negotiated, but in the ensuing referendum in 1994 many of the issues raised echoed those of 1972. Opponents of membership also made the additional argument that Norway had no need to join the EU since it was a prosperous country that, thanks to the EEA, already had the trading ties with the EU that it required. The people voted against membership by 52.2 per cent to 47.8 per cent.

Until December 1992, Switzerland was in much the same position as Austria and Sweden. That is to say, it had long been a member of EFTA, the end of the Cold War had removed one of the main obstacles to it becoming a member of the EC/EU, an application for accession had been made, and it anticipated entry some time in the mid-1990s. However, in December 1992, in a referendum on whether to ratify the EEA, the Swiss people narrowly voted – by 50.3 per cent to 49.7 per cent – against ratification. As a consequence, the timetable for bringing the EEA into effect was delayed, and the Swiss application to join the EU necessarily had to be put aside.

Iceland considered the possibility of EC membership at the time of the 1973 enlargement but concluded that there were too many policy difficulties in the way, especially with regard to fishing. This continues to be the case and explains why Iceland did not join the other EFTA states in the 1990s when they sought EU accession.

The non-membership of Norway, Switzerland and Iceland in the EU means that EFTA continues to exist, with Liechtenstein as its fourth member.

Concluding Remarks

This chapter has described the three enlargement rounds in the EU's history prior to the 10 + 2 round. Clearly each round was, in important respects, distinctive – in terms, for example, of how it was managed, of the sorts of countries that joined, and of its consequences for the subsequent operation of the EU. But there were also similarities between the rounds, regarding, for example, the reasons why countries sought membership and why existing member states allowed applicants to join. These and other points of comparison are explored in Chapter 4.

Chapter 3

The Unfolding of the 10 + 2 Enlargement Round

NEILL NUGENT

This chapter chronicles the unfolding of the 10 + 2 enlargement round and identifies its key distinguishing features. The chapter begins by focusing on the three groups of applicant states featuring in the round: the Central and Eastern European countries (CEECs); the two small Mediterranean states of Cyprus and Malta; and Turkey, whose presence has very much loomed over the 10 + 2 round even though it is not formally part of it. The differing attitudes of EU-15 states towards the round are then considered. This is followed by an examination of how the EU prepared for enlargement to the 10 + 2. There is then a description of the accession process itself.

The Central and Eastern European Countries

The 10 + 2 enlargement round may be said to have formally begun with the applications of Cyprus and Malta in 1990, but it took on its main thrust with applications from former communist-controlled Central and Eastern European countries in the early to mid 1990s.

After gaining independence in 1989–1990 following the collapse of communism, most CEECs were soon openly expressing the hope that, as they established liberal democratic and market-based systems and as East–West relations were transformed, the way would be eased for their accession to the EU. They were motivated by a mixture of overlapping and inter-connected political, security and economic aims. Politically, there was a widespread desire to become (re)integrated into the European, and more broadly the Western, world. This resulted in CEEC governments necessarily seeking membership of the EU – the organization which both symbolized 'the new' Europe and embodied much of its drive. In security terms, EU membership was seen as offering a measure of 'soft' security protection to bolster the 'hard' protection of NATO, which most CEECs also were seeking to join, especially against any communist revival or nationalist surge. And economically, the EU market was clearly crucial for trade, whilst the EU as an entity offered a framework and policies to assist with and to underpin economic liberalization, re-structuring, regeneration and growth.

The (then) EU-12, prompted and guided by the Commission, were quick to assist CEECs as they set about economic and political reconstruction. As is shown later in the chapter, this assistance took various forms, much of it set within the framework of association agreements that were contracted between the EU and CEECs. The assistance was given on the assumption that this was but the first step in what was likely to be a very long transitional process. Certainly, EU membership for CEECs was not thought of by many EU decision-makers to be a realistic prospect for some considerable time to come. After all, the CEECs were still in the very early stages of post-communist reconstruction and were nowhere near being ready to meet the demands and disciplines of EU membership. Furthermore, from the very early 1990s the EU was itself pre-occupied with other matters, including the EFTAn enlargement round and negotiating and then applying the Maastricht Treaty.

However, notwithstanding the reservations of most of the EU-12 about moving too quickly, an incremental process of 'rhetorical ratcheting-up', in which increasingly specific promises about membership were made to CEECs, soon begin to unfold (on this rhetorical process, see Chapter 1). A key step in the process occurred at the June 1993 Copenhagen European Council where, in the knowledge that applications from CEECs were likely in the near future, EU leaders declared in the Conclusions of the Presidency (in effect, the official communiqué of summit meetings) that 'the associated countries in Central and Eastern Europe that so desire shall become members of the European Union. Accession will take place as soon as an associated country is able to assume the obligations of membership by satisfying the economic and political conditions required' (European Council, 1993: 12).

So as to ensure that the enlargement to CEECs would not threaten the functioning or continuing development of the EU, the Copenhagen summit also laid down – for the first time in the Community's history – conditions that countries aspiring to membership would have to meet. All that had existed hitherto was the very open Article 237 of the EEC Treaty which stated 'Any European State may apply to become a member of the Community . . . The conditions of admission and the adjustment to the Treaty necessitated thereby shall be the subject of an agreement between the Member States and the applicant State.' The Copenhagen conditions – or criteria, as they came to be known – were designed so that there would be a convergence between existing and new member states in respect of their political and economic systems and also their adoption of Union laws and policies. These laws and policies were generally referred to as the *acquis*. The key paragraph setting out the Copenhagen criteria stated:

Membership requires that the candidate country has achieved stability of institutions guaranteeing democracy, the rule of law, human rights and respect for and protection of minorities, the existence of a functioning market economy as well as the capacity to cope with competitive pressure and market forces within the Union. Membership presupposes the candidate's ability to take on the obligations of membership including adherence to the aims of political, economic and monetary union. (European Council, 1993: 12)

Between March 1994, when Hungary applied, and January 1996, when the Czech Republic applied, 10 CEECs formally applied for EU membership (see Chronology, pp. 276–7). The December 1995 Madrid European Council formally reacted to these applications by requesting the Commission to investigate the implications for the EU of enlargement to these countries and to produce Opinions on each of the CEEC applicants. This led to the issuing in July 1997 of the Commission's influential communication *Agenda 2000: For a Stronger and Wider Union* (European Commission, 1997), which claimed that enlargement could be achieved with little extra cost to the Union provided significant reforms were made to the existing main spending areas – agriculture and structural policies. As for the Opinions on the applicants, which were prepared on the basis of the Copenhagen criteria, the Commission recommended that negotiations should be opened with five of the 10 CEECs – the Czech Republic, Estonia, Hungary, Poland and Slovenia – plus Cyprus, but should be delayed with the other five – Bulgaria, Latvia, Lithuania, Romania, and Slovakia – until their economic (and in the case of Slovakia, political) transitions were further advanced. The European Council accepted the Commission's recommendations at its December 1997 Luxembourg meeting and negotiations with what came to be referred to as the '5 + 1 first wave' states duly began in March 1998.

Before long, however, the Luxembourg decision came to be viewed as having been mistaken. One reason for this was that the link between enlargement and security was put into sharper focus with continuing turbulence in the Balkans. In particular, the NATO campaign in Kosovo in early 1999 highlighted the continuing dangers in South-East Europe and the broader dangers inherent in letting 'second wave' countries believe they were being left on one side. A second reason was that some of the second wave countries began to narrow the gap between them and first wave countries. And a third reason was that the Luxembourg summit had not only differentiated between first and second wave countries, but had also decided that Turkey – which had applied for membership as long back as 1987 – was not yet eligible to be even considered. Strong expressions of dissatisfaction by the Turkish government about how Turkey was being treated, coupled with suggestions that it might be forced to look elsewhere for friends, resulted in the EU having to reconsider its position on Turkey.

Accordingly, the enlargement strategy was revised at the 1999 Helsinki summit, where it was decided that: negotiations with the second wave 5 + 1 states would be opened in early 2000 (the 1 being Malta – see below); decisions on the preparedness for membership of all 10 + 2 states to become EU members would be made solely on the basis of their progress in negotiations, not on when the negotiations with them were opened; and Turkey would be given the status of being a 'candidate country'.

Such was the progress in the accession negotiations with the second wave states, which opened in February 2000, that it soon became apparent to both participants and observers that far from enlargement proceeding in a series of stages, as had been assumed, there was likely to a 'big bang' enlargement round some time before the June 2004 EP elections – with perhaps all negotiating states other than Bulgaria and Romania joining the EU. In November 2000, the Commission set out a revised enlargement strategy, incorporating a more flexible framework and a 'roadmap' allowing for negotiations with the more prepared states to be completed by December 2002. The Commission's strategy and targets were welcomed by the December 2000 Nice summit and the June 2001 Gothenburg summit confirmed that EU-15 leaders hoped negotiations with applicants that were ready could be concluded by December 2002. This hope was realized at the December 2002 Copenhagen summit when the European Council, on the basis of reports and recommendations from the Commission, decided that an accession treaty could be signed in April 2003 with all negotiating states apart from Bulgaria and Romania, with a view to them becoming members in May 2004 – that is, in time for them to be able to participate fully in the June 2004 EP elections. It was further decided that if Bulgaria and Romania made satisfactory progress in complying with the membership criteria, they could anticipate membership in 2007 (European Council, 2002c).

An Accession Treaty with the 10 states – eight CEECs, plus Malta and Cyprus – was duly signed in April 2003. By September 2003, all eight CEECs had held successful ratification referendums (see Chronology).

Cyprus and Malta

Although they are geographically distant from the Western European heartland, the two small Mediterranean states of Cyprus and Malta are usually thought of – and have usually thought of themselves – as being part of the west European tradition. Both countries applied for EC membership in July 1990, but their applications were received unenthusiastically. This was partly because of a reluctance by the EC to tackle the institutional questions that would be raised by the accession of very small

states. In the case of Cyprus it was also because it was the view of most
EC decision makers that the problem of Turkey's occupation of North
Cyprus – over 30 000 Turkish troops had been based there since a
Turkish invasion in 1974 occasioned by a right-wing Greek coup on the
island – must be resolved before the accession of Cyprus could be
contemplated. However, the prospects for both countries improved in
June 1993 when the Commission issued its official Opinions on the two
applications. Whilst recognizing that there were many difficulties ahead,
the Commission generally supported the applications and, in a significant break with the past, indicated that it did not favour allowing the
partition of Cyprus to be a reason for permanently excluding the accession of Greek Cyprus. The European Council moved the process further
forward when it decided at its June 1994 Corfu meeting that 'the next
phase of enlargement of the Union will involve Cyprus and Malta'
(European Council, 1994a). In March 1995 the Council of Ministers was
even more specific when it announced that negotiations with Cyprus and
Malta would open six months after the conclusion of the
Intergovernmental Conference (IGC) that was scheduled to begin in
1996. An election in Malta in 1996 then delayed Malta's plans, by bringing to power a government that put the EU application on hold.
Nonetheless, the Cyprus application continued to be advanced and
accession negotiations opened in March 1998 in parallel with the opening of accession negotiations with the five first-wave CEECs. In
September 1998 a further change of government in Malta resulted in the
country's membership application being revived and accession negotiations were opened along with those of the second wave CEECs in
February 2000.

Cyprus's situation within the 10 + 2 round was extremely difficult
and sensitive. In accordance with its established position in international law, the Greek Cypriot government, acting in the name of the
Republic of Cyprus, insisted from the very outset of its attempt to join
the EU that it represented the whole island and would be conducting
accession negotiations on that basis, even though in practice its writ
ran only in the south. The Turkish Cypriot leadership in the north,
strongly supported by Turkey, totally rejected the right of the Greek
Cypriots to claim to be negotiating on behalf of all of Cyprus. EU leaders hoped that a solution to what is commonly referred to as 'the
Cyprus Problem' would be found before the end of accession negotiations, but this was always based more on hope than on belief.
Delaying Cyprus's accession until the Cyprus Problem was resolved
remained a possibility throughout the accession negotiations, but not
a very realistic one because Greece threatened to veto all EU applications if Cyprus's accession was delayed. At the same time, however,
accepting a divided Cyprus as an EU member risked damaging the
EU's relations with Turkey.

At the December 1999 Helsinki European Council meeting, the EU-15 leaders agreed on how they would manage the conflicting pressures associated with the Cyprus application. Whilst making it clear that a settlement was much desired, they declared, on the one hand, that the lack of a settlement would not in itself be a pre-condition for Cyprus's accession, but on the other hand sought to mollify Turkey by stating that 'Turkey is a candidate state destined to join the Union on the basis of the same criteria as applied to the other candidate States' (European Council, 1999c: 3). Hopes that the Cyprus Problem would still be resolved prior to accession were raised in 2002 when talks – they did not amount to negotiations – were conducted under United Nations auspices between the leaders of the Greek and Turkish Cypriot sides. However, with no solution reached by the time of the key December 2002 Copenhagen summit – the summit that took final decisions on which of the 10 + 2 applicant states had completed accession negotiations and the target date for their accession – the EU 15 leaders acted on the basis of their Helsinki decision and decided Cyprus could join the EU in May 2004, along with the eight CEECs and also Malta. A consequence of this decision was that if no settlement could be reached before Cyprus's accession, then because in legal, though not practical, terms the whole of the island of Cyprus would be joining the EU, a foreign power, Turkey, would be occupying EU 'territory'.

Subsequent to the Copenhagen summit, a ratification referendum was held successfully in Malta in April 2003. In Cyprus it was decided that a referendum would not be held unless it could be tied in with a resolution of the Cyprus Problem. With no such resolution seemingly pending, Cyprus's membership was ratified by the Cyprus parliament in July 2003, thus resulting in Cyprus being the only one of the 10 acceding states not to seek the approval of the national electorate. (For a fuller analysis of Malta and the EU, see Pace, 2001. For more on Cyprus and the EU, see Brewin, 2000, Nugent, 1997 and 2000).

Turkey

Turkey applied for EU membership in 1987: that is, three years before Cyprus and Malta and between seven and nine years before the CEECs. Yet of all these 13 countries, Turkey is the only one with which accession negotiations had not been opened by the end of 2003.

The official reason – given initially in the Commission's 1989 Opinion on the application and since 1998 in the Commission's annual reports on progress towards accession – is that whilst Turkey has made great strides towards meeting the political and economic aspects of the Copenhagen criteria, there remain important areas where further progress is necessary. Regarding the political criteria, the EU has criticized Turkey's record on human rights, especially in relation to the treatment of Turkish Kurds, and has expressed concerns about aspects of the functioning of Turkish democracy, including the political role of the military. Regarding the economic criteria, Turkey has been advised that its economy needs further liberalization and modernization before it can meet the rules of and be able to compete in the internal market.

But beyond the official reasons given to Turkey for not opening accession negotiations – reasons that since 1993 have amounted to saying it does not meet the Copenhagen criteria – there have also been other reasons behind the lack of enthusiasm of EU member states for Turkish membership. Questions have been raised about whether it is in the EU's interests to admit an Islamic country, most of which is geographically in Asia. Would admitting Turkey, it is asked, not end any prospect of the EU being based on a sense of shared identity. Another area of concern has focused on the interrelated issues of Turkey's relative lack of development, large agricultural sector, and population size (it currently has a population of over 65 million, which is projected to increase to 100 million by about 2020). These characteristics would combine to make Turkey a major 'drain' on EU resources, at least as long as the CAP and the Structural Funds continue in something like their present form.

However, though the EU has been reluctant to open accession negotiations with Turkey, it has been anxious to maintain good relations with it. This has been partly for economic reasons – Turkey is a large market and is the EU's sixth largest trading partner. It has been partly also for political and security reasons: Turkey is a NATO member, and – being an Islamic country with considerable influence in the Balkans, the Middle East, and several states of the former Soviet Union – is also an important bridge between east and west.

Throughout the 1990s and into the early 2000s the EU's strategy towards Turkey was, therefore, to establish as close relations with it as possible short of opening accession negotiations. As part of this strategy, and as noted above, at the 1999 Helsinki summit Turkey was accorded the status of being a candidate country. Further to this, an Accession Partnership designed to assist Turkey to make the changes that will result in it meeting the Copenhagen criteria was adopted by the Council of Ministers in March 2001. The priorities identified in the Partnership were then reflected in Turkey's own National Programme for the Adoption of the Acquis which was adopted, also in March 2001, by the Turkish government.

However, as the crucial December 2002 Copenhagen summit approached, pressure on the EU to give Turkey a date for the opening of accession negotiations intensified. One source of such pressure came from Turkey's traditional friend in western power circles, the USA. President Bush even telephoned the summit's chair, Danish Prime Minister Anders Fogh Rasmussen, on the eve of the summit to stress the strategic importance of Turkey (*European Voice*, 12–18 December 2002). Another source of pressure stemmed from the fact that the Turkish case was strengthened by recent reforms to the Turkish constitution and changes in political and administrative practice designed to improve Turkey's credibility under the democratic and human rights dimensions of the Copenhagen criteria. And a third source was the overwhelming victory of an Islamic party – the Justice and Development Party (AKP) – in the Turkish general election of November 2002. The new government quickly made clear that it was as resolved as its seemingly more pro-Western predecessors to seek a date for the early opening of accession negotiations.

At Copenhagen the leaders of the EU-15 did not quite meet Turkey's demands to set a definite date for the opening of accession negotiations, but came much closer to doing so than had been anticipated. It was decided that the December 2004 summit would authorize the immediate opening of accession negotiations if the Commission so recommended on the basis of Turkey having continued with its reform programme. The Copenhagen summit did not explicitly link the opening of accession negotiations to the Cyprus Problem, but the December 2003 Brussels summit did so by incorporating the following in its Conclusions: 'The European Council underlines the importance of Turkey's expression of political will to settle the Cyprus problem. In this respect, a settlement of the Cyprus problem [based on UN proposals] would greatly facilitate Turkey's membership application' (European Council, 2003b). Significantly, and helped by elections in northern Cyprus in December 2003 when pro-EU parties polled a narrow majority, 'serious' negotiations on a settlement opened in February 2004.

Attitudes in the EU-15

The 10 + 2 enlargement round is sometimes thought of as having been conducted at too slow a pace. After all, the gap from the collapse of communism in CEECs to the May 2004 accession date is almost 15 years. It is 15 years also from the 1990 applications of Cyprus and Malta to May 2004.

In fact, leaving aside the special cases of Cyprus (and the Cyprus Problem) and Malta (which froze its application for a time), these time spans are not so long or excessive as they might at first appear. One reason for this is that although communism collapsed in 1989/90, CEECs did not actually apply for EU membership until the mid-1990s. The gap between applying and joining is thus 10 years or less, which is much the same as was the gap for Portugal and Spain. Another reason is that the 10 + 2 round has been not only the biggest but also the most complex enlargement round that the EU has had to manage. It has been so partly because of the ever expanding nature of the *acquis* and partly because the CEECs have been in political, economic and administrative transition and so have had to make many more changes to domestic laws, structures and practices than previous applicants.

That all said, it is possible that the 10 + 2 enlargement round could have been pushed forward more quickly had there been a strong political drive amongst the EU-15 to do so. But the existing member states differed in their views, both about the enlargement process as a whole and about particular applicants. So, for example, amongst the customary integration enthusiasts, Germany, Italy and the three Benelux countries were all ultimately in favour of enlargement, but in the early stages of the process they were concerned that it might threaten EU institutional and policy deepening, including the movement towards EMU. The UK was perhaps the most consistent supporter of enlargement, but in its case a major part of the attraction was precisely that it might threaten deepening. France was prominent in the 'doubtful and hesitant' camp, partly because of concerns that its privileged axis with Germany might be weakened and partly because existing support mechanisms within CAP, from which it is the largest single beneficiary, would inevitably be brought into question. Beneficiaries from the EU's Structural Funds – especially Spain and Portugal – also harboured reservations because of fears that funds from which they benefited would be re-directed to CEECs.

Regarding attitudes to particular applicants, some applicant states were advantaged by having a member state or states that took a special interest in their cause, and in a few instances almost acted as their patron. For example, Germany, virtually sponsored Poland, and less so Hungary and the Czech Republic. This led to Germany making it clear, when Poland began to slip behind in the accession negotiations, that there could be no question of Poland not being included in the first wave of CEEC accessions. For a mixture of cultural and strategic reasons, the Scandinavian member states promoted the interests of the Baltic applicants. And, most openly of all, for national, cultural and strategic reasons, Greece strongly supported Cyprus, to the point of indicating that Greece would veto the whole enlargement process if Cyprus was not a first wave acceding state.

EU Preparations for Enlargement

The 10 + 2 enlargement has not proceeded according to the 'classical method' (Preston, 1995) in which the focus was on the willingness and ability of applicants to accept the *acquis communautaire* and accession negotiations were much taken up with the extent and length of transition periods. These features certainly have been important parts of the 10 + 2 round, but it has also had to be an 'adaptive' enlargement round in the sense that the EU has had to do much more than in previous rounds to assist applicants to meet the conditions of EU membership and has had itself to change and adapt more than it had in previous rounds.

There have been three main ways in which the EU has prepared for, and sought to protect itself within, the 10 + 2 round. First, it has worked with and assisted applicant states as they have sought to adjust to the requirements of membership. Second, it has set the entrance bar high, with stringent requirements designed to ensure that applicants do not threaten or endanger existing arrangements and practices. Third, it has adjusted itself so that applicants can be accommodated without causing too much disruption or threatening the functioning of the EU system.

Working with applicants

Soon after the collapse of communism the EU began working closely with CEECs as they sought to transform their economies and consolidate their new democratic political systems. Initially, the EU concentrated on providing financial aid and technical assistance, but as the CEECs began to move towards EU membership an increasingly wide range of activities were covered as part of what came to be known from the December 1994 Essen summit, which agreed on a comprehensive strategy for preparing CEECs for EU membership, as 'pre-accession' preparations (European Council, 1994b). These preparations necessitated, and resulted in the creation of, a number of frameworks and mechanisms to manage the process: frameworks and mechanisms that were quite new in the history of EC/EU enlargement, and that became ever more wide-ranging as the enlargement process unfolded. Whereas in previous enlargement rounds applicants had been left largely to themselves to effect necessary changes before accession, but were then assisted by being given transitional time in particularly difficult policy areas, there was a recognition from an early stage of what became the 10 + 2 round that this earlier approach was not feasible. It was not so for three main reasons. First, the CEECs were much less developed, both politically and economically, than previous applicants. For example, whereas GDP per head in Portugal and Spain was around 70 per cent of the EU average at the time of the opening of their accession negotiations, in the CEECs it averaged only about 40 per cent, and in Bulgaria and Romania was even below 30 per cent. Second, the large number of applicants would make for a highly confused and fragmented EU if too much use was made of transitional criteria. And third, the *acquis* was much more extensive and complex than it had been at the time of the most comparable previous enlargement round, the Mediterranean round. So, if the EU did not provide extensive pre-accession assistance to applicants then either accession would be inordinately delayed or arrangements would have to be made for far more extensive transitional arrangements than EU-15 states were prepared to countenance.

The main pre-accession frameworks and mechanisms to be established were:

- *Financial and technical assistance.* This was quickly channeled to CEECs after their communist regimes were replaced by fledgling democratic and market-based systems in 1989–90. The first major programme to be established was PHARE – initially the acronym for Poland and Hungary: Aid for the Restructuring of Economies, but later used as the name for the broader Programme of Community Aid for Central and Eastern European Countries. Poland and Hungary were the first recipients of PHARE aid because they were the first countries to initiate democratization and economic liberalization programmes, key considerations for the EU in its relations with CEECs even before the Copenhagen criteria were laid down in June 1993. PHARE has been used primarily for infrastructure development, for promoting economic and social cohesion, for investment in intra-regional cooperation and, especially since the December 1995 Madrid European Council emphasized the need for CEECs to improve their administrative systems, for training public officials. Between 1990–1999 PHARE was allocated a total funding of €6.8 billion and between 2000–03 a total of €6.4 billion. Large though these sums are in absolute terms, an indication of their modesty in relative terms is seen in the fact that the 2000–2003 allocation is equivalent to only 0.16 per cent of the EU-15 GNP. The other main pre-accession programmes have been: (i) ISPA, which was created in 1999, which is mainly for transport and environment investment support, and which was allocated €4.2 billion for 2000–03; (ii) SAPARD, which also was created in 1999, which is for agricultural and rural development support, and which was allocated €2.8 billion for 2000–2003; and (iii) a number of programmes involving co-financing with the European Investment Bank (EIB) and several international financial institutions. (Figures given in this paragraph are taken from Kok, 2003: 45–7.)

For the immediate post-accession period, the December 2002 Copenhagen summit assumed that 10 states would become EU members on 1 May 2004 and on this basis updated and adjusted post-accession expenditure that had been agreed at the 1999 Berlin summit. For 2000–2004, a maximum of €40.8 billion was allocated at Copenhagen. Of this, €21.7 was assigned to structural actions, €9.78 to agriculture and rural development, and €4.2 to other internal policies (European Council, 2002c: Annex 1). The sums to be allocated beyond 2006 will form part of the 2006–2013 EU financial framework, which has not been negotiated at the time of writing.

- *Association Agreements*, or, as they soon came generally to be called, *Europe Agreements*. These Agreements form the legal bases for association between applicant countries and the EU and have come to have as a central objective the provision of frameworks enabling applicants to gradually integrate into the Union. They mostly cover the establishment of free trade areas, the liberalization of economic activity, technical and legal assistance, participation in some EU programmes (including research, energy, public health, education, and environment), and political dialogue.

  Association agreements with the three non-CEEC applicants were long-standing: the first version of the agreement with Turkey was signed in 1963, that with Malta in 1970, and that with Cyprus in 1972. At the time of these initial versions of the agreements, EU accession was not promised and the liberalization of trade between the two sides was scheduled to be introduced only over a long period.

  The association agreements with the CEECs were signed between December 1991 (Hungary, Poland, and the Czech and Slovak Federal Republic) and June 1996 (Slovenia). Initially they were seen, as Maresceau (2003: 14) has observed, more as alternatives to enlargement than preparations for it. So though EU membership was proclaimed as an 'ultimate objective' of the signatories, they did not explicitly promise it. However, after the 1993 Copenhagen summit they did, in practice, come to be seen as and to be used as pre-accession frameworks.

  By February 1998 association agreements were in force with all of the 13 applicants.

- *Regular Reports on the Progress of Applicants Towards Accession*. Since 1998 the Commission has drafted, and in October/November published, annual reports – called Regular Reports – on all candidate states, including Turkey, plus a composite report called the 'Strategy Paper'. These reports are extremely detailed, covering all of the issues featuring in the accession negotiations and identifying where matters are proceeding satisfactorily and where they are not. A particular focus of the reports is on the measures taken to transpose the *acquis* into national law and the extent to which there is national administrative and judicial capacity to implement EU law. The reports have the effect of creating, as Maresceau (2003: 33) puts it, 'an atmosphere of permanent follow-up and contributes considerably to the enhancement in the candidate countries of an awareness that the necessary measures must be taken for the credibility of the enlargement process as such and to move forward in the accession negotiations'.

- *Accession partnerships*. Launched for the CEECs in 1998, and later for Cyprus, Malta and Turkey, as part of a reinforced pre-accession strategy, these provide a single framework for activity involved in the transition to membership. As such, they build on and extend existing pre-accession structures and assistance, especially the Europe Agreements. The partnerships identify priority areas in which the *acquis* is to be adopted, plan and coordinate the various financial assistance programmes, and monitor progress in meeting the accession conditions. An important element of the partnerships is National Programmes for the Adoption of the *Acquis* (NPAAs), which all candidate countries are obliged to adopt as part of the partnership. NPAAs involve candidate countries specifying the laws, the institutional and administrative reforms, the human and budgetary resources, and the timetable they intend to deploy in the priority areas identified in the partnerships. The partnerships, which necessarily require periodic updating, are thus a key element in meeting the conditions of and preparing for EU membership.

Setting the bar high

All organizations set conditions for new members. At a general level, they do so to protect the nature of the organization as it has developed and often also to protect the organization against the possibility of new members wanting to change it when they assume membership. At a more specific level, conditions may be set to safeguard the interests of particular existing members.

EU states were concerned from the outset of what became the 10 + 2 round about many aspects of accession by CEECs. Across the EU-15 as a whole, concerns included: whether CEEC accessions would disrupt the operation of the internal market; whether lower wages in the CEECs would result in over-stiff competition and in the diversion of investment from the EU-15; whether EU policy processes would be slowed down; and whether administrative, judicial and police structures in CEECs were such as to be capable of ensuring that EU laws and policies would be implemented with levels of efficiency and honesty that were comparable to those in the EU-15. Specific concerns of some EU-15 states were: whether they would suffer a net loss of EU subsidies from the Regional and Social Funds (of particular concern to Greece, Portugal and Spain); whether pressures for further reform of the CAP would increase (of particular concern to France); and whether there would be significant flows of immigrants from the CEECs (of particular concern to Austria and Germany).

So as to protect both the EU as an entity and themselves individually, the EU-15 sought to ensure that no applicant would enter the EU unless it met demanding entry terms. The first protective step taken was the formulation of the Copenhagen accession criteria, which set out requirements that candidate countries must have met, or be capable of meeting, before accession negotiations could be opened. The criteria were set out above – on p. 36 – and, in essence, specified that to be considered a viable candidate a country must: be a liberal democracy in which the rule of law is respected; have a functioning market economy that can cope with the competitive pressures of the market forces in the Union; be capable of implementing the *acquis communutaire* – that is, the established body of EU law; and be willing to be a full participant in EMU and the CFSP. Clearly these criteria are very general in scope and give to the Commission and existing member states considerable discretion in deciding just how the criteria are to be interpreted and whether or not applicants meet them (see, for example, Smith K.E., 2003: 115–19 on how the Commission interpreted the criteria in respect of the CEECs in its 1997 *Agenda 2000* document).

The second protective step was to set stiff entry requirements during the accession negotiations These requirements included obliging the applicant states to incorporate the 80 000 or so pages of the *acquis* into national law, to accept unfavourable terms in respect of financial support from the CAP and Structural Funds, to be permitted relatively few transitional measures, and to have to make significant changes to national administrative structures and practices. The approach, in short, was virtually to try and make acceding states into EU prototypes before they became members of the club.

Adjusting the EU for enlargement

In previous enlargement rounds the burden of adaptation fell largely on the applicants. However, in the 10 + 2 round the EU has been obliged to make considerable adjustments itself, both to its institutional and decision-making systems and to some of its policies.

Institutional adjustments

The 1996–1997 Intergovernmental Conference (IGC) was supposed to deal with the changes to the institutional and decision-making systems required by enlargement. It was to do so by thoroughly overhauling the arrangements that were still recognizably based on those that had been created for 'the Founding Six' in the 1950s. In the IGC, however, the governments of the EU-15 were unable to agree on all the changes that would be necessary, mostly because they knew enlargement was not imminent and EU governments are usually inclined to postpone contested 'historic' decisions, be they on treaty reform, financial perspectives, enlargement, or any other major matter, until the timetable gives them no option but to resolve matters. As a result, the treaty that emerged from the IGC – the Treaty of Amsterdam – made only a few relevant institutional changes. Rather, the governments decided to convene another IGC when enlargement was more imminent, though they did indicate in a protocol attached to the Treaty the outlines of some of the changes they envisaged making in the next IGC. This next IGC duly opened in February 2000. It produced the Treaty of Nice, which was agreed at the December 2000 Nice European Council meeting, was formally signed in February 2001, and came into effect – after a delay caused by a ratification difficulty in Ireland (see Chapter 2) – in February 2003.

The Amsterdam and Nice treaties did not make the radical institutional changes that many observers and some participants thought enlargement demanded, but between them they did at least make sufficient changes to permit enlargement to proceed. These changes are considered at length in Chapter 8, so only an outline of the most important of them is given here:

- upper limits were set on the overall size of the Commission, the EP, the ESC, and the CoR (an upper limit of 700 on the EP that was set at Amsterdam was raised to 732 at Nice);
- from 2005 and until such time as the EU has 27 members, each member state will have one Commissioner (Nice);
- national representations in the EU's other institutions were set (Nice, with minor adjustments to EP representations made in the 2003 Act of Accession);
- allocations of votes in the Council and the size of QMV majorities were set, it was stipulated that qualified majorities must include a majority of states, and it was determined that any state could request verification that a qualified majority represented at least 62 per cent of the total population of the Union (Nice);
- QMV was extended to more treaty articles (mainly Amsterdam, with only minor extensions at Nice);
- provision was made for enhanced, or flexible, cooperation (established at Amsterdam and made easier to apply at Nice).

Beyond treaty adjustments, other changes that have been made over the years in the operation of the EU will also help it to meet the challenges of enlargement. One of these changes is the much greater acceptance than formerly of the use of QMV where it is legally permitted. Another is the increasing use of flexible coalitions wherein initiatives are developed without the involvement of all member states. Schengen and EMU are the most developed of these, but aspects of defence and social policy are also included. A third change is the use since the late 1990s of what is known as the 'open method of coordination' (OMC) in which EU governments set non-legally-binding targets for themselves and then attempt to meet the targets through monitoring of each other's performance. And a fourth change is the movement towards 'Brussels-ization' of less delicate external policy matters, with policy control shifting from national external ministries to key actors in the Council and Commission systems.

These various institutional changes add up to a set of reforms that enable enlargement to go ahead, but they hardly constitute the more comprehensive reform of the EU that many believe is necessary in an EU of 15 plus, and even more so 25 plus, member states. Aware of this, it was agreed at Nice to open up a debate on the future of the EU and to convene another IGC in 2004. To facilitate the debate and prepare for the IGC, the December 2001 Laeken summit decided that a Convention on the Future of Europe, chaired by the former French President Valery Giscard D'Estaing, should be convened. Composed mainly of national government, national parliament, and EP representatives, the Convention duly deliberated from March 2002–June 2003 on the contents of a constitution for the EU. Many of the contents of the draft constitution it produced had enlargement very much in mind, including: replacing the rotating six-month Council presidency between all member states by a new and more flexible system designed to give the post greater solidity; the European Council to appoint its own President, by QMV, for a 2½-year term which could be renewed once; and – from 2009 – the size of the College of Commissioners to be reduced to fifteen, but with non voting Commissioners also to be appointed (European Convention, 2003).

Most of the recommendations of the Convention were duly accepted by the IGC, which was opened in October 2003. However, no agreement could be reached on QMV provisions in the Council. The Convention had recommended that QMV voting weights be abandoned in favour of a double majority system in which majorities would be deemed to exist for proposals that were supported by a majority of states representing at least 60 per cent of the EU's total population. Germany was especially anxious to accept this recommendation since the Nice arrangements had assigned to it a proportionately small voting weight – only 29 votes despite it having a population of just over 80 million. However, Poland and Spain, which were favourably treated under the Nice formula – 27 votes each despite both countries having populations of just under 40 million – were not willing to accept the Convention's proposal. Such was the implacability of both sides, that the IGC could not be concluded, as had been the intention, at the December 2003 Brussels summit.

Policy adjustments

The changes made to policies concern mainly the two policy areas that account for most of the EU's budgetary expenditure: the CAP and the Structural Funds. These changes are examined in Chapters 1 and 13 so, as with institutional changes, only a brief outline will be given here.

The Commission did much to set the reform agenda with the publication in 1997 of its communication *Agenda 2000: For a Stronger and Wider Union* (European Commission, 1997). Key recommendations in the communication were: a continuing movement of CAP away from price support to direct income support; targeting Structural Funds more tightly so as to deal with economic and social deprivation; and keeping EU budgetary expenditure within its existing limit of 1.27 per cent of total EU GDP. The Commission's recommendations were, after the customary horse-trading between member states on particular matters – which included some watering down of the CAP and Structural Fund proposals – subsequently accepted by the Heads of Government at their March 1999 Berlin summit, and were later translated into legislation.

It was always doubtful whether the Berlin arrangements would be adequate to permit enlargement to proceed without creating major funding difficulties. Certainly, the Commission's view was that a more radical reform of the CAP and the Structural Funds was necessary, given that acceding states would be beneficiaries – and some would be major beneficiaries – of both policy areas in their existing form. Significantly, when in February 2002 the Commission produced proposals for the application of the two policies to the prospective new member states, the most striking feature of them was long transition periods – of up to 10 years – before new member states would be treated on the same basis as existing member states. Hardly surprisingly, the proposals were received with dismay in most CEECs, but were largely accepted by the EU-15 and imposed on the applicants.

Accession Negotiations

The manner in which, and the reasons why, the EU moved from initially conducting accession negotiations with only six of the 10 + 2 candidate countries to conducting them with all 12 were outlined earlier in the chapter. This section will not re-cover that ground, but rather will focus on the nature and features of the accession negotiations.

With all 12 states, negotiations were preceded by a so-called 'screening process', which consisted of the Commission working with the applicants to establish their state of preparedness for accession and to identify what they needed to do to meet the conditions of membership. The main screening exercise for all of the states was conducted over a few months from April 1998, followed by updating as necessary.

For the six first-wave countries, once the screening process was completed, 'real' negotiations began in November 1998. For the six in the second wave, the negotiations began in February 2000

For all candidate countries the negotiations were divided into 29 chapters, plus two chapters that were left until all other chapters were closed. The 29 chapters covered the full range of the *acquis* and so included the likes of agriculture, energy, competition and free movement of capital. The two chapters left to the end were institutions and other matters (see Appendix 2 for a complete list of the chapters). One of the consequences

of dividing the negotiations into sectoral areas was that though the rationale for enlargement was presented by EU leaders in broad, visionary
and sweeping terms covering issues of peace, stability, security and prosperity (see Chapter 1), these justifications barely featured in any direct
way in the negotiation of accession terms. Rather, the focus in the negotiations was mostly on highly detailed and technical issues. (Note, this
section is written in the past rather than the present tense because negotiations with 10 of the 12 candidate countries were completed in
December 2002. It must, however, be emphasized that, at the time of
writing, negotiations continue with Bulgaria and Romania, and therefore
for them 'has/have' is usually more appropriate than 'was/were'.)

An important input into the negotiations were the Regular Reports on
the Progress to Accession that the Commission produced on candidate
countries from 1998. These reports were extremely detailed, covering
both general issues and each of the individual chapters around which the
accession negotiations were conducted. The reports served both as an
update on progress and as a guide for future action.

As regards the negotiation process on individual chapters, the procedure was as follows:

- Applicants presented position papers, which may have been only a
  couple of pages in length if it was being claimed that the *acquis* had
  already been met, no transitional measures were being sought, and
  implementing arrangements were thought to be satisfactory. Where
  there were problems, however, position papers were sometimes long.
- The Council – working through COREPER and, at ministerial level,
  the General Affairs Council – agreed a common position, by unanimity, on each chapter. Common positions were drafted by the
  Commission, but invariably were amended in Council before being
  given approval: the amendments often took the form not so much of
  changes in substance but rather of formulation, so that the position
  could be made acceptable to all of the EU-15. This need for common
  positions to be acceptable to all EU-15 states made this stage of the
  accession process often more difficult and protracted than the accession negotiations themselves.
- Insofar as detailed negotiations were necessary, these were conducted
  between the Council Secretariat – working in close liaison with the
  Commission – and officials from candidate countries. Much of this did
  not involve the classic image of negotiators from the two 'sides' facing
  each other across a table, but rather extensive informal communications between relevant and technically informed officials. In these
  communications the EU and candidate country officials sought to
  advance the accession process by, for example, establishing what
  needed to be done, by when something could be done, and where there
  might be flexibility on an apparent stumbling block.

- Formal negotiating rounds, attended by EU Foreign Ministers or their representatives and by the chief negotiators of applicant countries, usually were held about half way through a Council Presidency and in a 'rounding-up' session towards the end of a Presidency. These were largely set-piece occasions at which few 'real' negotiations occurred. At the rounding-up sessions, attempts were made – largely on the basis of agreements at COREPER level – to 'provisionally close' as many chapters as possible. Chapters were 'provisionally closed' when the EU decided no further negotiations were required and when the candidate country accepted the Council's common position. Closures were provisional rather than complete so as to enable a return to chapters if new *acquis* were adopted or if a candidate country failed to implement commitments made in the negotiations.
- Chapters were opened not on a differentiated basis according to the circumstances of applicants but rather on a schedule set by the EU (Glenn, 2003: 8). In this schedule, the first-wave applicants followed an identical sequence whilst the second-wave applicants followed a sequence almost identical to the first wave. For all applicants, what were thought to be the more problematic chapters, including those with the most significant budgetary implications – agriculture and regional policy – were left until the end. With second-wave applicants anxious to catch up, and with the EU recognizing from early 2000 that a 'big bang' enlargement round was both desirable and possible, chapters with second-wave applicant were opened more quickly than they had been with the first wave. For example, whilst the Czech Republic opened eight chapters in its first year of negotiations, Slovenia opened 15 (Glenn, 2003: 8).
- The length of time chapters were open varied both between chapters and between applicants in respect of particular chapters. Of particular importance in determining the lengths were the extent and complexity of the *acquis* covered by the chapter, the importance of the chapter to applicants (not all applicants, for instance, had a great stake in the Common Fisheries Policy), and the extent to which the governments of applicant states chose to contest the EU's position on points in the chapter. For example, on this last variable, Estonia, Latvia and Slovakia were amongst applicants that largely accepted the EU's position on free movement of capital, with the consequence that negotiations on the chapter lasted only six months, whilst Poland – anxious about the prospect of non-nationals buying Polish land and property – pressed for a longer transition period than was initially on offer, with the consequence that its negotiations on the chapter lasted for 30 months. (Glenn, 2003: 11)

Whether the above process really merits the description of 'negotiations' is perhaps open to question. Certainly, negotiations in the commonly understood sense of the word were conducted on only a rather limited range of issues, and when they were so conducted the balance of power was tilted very heavily towards the EU side. The fact is that the 'negotiating process' largely consisted of the applicant states trying to satisfy the EU that they had both incorporated the *acquis* into national law as required and had suitable administrative structures and arrangements in place to be able to fully apply the *acquis*. Applicants had no choice but to transpose virtually all of the 80,000 or so pages of the legislative *acquis* and to be able to demonstrate they had an administrative capacity to apply it in practice. In other words, applicants had to adopt the EU model. (For a fuller account of the conduct of the accession negotiations, see Baun 2000; Avery 2004.)

Insofar as there were 'negotiations', they mainly involved applicants seeking to be given long(er) transition periods to be able to adjust to EU policies and laws. Since, however, the EU was much more resolved than in previous rounds to keep lengthy transition periods to a minimum, the room for manoeuvre available to applicants was limited. The average number of transitional arrangements that was eventually 'conceded' was only between 15 and 20 per member state, with few of them lasting more than three to four years. Amongst the policy areas where many of the transitional arrangements were given were: free movement of capital (where, in a high profile and successful campaign, some CEECs fought to be allowed to prevent non-nationals from buying agricultural land for at least seven years), free movement of services, competition, agriculture, energy, the environment and taxation. A flavour of the highly specific nature of most of the transitional arrangements agreed is seen in the following examples:

- *Freedom to provide services*. Under the Investor Compensation Scheme, 'Estonia, Hungary, Latvia, Lithuania and Poland have been granted transitional arrangements until the end of 2007 to reach the minimum level of compensation.'
- *Competition policy*. 'A transitional arrangement is agreed with Cyprus and Hungary for the phasing-out of incompatible fiscal State aid for offshore companies by the end of 2005.'
- *Agriculture*. 'Slovenia may grant degressive State aid for the production of oil pumpkins for a period of 5 years from the date of accession.'
- *Environment*. 'The requirements for the storage of petrol and its distribution from terminals to service stations (Directive 94/63/EC) will be gradually achieved in Estonia (end 2006), Latvia (end 2008), Lithuania (end 2007), Malta (end 2004), Poland (end 2005) and Slovakia (end 2007)' (all these examples are taken from European Commission, 2003f).

Significantly in terms of displaying the resolve of the EU in the negotiations, whilst in numerical terms most of the agreed transitional arrangements were designed to assist the new member states, some of the more important ones were at the EU's insistence and were in the interests of the EU-15. The most notable of these concerned: free movement of persons, where the EU insisted on being protected from the risk of the immediate movement of people from Central and Eastern Europe to Western Europe after enlargement by insisting on a five-year transition period, with up to seven years in some circumstances, from the date of accession; CAP support, where – mainly for cost reasons, but partly also because it was felt giving subsidies to CEECs at EU-15 levels immediately on accession would delay a much needed re-structuring of the agricultural sector in CEECs – the EU was prepared to phase-in subsidies only gradually; and support for structural operations where, again mainly for cost reasons, payments to acceding states were to be phased-in only gradually and were also to be capped.

In addition to the EU's negotiating resolve, two other factors also limited the applicants' power in the negotiations. First, because all the negotiations were bilateral – between the EU and each applicant state – the applicants found it difficult to present a common front, though there were attempts to do so on CAP and budgetary issues. Second, the applicants were constrained precisely because they were applicants: it was more important to them than to the EU that the negotiations should succeed, and they were more anxious than the EU – or, at least, many EU member states – that the negotiations should be completed as quickly as possible.

*   *   *

With the December 2000 Nice summit having set the December 2002 summit as the target date for the conclusion of negotiations with the most prepared candidate states, and with subsequent summits having confirmed this as the aim, the accession process quickened in the months before the issuing of the Commission's 2002 Regular Reports. For, unlike in previous years, it was known that these Reports would not only provide an update on the accession process but would also make recommendations to the European Council on which states were now ready for membership. As anticipated, the Commission stated that negotiations had been completed successfully with all applicants apart from Bulgaria and Romania and that the ten states concerned should now proceed to membership. The European Council accepted the Commission's recommendations and determined that the Treaty of Accession would be signed in April 2003 with a view to ratification processes being completed in time for the new states to join the EU on 1 May 2004 – in time for them to be able to participate fully in the June 2004 EP elections. In addition, the European Council anticipated Bulgaria and Romania joining the EU in 2007 if they continued to make satisfactory progress in meeting the requirements of membership. This anticipation was reinforced at the 2003 June Thessaloniki and December Brussels summits, with the conclusions of the latter declaring: 'Welcoming Bulgaria and Romania in January 2007 as members of the Union, if they are ready, is the common objective of the Union of 25 . . . Bulgaria and Romania should continue energetically their preparations . . . so that accession negotiations can be brought to a successful conclusion in 2004 . . . and the Accession Treaty can be signed as soon as possible in 2005' (European Council, 2003b).

Accession treaties require EP assent by an absolute majority – that is, 314 out of 626 votes for the 10 + 2 round – before they can be formally signed by representatives of the Council on behalf of the EU. In April 2003, the EP duly gave its assent, with overwhelming majorities for each of the 10 states with which accession negotiations had been concluded and for the accompanying non-legislative resolution on the overall outcome of the negotiations.

Following the EP's assent, the Accession Treaty was formally signed one week later at a grand ceremony attended by Heads of Government in Athens (Greece held the Council Presidency).

The final stage of the accession process was for the Accession Treaty to be ratified by the EU-15 and the candidate states. In the EU-15 states, ratifications were processed via parliamentary votes. In all acceding states apart from Cyprus, national referendums were held, with a variety of rules concerning whether they were mandatory or advisory and on whether minimum turnouts were required for them to be valid. All the referendums endorsed membership (see Chronology, pp. 278–9). As was explained earlier in the chapter, the absence of a resolution of the 'Cyprus Problem', resulted in the Cypriot government deciding to ratify by a parliamentary vote only.

Concluding Remarks

The 10 + 2 round is the most momentous enlargement round in the history of the EC/EU in that it marks the point at which the EU is transformed from being a Western European organization into being a European-wide organization. By the time the round has been completed, the EU will have almost doubled in size in terms of the number of its member states and it will embrace countries of Central and Eastern Europe from which Western Europe was estranged for most of the second part of the twentieth century.

The 10 + 2 round has not only been momentous in its impact but also has been unique in many respects. This has been because of the sheer number of applicants with which the EU has had to deal, their very different character-istics compared with EU-15 states, and the fact that the scale of the enlarge-ment has forced the EU to examine aspects of its own operation in a way previous rounds have not. However, the 10 + 2 round has also displayed a number of important similarities with previous enlargement rounds. These contrasts and comparisons are explored in the next chapter.

Chapter 4

Distinctive and Recurring Features of Enlargement Rounds

NEILL NUGENT

The Distinctiveness of Enlargement Rounds

At first sight, the 10 + 2 enlargement round appears to be rather like a larger and more challenging version of the Mediterranean round. Certainly, it shares some of the characteristics of that earlier round: applicants just emerging from dictatorships; applicants with low per-capita GDPs; applicants with proportionately large agricultural sectors; and an EU with no wish to rush the application process through.

However, further inspection reveals the differences between the two rounds to be far greater than the similarities: the Mediterranean dictatorships were internal in that they were not engineered or controlled by another country and they had a much less embracing grip on society than did the communist regimes in the CEECs; the Mediterranean applicants had most of the features of a market economy, whilst the CEECs were just emerging from centrally planned economic systems; the Mediterranean states were all firmly within the Western zone of influence in the post-World-War-2 era, not least through NATO membership, whilst the CEECs were part of the Soviet bloc; and by the late 1990s and early 2000s the EU was much more integrated in respect of both institutional arrangements and policy responsibilities than had been the EC in the late 1970s and early 1980s when the Mediterraneans were negotiating accession terms.

These differences serve to make the point that all enlargement rounds are unique. They are so, most obviously, in terms of:

- *The number of applicants*. There were four applicants in the first round – Denmark, Ireland, Norway and the UK – with all but Norway joining; one plus two applicants in the second round – Greece, plus Portugal and Spain; four applicants in the third round – Austria, Finland, Norway and Sweden – with, again, all but Norway joining; and the 10 + 2 (or + 3 if Turkey is included) in the fourth round.
- *The characteristics of applicants*. These have varied enormously both

between applicants in the same enlargement round and, in more general terms, between rounds. Focusing just on differences between rounds, examples of variations include: geographical location – the first enlargement brought in northern countries, the second Mediterranean countries, the third two very northern countries and one central country, and the fourth central and eastern countries and two Mediterranean countries; political inheritance – the countries which joined in the first and the EFTAn enlargement rounds all had well-established and solid democratic political systems, whilst those that joined in the Mediterranean and 10 + 2 rounds had recent histories of authoritarian/military/one party rule; and GDP per capita – the EFTAns joined the EU with an average per capita GDP well above the EU average, whilst the average of the applicants in the first round was 90 per cent, in the Mediterranean round was 70 per cent, and in the 10 + 2 round was 40 per cent.

- *The level of development of the EC/EU.* As European integration has advanced, accession processes have necessarily embraced an ever wider range of issues and, in turn, have necessarily become more complex. So, for example, the first enlargement round did not stray much beyond market-related issues, and even on these the *acquis* was much narrower than it has subsequently become. The fact is that in the early 1970s the EC did not have a foreign and security policy, a justice and home affairs policy, coordinated macroeconomic policies and a single currency, or much in the way of environmental policies. In consequence, unlike in later enlargement rounds, especially the 10 + 2 round, these issues barely arose during the accession processes that led to Denmark, Ireland and the UK joining the EC.

- *The number and nature of policy issues creating difficulties.* All applicants come to accession negotiations with policy issues about which they are particularly concerned. This can create problems, on both sides, during the accession process. For example, a key issue for the UK was protection of its historically important trading links with Commonwealth counties; for Spain, the Common Fisheries Policy was an important issue because on entry it would have the largest fishing fleet in the EC; and for most CEECs – but especially Poland – there was a desire to secure early access to the full benefits of the CAP.

- *The length of the accession process.* It might be assumed that the process would have become progressively longer as the *acquis* has developed, but this is not so. It certainly is the case that the rapid completion of the first enlargement round – the negotiations themselves lasted only around 18 months – was assisted by the relatively undeveloped nature of the *acquis*, but of equal importance was the fact that the applicants were all well-established democracies with solid market-based economies. That is to say, though there were many specific points on which agreements had to be negotiated, all of the applicants were adjusted to the main bases of membership. Such was not the case in the second round, where the political and economic bases of the applicants were much less secure and where many more adjustments were necessary to meet the requirements of Community membership. In consequence, five and a half years elapsed between Greece's application and its entry, for Portugal the gap was almost nine years, and for Spain it was eight a half years. For the 10 + 2 applicants the necessary adjustment were, of course, even greater than they had been for the Mediterraneans, with the consequence that for the CEECs the gap was on average 10 years, whilst for Cyprus and Malta – each of which had special problems – the gap was over 13 years. But, squeezed between the Mediterranean and 10 + 2 rounds was the EFTAn round, which was completed very quickly: the negotiations lasted only 13 months and less than three years elapsed between the last EFTAn application – from Finland in March 1992 – to the three accessions in January 1995. There were two main reasons why the round was completed so quickly: all the applicants more than met the broad political and economic criteria of membership, and many of the technical matters that feature in accession negotiations had been cleared in the earlier negotiations to create the European Economic Area (EEA).

All enlargement rounds, therefore, have been in important respects distinctive, indeed unique. They have been so because of features of the applicants on the one side and of the EC/EU on the other.

Recurring Features of Enlargement Rounds

Although all enlargement rounds have been distinctive, they have also displayed a number of recurring features. These features will now be examined.

Motivations of applicants

All states applying for EU/EC membership have done so for a mixture of economic and political reasons. The particular nature of, and balance between, these reasons has naturally varied from case to case, but all potential applicants have had to weigh the respective advantages and disadvantages presented by the two sets of reasons and relate them to their particular circumstances.

The prime economic reason for seeking membership has been that the EC/EU has been seen to be successful in terms of the usual benchmarks of economic success: promoting trade, growth, and prosperity. The main explanation for this success has been held to be the opening of the internal market to an ever-increasing number of people. The main economic disadvantage of membership has been the restrictions placed on national economic manoeuvrability. Initially, the restrictions applied primarily in the sphere of trade, following the construction of the customs union in the 1960s. Later, restrictions also came to apply in many other spheres as, especially following the 're-launch' of the Community in the mid-1980s, most key economic decisions – on matters ranging from competition law to macro-economic management – have come to be either taken at, or at least be heavily guided from, the EU level.

Two main sets of possible political advantage have offered themselves to potential member states. The first has been to be part of an organization with the potential to exercise a considerable influence on the world stage. No EU state, not even Germany, which, with a population of over 80 million, is the largest member state by some 20 million, has the resources to be an international power of the first rank. The second possible political advantage for many applicants has been that the EU has offered the prospect of bolstering fledgling democracies and/or has offered soft security protection. Bolstering their newly-established democratic systems was important for all of the Mediterranean and CEEC applicants, whilst offering soft security protection has been important for the CEECs and also Cyprus.

Motivations of existing member states

Just as applicants have sought membership for varying mixtures of economic and political reasons, so have existing member states been willing to open the doors for such reasons. The central economic reason has been the perceived opportunities and advantages that have been anticipated as flowing from widening the internal market. However, other economic considerations have played a part too, as with, for example, the EC-6 welcoming the fact that the UK would be a net contributor to the EC's budget. Political reasons have included the potentially greater global role and impact for the EC/EU, the security advantages of bringing together the European continent – especially important in the 10 + 2 round – and, in the Mediterranean and 10 + 2 rounds, a strong desire to help applicants to consolidate their new democratic systems. Such has been the perceived importance of this last reason that in 1976 the European Council did not follow the Commission's advice that accession negotiations with Greece should be delayed because the country was not ready for membership in economic terms but rather instructed that negotiations should be opened so as to help underpin Greece's newly restored democracy.

But whilst existing member states have recognized reasons for being open to applicants, all enlargement rounds have also been accompanied by concerns that enlargement might create too many difficulties for the

EC/EU and/or might damage national interests. This has resulted in a certain hesitation, even reluctance, to embrace new members too quickly. It is a reluctance that is understandable. Existing member states have, after all, helped to build, and are part of, an organization they believe furthers their interests and they do not want to see this endangered. President de Gaulle's two vetoes of the UK were but a particularly blatant and overt instance of national considerations and calculations guiding reactions to attempts by outsiders to join the club. When de Gaulle's successor, Georges Pompidou, lifted the French veto he did so not because of any attachment to a pan-European spirit but because he judged UK membership would be useful to France by helping to open the British market and providing a counter balance within the Community to the increasingly powerful West Germany.

In the EFTAn and 10 + 2 rounds, the concerns of some member states have been such as to lead the EU to attempt to satisfy applicants with arrangements that have stopped short of accession. In the EFTAn round, the concern – which was encouraged by the then President of the Commission, Jacques Delors – was that an enlargement at that stage might deflect the EU from its efforts to forge further political and economic deepening (the latter including the EMU project.) Such concerns lay behind the creation of the EEA. In the 10 + 2 round, the main concern was that the applicants were so far from being prepared for membership that their accession would be both hugely disruptive and too expensive. This concern formed part of the background to the Europe Agreements and the assumption by existing EU member states in the early 1990s that these would serve to help put CEEC EU memberships on a long hold. Of course, such was the attraction of EU membership for the EFTAns and the CEECs that the EEA and the Europe Agreements did not delay membership applications, or indeed membership itself.

Managing applications

The ways in which membership applications are handled have become progressively sophisticated and fine-tuned over the years. So, in the 10 + 2 round, innovations included the increasingly elaborate pre-accession preparations, the devising of a 'roadmap' to provide target dates for the closing of chapters, and the creation in the Commission – at the beginning of the College that assumed office in September 1999 under the Presidency of Romano Prodi – of a DG for Enlargement.

But although the mechanics of dealing with enlargement have been developed, they have mostly conformed to a similar overall pattern in each round. The 1973 enlargement was the most 'rudimentary', but then the EC was much less developed in institutional and policy terms at that time and had no 'template' from which to work. However, even that enlargement displayed many of the central features that are still very much present today: the decision to open the round was taken at a summit of national leaders (the Hague summit of December 1969, which was an informal summit since the European Council had not then been created); the detailed negotiations were conducted by teams of expert officials from the applicant states on the one side and from the Commission and Council on the other side; and final decisions to conclude negotiations were taken by politicians on both sides (on the EU side, key political decisions of this nature usually were taken in the Foreign Ministers Council, but since the creation of the European Council in 1974 they mostly have been taken at summits).

The accession procedures as they applied in the 10 + 2 round were described at some length in Chapter 3, so only an outline of the main stages as they have become 'standardized' will be given here:

- The European Council decides whether an application is acceptable in principle. Only one application has been rejected to date – that of Morocco because it is not a European state.
- When an application is deemed to be acceptable in principle, the European Council asks the Commission to produce a report on whether the applicant meets the conditions of membership and to evaluate the strengths and weaknesses of the application.
- The Commission's report on an application, which normally takes some months to produce, is known as its Opinion (or *avis*). All Opinions contain a recommendation on whether or not to proceed to accession negotiations. Amongst the recommendations that have been made are: that accession talks be opened in the near future – Spain and Portugal, the EFTAns, and the first wave CEECs; that applicants are not ready for negotiations and should wait until they are further developed – Greece (the only Commission recommendation to have been rejected), Turkey, and the five second wave CEECs; and that a state is ready according to the normal criteria but circumstances suggest the opening of negotiations should be delayed – Cyprus and Malta.
- The European Council sets the date for the opening of accession negotiations.
- The negotiations are divided into sectoral areas. Before detailed negotiations between the applicants and the EU can begin in any sectoral area, the latter must agree, by unanimity, on its common position. The most difficult and longest part of the negotiating process is usually not the exchanges between the EU and applicants, but these internal deliberations in the EU as the member states search for common negotiating positions.
- The negotiations between the EU and applicants are overseen by the Council of Ministers (Foreign Ministers) working with the Commission on the EU side and by national governments on the applicants' side. The detailed deliberations and exchanges – most of which

are conducted through memos, papers, and documents rather than through across-the-table discussions – are handled by subject specialists.
- When all of the negotiations are deemed by Ministers to have been finalized, they are referred to the highest political level – the European Council on the EU side – for formal completion. The European Council sets the date for the signing of an accession treaty and a target date for EU admission.
- Accession treaties must be ratified by the EP and by all existing and applicant states according to their own preferred procedures.

An elite-driven process

Decision-making in European liberal democratic states is elite-driven and elite-managed. Citizens do input into decision-making – most obviously and commonly through elections and public opinion soundings – but they do not directly control decisions, except in the rare circumstances when referendums are held. Elected decision-makers are expected to provide a lead, and because they are representatives rather than delegates they are able, and arguably are obliged, to take what they believe to be the best decisions in the circumstances they meet even if their electorates are sceptical or are opposed.

All EU enlargement rounds have been controlled by political elites, in both existing and applicant states, on the basis of the principles that have just been outlined. Or at least they have been so up to the point of ratification of accession treaties. Even though EU membership has immense implications for acceding states and important implications for existing member states, no government has ever consulted its electorate on whether accession negotiations should be opened. Moreover, no existing member state has ever consulted its electorate after the signing of accession treaties: ratification has always been channelled via national parliaments.

In existing member states this control by elites has been especially important in the 10 + 2 round. It has been so because opinion in the EU-15, for most of the period of the accession process, has, on average, been reasonably evenly divided for and against enlargement, though in a minority of states it has leant against. So, for example, in 2001, *Eurobarometer* (which measures opinion in EU states) reported that, across the EU-15, 43 per cent of respondents indicated they were in favour of enlargement, 35 per cent were against, whilst 22 per cent expressed no opinion. Support was strongest in Greece, Ireland and Spain, and weakest – there were majorities against – in Austria, France and Germany (Eurobarometer: 55, October 2001).

Occasionally, the government of an existing member state has indicated that it might hold a referendum on accession ratification but this has tended to be done either to deflect a temporary domestic problem or to put pressure on applicants that are causing 'difficulties' in negotiations to be more compliant. Whatever the reason for indicating that a referendum might be possible, the fact is that no such referendums have been held, even when particular enlargement rounds have had major and very direct implications for existing member states, as when borders are shared with applicants. A key reason why they have not been held is that, as with the very limited use of referendums in domestic politics or on such important EU subjects as treaty reforms and the introduction of the euro, governments prefer to remain in control of events and they lose control if they permit referendums to be held. That this is so is seen in EU governments having lost referendum votes on the ratification of the Maastricht Treaty (Denmark in 1992), the adoption of the euro (Denmark in 2000 and Sweden in 2003), and the ratification of the Nice Treaty (Ireland in 2001). So, even when some thought has been given by governments of existing member states to holding referendums on accessions, and this itself has been only an occasional occurrence, it has in the event been judged to be just too risky to go ahead.

The most significant exception to the pattern of elite dominance is the ratification of accession treaties in acceding states. With the exception of the UK in the 1973 round, all three states that made up the Mediterranean round, and Cyprus in the 10 +2 round, all acceding states have held a referendum on the terms of accession. The rules of these referendums have varied greatly, including in respect of whether their outcome has been binding or merely advisory and also in respect of whether a specified percentage of the electorate has had to vote in order for the referendum to be valid. Though there have been concerns in some states as to whether the necessary majority would be obtained – Malta was seen as being the most doubtful in the 10 + 2 round – the only country which has rejected accession terms negotiated by its government is Norway – in both 1972 and 1984 (see the Chronology for all referendum results).

The impact on widening and deepening

The nature of the relationship between the widening and deepening of the European integration process has been raised and debated at every enlargement round, but especially since the Mediterranean round. Widening refers to the accession of new member states whilst deepening refers to the extension of EU-level policy competencies and the strengthening of EU institutions.

The debate has focused particularly on whether, to what extent, and in what ways widening and deepening are in potential conflict with one another. The essence of the case that widening threatens deepening is that the larger, the more diverse, and the less cohesive the EU becomes then so does decision-making become more difficult and, therefore, policy development more problematical. All member states have recognized that there is at least something in this case, whilst the UK, for long the member state least willing to support integrationist advance, has also *hoped* there is much in the case. Because of the concerns of most states that widening might threaten deepening in this way, a cautious approach has tended to be taken towards new applicants. So, for example, as noted earlier in the chapter, a major reason the EU promoted the EEA with the EFTAns and Europe Agreements with CEECs was a hope that these would postpone membership applications.

Because of their concerns that widening might endanger deepening, the more integrationist states have taken a lead to ensure that precisely the reverse happens. This has been achieved by preceding, or at least accompanying, each enlargement round since the Mediterranean round with treaty reforms that have had as at least part of their purpose advancing institutional and policy deepening before they can be threatened by widening: the major component part of the Mediterranean round – the Spanish and Portuguese accessions – was accompanied by the SEA; the EFTAn round was preceded by the Maastricht Treaty; and the 10 + 2 round was preceded by the Amsterdam and Nice Treaties. All of these treaties provided for both institutional deepening – including provisions for increased supranational decision-making – and policy deepening, including by adding new policy areas to the treaties and by making it easier for many policy decisions to be made. Furthermore, the 10 + 2 round provided an important part of the background to the convening in 2002 of the Constitutional Convention on The Future of Europe, followed by the convening in 2003 of an Intergovernmental Conference (IGC) charged to finalize a constitution for the EU. Widening has thus been an important factor in driving deepening.

The case that deepening threatens widening rests mainly on the argument that deepening raises the barriers for would-be member states by making the conditions of entry look too intimidating and the *acquis* ever more difficult to meet. That the barriers are raised by deepening is indeed indisputable, but there is little evidence to indicate that this discourages possible applicants. On the contrary, deepening has promoted widening by increasing the importance of the EU and hence the desirability/necessity of joining before deepening proceeds even further. This does, of course, create the possibility of states seeking membership not so much for the 'positive' reason of what is to be gained but more for the 'negative' reason of fear of being excluded. In turn, as Redmond and Rosenthal have observed (1998a: 5), this possibility 'raises the specter of some of the newer member states not wanting to pursue integration beyond a certain point and/or in certain areas; from here it is but a short step to "variable geometry" '.

Far from being in conflict, widening and deepening have therefore proceeded hand-in-hand – indeed have even promoted each other. This is not, of course, to suggest that they have been the *only* promotional factors. Deepening has also been promoted by the pursuit of greater economic prosperity, of greater security, and of a greater voice for the EU in international affairs. Amongst other factors promoting widening have been changing international power balances (which encouraged the UK, and in its slipstream Denmark and Ireland, to join), the end of authoritarian dictatorships (the Mediterranean round), the end of the Cold War (the EFTAn and 10 + 2 rounds), and economic interdependence (all rounds).

But though deepening and widening have proceeded alongside one another, the nature of the deepening has been changed in some respects by widening in that it has had to assume a more flexible character. As EMU, Schengen, and the Amsterdam and Nice provisions for enhanced cooperation show, it has come to be accepted that beyond the internal market core there are circumstances in which it is permissible for institutional and policy development to occur without all member states participating. This development is a direct consequence of the EU becoming larger and taking on a more heterogeneous membership. Most observers and practitioners believe the 10 + 2 round will, because of the number and diversity of the acceding states, greatly boost this movement in the EU towards flexibility or differentiation.

Impact on the European Union

It is evident that all enlargement rounds have had a significant impact on the nature and operation of the EU. They have done so, most notably, in terms of institutional composition, the rules and functioning of decision-making processes, and policy development.

Institutional composition

The most obvious impact of enlargement on EU institutional composition has been the need to incorporate representatives and officials from acceding states into the EC/EU institutions. At the 'political' level, this incorporation was, until the 10 + 2 round, relatively straightforward, with acceding states given their 'due' allocation of a Commissioner (or two in the case of the UK and Spain), an ECJ judge, a seat in the European Council and Council of Ministers, a proportionate number of MEPs, and appropriate allocations in the other institutions. The 10 + 2 round, however, was more problematical, with many practitioners and observers taking the view that if the institutions were to be able to operate efficiently after such a large intake there would have to be a radical re-think of their composition with, for example, an end to the system of each member state having at least one Commissioner and a tight cap put on the overall size of the EP. In the event, the IGCs leading up to the Amsterdam and Nice treaties, which were established largely to tackle the institutional implications of the 10 + 2 round, failed to provide for fundamental reforms (unless the restriction of all member states to one Commissioner and the cap on the size of the EP can be so described) and largely settled for the customary 'easing in' arrangements.

At the administrative level, the number of additional posts created depends on the number and size of new states acceding plus the outcome of budgetary negotiations between the EU's institutions. In the 10 + 2 round, for example, the Commission recruited 500 temporary staff in the period leading up to enlargement – primarily to deal with languages work and with agriculture policy and regional policy (*European Voice*, 2–8 October 2003). In the first year of enlargement (2004) the Commission was assigned an extra 780 permanent posts, whilst the Council was assigned 286 and the EP 355 (*EUobserver*, 20 December 2003). Further additions were planned to be phased-in over a five year period.

Some senior administrative positions have virtually been assigned to new member states in the early post-accession period, which has led to pressure on some established officials to take early retirement and also to (seemingly justified) complaints about people being appointed who would not qualify in the normal way. However, in a short space of time, officials from acceding states have become subject to the same entry and promotions requirements as established officials. An important effect of enlargement on the EU bureaucracy has, of course, been to make it more multi-national and multi-cultural in composition, which has led to suggestions that the work of the bureaucracy has been increasingly influenced by the existence of different national administrative cultures (see, for example, McDonald, 2000).

The changed composition of the EU's political and administrative institutions has served to undermine the dominance of French as the EU's, and especially the EU bureaucracy's, working language. The 1973 enlargement brought in two countries (the UK and Ireland) which had English as their first language and one (Denmark) which had it as its second language. The 1995 enlargement brought in three countries in which English was much more the second language than French. Of course, the increasing role of English as the language of international communication has been important in this context too, but English would not have made such an 'advance' without enlargement.

The rules and functioning of decision-making processes

The approach to adapting the rules and functioning of decision-making processes so as to accommodate new member states has, for the most part, followed a similar pattern to the adjustments made to the composition of institutions. That is to say, changes that have been judged to be necessary to enable new members to join have been made, but they have stopped short – until the 10 + 2 round at least – of using enlargement as the occasion for radical re-structuring.

Little was done to decision-making rules or functioning at the time of the 1973 enlargement round. However, subsequent enlargement rounds have always been accompanied by calls for reforms in the interest of improving decision-making capacity. Attention has focused primarily on the anticipated greater difficulties of achieving unanimity in the Council with more members at the table. Concerns that this would lead to decisions not being taken in key policy areas provides much of the explanation for the convening of IGCs and for the intense focus at IGCs on QMV. Some changes made to QMV rules consequent upon enlargement have been unavoidable, including the allocation of Council votes to new member states and setting the number of votes that constitutes a qualified majority. Other changes, however, have been more discretionary, including determining the treaty articles to which qualified majority voting (QMV) should be extended and the political willingness to actually use QMV when it is available.

Because member states had avoided making certain much-needed difficult decisions on rules and functioning in previous rounds, and because too of the scale of the round, it was generally recognized by the EU-15 that the 10 + 2 round would require attention being given to neglected aspects of the rules and operation of the EU. The Amsterdam and Nice IGCs were supposed to do this but, in the event, they largely limited themselves to the bare essentials to make enlargement possible. However, with significant, and arguably fundamental, reform clearly required, the Constitutional Convention on the Future of Europe that was convened in March 2002 to help lay foundations for the next IGC was charged by the 2001 Laeken European Council meeting with the task of taking a broad view of the nature and functioning of the EU's institutions and decision-making processes. As was shown in Chapter 3, several of the most important recommendations of the Convention – which were formally presented to the June 2003 Thessaloniki summit in the form of a draft constitution – stemmed directly from the increasing size of the EU. These included recommendations for a new European Council President, for the abolition of the rotational Council presidency, and for a smaller College of Commissioners. Most of the recommendations were duly accepted by the IGC, which convened the following October. However, recommendations on Council voting – centred on abolishing national voting weights and basing majorities on a majority of member states representing at least 60 per cent of the total EU population – were not accepted, which led to the IGC being, in effect, suspended at the December 2003 Brussels summit.

Policy development

EC/EU policy development has been affected in many ways by each enlargement round, with all newcomers bringing their own policy preferences, priorities, and needs with them. One of the effects has been to intensify the importance of some policies. Such was, for example, the case with the Common Fisheries Policy after the UK and Ireland became members. Another effect has been to add new dimensions to existing policies, as, for instance, with Greece, Portugal and Spain seeking to shift the balance in CAP spending from northern temperate produce to Mediterranean produce. And a third effect has been to make it more difficult for all members to be full partners in policy initiatives, for the more member states there are the more diverse are the interests and policy preferences that have to be accommodated. The differentiated character of EMU and of Schengen illustrate this, as do many foreign and security policy actions.

Regional policy provides, as Preston (1997: 138–43) shows, another good example of how a policy area can both assume salience and also be changed as a result of enlargement. A Directorate General for Regional Policy was created in the Commission in 1967, but it was only with the 1973 enlargement that regional policy assumed real significance. It did so because the enlargement resulted in the establishment of the European Regional Development Fund (ERDF), which was devised not only to assist less prosperous areas, including Ireland, but also to enable the UK to receive transfer payments that would partially offset its budgetary deficit with the EC caused by its relatively small agricultural sector. The Mediterranean round then led to a major upgrading of regional policy, and, more broadly, 'cohesion' policy, with the Single European Act adding a new 'Economic and Social Cohesion' title to the EEC Treaty, and with the 1988 'Delors 1' package of budgetary reforms doubling the size of the Structural Funds (composed mainly of the ERDF and the European Social Fund) between 1988–1992. As Preston observes of this period, 'The focus on 'cohesion' was part of the grand bargain underpinning the development of the Single European Market and it was the price exacted by the poorer, mainly southern, EC members for their consent to further internal deregulation' (pp.140–1). In the early 1990s, the four poorest member states – Greece, Portugal, Spain, and Ireland – bargained hard again over the replacement to the Delors 1 package, and were instrumental in securing another doubling of Structural Fund expenditure in the 1993–1999 financial perspective. Even the EFTAn enlargement round affected regional policy, not in its case by leading to an increase in expenditure but by producing an additional criterion for Structural Fund payments: under the new Objective 6, areas with low population density in Arctic and Sub-Arctic regions were to qualify for financial support.

External policies – both economic and political – also serve to illustrate how enlargement can impact on existing EU policies. The main impact here has been in the way new member states have sought to protect many of their pre-accession external arrangements and interests, either by seeking to persuade the EU to enter into new arrangements with third parties and/or by seeking to raise the profile and importance of issues, interests and geographical areas already on the EU's external policy agenda. As Cremona (2003: 185) has noted, examples of this phenomenon include the following: the 1973 enlargement promoted the negotiation of a free trade agreement with the remaining EFTA states, an increased engagement with the Nordic states arising from Denmark's membership, and a similar increased engagement with the ACP states and the US arising from the UK's membership; the Mediterranean enlargement stimulated the development of policy towards Latin America and the Mediterranean region; and the EFTAn round led directly to the so-called Northern Dimension initiative and raised interest in relations with the Baltic states and Russia. It can be anticipated that the 10 + 2 round is unlikely to have much impact on the EU's relations with the 'far abroad', but is likely to heighten the importance of relations with the (in many cases new) near neighbours of the Western Balkans, of the former Soviet Union, and of the southern Mediterranean.

Concluding Remarks

This chapter has compared enlargement rounds in order to bring out a number of differences and similarities between them.

Differences between rounds have been occasioned by a number of factors related to both the applicants and to the EC/EU. Regarding applicants, amongst important factors that have been different between rounds have been their number, their levels of political and economic development and their historical legacies. Regarding the EC/EU, the key factor has been that it has become much more integrated over the years and so has imposed ever expanding membership requirements on applicants.

The similarities between rounds are such as to testify that, notwithstanding the many distinctive features each round has displayed, there is a considerable measure of continuity and evolution in the enlargement process. This is seen, for example, in the motivations of both applicant and existing member states, in the necessity of all newcomers having to make many domestic adjustments before admittance, and in the elite-driven and elite-dominated nature of enlargement processes. The 10 + 2 round may not have proceeded in quite the classical manner described by Preston (1995 and 1997) and may have required more adaptations on both the applicant and member states sides than had been seen before, but much of it was still conducted within a recognizably inherited framework.

Chapter 5

What the New Member States Bring Into the European Union

*HEATHER GRABBE**

Introduction

Does the European Union really face a dilemma between widening or deepening? Both academic work and press comment on the EU frequently assume there is a tension between enlargement and further integration. Behind this assumption lies the belief that if more countries are involved in the EU's decision-making, the Union will be less able to develop new projects that will extend the scope of European integration. This chapter challenges that view, arguing that the new members joining in 2004 will, in fact, encourage the EU to develop new areas of integration. The effects of enlargement will force the member states to work more closely together on issues where they already have significant cooperation either inside or outside the framework of the EU's treaties.

The 2004 enlargement increases the number of member states by two thirds, which creates a major impact on the EU's institutions and budget. But the new members also bring specific policy problems that open up new opportunities for integration. For example, the EU-25 has wider social and economic disparities; it has new borders witheven poorer countries to its east; and it becomes more diverse politically and ethnically. This chapter addresses some of the specific challenges that the new members bring in, notably increased economic diversity, administrative weakness, and new perspectives on the EU's external role. In responding to these features and challenges, the enlarged EU will have to develop new policies, which will take it into new fields of integration.

* Parts of this chapter draw on joint work by the author and Katinka Barysch (published as Barysch and Grabbe, 2002).

Economic Challenges

Key economic features of acceding states

The 10 new members change the EU by increasing its population, by increasing its economic disparities, and by bringing in more diversity. The number of people living in the Union grows by a quarter, but the new members add just 8 per cent to the EU's GDP (at purchasing power parity), so they are unlikely to have a dramatic effect on its economy. Moreover, most of the economic effects of enlargement have already been felt, as a result of trade liberalisation and investment flows over the 15 years of preparations for accession. However, more trade could result from the abolition of frontier controls on the movement of goods and the removal of the remaining trade barriers. Foreign direct investment is also likely to continue to increase, in an unspectacular but steady flow.

The most significant economic change that the new members bring to the Union is in extending its range of poverty and wealth. The acceding states have income levels of between one-third and two-thirds of the EU average, as is shown in Appendix 1. However, there is a diversity of income levels among the EU-15, so the top end of the new members' incomes overlaps with the bottom of the EU 15's income range. The per capita incomes of Slovenia and Cyprus are not much different from those of Greece and Portugal. However, incomes in Latvia are only one-third of the EU average. The enlarged EU therefore has to consider how to help many of the new members to catch up economically, but, contrary to widely held beliefs, not all of the new members are dramatically poorer than EU-states.

There are some differences in the economic problems faced by the new member states and the EU-15. These differences are explored in Chapter 10, but a few of the key differences merit a mention here, since they will affect what kind of policies are suitable to encourage the new members to catch up with the richer EU-15 members. Poland has a large rural population (as do the candidates that are not entering in 2004 – Bulgaria, Romania and Turkey), and needs help with transforming its farming sector. However, the other countries have a much smaller proportion of the workforce in agriculture. They will thus be less keen than Poland to see a large proportion of the EU's budget devoted to the Common Agricultural Policy in future. Instead, most of the new members will prefer to see EU financial transfers devoted to other ways of making their economies more competitive.

Labour market problems are also somewhat different. Unemployment rates are high in the CEECs, especially in declining industrial heartlands and rural areas. In counties such as Poland and Slovakia unemployment is as high as 20 per cent. Only the Czech Republic and Slovenia have employment levels that match or surpass the EU-15's 64 per cent average. But the main problems with CEEC labour markets are geographical and skills mismatches, not over-regulation as in the EU-15: laid-off workers in

CEECs lack the transport links, flexible housing markets, and skills to take advantage of new employment opportunities in faster-growing sectors.

The Single European Market

It is evident that the new members will be able to compete in the Single European Market (SEM), because they are already doing so. From the economic point of view, enlargement was a reality long before 2004, with the candidates and the EU having almost completely dismantled barriers to bilateral trade, except in the important sphere of agriculture. CEECs have benefited from over a decade of massive investment by Western European firms. Thousands of Central and Eastern European manufacturers are part of pan-European supply networks. The new members have also opened up their markets for services. Western banks have taken over and restructured financial institutions in the region. And the economies of Central and Eastern Europe have flourished, despite the massive pressures exerted by this steady market opening: for example, since the late 1990s, Estonia, Hungary, Poland and Slovenia have managed growth rates of more than 4 per cent a year, compared with an EU average of 2.6 per cent.

However, the Central and Eastern European economies need to continue to upgrade their competitiveness, moving from labour-intensive industries to high-tech goods and knowledge-based services. To do this, they need massive further investment in technology and education. The EU probably will end up devoting much more of its budget to policies that will help CEECs to catch up. One of the priorities in EU economic policy to which the budget could be devoted is the 'Lisbon agenda' for economic reform. The aim of the Lisbon agenda is, as is shown in Chapter 11, for the EU to become 'the world's most competitive and dynamic knowledge-based economy by 2010'. How far will the new members make this goal easier or harder to reach?

The new members have signed up to the Lisbon process with some enthusiasm. They compare well with the EU-15 states on market liberalisation, but they do less well when it comes to employment, social inclusion, and sustainable development (see Murray, 2003). The new members make it harder for the EU to meet targets such as raising the average employment rate to 70 per cent and increasing research and development spending to 3 per cent of GDP. On the other hand, they bring in fast-growing, dynamic economies with low-cost workforces. The overall impact on the EU economy will be higher competitive pressures within the SEM, which will encourage structural reform, particularly in the Union's more sclerotic economies.

Three of the SEM's four freedoms are already in place, with movement of goods, services and capital substantially as free across the new member states as the old ones. However, during the accession negotiations the EU-15 insisted on a transitional period on free movement of labour, whereby

EU-15 states can keep their national restrictions on the movement of workers from Eastern Europe for at least two years after accession, and possibly for as long as seven years. A special arrangement exists for Malta, which has access to a safeguard clause should accession give rise to difficulties in relation to free movement of workers. Labour is thus the factor of production that is the least mobile in the European economy.

Some workers, particularly Eastern Europeans living in border regions close to Germany and Austria, are likely to migrate to work, or to commute from their current homes to the higher-wage economies over the border. However, extensive academic studies suggest that the total movement is unlikely to be great (see Boeri *et al.*, 2002, for a survey). The restrictions on CEEC workers will probably be lifted after two to five years, opening up EU labour markets to greater competition.

Joining the eurozone

The new member states have already made huge changes to their economies, spurred on by their ambition to join the EU. The next major challenge will be to adopt the EU's single currency. The new members will all join EMU at some point, but, as Michele Chang shows in Chapter 13, it could be several years after accession before they become part of the eurozone. They have not been given the option of an opt-out from the euro like those negotiated by the UK and Denmark. However, this is not a problem as most of the new member states want to join the eurozone as quickly as possible after accession, and they nearly all have some form of peg to the euro in place. They see the eurozone as removing exchange rate risk and further boosting their trade with the other eurozone members. It would also result in lower interest rates, in turn encouraging investment and growth.

However, there is no fixed timetable for when they join, and the EU's institutions – particularly the Commission and the European Central Bank – are increasingly cautious about precipitous enlargement of the eurozone. The earliest possible date when the new members could adopt the euro is 2006, because they have to peg their exchange rates to the euro for two years within the revamped Exchange Rate Mechanism (known as the ERM II) in order to qualify for monetary union. However, most of them are likely to move into the eurozone several years after that, because the pressures of trying to meet the convergence criteria for monetary union by 2006 will conflict with other economic goals.

The would-be euro members are unlikely to suffer exchange rate crises like the one that forced Britain out of the original ERM. The ERM II is less rigid than its predecessor, with currencies allowed to fluctuate by 15 per cent on either side of the central rate. Some EU policy-makers would like to narrow the fluctuation band before the new members' currencies can qualify. But the flexibility of the wider band will be sorely needed in the years ahead. Economies undergoing rapid structural change – like those of the new members – tend to experience significant upward movements in their real exchange rates (this is the much-discussed 'Balassa-Samuelson effect'). This real appreciation will show up in either nominal appreciation of the currency or in higher domestic inflation, or both. The new members' governments may therefore find it hard to hold nominal exchange rates stable while also bringing down inflation.

In addition to keeping their exchange rates relatively stable, would-be euro members have to meet the four 'Maastricht criteria', which concern public sector debt, budget deficits, inflation and interest rates. Eastern European inflation rates have fallen rapidly since the late 1990s, although this has been largely because of external, one-off factors, such as falling oil prices, good harvests, strong currencies and sluggish growth. Some countries will struggle to keep inflation below the level required by the Maastricht Treaty – which is no more than 1.5 per cent above the average of the three best performing eurozone members. Ten-year bond yields will also have to fall to no more than 2 per cent above those in the three eurozone countries with the lowest inflation. That criterion should be easy to satisfy, for interest rates will converge towards eurozone levels as soon as financial markets believe that the country will join the euro – and in fact this process has started already.

Where the new members will have problems is with the fiscal criteria. All the candidates have public debt levels below the Maastricht threshold of 60 per cent of GDP, but public borrowing is growing. In 2003, the Czech Republic, Hungary and Poland were heading for budgets deficits of between 5 and 10 per cent of GDP. If they want to join the euro in 2006, they will have to reduce this to the Maastricht Treaty's 3 per cent threshold by 2005 – a major challenge given that their growth prospects are uncertain and they will have to make many costly reforms after accession (see Barysch and Grabbe, 2002).

Fiscal challenges after accession

The Finance Ministers of the new member states face fiscal pressures in the EU. One reason is that EU-related spending will increase as the new member states implement the more expensive parts of the EU's rules and regulations, such as environmental standards. At the same time, the new members' Finance Ministries will have to find more money to co-finance infrastructure projects in order to qualify for EU budgetary transfers. Poland and Slovenia will also have to find a lot of money to top up the level of direct payments to their farmers, as their governments have promised to give extra money on top of transfers from the EU.

Since most public spending is fixed in advance – to pay for social welfare or the state administration – public investment is likely to take the brunt of any cuts. However, the new members will need high rates of public investment in order to bring their infrastructure up to western standards and modernize their education, pension and health systems. This implies that any concerted efforts to squeeze budgets into the straitjacket of the Maastricht criteria might not only choke off growth in the short-term, but also reduce the economies' growth potential in the medium- to long-term.

The EU has tried to ease the burden on the fiscal side by providing the new members with a cashflow facility. Although all the new members will receive much more money from the EU than they will pay in, the EU-related spending in their own countries will cause the level of fixed expenditure in the national budgets to rise, with less discretionary spending available in the event of unforeseen problems like floods or higher unemployment. The likely outcome is a fiscal squeeze in the first few years of accession, which could result in higher levels of public borrowing.

Over the medium-term, all of the new member states are likely to undertake structural reform of public finances, partly as a result of these pressures from the EU. That could mean both cuts in public expenditure and tax rises. If the Central European Finance Ministers blame the EU for these measures and their fiscal troubles, the Union could become unpopular.

Administrative Capacity and Implementation of the Acquis

Do the new member states have appropriate and sufficiently strong legal frameworks and enforcement mechanisms in place to enable them to meet the requirements of being EU members? The Commission's annual Regular Reports on the candidates' progress towards accession (see Chapter 3) have painted a mixed picture since they were first issued in 1998. Some legal shortcomings could indeed threaten the smooth functioning of the SEM. For example, the Commission has criticized some of the new member states for not adequately applying EU food standards. This may impede trade, especially since Western European consumers are much concerned about food quality in the aftermath of the BSE ('mad cow') crisis. Another potential problem area is that some new member states have restrictions on foreign investment in certain sectors, which goes against the EU principle of a free flow of capital. Others have not adopted EU rules on public procurement and may discriminate against foreign companies in public tenders.

These shortcomings need to be rectified. However, they should be placed in the context of the fact that EU-15 states themselves have not managed to transpose (that is, adopt into national law) the entire *acquis*. Commission figures show that in 2003 the percentage of single SEM laws that EU-15 states had failed to transpose stood at 2.4 per cent, up from 1.8 per cent in 2002 (European Commission, 2003a). Only five of the EU-15 states – Denmark, Sweden, Finland, Spain and the UK –

meet the European Council's target of a 1.5 per cent deficit or less. Nevertheless, the SEM functions reasonably well despite this uneven transposition of some elements of EU law.

The important difference between EU-15 states and new member states will, therefore, not be in the domain of written law, but in day-to-day implementation and enforcement. The EU-15 are not perfect role-models in this respect either: in 2003 the Commission was pursuing 1500 infringement procedures against member states for failing to implement SEM legislation properly. But the EU-15 states enjoy the advantage of long experience in adjusting their laws and administrative practices to the requirements of EU membership. The new member states have made tremendous progress in recent years in building up the administrative bodies that are needed to implement the *acquis*. Amongst the bodies to have been established are food standards agencies, telecoms regulators, labour inspectorates and insurance market supervisors. However, many of these bodies are understaffed, poorly funded or not sufficiently independent of political influence.

The candidates can close legal gaps in the *acquis* relatively quickly, especially since most have 'fast track' procedures in place to push through EU laws. But to strengthen their administrative capacity requires substantial financial investment in building up new bureaucracies, training officials and, in many areas, the development of a new culture of compliance and cooperation.

Will the EU improve governance in Eastern Europe?

Perhaps the biggest problem in the new members' bureaucracies is a lack of well-trained, experienced and motivated staff. Many of those with marketable skills – foreign languages, IT proficiency, legal expertise, or an understanding of economics and business – have long since switched to better-paid jobs in the private sector. As a result, those stuck in underpaid civil service jobs are often poorly trained and motivated. Many supplement their meagre salaries with bribes. Petty corruption is still a serious problem in many of the CEECs.

The Commission has also highlighted the problem of a weak and understaffed judicial system in some accession countries in its annual reports on their progress. Although the Commission lauds the steps undertaken by the new member states in recent years, it warns that judicial reform is far from complete. The 'brain drain' that has weakened state bureaucracies has also ravaged the judiciary. The Czech Republic, for example, had more than 270 unfilled posts for judges and the same number for prosecutors in 2003. Many court officials do not have access to computers. Court cases can take years to wind through the system. Slovenia has a backlog of about 300 000 unresolved cases. And, in many CEECs, some judges are less than fully insulated from political influence.

Most CEEC governments are credibly committed to strengthening their court systems, rooting out corruption at all levels and making their bureaucracies more efficient. They have drawn up comprehensive strategies and devoted more financial and human resources to this task. But implementation will take time. In particular, governments will take many years to restructure civil services in a way that makes public sector careers attractive for educated young people.

EU membership as such does not necessarily force countries to root out corruption and improve the quality of their bureaucracies. Indeed, several of the EU-15 states continue to struggle with corruption. Transparency International, a corruption watchdog, ranks Estonia and Slovenia as less corrupt than Greece and Italy (Transparency International, 2003). Similarly, the Open Society Institute, in another monitoring exercise, has also found that corruption is worse in some EU-15 states than in the best-prepared new member states (Open Society Institute, 2002). Moreover, some EU-15 states have bureaucratic procedures that are as lengthy and cumbersome as those found in some CEECs. And in Italy there are worries about the independence of the judiciary.

The EU's *acquis* provides little guidance for addressing these reform issues. Peer pressure within the EU can help to encourage governments to tackle administrative weaknesses and undemocratic practices. But the EU's institutions themselves have little leverage over bureaucracies and different levels of government within the member states. However, the Commission is now starting to use a new 'safeguard mechanism' that allows it to police the new members' enforcement of the *acquis* by warning them about lax enforcement, without having to go through a lengthy and complex infringement procedure.

EU practitioners are concerned not only about the consistent implementation of EU laws. They are worried also about how the new members will spend the sums they will receive from the EU budget, mainly for farm support and the improvement of infrastructure. In the absence of transparency and efficient administrative procedures, government officials may distribute huge construction contracts in return for bribes or channel funds to their friends and cronies. Again, there are many precedents from EU-15 states, with fraud, for example, long having been a problem in respect of agricultural subsidies and with corruption being known to exist in EU-funded road-building projects in southern Europe.

The EU probably will also have to develop a firmer *acquis* on good governance and democratic standards – areas where the European Council has often expressed rhetorical support for higher standards, but almost never proposed more specific definitions of those standards. One area of democracy and governance where enlargement will force the EU to develop more coherent policies is on the status and protection of ethnic minorities. Enlargement will increase the number of national and ethnic minorities living in member states, which will oblige both new and old member states to co-operate to protect groups that suffer discrimination across Europe, especially the Roma.

The EU's External Role After Enlargement

Foreign policy will become increasingly important in the enlarged EU. An important reason for this is that with the accession of additional members the EU acquires new responsibilities – it covers another third of the European continent and shares a border with poor and often unstable countries such as Russia, Ukraine and Belarus. Eastward enlargement has taught the EU valuable lessons in how to manage relations with countries that aspire to join the EU. But membership is not a foreseeable prospect for the enlarged Union's neighbours. The EU therefore needs to find a new way of forging bonds that are not based on membership aspirations. How it might do this is explored in Chapter 16.

The EU will need to pay more attention to external border controls, as well as internal security after enlargement. With enlargement, the CEECs no longer act as an external buffer-zone for illegal migration. Rather, they will eventually become members of the Schengen area of passport-free travel. This may add to existing concerns among the Western European public that CEEC governments are not coping adequately with new security threats, be they in the form of illegal immigration, drugs trafficking or terrorism.

However, the new member states are not allowed to join the Schengen area for at least two years after accession, and probably for several years longer. The EU-15 want the new members to raise the standards of their border controls further, and they have to wait for a computer upgrade before the EU's internal security database – the Schengen Information System – can handle 10 more sets of data.

This delay will cause frustration in Eastern Europe. For ordinary citizens, the freedom to travel is one of the few unambiguous benefits of the end of communism, and thousands of people have used it to visit Western Europe and other parts of the world that were hard to get to before 1989. The new members are likely to push hard to join Schengen fully as soon as they can. But in defending its external borders more rigorously, the EU must make sure it does not cut off the countries that remain outside. The new controls must be balanced with measures that facilitate travel by legitimate business people and tourists.

Strategic orientation

The new members of the EU have been forced to choose their strategic friends sooner than they wanted to. During their accession negotiations, the candidates were cautious about expressing opinions that might alienate one or another EU member, every one of which had to approve their accession.

But the crisis over Iraq in 2003 forced them to stake out a public position on the EU, NATO and the United States. The three NATO members – the Czech Republic, Hungary and Poland – signed the 'letter of eight' in January 2003 that called for unity with the US in the UN Security Council, and the ten Eastern European candidates for NATO later sent their own letter of support. These countries were angered that France and Germany claimed to speak for the whole of Europe without consulting them. Moreover, their leaders believed that support for the US on the enforcement of the UN's Resolution on Iraq was more important than forging a common European position.

On Iraq policy, US Defence Secretary Donald Rumsfeld's prediction of a division between the 'old' and 'new' Europes was over-simplistic, but largely true. Poland, especially, supported the US strongly and even took responsibility for one of the post-conflict zones into which Iraq was divided. As two leading scholars on Poland's strategic orientation put it: 'It is clear that Poland belongs to Rumsfeld's 'new Europe', a fact confirmed by Warsaw's active support of US policy towards Iraq and its role in the post-war occupation' (Zaborowski and Longhurst, 2003: 11). However, Poland stands apart from the other new members in being much larger – four times the population of the next largest acceding state – and more stridently Atlanticist than the other Central European countries.

The dividing lines that followed the end of the old East–West fissure are not so clear-cut on foreign policy questions beyond Iraq, as the new EU members have similar views to the EU-15 on questions such as the role of the International Criminal Court, the Kyoto Protocol, and the importance of working through multilateral institutions. Moreover, on defence, the new members are close to the position of the UK Prime Minister, Tony Blair. Like him, they see no contradiction between supporting NATO and building up a European security and defence policy at the same time – and they do not want European capacities to be built up as a rival to NATO or a counterweight to the US. The new members believe in a strong transatlantic alliance, but they generally also want the EU to have an effective foreign policy, especially in the Balkans and the Union's 'near abroad' to their East.

How Will the New Members Behave in the Union?

New political dynamics

Although ten states join the EU at the same time, this does not mean that their interests on EU issues always coincide. Some issues unite them

– for example, they all favour financial transfers to poor regions – but they are in different situations and have different views on many other issues. Estonia, for instance, is among the most liberal countries in Europe in economic terms, whereas Polish and Slovak instincts are more protectionist. A small rural country like Lithuania does not share all the objectives of relatively wealthy Central European countries, such as the Czech Republic and Slovenia, with their diversified, export-oriented industries. And Poland, with nearly 40 million people, has a much greater range of policy interests than Malta, with its population of 400 000.

Rather than acting in unison, the new members will therefore team up with each other and with EU-15 states according to the issues at hand. Enlargement could thus change the debate in areas such as tax harmonization or defence policy, with new member states teaming up with old ones on one side of the argument or the other. The enlarged Union is thus likely to be characterized by shifting coalitions of countries that change according to the subject under discussion. Certainly it is unlikely to break up into blocs of member states that always vote together. (The nature of likely coalitions in the post-enlargement EU is explored in depth by Michael Baun in Chapter 9.)

In the EU-25, and later EU-27 plus, the ties between member states will not be based just on factors such as geography, size or attitudes to the US. Instead, friendships will depend on the issue in question. Until the early 1990s, a Franco–German deal was the necessary, and at times almost sufficient, condition for any initiative to move ahead. These two countries seemed almost to represent the main divisions in the Union – between South and North, West and East, Catholic and Protestant, agricultural and industrial, and inter-governmentalist and federalist. A deal between them could thus serve as a compromise between the other competing interests in the Union. But French and German views no longer represent the main dividing lines, as other divisions – including one between big and small countries – have become more important. After enlargement, Franco–German agreement is not even necessary for an initiative to proceed. Instead, new member states are able to team up with old ones to push initiatives that suit their interests. Short-term, pragmatic liaisons will replace the emotional, history-laden marriage between Germany and France. The trade-offs will become more complex as member states bargain across different issues. Poland is likely to stand with Britain in opposing tax harmonization, for example, but Warsaw will support Madrid against London in demanding a larger EU budget. By contrast, Estonia is strongly against subsidies and will favour reform of EU agricultural policy, along with the Czech Republic and possibly Hungary. But Estonia will have similar interests to the Danes and other small countries in wanting Europe to protect its cultural inheritance and its minority language films.

In addition to joining existing debates, the new members bring in their own ideas and priorities. They have a decade of experience behind them with economic reform and democratization, so they may be impatient with the EU's slow progress in structural reform. Several of them have active relationships with important neighbours that will be an asset to the Union. Poland's engagement with Ukraine will make Warsaw a strong advocate of a more active eastern policy for the Union, while Hungary will contribute to the EU's thinking on its southern neighbours in the Balkans.

The enlarged EU's political dynamics also change because it will have to become more flexible. The ability and willingness of member states to be integrated into the EU's policies will vary much more than in the EU-15. The EU as a whole needs to consider how to manage flexible coalitions successfully. It already has a number of areas of flexibility, where the member states are involved in a policy area to different degrees, the most important being participation in the single currency, border policies and defence. More issues like this will emerge where the new members are unwilling or unable to participate fully: higher eco-taxes are one example. The key is to ensure that the Union can maintain a consensus on the broad principles of European integration, even if not every member is fully involved in every policy. The CEECs are united in opposing the idea of the EU breaking up into first- and second-class members.

In terms of ambitions, the enlarged Union should become a more important actor on the world stage because of its greater size and because of the United States' need for a strong ally. But it will have to square a circle, between the small group of large countries which will drive foreign policy – owing to their size, and military and diplomatic assets – and the others, which will want to be involved, but are unwilling or unable to play a major role. The EU needs to find an answer to the question of how member states can meet in groups numbering between two and the total membership, without provoking resentment that just the large states are running foreign policy. The answer may lie in informal coalitions of countries with an interest in particular parts of the world: for example, the southern member states in the Mediterranean and North Africa, or the Nordic and Baltic states in the EU's Northern Dimension.

Budgetary issues

The EU's budget is the first difficult policy issue faced by the new members, although they will already have experienced a bruising fight over institutional reform in the 2003–2004 IGC. The negotiations on the post-2006 financial perspective start in 2004, so the new members are fully involved in the process that will produce a new medium-term budgetary framework. Disputes about fiscal matters tend to be the most acrimonious and difficult that member states have to face, so the new members are thrown into one of the hardest and most contentious areas of inter-governmental and inter-institutional bargaining soon after their entry.

Moreover, the new members themselves have strong interests in the budget debate. They are all considerably poorer than the EU average, with income levels of between one-third and two-thirds of the EU average (see Appendix 1). The new members can, therefore, expect to receive significant funds from the EU's budget to help their economies to catch up. In the accession negotiations, the would-be members had little clout, and they received a relatively ungenerous deal from the EU as a result. Many of them are keen to get more from future budget negotiations, when they will be able to negotiate on a par with the old members.

The danger is that the negotiating style of some of the new members might be set during the negotiations on the post-2006 financial perpective. Like Spain, which has fought hard for EU subsidies throughout its membership of the Union, some of the new members could make budgetary transfers a priority in their European policy. This is particularly likely in the case of Poland, which has the largest number of farmers and a lively domestic debate about the costs and benefits of accession. Already, some Poles are worried that the priority to fiscal flows could diminish their country's influence in other areas. An advisor to the Polish Prime Minister during the accession negotiations expressed the concern thus:

> If confined to defending ferociously only our own interests (understood narrowly as a 'consumption of money' from the EU), we would consequently lose allies in other fields of integration: foreign and defence policy, infrastructure development . . . Poland would in the long run probably achieve more by systematically building up its influence throughout the EU institutions. (Jesień, 2002: 36–7)

Conclusions

The idea of 'deepening versus widening' is a false dichotomy because the Union after 2004 is not just a bigger version of the pre-enlargement EU. More member states and greater diversity may put the structures under strain, but the differences are more than arithmetical. There is a qualitative change in the Union's ambitions and responsibilities. These changes will affect how the EU works, but also will cause it to develop new policies that deepen its integration overall.

Previous enlargements have not generally prevented the EU from developing existing policies or from moving into new fields of integration. The EU evolved new dimensions to its regional policy as a result of the arrival of Greece in 1981, and it developed the single market programme as Portugal and Spain were joining in the mid-1980s. The entry of Austria, Finland and Sweden in 1995 did not prevent the expansion of the Schengen area and the launch of the euro after they joined. In the 10 + 2 round the challenges are much greater, so the institutional and policy reforms should have started earlier. But the EU proved unable to achieve meaningful change without a firm deadline. Indeed, enlargement was an important catalyst for reform: for example, the EU might never have embarked on the project of consolidating its treaties into a constitution if such a massive expansion had not been in prospect.

The 'big bang' enlargement of 2004 is unlikely to slow the pace of integration. On the contrary, it will raise new challenges that invite the member states to work together more closely – on issues ranging from economic policy co-ordination to internal security to environmental degradation. However, although the scope of European integration is likely to stretch over more policy fields, it may develop in untraditional ways. At 25-plus members, the Union is likely to experience differentiated integration, as some member states become frustrated with the slow progress of the Union as a whole on issues like defence and energy.

The acceding states bring problems to the EU, not least by bringing their own ambitions for the Union. But they also bring new opportunities for cooperation to improve the lives of Europeans. If the Union can respond adequately to these challenges, the 10 + 2 round could open a highly beneficial new chapter in the history of European integration.

Chapter 6

European Identity

LAURIE BUONANNO AND ANN DEAKIN

Introduction and Background

'What kind of European am I? One needs to speak a language,' a young Polish respondent tells Meinhof and Galasinski in their 2002 study of intergenerational identity in German and Polish border communities. 'We are laughing that we are going to this Europe barefoot.' For him, to be European is to speak German, French, or English. But for the German brother and sister across the Neisse, the river border dividing the German city Guben from the Polish Gubin, Europeans dwell in pulsing, glittering cities, a world away from their humdrum provincial city in the former German Democratic Republic (GDR).

A European lives in Europe. This much we know. But what is Europe? Is it a continent or is it, as the nineteenth century Russian 'culturologist' Nikolai Danilevsky (1964) dismissively wrote, merely a peninsula of Asia? In a peninsular Europe, Turkey Spain, Italy, the Balkans, and Greece are tendrils, and so ends the squabble over Turkey's continental classification.

Europe's borders are tidal (WRR, 2001: 32) because they are social constructions. In the Middle Ages, Europe stopped at the River Don. By the eighteenth century, it had expanded to the Urals to accommodate Russia's turn to the West. Moscow's joining the ranks of European cities transforms Italian Prime Minister Silvio Berlusconi's proposal to invite a Russian application for membership in the EU (*European Voice*, 12–18 June 2003: 4) from the ridiculous to the conceivable.

Europe is also understood as a 'community of shared values in a given geographical area' (Schwimmer 2001). In this chapter we consider identity in the context of enlargement. We do so for three reasons. First, as the EU increasingly resembles a state, identity becomes less luxury, more necessity, becoming a stabilizing force in the state (Easton, 1965; Weiler, 1998: 8). Post-Maastricht Europeanization requires new member states to adopt a broad and deep *acquis*. The skeletal staffing of the EU's regulatory and judicial bodies virtually ensures that much of member state compliance depends upon civic virtue – the *sine qua non* of the well-functioning European state – and that identity becomes a powerful inner

dynamic of a European state. The standard alternative to territorial identity – religion (see de Tocqueville [1969: 44] on this point) – is not a prac-
ticable alternative in modern Europe. Second, the EU has actively sought
to build an affective European identity. In this context, Jean Monnet once
remarked, 'If we were beginning the European Community all over
again, we should begin with culture' (quoted in Van Ham, 2000: 31).
Third, a continuously expanding literature emphasizes the importance of
identity to the integration project (see, for example, Cederman, 2000;
Fossum, 2001; Howe, 1995; Malyarov and Hendrick, 2003; Milward,
1992; Weiler, 1996).

We will pose a number of questions in this chapter in order to examine the implications of enlargement on the EU's future identity. Does a
European identity exist? If so, can we discern characteristics distinguishing it from other territorially linked identities? Under what conditions
will European identity form and/or intensify among citizens in the new
member states? Will identity conflicts impede the pace of integration?

A European Identity . . . Gemeinschaft or Gesselschaft?

While there is substantial agreement amongst informed observers that
there *is* a Europe *and* even Europeans (see, for example, see Ash, 1989;
Van Ham 2000; Schwimmer, 2002; WRR, 2001), there is less agreement
on who they are and in what they believe. What factors engender
Europeaness – to the extent that such an identity exists – as opposed to
being German, Maltese, or Czech? What is the causal variable? Does
identity precede political legitimacy or does the modern state, through its
control of instrumental benefits, produce over a certain period of time, as
Easton (1965) argued, identification? EU policy makers need to understand the causal sequence if they are to nurture a European identity.

The German sociologist Ferdinand Tönnies (1957) distinguishes
between identity as *gemeinschaft* and as *gesselschaft*. The former may be
thought of as identity in its original form – exemplified by family, neighbourhood and village; that is, as a deep sense of belonging, an affective
identity. *Gesselschaft* is the modern manifestation of identity, involving
the 'artificial construction of identity through state builders' production
and distribution of benefits in exchange for citizen loyalty. *Gemeinschaft*
produces the more stable, satisfying identification, but modern society,
with its emphasis on utilitarianism and instrumentalism, roots out
gemeinschaft whenever it impedes state-builders' goals. We will see how
scholars draw on this tension between community and society in shaping
their opinions about European identification.

There are, broadly speaking, four distinct explanatory theories on identity formation: primordial/essentialist, postmodernist, postnational-ist, and modernist. Each can be used to aid our understanding of European identity.

Primordialists and essentialists

Primordialists and essentialists view identity as natural and self-generat-ing; its absence is indicative of political repression (Gellner, 1983: 129). *New* states need *old* nations; without the embedded pre-rational memory of nation (myths, legends, artifacts and heroes), the polity resists each incremental step in state-policy growth. If the primordialist interpreta-tion correctly captures the inner dynamic of state stability, new member states' citizens would check EU policy deepening. Not surprisingly, the more integrationist EU-15 states expressed this very concern in relation to the 10 + 2 enlargement round.

Without this *affective* identification, primordialists – for example, Anthony Smith (1992) – believe it will take generations for a European identity to emerge. *Eurobarometer* results help us to evaluate the primordialist claim. In terms of how 'European' EU-15 citizens feel as compared to their respective nationalities, respondents in the spring of 2003 reported that they consider themselves either in terms of their own nationality or their own nationality *and* being European (see Table 6.1) Given the special circumstances in Luxembourg – where there are a large number of Eurocrats and Portuguese immigrants rela-tive to the size of the country – it is perhaps not surprising that it stands out with the most citizens who consider themselves 'European Only', at 20 per cent. The next closest countries – Belgium, Germany and France – are at 6 per cent, with the lowest being Finland and Sweden at 1 per cent. The United Kingdom, with 64 per cent, has the highest percentage of respondents who claim only their own national-ity.

The same overall tendency for people to have more affinity with their own nationality or their own nationality *and* Europe is evident among the new member and candidate EU states. Six per cent of the Latvian and Slovak *Eurobarometer* respondents consider themselves 'Only European', while none of the Hungarian respondents consider them-selves 'Only European'. In the 'nationality only' category, the lowest countries are Cyprus and Slovakia, both of which have 25 per cent of their respondents claiming only Cypriot or Slovak as their nationality. Across the states surveyed the results are thus mixed; however, many citi-zens do clearly identify themselves, at least in part, as being European.

Whether the respondents see membership of the EU to be a 'good thing' or a 'bad thing', results for the EU-15 and the new member states are similar, though the latter have a more optimistic sense of what EU membership will do for their respective countries (see Table 6.2).

Table 6.1   *National and European identification in the EU-15,*
*new member and candidate states**

Country	% Nationality only	% Nationality & European	% European & nationality	% European only
EU-15 states	40	44	8	4
Belgium	45	36	9	6
Denmark	37	52	7	3
Germany	34	45	12	6
Greece	53	41	3	3
Spain	34	52	8	3
France	34	49	9	6
Ireland	48	39	5	3
Italy	26	59	10	3
Luxembourg	21	45	10	20
Netherlands	46	43	7	3
Austria	51	34	8	3
Portugal	49	43	4	3
Finland	56	38	4	1
Sweden	55	39	4	1
United Kingdom	64	24	4	3
New member states	33	54	6	2
Cyprus	25	63	8	2
Czech Republic	37	39	9	2
Estonia	39	36	10	5
Hungary	39	53	6	0
Latvia	31	41	7	6
Lithuania	35	39	9	3
Malta	30	59	6	1
Poland	32	60	5	1
Slovakia	25	49	13	6
Slovenia	32	57	5	2
Candidate States	42	45	4	3
Bulgaria	37	44	5	2
Romania	36	50	5	3
Turkey	52	41	3	3

Source: adapted from Table 5.1a. *Eurobarome*te*r* 59.1 and Table 3.1 *Candidate Countries Eurobarometer* (Spring 2003).
* The question asked was: 'In the near future do you see yourself as . . .?'
– '(Nationality) only'
– '(Nationality) and European'
– 'European and (Nationality)'
– 'Don't know'

Table 6.2 Attitudes toward EU membership in EU-15, new member and candidate states[*]

Country	% A 'good thing'	% A 'bad thing'	Neither 'good' nor 'bad'
EU-15 states	54	11	27
Belgium	67	7	20
Denmark	63	16	17
Germany	59	8	26
Greece	61	8	29
Spain	62	6	27
France	50	12	34
Ireland	67	5	16
Italy	64	6	22
Luxembourg	85	4	11
Netherlands	73	5	18
Austria	34	19	41
Portugal	61	9	24
Finland	42	17	37
Sweden	41	27	30
United Kingdom	30	25	31
New member states	58	8	26
Cyprus	72	4	21
Czech Republic	46	13	32
Estonia	31	16	42
Hungary	63	7	23
Latvia	37	15	40
Lithuania	65	9	23
Malta	51	19	24
Poland	61	7	23
Slovakia	59	5	30
Slovenia	57	7	33
Candidate states	70	5	46
Bulgaria	70	3	17
Romania	74	2	15
Turkey	67	11	14

Source: adapted from Table 3.6.a. *Candidate Countries Eurobarometer* and Table 6.1a. *EuroBarometer* (Spring 2003)

[*]The question asked was: 'Generally speaking, do you think (our country's) membership of the European Union is/would be . . .?'
– 'a good thing'
– 'a bad thing'
– 'neither good nor bad'
– 'don't know'

Overall, a majority of the respondents in EU-15 and new member states believe EU membership to be a 'good thing', at 54 per cent and 58 per cent respectively. Of the EU-15, Luxembourg, again, is the highest, with the UK and Austria the lowest. Among the new member states, Cyprus is the highest and Estonia the lowest. Across the new member states, an average of 70 per cent think EU membership is a 'good thing'.

Some caution should be exercised when interpreting Eurobarometer data as evidence for a widespread European identity. One reason for this is that some observers – for example, Meinhof and Galasinski (2002) – have found that European identity emerges only when survey respondents are prompted (as they are in *Eurobarometer* surveys), and even then identification varies, with some respondents thinking in terms of European culture, some in terms of a supranational (EU) state, and some in terms of a mix of the two. Another reason for caution centres on the longitudinal results of Eurobarometer identity questions; specifically the number of respondents identifying as 'European', alternately weakens and strengthens (Dalton and Eichenberg, 1993; Duchesne and Frognier, 1995; Gabel and Palmer, 1995; Gabel, 1998), prompting some scholars to conclude European identification is shallow rooted, affected by recent and personal events.

These findings seem to at least partly confirm the primordialist prediction of weak European identity. Nevertheless, we cannot discount the fact that some respondents *do* report a European identification, whether or not they are prompted to do so. The inconsistent percentage of identifiers across time is a different matter altogether as it concerns the *nature* of identification; if it is affective then stability would be expected, whereas if it is instrumental instability would be anticipated. We will return to this issue of the nature of identity later in this chapter.

Postmodernists

While the literature often treat 'postmodernism' and 'postnationalism' as synonyms, they represent opposite philosophical perspectives. For postmodernists, no identity trumps the other (Flynn, 1991). In a world devoid of universal realities, ethnic and national identity co-exists on a horizontal plane with lesbian, football enthusiast, political party and environmental identities, even across borders. Yuppies, Goths, 30-somethings, holiday-loving pensioners, and vegans shape the EU in a 'free market of identities' (Billing, 1995). Postmodernism thus asserts a perhaps unsettling notion of 'anything goes' – that being a member of a running club is equivalent to being Slovakian. The postmodernist would ask us to look forward to the many ways in which Western and Eastern Europe will forge cross-border identities.

Postmodernists, in focusing on identity, capture an important element of modern democratic society; namely, the proliferation of groups.

Democratic theorists, indeed, call these 'groups' rather than 'identities' and point to their proliferation as evidence of a trend toward democratization in advanced industrialized societies rather than an explicit challenge to national identity. The issue becomes confused because identity, as we have seen, exhibits both affective and instrumental dimensions; groups, too, offer their members both instrumental and affective benefits. Yet, most of us would not think to use the term 'identity' and 'group' interchangeably; for example, does anyone believe that German and British holiday pensioners have a shared identity when their motivation is finding the most affordable holiday in a half-day's journey?

While useful in recognizing the subnational interactions among East and West, postmodernism stumbles both descriptively and prescriptively. It does so partly because while there are EU state borders there cannot be a free market in identities (Faist, 2001: 46). It also elevates to the level of 'identity' what are more properly 'shared interests'. Finally, postmodernism, in denying extraneous, universally rational standards as myth, promotes 'virulent nationalism', a possibility Europeans clearly cannot afford to dismiss (Gellner, 1983: 120).

Postnationalists: globalization, cosmopolitanism, and social democracy

From a postnational perspective, globalization, cosmopolitan democracy, and social democracy predict that international or transnational identities will supplant national identity.

Globalization

Globalization emphasizes a Europe of multinational corporations and mobile professionals. Friedman (quoted in Van Ham, 2001: 34 as an example of an 'updated and vulgar version of Kant') suggests 'no two countries that both have a McDonald's have ever fought a war against each other'. Laffan (1996: 95) calls this EU a 'soulless market'. It is a Europe of elites: Edmund Burke thought that 'no European can be a complete exile in any part of Europe' (Hay, 1968: 117); Lenin (1915) argued that Europe's leisure and business class is and always will be 'European'; and Trevor Lloyd (1997: 548) has suggested that 'most people who think themselves as 'Europeans' [probably] have at least a Master of Arts degree'. On this basis, if the number of European identifiers is increasing it can be attributed to a shrinking working class and growing professional class.

This interpretation is clearly limited by the fact that globalization is seen as benefiting directly and significantly a relatively small number of citizenry. For, as Anderson (1983: 203) states, 'the problem has always been how to create nations out of the everyday man. There has always been a connectedness among the elites'. Modern territorially-based identities must be felt equally by all citizens.

Cosmopolitanism

While cosmopolitans are sometimes labeled postmodern (see discussion above), their orientation is fundamentally different. Cosmopolitans, in predicting a diminishing role for states, point to the power international organizations wield in setting standards for respecting and protecting human rights, democracy, and the rule of law (Schwimmer 2001).

No one would describe the European Community's founding as European *gemeinschaft*. Why, then, would cosmopolitans describe the European Union as a community of Europeans? Many of them would start with 'Maastricht', where they would see the creation of a legally recognized European citizenship and the legal recognition accorded to the Social Charter as laying the basis of a new *gemeinschaft* based on a civic code of collective identity (Eisenstadt and Giesen, 1995: 81).

Western Europe has achieved a civil society where corruption, while not eliminated, attracts strict sanction and harsh punishment. Respect for human rights is enshrined in modern democracy. Yet corruption remains stubbornly common in the CEECs (European Commission: 2002c) and the EU, while achieving some success in promoting minority rights (such as for the Hungarians in Slovakia, the Roma in most of the CEECs, and Russians in Latvia), cannot monitor all political campaign rhetoric, each speech in parliament, every local law. Cosmopolitans, ironically criticized as idealists, point to the limited financial capacity of the CEECs to root out corruption, improve administrative capacities, and protect the rights of minorities and women.

Cosmopolitans, too, point to a tendency to blur democracy and capitalism in the minds of the citizenry in former communist countries. According to Habermas (1999: 118–19), constitutional patriotism 'can take the place originally occupied by nationalism if the people recognize that they are materially better off'. Democratic values emerge and harden into a civic culture as the people learn and grow in a market economy (Ash 1998: 53). CEECs, with their fledgling democracies and market economies, could import instability to the EU (Willis, 1996).

Cosmopolitans also suspect that the CEECs think of themselves as *natio* or *gens*, rather than civic nations (Fowler, 2002: 22; Habermas, 1999: 109). Without a democratic political culture, how will the new member states' polities react to economic downturns (Breton *et al.*, 1995: 25)? Will opportunistic politicians exploit CEEC insecurity?

Cosmopolitan democracy, as we have seen, is based on rational enlightenment. Herein perhaps lies its major flaw. Whether the majority of the polity can be reasoned with and will, in turn, reason with others, is a philosophical conundrum generating as much debate today as it did in the eighteenth century.

Cosmopolitans suggest that Europeans are *weltbürger* [world citizens] (Gottdiener, 1995: 233) living under *weltbürgerrecht* [world/cosmopolitan law] (Habermas, 1999: xxvi). Yet identity is tied to 'otherness' (Anderson 1983: 73). A nation is 'a people with a common confusion as to their origins and a common antipathy to their neighbors' (Harmelink, 1972, quoted in Cohen, 1998: 33). People have a deeply-felt psychological need to distinguish themselves from those whom they are most alike: what Freud (1985) called the narcissism of small differences. Cosmopolitan democracy fails to explain the tendency of people to behave 'irrationally' and Kant's pacific union overlooks the plainly observable phenomenon that substantial numbers of people enjoy the solidarity of otherness that nationhood offers.

Does this mean that cosmopolitan democracy has nothing to teach us about identity formation in the EU-25? Not at all. We should be cautious about dismissing the influence of cosmopolitan democracy among the CEECs' elites who are in the driving seat of enlargement. For many of these elites have been strongly influenced, directly or indirectly, by Habermas' Frankfurt School, with its reincarnation of enlightenment philosophy and its perception of the possibility of the postnational state. We will return to this point later in the chapter.

Social Democracy

Despite the fact that Europeans created postmodernism – Foucault, Derrida, Levi-Strauss – it has colonized entire academic departments only in the US. Perhaps this is because the postmodern contention that identity politics has replaced class-based politics is less applicable to continental Europe. Plurality manifests itself in groups, a critical distinction in an American democracy lacking the class-based parties and proportional representation electoral systems of continental Europe. Lenin (1914) wrote: 'Our banner does not carry the slogan "national culture" but *international* culture, which unites all the nations in a higher, socialist unity.' Could the intellectual legacy of European Marxists/Leninists hold the key to a unique European identity?

If we can argue for the moment that states nurture identity, then European states have produced a common culture that supports social democracy; this, then could be a fundamental element of European identity. Certainly the European left sees matters this way. This point of view is exemplified by Žižek's (1998: 77) comment that 'from the sublime heights of Habermas' theory to vulgar market ideologists, we are bombarded by different versions of depoliticization'.

Is it realistic to suggest there could be a European cultural and political identity rooted in class solidarity? It has become a truism that national identity trumps class-based identity since the 1907 resolution of the Second International, pledging worker solidarity in the event of war, fell to pieces when the majority of the socialist parties of Europe ignored their own resolution in August 1914, voting to support their respective countries in World War 1.

Neverthless, Faist (2001: 51) reminds us that welfare state institutions were developed first and collective identities resulted from them. Who then better to understand the benefits of social democracy than the citizens of the CEECs? Nor can we discount the opposition to EU membership in some of the new member states, where in Poland 22 per cent, in the Czech Republic 23 per cent, and in Hungary 16 per cent voted against joining the EU (see the Chronology for the results of all the accession referendums).

Perhaps the CEECs could be attracted to a European identity that distinguishes itself from all other advanced industrialized democracies: one based on homegrown European social democracy. Western Europe has consistently been more favourable to welfare spending than the United States, and European political parties of the centre-left describe their platforms as putting a human face on capitalism. Does this hold true for the CEECs as well, or has the reaction against the communist era moved citizen attitudes to the right, thus nearer to American-style capitalism? The empirical evidence suggests that the CEECs may, in fact, have *more* favourable attitudes toward social welfare spending than exists in Western Europe, with Lipsmeyer and Nordstrom (2003) finding a statistically significant difference between the two regions.

While this may take us closer to answering the question 'whither European identity?', we are no closer to understanding causality. While European social democracy may form the basis of 'otherness', we have not addressed the process by which this identity forms. We know intuitively what the research has long shown: individual characteristics – skill levels, family status, age, education, income – shape support for welfare spending. How might self-interest shape and reinforce European identity? To answer these questions, we must turn to the explanations offered by 'Modernists'.

Modernists

Transnationalists place national identity in a transitory phase between ethnic and civil culture; modernists, on the other hand, are more sceptical of an evolving dynamic. Both traditions recognize capitalism as a precondition for nations because labour mobility is a precursor to industrialization and national identity encourages this mobility (Gellner 1983: 105). Postnationalists and modernists part company in postnationalist predictions of a progressive irrelevance of state and nation, although modernists will concede that nationalism in advanced industrialized societies is in 'a muted, less virulent form' (Gellner, 1983: 122). Unlike the primordialists who believe most existing nations preceded their respective states, the modernists counters 'the mere fact of existing for a few decades, less than the length of a single lifetime, may be enough to establish at least a *passive* (emphasis added) identification with a new nation-state' (Hobsbawn, 1990: 86). The modifier 'passive' is key to this perspective, a point to which we will return below.

What type of identification does the state foster? David Easton believed that specific support (utilitarian or instrumental) precedes and shapes affective identification, but that inevitably state builders strive to build affective identification because of its 'reservoir of favorable attitudes or goodwill that helps members to accept or tolerate outputs to which they are opposed' (1965: 273). The danger, scholars suggest, is that short-term identification based on self-interest runs only as deep as immediate benefits (Almond and Verba, 1963; Dahl, 1989; Putnam, 1993). Has the EU fostered affective or instrumental identity, and should it have?

Laffan (1996: 100) recommends 'the affective dimension of the European project is critical to the Union', asserting that 'the Monnet method has reached its limits'. The EU has certainly attempted to promote the affective dimension. It did, for example, implement many of the recommendations of the 1985 Adonnino Report on 'A People's Europe' (European Commission 1985), which had been requested by the 1984 Fontainebleau summit, including those on a European passport, student and teacher exchanges, European sporting events, and the twinning of towns and cities. Moreira (2000) documents the European Commission's preference for funding projects that celebrate a concept of Europe – unitary, republican citizenship – rather than a multicultural Europe, whilst Theiler (1999) reviews EU attempts to promote a European identity through cultural, audiovisual policy, and education. Even the euro could have an affective component: Helleiner (1998:1419) believes that the euro bolsters identity because its enables its users to communicate in the same economic language when discussing pensions, wages, and retail prices.

But notwithstanding this involvement in promoting affective identity, the EU has been and continues to be most actively engaged in policies and activities that build instrumental identity. The citizens actively support the state in exchange for security and prosperity – a Hobbesian rather than a postnational Rousseauian view of citizen–state relations (Van Kersbergen, 2000: 8). Instrumental or utilitarian identification relies on motives. For instance, the opportunity for a Czech national to identify as a European rather than lose her Czech identity and family roots by emigrating to the USA could hardly be thought of as an affective choice:

the Czech emigrates to Western Europe because its proximity enables her to achieve personal and professional goals with fewer trade offs. The effects of new member states' compliance with the Schengen *acquis* support the instrumentality of citizenship (Fowler, 2002: 35): surveys have found that Croatian-Romanians began applying for Croatian citizenship when Croatia was removed from the EU's visa blacklist and Romanian-Moldovans increased their demands for Romanian citizenship after the 1999 Helsinki Summit where the European Council decided to open accession negotiations with Romania. Furthermore, individuals expected to benefit from integration report higher support for the EU: people living closer to the borders (Anderson, 1996a, 1996b); citizens in states receiving substantial EU financial support (Carrubba, 1997); the more educated; and the young seeking study opportunities (European Commission, 2002e, 2003c). Gabel (1998) and Gabel and Palmer (1995) find that the combined effect of socio-demographic differences (divided according to expected benefits) has as strong an effect on integration support as nationality.

Given that Europeans are more likely to form instrumental, rather than affective identities, how will this tendency shape relations between the citizens and governments in the enlarged EU? And how might this affect the integration efforts of EU policy-makers?

Attitudes in the New Member States: Costs and Benefits

We have argued that the extent to which citizens identify as Europeans can be attributed (primarily) to instrumental benefits. This is so for two main reasons. First, support for integration tends to be strongest among those individuals most likely to benefit from EU membership. Second, the fluctuations in identity support probably reflect changing individual assessments of the immediate benefits offered at the European level of government. This conclusion corroborates Easton's prediction that instrumental identity precedes affective attachments, precisely what we would expect in an organization existing less than five decades.

As regards the expected benefits of accession, we have two pieces of evidence from the new member states of the importance of instrumental needs: Eurobarometer data and attitudes during the accession negotiations.

Taking 2003 *Eurobarometer* data, when asked, 'taking everything into consideration, what will the EU have brought in 10 years' time for the European citizens?', 48 per cent of positive responses were for economic reasons, whilst only 3 per cent mentioned identity (European Commission 2003c: 49). When respondents were asked to rank-order answers to 'what the EU means to you personally', 70 per cent listed 'better future for youth', 61 per cent 'freedom of movement', 58 per cent 'a way to create jobs', 52 per cent 'lasting peace', 49 per cent 'protection of citizens' rights', and 45 per cent 'improving the (national) economy'. 'Being a citizen of the EU' meant 'right to work in any country in the EU' for 72 per cent of the respondents, 'being able to study in any EU country' for 69 per cent, 'the right to move permanently to any country in the EU' for 68 per cent, and 'the right to vote in EP elections in the member state in which one resides or lives, regardless of nationality' for 32 per cent (European Commission, 2003c). 'Political rights' simply did not appear as one of the top three rights in any of the then candidate states.

On the other hand, only 34 per cent showed concern 'for the loss of national identity', 39 per cent concern for 'one's language used less and less', while 50 per cent showed more concern about increased drug trafficking and international organized crime (European Commission, 2003c: 121).

Following Easton's theory, it follows that the EU can forge a European identity, or at least a loyalty, among new member states by ensuring the benefits of joining outweigh the costs. As illustrated in other chapters in this book, benefits are expected in some policy areas, but disappointments are equally likely in others.

Among the most controversial chapters of the accession negotiations in the CEECs – as measured by protracted talks and public grumblings – were those concerning labour mobility and Justice and Home Affairs (especially Schengen). How are these two policies affecting the CEECs and what is the likely impact on the forging of a European identity among the citizenry?

Free movement of labour

In the modernist explanation of identity, particularly Gellner (1983) and Deutsch *et al.* (1957), labour mobility is the determining factor in both geographical identity formation and successful political integration. In fact, Deutsch *et al.* (53–54) speculated that mobility of persons might be *more* important than either goods or money. This issue continues to concern governments in the new member states. Viktor Orban, Hungary's former centre-right Prime Minister, for instance, has argued that without free labour mobility an enlarged EU would resemble a class-system (Jileva, 2002). In preparing the EU's common position for the accession negotiations, however, most of the EU-15 were unwilling to concede immediate free movement of labour to CEECs and insisted that they be subject to a transition period of up to seven years. This was duly incorporated into the accession agreements, with each EU-15 state left to choose whether to take advantage of it. In the event, all of the EU-15 did announce restrictions of some kind on CEEC workers. This derogation on labour mobility would probably be a less bitter pill for the new member states if the EU did not encourage labour mobility amongst themselves. It certainly seems that Germany and Austria are gaining the most advantages of the CEECs' enlargement with regard to trade and investment, but are unwilling to accept potential costs to disrupted labour markets in border towns and cities. The perception of unfairness is palpable. Meinhof and Galasinski (2002, 81) cite the following informant's response as typical of the Polish attitude toward accession: 'It is now known that a German in Poland when we join the Union will be able to do everything, including work and we (not until) 10 years' time'.

What is the likely effect of derogations on European identity in a Europe of 'metics' – long-term residents excluded from the polis (Walzer, 1983)? Clearly there is a sense of unfairness, reinforcing the notion of 'otherness'. We alluded earlier to Anderson's (1983) historical research in which he discovered a causal link between lack of opportunities for the more ambitious inhabitants of a region and nationalism. How can the EU forge a European identity among the new member states if their otherness is reinforced in an area of such paramount concern to their citizenry?

While it is often thought that limiting emigration from third countries is necessary to protect the jobs of citizens in the EU-15, this does not in fact appear to be the case. There are several reasons for this.

First, survey data indicate that CEEC citizens desire to work, but to a lesser extent settle, in Western Europe. Claire Wallace's (2002: 605) analysis of the International Organization for Migration's 1998 survey data concludes that Poles, Czechs, Hungarians, and Slovaks prefer Germany to other EU member states for work, but a smaller number actually wish *to settle* in Germany compared to the US (see Table 6.3). And while substantial numbers of the CEECs' citizens would like the experience of working abroad, only a small number would choose to

Table 6.3   *Attitudes in selected CEECs to working and settling aboad*

	Working abroad, Germany (%)	Settling abroad, Germany (%)	Settling abroad, US (%)
Poles	36	5	20
Czechs	38	6	14
Hungarians	25	2	7
Slovaks	17	<1	7

Source: adapted from the 1998 survey data of the International Organization for Migration, as analysed by Wallace (2002).

dwell permanently outside of their countries. Wallace (2002: 621) concludes that migration is 'short-term, circulatory, commuting' (sometimes characterized as *pendeln*) (Favell and Hansen, 2002) – involving back and forth movement. She speculates that EU-15 states closing their labour markets to the CEECs' citizens will actually *increase* long-term resettlement by hindering frequent migration. This situation may be exacerbated when low value-added industry originating from the EU-15 abandons the EU 10 + 2 for lower wage countries in Asia, for this could lead to short-term demand to emigrate to the EU-15, thus further fueling resentment over the labour mobility derogation (see, for example, Dyker, 2000: 16; Hudson, 2002: 11; Willis 1996: 156.)

Second, there is the commonly known psychology of emigration: push is a stronger force than pull. With average growth rates in recent years of around 5 per cent in the CEECs (compared to 1 per cent in the EU-15), the continent may experience reverse migration as more Western Europeans are attracted to increased opportunities available to them in the East in an integrated Union. This conjures an image of Westerners being able to cross the EU's borders freely, whilst Easterners cannot.

Third, the very individuals whom the EU should be trying to reach – young people – are most negatively affected by derogations. Their situation is captured by Slovakian student Ivana Holeciova's comment to a *BBC News* reporter (2002):

> All young people support the EU. It will make it easier for us to study and work wherever we want in Europe. It's not that we all want to move away from Slovakia and get rich in the west, it's just that being able to travel is part of our freedom, something that our parents and grandparents have not always had.

Fourth, the EU-15's low population growth rate (3.7 per cent until at least 2025) ensures that the EU-15 will increasingly experience labour shortages. By 2025, 22.4 per cent of the EU-15 population will be over 65 (Geddes, 2002). But, in fact, the CEECs' population rates are mimicking those of the EU-15, so they may well not be able to provide the working age people needed to compensate for Europe's aging workforce! The EU will need to *stimulate* labour mobility to at least the levels of fluidity of the United States. While identity is certainly not the only factor promoting mobility – the EU has much work ahead of it in creating, for example, portable pensions and health benefits and in harmonizing tax policies – creating a sense of *continental* identity to encourage all Europeans to move about in search of better, more satisfying employment should have a non-trivial effect on EU growth rates.

Finally, Europe still lacks in diversity compared to the traditional recipients of immigrants. Only 5.3 per cent of Europeans are foreign-born, compared to 10.3 and 25 per cent in the US and Australia, respectively

(Schifferes, 2002). Diversity is considered by many experts to be an important contributory factor in the energetic economies of Australia, Canada and the United States.

So, although labour mobility may be seen as being essential for creating a sense of Europeaness, this historic (and seemingly costless) opportunity to create good will and to afford restless and curious citizens of the CEECs the opportunity to move about the West for school and work, may be lost. Or at least it could be so if the EU-15 fail to recognize that the benefits to the EU-25 of free labour mobility far exceed the costs and that one of these benefits – strengthened identity – will produce synergistic effects throughout the Union.

Schengen

Another area of concern for new member states is the way the Schengen *acquis* – which involves the gradual abolition of checks at participating states' common borders – interrupts historical ties of countries in the region. Jileva (2002) reminds us that despite proscribed travel to the West, visiting Socialist countries was routine for the citizens of CEECs in the late communist period. But Schengen creates new barriers at traditional border crossings between the CEECs and neighbouring countries. Schengen, thus, disrupts movements of goods and people among Slavic countries and requires CEECs to distance themselves from peoples with whom they share historical and linguistic ties, thus undermining both affective and instrumental identification with peoples to their east. This reinforcement of 'otherness' also risks engendering a mixed sense of guilt and insecurity – with the latter being exemplified by CEECs' citizens' fears about cross-border crime.

Poland's 1998 Act on Foreigners, Migrants and Border Traffic, designed to bring it into line with Schengen, introduced visas and vouchers for Belarussians and Russians at $60 a visa – at a time when a Belarussian earns, on average, $30 per month. After implementation of the 1998 Act, the number of Russians crossing the border decreased by 48.5 per cent and of Belarussians by 35.8 per cent (Kisielowsa-Lipman, 2002: 147). Schengen also disrupts border trade between Poland and the Ukraine, despite Korczow/Krakowiec being one of the busiest border crossings in Europe (Kiseilowsa-Lipman, 2002: 148), and despite too the importance of the economic relationship between Poland and the Ukraine – the Ukraine is Poland's third largest trading partner.

These type of situations are being mirrored throughout the CEECs, with disruption to trade and employment, particularly among small- and medium-scale traders and businesses. The EU has virtually made the CEECs 'migration buffers', resulting, in the words of Poland's Foreign Minister, Wlodzimierz Cimoscewicz, in the imposition of a 'glass curtain' between CEECs and their eastern neighbours. Most of the CEECs have attempted to implement policies to skirt Schengen, especially so as to maintain links with their ethnic minorities in non-EU states (Fowler, 2002: 7), but this has then naturally created problems with the EU

Zielonka (2001: 525) calls the Schengen *acquis* a symbol of 'inequality, division, and exclusion'. Indeed, while the EU offers permanent Schengen derogations to the UK and Ireland, and two non-EU countries – Iceland and Norway – have been admitted to the Schengen system, the EU required the new member states to adopt the whole Schengen *acquis* as an accession condition (Jileva, 2002). Furthermore, EU negotiators left the new member states little room for discretion in implementing Schengen (Mitsilegas, 2002).

Schengen brings us back to the beginning of our discussion: what is Europe? If the heart of Europe is in Prague, then the EU-25 will need to find the means to include the Ukraine, Russia, and Belarus in Schengen. Otherwise the EU-15 demands too much of its eastern frontier members: to turn their backs on their neighbours to the East and watch helplessly as their eastern border towns languish due to tightly restricted crossings. The EU risks creating a situation in which at least some CEECs may have to choose between a European and a pan-Slavic identity, when no such choice is necessary.

Schengen also places the new member states in the costly and politically sensitive position of policing borders with their less prosperous neighbours to the south and east. Looking in from the outside, the peoples of Turkey, the Balkan states, Ukraine, Belarus and Russia may thus become more estranged from the European cosmopolitan project, further exacerbating security concerns for those states on their borders.

Conclusions

What are the expectations of the new member states? Deutsch *et al.* (1957: 202) found that earlier successful integration experiences were shaped by 'the expectation of economic gains'. They stated that 'it was sufficient (even for amalgamation) if such expectations were fulfilled in part rather than completely, *provided that a substantial portion of this fulfillment came at an early stage*' (emphasis added).

Constructing a nation of Europeans loyal to a state-like EU will require a careful balance between rights and obligations. If new member states' citizens experience difficulty in arranging to work and study in the enlarged EU, and if the EU continues to ask the CEECs to abandon the peoples on their eastern borders, these concerns could, among others, unnecessarily delay the formation of a sense of Europeanness.

Whither identity? In this chapter we have reviewed the four principal interpretations of identity formation: primordialist, postmodern, post-national and modern. How have they contributed to our under-standing of identity formation in an enlarged EU?

Primordialists reject the modernist assertion that states foster nations to assist industrialization. Some nations existed prior to industrializa-tion, even if imagined. To deny a sense of shared history – even if not all moments were experienced equally in all quarters of Europe – is to ignore the diffusion of ideas and goods simply due to propinquity. Although only a small percentage of the polity feels 'European', those individuals tend to be the decision-makers in European states. This is clearly a prob-lem, but we believe the evidence supports the primordialist contention that a widespread affective attachment has yet to be formed.

Postmodernist scholarship also contributes to our understanding of European identity, although perhaps less directly than primordialist thought. Particularly interesting is the possible linkage between 'identity' and 'interests'. What in other federalist systems passes for 'identity poli-tics' in Europe may be simply classic interest group behaviour. Interest groups, indeed, could play an increasingly important role in building cross-national linkages among the citizenry of the enlarged EU. This, in turn, would reinforce Europeaness.

Within postnational perspectives, cosmopolitan enlightenment has gained currency as an explanation for the way in which European iden-tity might be forming. A major weakness in this neo-Kantian interpreta-tion of European identity, however, is that apart from a few disagreements at the margins – for example, with the US maintaining the use of capital punishment and questioning aspects of the jurisdiction of international courts – Europe looks very much like its allies in the other advanced industrialized countries. Cosmopolitanism reinforces Europe's image as a 'higher civilization', but provides little in the way of 'other-ness'.

As for the modernist emphasis on the *raison d'être* of identity, we conclude that a sense of identity will be integral to the ability of Europe to develop a seamless, integrated market, such as is found in large feder-alist states. A sense of belonging, which a common identity provides, is, for example, the *sine qua non* of labour mobility.

*   *   *

Where Europe differs markedly from other advanced industrialized democracies is in the way its individual states have struggled and resolved the classic balance between efficiency and equality. This debate was to split Europe – the West choosing efficiency, the East, equality (even if it was imposed largely from outside) – but even the West produced working-class political parties and adopted socialist policies far beyond that of any other modern capitalist state. It is not an exagger-ation to say that Western Europe invented social democracy. During the

Cold War many Western European socialist and communist parties (particularly in Italy and France), assiduously and indefatigably worked to keep open the links between West and East. Despite the metaphor of the iron curtain, the East was never completely isolated from the West – largely because of this sense that Western Europe had found a middle way between America and the Soviet Union. In this context, the centrality of social democracy clearly delineates the European from the American approach to economic competitiveness.

This identity – whether it is called social democracy, the human face of capitalism, the Third Way, or the sensible middle – is instrumental. It precedes the affective identification that might begin to form in the years to come.

It has been said that Europeans are Americans who are afraid to get on boats. A less politically conservative interpretation of migratory patterns seems equally valid: Europeans are people who remained behind to do the hard work of turning something old to something new, refurbishing an old and stately house one copper pipe at a time. This reluctance to leave, or rather determination to stay, is an identity in and of itself that has manifested itself in Europe's social democracy. Thus, in the end it may be this European social democracy that sets Europe apart from the other advanced industrialized countries of the West, particularly the United States, but also Canada and Australia. That could well be the internal dynamic that links Western, Central, and Eastern Europe into a transnational state and produces a European identity.

Chapter 7

The Citizenry: Legitimacy and Democracy

JANET MATHER

This chapter looks at the impact of enlargement on the EU's legitimacy and democracy. First, it considers the derivation of legitimacy, focusing upon empirical as well as normative means, particularly those derived from democratic practices. Second, it looks at the relevance of legitimacy to the EU, asking why the EU, which is not a state, requires legitimacy. Third, it examines the correlation between enlargement and legitimacy and its relevance to the EU's form of liberal democracy. Fourth, it looks at the potential effects of enlargement upon normative and empirical legitimacy, arguing that legitimacy may be derived from the EU's performance as well as from its political and constitutional construction. Hence, the chapter considers both the internal impact of enlargement on longer-standing and new citizens, and the external impact of an enlarged EU on the international community.

What is Legitimacy?

Analyzing legitimacy has always been something of a problem. As Schmitter (2001) remarks: 'It ranks up there with "power" in terms of how much it is needed, how difficult it is to define and how impossible it is to measure.' The literature on the subject tends to place its acquisition into two categories: the normative and the empirical. Normative theorists argue that forms of legitimization depend upon established ethics and principles – particularly those derived from democratic norms and values. A popular mandate for governmental activity and the need for a government to be chosen under and subject to a system that has acquired popular sanction (Beetham, 1992) are both ingredients of the *normative* legitimate polity. In relation to the EU, some theorists, for example Moravcsik (2002) and Zweifel (2002), argue that since the EU fulfils these criteria (and, Moravcsik adds, rather better than some existing western democracies) concerns about its 'democratic deficit', and hence its 'legitimacy deficit', are misplaced.

This may be, but this perspective ignores the alternative, empirical, justification that owes much to Weber's work (Gerth and Mills, 1967). Weber argued that legitimacy equates with the perception of legitimacy. He regarded the routes towards legitimacy as means to an end. Legitimacy could be derived from tradition, from the personal qualities of the ruler(s) or from the constitution. What was important was that governmental authority be accepted by the people. It is here, as evidence derived from electoral participation and satisfaction ratings indicates, where the EU falls short.

Whilst the normative version is almost entirely dependent upon popular *input*, empirical legitimacy has no prerequisites, and theorists have suggested that, particularly where the EU is concerned, governance might win the support and approval of its citizens by means of its *performance*. For example, Beetham and Lord (1998) suggest that one outcome could be the provision of a form of citizenship based upon human rights and perhaps also upon social and economic benefits, whilst Feldman (1999) suggests that the EU could, by gaining the acclaim of the international community, win the support and approval of its own citizens.

Both of these avenues seem more worth pursuing than that presented by normative theory when considering the impact of enlargement on legitimacy. As shown below, liberal democratic accessories like elections and voting do not transplant very effectively in the EU, but, as a nascent and developing polity, the EU does have the potential to deliver other desirable public goods to its citizens. This chapter, therefore, concentrates most of its attention upon the ways in which the EU can gain popular acceptance by means of its actions and activities.

Why Does the EU Need Legitimacy?

An additional problem of determining the nature of legitimacy in the EU is its own ambiguous status – as a political organization it has some, but not all, of the functions of a state. To what extent does the 'intergovernmental body' or 'confederation' – depending on the analyst's definition – need popular legitimacy? Some theorists, for example, Tsinisizelis and Chryssochoou (1998: 83–97 *passim*), argue that the EU does not need direct legitimacy. They have suggested that 'confederal consociation' defines EU modes of decision-making. In this model, the EU is managed by means of 'demoi' involved in mutual rather than democratic governance. By deduction, this makes EU legitimacy dependent upon the prior legitimacy of the member states that comprise it. This is a tempting idea, but it does not really address the question directly – the EU may not (yet) be a state, but it needs to govern.

Popular allegiance or unquestioning obedience may not be essential, since the implementation of EU decisions is in the hands of national governments and bureaucracies. However, consent and acceptance are necessary, if only because people are used to some sense of government being for their benefit – that is, government for, if not necessarily by, the people. Illegitimate governments are hard to sustain (Finer, 1988), and the longevity of the EU is needed particularly because of the challenge of enlargement.

Enlargement presents both an opportunity for and a threat towards the EU's legitimacy, as shown below. On the one hand, it offers the prospect of the largest peaceful and liberal polity known so far in the world; on the other, it endangers the slightly precarious balance in legitimacy achieved to date.

What Is the Correlation Between Enlargement and Legitimacy?

Any developments within the EU have a potential impact upon legitimacy. As the EU does more, each incursion into different policy areas raises the issue of the EU's right to widen its jurisdiction. In relation to enlargement, however, the issue is not generally seen as a question of whether the EU *ought* to enlarge – on the whole, this is seen as a natural extension, with potential benefits. However, this assumption needs to be analyzed.

Three potential effects are pertinent to this analysis. First, looking briefly at normative legitimacy theory, the impact of enlargement upon the EU's internal policy processes needs to be examined. Enlargement here looks set to dilute the EU's rather insecure democracy as more countries, offering higher heterogeneity as well as a greater numbers of citizens, join. Second, the potential for a new form of citizenship should be considered, not forgetting that, should new citizens' benefits appear to translate into longer-standing citizens' losses, EU-15 citizens may come to resent the political, social and economic gains made by their new fellow-citizens. Third, the question of the extent to which the newly enlarged EU can become an effective player on the world stage should be estimated, particularly in relation to foreign policy. This is the idea, suggested by Beetham and Lord (1998: 98–104 *passim*) and Feldman (1999), that the successful implementation of external policies can result in internal popular allegiance. Enlargement offers potential benefits in this direction, but the newer states have multi-faceted approaches towards questions of foreign relations, and they may sharpen the existing division between the EU's 'Atlanticists' and 'Europeanists'.

Legitimacy, Enlargement and the EU's Form of Liberal Democracy

Liberal democracy offers two benefits to its recipients. On the one hand, it promises them a degree of freedom (liberalism); on the other, it offers the potential for popular control (by means of elected representation). Liberal democracy, therefore, should be an appropriate system of governance for the EU. However, optimism about the 'end of history' (Fukuyama, 1992), wherein liberal democracy offers the ideal balance between governors and governed, now appears to have been misplaced. Some of the challenges to liberal democracy are external – for example, international terrorism – but internal challenges relating to a sense of declining legitimacy are more relevant in relation to the EU's enlargement.

Here, there is the problem of popular disengagement with party electoral politics, mostly demonstrated by declining electoral turnouts and increasing interest in non-governmental means of influencing policies and events. This tendency is exacerbated at EU level, indicating that there is a difficulty in 'copying and pasting' liberal democracy onto a larger and more remote polity. What works reasonably, if increasingly less, well at the nation-state level, does not seem to be readily transferable upwards.

Evidence for disengagement at the EU level is seen in turnouts in EP elections, which have declined consistently since the first set of elections in 1979. In addition, polls conducted about the EU indicate not only a sense of suspicion about its activities and lack of trust in its institutions, but also an alarming degree of ignorance about its policies and structure. There seems to be a shortfall between popular *input* through elections and popular *outcomes* in terms of public perception.

The *Eurobarometer 57* report (October 2002) demonstrates the relatively low level of faith in the EU amongst EU-15 citizens. The EU-wide average level of trust was 46 per cent. On the whole, people who approved of EU membership tended to claim to know more about it, but only a small majority – 53 per cent – of the EU-15 citizens approved of their country's membership. *Eurobarometer 57* shows that, according to respondents' self-perceived knowledge of the EU, on a scale of 0 ('know nothing') to 10 ('know a great deal'), the EU average was 4.35. Only 1 per cent of the EU-15 population regarded itself as 'knowing a great deal' about the EU.

Despite declining electoral turnouts, more people (89 per cent) had heard of the European Parliament than recognized the term 'European Commission' (78 per cent) or 'Council of Ministers' (63 per cent) (*Eurobarometer 57*, 2002). More people also 'trusted' the EP than other institutions. Of those EU-15 citizens surveyed in the *Eurobarometer 57* report, 54 per cent had faith in the EP, compared with 47 per cent for the Commission and 41 per cent for the Council of Ministers.

The EU, then, had a fairly low level of institutional support before the accession of new countries. Whilst it may be argued that one reason for this is the relatively limited knowledge that citizens have about the EU, the lack of knowledge itself must have something to do with a lack of interest and/or a sense of powerlessness.

Enlargement is a means whereby awareness may increase (although, according to *Eurobarometer 57*, only 21 per cent of respondents consider themselves to be 'very well informed' or 'well informed' about enlargement). However, whilst increased awareness could contribute to increased interest in EU affairs, it will not create a sense of effectiveness, since enlargement brings into prominence the 'representation deficit' that has existed within the Community since its beginnings. In other words, there are insufficient representatives to make meaningful the connection between them and their electorates (Mather, 2000: 105–14).

In 2002, about 370 000 000 citizens were represented by 626 MEPs – an average ratio of one MEP: 600,994 voters (although this varies considerably amongst the EU-15). In 2007, when 12 additional states are likely to have been admitted into the EU, 732 MEPs will represent 455 500 000 voters – a ratio of one MEP: 622 267 voters. Duff (2000) comments that the increased size of the EP is 'bad for the Parliament, which will be blamed for being too big'. However, it could also be argued that the EP is simply not large *enough* to act as a vehicle for representative democracy, if voting is to mean anything more than a vehicle for getting people elected to positions of power.

In the EU, however, it is normally assumed that representative democracy is conducted at second hand. The EU's citizens do not vote only for their MEPs, they also elect their government by one means or another, and, in turn, the elected government plays its part at EU level. Enlargement, however, reduces the significance of the part played by individual governments. It does this in two ways. First, enlarging without slowing down decision-making processes to an unacceptable level requires an extension of qualified majority voting (QMV) within the Council of Ministers. The Treaty of Nice extended QMV to 28 additional areas. Most of these have a limited significance, but they indicate a trend that may need to be continued to enable a much larger EU be able to operate. Second, the Nice Treaty also re-allocated voting weights in the Council of Ministers, with the result that whilst the majority threshold increases slightly after accession – from 71.3 per cent to an ultimate maximum of 74.8 per cent – each EU-15 state will have a lower percentage of votes after the accession of the new states. Interestingly, also, in relation to their respective populations, EU-15 states end up with lower percentages of votes in the Council of Ministers, and a smaller percentage of seats in the EP by comparison to the new states. This imbalance is mainly because so many applicants are small states, which have always had a favourable balance of voting rights in the EU (see Table 7.1 and also Tables 8.1 and 8.2):

Table 7.1   *Allocation of votes in the Council of Ministers and seats in the EP in the EU-25*

States	*Total population % of EU*	*% votes in Council*	*% seats in EP*
EU-15	78.2	68.7	73.1
New states	21.8	31.3	26.9
Total	100	100	100

Sources: Nugent (1999); Duff (2001, adapted).

The figures in Table 7.1 suggest that that faith in EU-15 states' governments' ability to stand up for national interests may decline after enlargement. However, one set of countries' loss is another's gain. Citizens of new member states are not only given slightly higher levels of representation on average in the Council of Ministers and EP, they also acquire representation simply by means of membership. According to *Eurobarometer* 2001, which indicated that 62 per cent of future citizens 'trusted' the EU, newer citizens already have a higher level of belief in the Union (*Candidate Countries Eurobarometer*, 2001). This suggests legitimization by means of liberal democracy may work better for the EU's newer citizens, although in the longer term, this may depend upon the outcomes they experience after accession, as considered below.

Towards a New Form of Citizenship

If legitimacy depends upon the EU's performance in relation to its citizens, it may be enhanced by enlargement to the extent that its newer citizens react favourably towards its governance. The *Candidate Countries Eurobarometer*, 2001 showed that most citizens in the acceding states were enthusiastic about membership before accession. Almost 60 per cent thought that it would be 'a good thing' for their countries and 52 per cent thought that the EU conjured up a positive image.

CEECs' previous experience of democratic citizenship

The CEECs' people have limited experience of citizenship under constitutional democratic government. As shown in Table 7.2, only four – Latvia,

Table 7.2 *Statehood and political regimes of CEECs during the twentieth century until the collapse of communism*

State	Experience of authoritarianism /dictatorship (including Nazi occupation)	Experience of communist control	Experience of democracy/ constitutional government
Bulgaria (unified and independent from 1908)	1923–1932 1934–1944	1920–1923 1944–1989	1908–1920 (constitutional monarchy) 1932–1934
Czechoslovakia (Czech Republic and Slovakia; under Austro-Hungarian control until 1918; separated in 1993)	1939–1944	1946–1989	1918–1938 (from unification)
Estonia (independent from 1920)	1933–1940	1940–1991	1920–1933 (unstable govts)
Hungary (Austro-Hungarian Dual Monarchy from 1867–1918)	1867–1918 1919–1945	1918–1919 1947–1989	1945–1947
Latvia (under Russian sovereignty until 1917)	1934–1940	1918–1920 1940–1991	1920–1934
Lithuania (under Russian sovereignty until 1917)	1795–1916 1926–1939 1941–1944	1939–1941 1944–1991	1917–1926
Poland (ancient state, but under Russian sovereignty and extinct as a political unit until 1918)	1918–1939	1939–1989	–
Romania (independent state from 1862, but additional territory in 1877 and 1918)	1938–1946 1958–1989 (Ceausescu)	1946–1958	1919–1938 (but domination by fascist Iron Guard)
Slovenia (part of Kingdom of Serbs, Croats and Slovenes from 1918 – renamed in 1929; Yugoslavia independent state from 1991)	1929–1931 1935–1939 1939–1945 (Hungarian/Nazi occupation)	1945–1990	1981–1929 (political unrest) 1931–1934 (limited democracy)

Lithuania, the Czech Republic and Slovakia – had longer than three years' continuous experience of constitutional government during the twentieth century. All, at some stage, have had authoritarian and/or dictatorial regimes. Many also have experienced only a very limited period of independent statehood. The majority are post-1918 creations, following the collapse of the Austro-Hungarian and Russian empires. Slovenia, despite a long national history, has only been an independent state since 1991. Nevertheless, there is a high degree of national pride – an average of 86 per cent, ranging from 60 per cent in Estonia to 92 per cent in Slovenia – amongst all CEECs and the Mediterranean states (*Candidate Countries Eurobarometer*, 2001: 33).

What securities does the EU offer to the Newly Independent States?

Their chequered past experiences mean that membership of the EU offers two significant securities to the CEECs. On the one hand it helps to assure their political autonomy and on the other hand it helps to guarantee their people the kind of citizens' rights obtainable from liberalism and democracy.

The potential for the EU to establish these securities may be assessed, although three points can be made at the outset. First, the CEECs achieved a degree of political autonomy and liberal democracy without the direct assistance of the EU, although attitudes may have been influenced by the EU's economic success and, as Pridham's (2002) studies of Slovakia and Romania indicate, by the dynamic of the accession process itself. Second, the condition of a state's polity is likely to be more dependent upon its internal governance and upon its people's behaviour than upon the input of the supranational association. The European Commission (2002c) acknowledged this when it commented that 'the credit for this success belongs mainly to the people of those countries themselves'. The third point is significant in the context of this chapter. The impact of the EU on any member state's sovereignty is a sensitive issue. The Eurosceptic version of a dilution of sovereignty conflicts with the more positive view of a pooling of sovereignty (see, for example, Nugent, 1999: 505–6). However, both these notions link with the exercise of democratic government inasmuch as, whether or not a state has 'diluted' or 'pooled' its sovereignty, the fact that powers are used at a non-state level affects direct popular control over those powers (see, for example, Fella, 2000: 83). In this case, popular democracy based upon the sovereign state, recently gained by the CEECs, will be conceded before its advantages can be realized by citizens. The substitution of supranational democracy may not be sufficient. This is considered further below.

Another possibility is that the EU's new citizens will regard the trade-off between national sovereignty and supranational governance as a price worth paying. EU membership promises, besides the reinforcement of liberal democracy, economic benefits. In addition, as partners in a supranational community with the status of an international power, the new states' citizenry achieve a prominence unavailable to any single country, let alone one that has had a variable and generally unhappy experience of occupation and external control for most of its statehood. Cyprus and Malta, too, formerly states with limited international significance given their size and their limited autonomy, will also share in these benefits, should they be realized (see below).

What political benefits does enlargement offer to the EU's new citizens?

In political terms, the application of the Copenhagen accession criteria (see Chapter 3), along with the need to measure up to the EU's *acquis*, ought to provide the framework for constitutional and institutional liberal democracy for CEECs. Meeting expectations may prove challenging – and Pridham (2002) warns that the pace of implementation can be burdensome on 'fragile new democracies' – but the level of trust in indigenous public institutions in the new states before accession was low (although results varied from country to country). According to the *Eurobarometer* (2001: 23), only 30 per cent of the people had trust in their own public institutions – national governments, parliaments, civil service, and political parties. There is, one may assume, something to be gained if EU membership succeeds in improving the integrity and status of new member states' public institutions to the advantage of their citizens.

Nevertheless, the Commission's 2002 *Annual Strategy* report, issued alongside the *Regular Reports* on the applicants, seemed satisfied that all candidate countries had met the Copenhagen criteria (European Commission, 2002c: 13). All had functioning democratic governmental systems; all had held 'free and fair' elections; and matters relating to public administration had been clarified to show a definition between political and administrative responsibilities and to allow access to information. Judicial improvements were also noted, although corruption was still seen to be a problem. The candidate countries had ratified most of the UN Human Rights Conventions. The problem, which was illuminated in the individual country reports, seemed to be the difference between enshrining the letter and operating within the spirit of the law.

So, for example, although all CEECs plus Cyprus and Malta had ratified the Convention on the Elimination of all Forms of Racial Discrimination, the Commission's *Regular Reports* made it clear that the matter went beyond the promulgation of constitutional and legislative measures. CEECs, as Leibich (2002: 118), points out, adopt culturally different approaches towards minorities, ranging from the 'friendliness' of Hungary to the confrontational stance of Latvia and Estonia. The treatment of minorities, especially of the Roma, which are seen as having human rights implications, gave cause for concern. The 2002 Commission *Regular Reports* on Slovakia, the Czech Republic and Poland (European Commission, 2002c) commented adversely upon the treatment of the Roma in all three countries, and in its summary paper on accession in 2002 the Commission hinted that more needed to be done.

The message was mixed, therefore, for ethnic minorities in the new member states, potentially undermining their consequent support for EU governance. There seems no doubt that EU monitoring efforts will continue beyond enlargement, but a final resolution of human rights issues within the new member states has not yet been achieved.

The situation of minorities within the EU-25 states raises another issue that needs to be considered in relation to legitimacy. It is taken for granted that the EU should be comprised of some kind of grouping of sovereign *states*. However, there is the question of whether groupings of Europe's *population* are best served by it. Judy Batt and her colleagues have explored the idea of 'Fuzzy Statehood' and have suggested that Europe is better defined in terms of 'political fragmentation, the resurgence of regional and ethnic minority identities, and the devolution of state power' rather than in terms of the re-emergence of the sovereign nation state after the fall of communism (Batt, 2001). If this analysis has validity, there is a role for the EU in helping legitimize sub-state nationalities and movements, whilst providing a supranational security in relation to the world outside its borders. It is not, though, the role that its leaders have carved out for the EU (Newman, 1996: 172). If the EU can encourage or force national governments in EU-25/EU-27 states to take on the concerns and needs of groupings within their own borders, it may succeed in dampening down sub-national groups' demands. If it does not, then the EU may have taken on the wrong kind of role at the wrong moment. The price may be paid in an entrenched and institutionalized lack of legitimacy.

Will economic benefits convince new citizens of the EU's legitimacy?

Minority groups, along with the rest of their fellow citizens, may find compensation in terms of an improved quality of life. If so, the potential shortfall in legitimacy generated by a reduction in their support may be lessened. There are high expectations in relation to economic benefits. The highest number (38 per cent) of respondents from the applicant states to the 2001 *Candidate Countries Eurobarometer* cited a positive view of the economy as their main reason for regarding the EU favourably (p. 42). It is not too difficult to see the origins of this belief. The enlargement process itself has helped contribute to rising economic standards and the vision of the economic growth of the EU-15 has also encouraged applicants.

New citizens, moreover, are starting from a relatively low basis of personal affluence. For example, before accession, 58 per cent did not own a car (*Candidate Countries Eurobarometer*, 2001: 10). General satisfaction with life was also low. Taking candidate country citizens as a whole, only 51 per cent claimed to be satisfied, compared with 83 per cent in EU-15 states (*ibid*.: 11).

The extent to which expectations will be met is, however, uncertain. A key reason for this is, as other chapters in this book show (see especially Chapters 3 and 12), that EU-15 governments have been more concerned with protecting their own interests than with assisting the acceding states, with the result that new states will not benefit from EU resources on the same basis as existing members. The main argument for this approach, put forward, for example, by Germany, backed by France and the UK, at the October 2002 Brussels European Summit (European Council 2002b) was that the new members would not be able to spend the full amount of subsidies (Czerwińska 2002). This argument was applied to a less-than-thoroughly reformed CAP. After discussions between French President, Jacques Chirac, and German Chancellor, Gerhard Schröder, a Commission proposal to give farmers in all accession states initially only 25 per cent of the direct aid available to EU-15 states' farmers for agricultural subsidies was confirmed by the Brussels European Council. A phasing in of the CAP was agreed so that for the initial years of their membership new member states will receive proportionately less funding than EU-15 states (see Chapter 12). The European leaders also made it plain that delays in adjustment on the part of new states could mean exclusion from the subsidies (Czerwińska, 2002).

The question of CEECs being able to make effective use of monies available has been considered by a number of commentators. For example, Sándor Richter (2002) estimates that new members may be able to utilize only between 30–75 per cent of the available resources, depending upon whether they are able to improve on their pre-accession effectiveness. Richter notes that the opportunity costs of remaining outside the EU would be higher, but comments that the new citizens may be disappointed in their first experiences of EU membership.

In the longer term, new countries are likely to benefit. For example, Peter Havlik (2001) suggests in his study of the prospects of five new countries that Poland and Hungary may add 8–9 per cent to their GDP from 2001–2011, whilst the Czech Republic and Slovakia are likely to gain between 4 and 6 per cent. The issue, however, is whether benefits will be sufficiently apparent soon enough after accession. Whilst there are long-term political and economic benefits to be derived, there is likely to be an uncomfortable transition period, during which cultural differences and required changes in established practices may become a focus for apprehension.

Enlargement and the International Community

Enlargement also has the potential to enhance the EU's performance legitimacy by means of increasing its international standing, and thereby qualifying for increased support and approval from amongst its citizens (Feldman 1999). 'At a stroke', according to Dunkerley *et al.* (2002: 154), enlargement makes the EU a more powerful and influential player on the world stage, and at the same time reduces its dependence upon the US in security terms and increases its input into global security. The Commission (2002c) agrees that:

> On the basis of political and economic stability, the enlarged Union will be better equipped to confront global challenges. An enlarged Union will add weight to the EU's external relations, in particular to the development of a common foreign and security policy.

If these contentions are borne out, all the EU's citizens are likely to bear out the neofunctionalists' customary claim that the EU will be 'cumulatively legitimated by a record of superior performance' (Beetham and Lord 1998: 95).

The problem is that the EU's foreign policy is 'sharply contested' (Feldman, 1999: 80) and, unfortunately, there have been few examples to date of a common EU approach to world crises. The fear is that increased heterogeneity may bring about additional barriers. This risk was highlighted during the 2003 crisis over Iraq, where it was clear that the (then) candidate countries' acceptance of the UK/US line added to, rather than detracted from, internal EU divisions (see Chapter 16).

One major issue for the new EU is its relationship with the US, and it is difficult to ascertain whether a common approach is made more or less likely by means of the accession of the CEECs. Feldman (1999: 80) notes that 'the United States recognizes the unique contribution EU enlargement can make to the stability of Central and Eastern Europe, and Europe as a whole'. The US may indeed want increased stability within Europe, but not, one may surmise, at the price of acquiring a serious rival to its own hegemony.

The problem here is that the continuing respect of the international community depends upon the *success* of enlargement – or, in other words, the extent to which enlargement contrives to bring about peace and reconciliation throughout Europe. And, in turn, this depends upon the extent to which new citizens regard the EU as an instrument of peace and reconciliation. An early resolution of 'the Cyprus Problem' would provide an encouragement for them to trust the EU's capabilities in this respect.

Nevertheless, enlargement offers the prospect of a united Europe forming the largest area of peaceful liberal democracy in the world. By examining the progress that the accession states have made towards achieving the EU's *acquis* in foreign and security policy, the likelihood of enlargement leading to more rather than less commonality of purpose in that field can be established. In the accession negotiations the *acquis* on foreign and security policy covered essentially three areas. First, an applicant state needed to demonstrate its capacity to contribute to EU initiatives; secondly it needed to share the EU's broad positions on foreign policy, including international peace-keeping; and thirdly, it should have achieved reasonable relations with its neighbours and, where applicable, traditional adversaries. The EU is not anxious to import strained foreign relations.

In all of these areas, there appears to be little to concern the EU, and the chapter on foreign and security policy was closed provisionally early in the negotiations by all countries, suggesting that this was a relatively easy set of conditions for the applicant states to fulfil. The Commission was satisfied that each country had made sufficient substantial as well as formal progress in respect of the CFSP *acquis* and no countries asked for transitional arrangements.

The Commission's findings show that each new member state can take part in the EU's foreign policy ventures. According to the Commission's 2002 Regular Report (2002c), all, with the exception of the Czech Republic and Estonia, are able to contribute to the EU's Rapid Reaction Force and all, except Estonia, are ready to be associated with the EU Police Force/Mission. All new member states have aligned their foreign policy positions with EU foreign policy statements and declarations and have associated themselves with EU joint actions. The prospect of an EU presenting a reasonably united front towards the rest of the world seems likely to be fulfilled, thereby increasing the likelihood that it can gain legitimacy on the back of its international status.

In addition, the prospect of membership seems to have encouraged new member states to settle most significant differences with their neighbours and traditional enemies (Cyprus apart). Nello and Smith (1998: 56) have argued that:

> In the case of the CEECs, enlargement will inevitably mean that there will be a larger 'lobby' concerned with relations with Russia, in particular . . . Once in the EU, the new member states could push for a harder stance against Russia. Current attempts by the EU to strengthen economic and political relations with Russia could be jeopardized.

Likewise, EU relations with other 'outsiders' in Central and Eastern Europe could also worsen where there have been problems between them and the acceding CEECs.

There is also the reverse problem: Russia may seek to pressure the EU and the new member states, particularly the Baltic republics . . . Estonia has had serious difficulties with Russia (over, among other issues, its treatment of the Russian minority), and it is not clear how the EU would handle a deterioration in Russian-Estonian relations.

These predictions do not seem to have been borne out by events. The Commission, in its *Regular Report* on Estonia (2002c), stated that 'relations with Russia have remained stable', and seemed satisfied that Russian-origin minorities were being treated with more fairness in terms of their language and voting rights. A border agreement with Russia, although not formally ratified by the Russian Parliament, had been applied in practice (2002c: 100). Latvia, Lithuania and Poland are also enjoying good relations with Russia. Cyprus and Malta have 'constructive', 'intensive' relationships in their areas. Additional funding for cross-border cooperation programmes for Slovenia has led to strengthened relations with Austria, Hungary and Italy.

The picture that emerges is one that shows an enlarged EU in which former differences amongst its new members have been primarily resolved, and which has at least the political right to speak with one voice as had the EU-15. This may be a limited vision, reflecting only the reality that the EU's foreign policy is embryonic, and that 'common positions' are so broad as to be lacking in content, in particular when facing the significant question of the EU–US relationship. However, it may be that the new member states, not fully conscious of the problems surrounding the development of new foreign policies, will encourage a larger EU to move forward faster towards converging its foreign policies at least inasmuch as it affects its newest members.

International opinion may therefore be influenced by small, as opposed to all-encompassing, initiatives in the field of foreign policy. The extent to which the enlarged EU wins respect from the international community by these means may help to determine the responsiveness of its citizens to EU governance in the future.

Conclusions

This chapter has examined three main avenues that may lead the EU, through its enlargement process, towards heightened legitimization. It has shown that enlargement is a challenge for the EU's legitimacy. It stretches the concept of traditional normative legitimacy, but at the same time paves the way for a newer empirical form derived from EU performance either by means of endowing its citizens, particularly its new ones, with meaningful citizenship, or by means of increasing its status on the world stage. All the people of the EU, in the end, will decide for themselves whether the enlarged EU commands sufficient legitimacy to be an effective organization within a political ethos that takes democratic input and outcomes for granted. The paradox is that an enlarged EU may demand and/or need less legitimacy because its greater heterogeneity makes it less likely to become an integrated polity. However, because it is less likely to become an integrated polity, the EU is correspondingly less likely to be able to deliver the benefits that could result in its enhanced popular legitimacy.

There are favourable and less favourable signs, but the outcome of enlargement is bound to provide useful evidence about the process of legitimization in 'state building' – which may be of use to political scientists, if not of direct benefit to the people of the EU.

Chapter 8

Institutions and Governance

DAVID PHINNEMORE

Whenever the EU is faced with the prospect of enlargement, concerns are invariably raised about the impact more members will have on its capacity to function. The lead up to the 2004 enlargement was no exception, with much attention from the mid-1990s onwards being focused on how to ensure that an EU with a membership of 25 or more states would be able to operate. The matter was supposed to have been addressed at the 1996 intergovernmental conference (IGC), but the resulting Treaty of Amsterdam failed to resolve many of the issues being raised. Hence, it was left to the 2000 IGC to prepare the EU for the challenges raised by an enlarged membership. The Treaty of Nice that emerged, according to its authors at least, prepared the EU institutionally for enlargement (Galloway, 2001; de Witte, 2003). Technically, however, it did not establish the actual institutional arrangements for an enlarged EU. These were agreed during the course of the accession negotiations and, in most cases, inserted into the Act of Accession annexed to the Treaty of Accession signed on 16 April 2003 (European Commission, 2003h), which was subsequently ratified by the EU-15 and the 10 acceding states.

Neither the Treaty of Nice nor the Act of Accession brought about any major overhaul of the EU's institutional structure. Equally, developments in the years up to enlargement addressed only some of the many challenges the EU faces as a system of governance. As the European Commission has acknowledged, the EU is some way from being a model exponent of principles of good governance such as openness, participation, accountability, effectiveness and coherence (European Commission, 2001b). And enlargement only adds to the challenges with which the EU is faced. More members mean greater diversity, more interests and a larger electorate. This has long been recognized.

The promotion of good governance as well as institutional reform featured, therefore, in the deliberations of the European Convention that produced the *Draft Treaty Establishing a Constitution for Europe* in 2003 (European Convention, 2003). They also provided a backdrop for the negotiations that took place within the IGC that began its work in October 2003. Further reforms affecting the institutions and governance are, therefore, likely to come into force in the first few years after enlargement. For the time being, however, institutional arrangements and governance practices in the EU will be determined by existing approaches, in some cases amended, and the changes introduced by the 2002 Act of Accession. They will nevertheless change. In part this will follow from the seemingly continuous process of constitutional reform. It will also come about as the EU faces the reality of a much enlarged membership.

This chapter outlines the institutional changes accompanying enlargement and highlights some of the governance challenges the enlarged EU faces.

Institutions and Decision-Making in EU-25

The most obvious impact of any enlargement round is that each of the EU's main institutions increases in size to accommodate the new member states. In the case of the 10 + 2 round, this has been done either in line with existing distributions among the EU-15 or in accordance with agreements reached at the Nice European Council in December 2000. These were set out in a *Declaration on the Enlargement of the European Union* (Official Journal, 2001a: 80–4). Another important impact of enlargement rounds is that they lead to changes in the operation of qualified majority voting (QMV) in the Council. The total number of votes available increases following the allocation of votes to the new member states and there is an adjustment to the QMV threshold. In addition to these two impacts, there has been a further impact in the 10 + 2 round on the institutions and decision-making. This is the entry into force of the institutional changes affecting the Commission and the Council envisaged in the *Protocol on the Enlargement of the European Union* (Official Journal, 2001a: 49–52). These were agreed as part of the Treaty of Nice and scheduled to enter into force on 1 January 2005. During the course of the accession negotiations, however, it was agreed to advance the date for the changes affecting the Commission and the Council to 1 November 2004. As a consequence, there is a separate set of arrangements governing the interim period from 1 May until then.

The Commission

Although there have long been questions raised over the merits and necessity of a large Commission, the 2004 enlargement sees the Commission increase in size. Initially, the increase is to 30 Commissioners as each new member state appoints one of its nationals to the Commission for the remainder of the 2000–2004 term. Thereafter the size falls. In line with the agreement reached at Nice, that following enlargement the Commission would include a national from each of the member states, the five largest member states – France, Germany, Italy, Spain and the United Kingdom – lose their second Commissioner. The 2004–2009 Commission therefore has 25 Commissioners appointed in line with the revised procedure introduced by the Treaty of Nice. Hence, the President is nominated by the European Council (minus, obviously, the incumbent Commission President) acting by a qualified majority. The Council, also acting by a qualified majority and in accord with the nominee for Commission President, then draws up a list of nominees for Commissioners. The list and the nominee for Commission President are then approved by the European Parliament (EP) before being formally appointed, on the basis of a qualified majority, by the Council.

The size of the Commission may in due course change. When there is a further enlargement of the EU – as there could be in 2007 to include Bulgaria and Romania – new Commissioners probably will be appointed. However, according to the *Protocol on the Enlargement of the European Union*, once the EU consists of 27 or more member states the number of Commissioners will be less than the number of member states. There is a proviso, however. The reduction will only take effect if the Council can unanimously agree a system for the equal rotation of Commissioners that reflects 'satisfactorily the demographic and geographical range' of the member states. Whether that will be possible remains to be seen, although the details of possible systems were circulated to member states at the time of the 2000 IGC. More recently, the European Convention proposed a rotation system with 15 Commissioners having full voting rights with additional non-voting Commissioners being appointed from all other member states. This was opposed by various smaller member states. In an attempt to find a compromise, the Commission subsequently proposed that a national from each member state be appointed as a Commissioner but that the Commission be structured in 'groups' covering its main areas of competence. Each group would consist of at least seven Commissioners (European Commission, 2003n: 19).

The European Parliament

In a similar manner to the Commission, enlargement results in an initial increase in the size of the EP. This is because enlargement takes place a month before the June 2004 EP elections and the scheduled reduction in the number of MEPs allocated to the member states of EU-15 heralded in the *Protocol on the Enlargement of the European Union*. For the short interim period from 1 May 2004 to the end of the 2000–2004 term of the EP, the existing 626 MEPs are joined by 162 appointees from the parliaments of the new member states. These will be the same individuals as those who from 5 May 2003 to 31 April 2004 were present in the EP as observers. As ever, the distribution of MEPs depends on population size.

Poland, the largest of the new member states, has 54 MEPs while Malta, the smallest newcomer, has only five MEPs (see Table 8.1).

With the 2004 elections, the size of the EP falls to 732 MEPs. This is the same size as that envisaged at Nice for an EU of 27 members. During the accession negotiations, however, the 'spare' seats provisionally allocated to Bulgaria and Romania were redistributed. With the exception of Germany and Luxembourg, whose allocations remain unchanged, each of the EU-15 states experienced a smaller reduction in the number of MEPs than envisaged at Nice. Likewise, the larger of the new member states were allocated a slightly higher number of MEPs. In the cases of the Czech Republic and Hungary the number of extra seats (4) is comparatively high, reflecting the acknowledged shortfall in the allocations of seats assigned to them at Nice – where both countries were allocated

Table 8.1   *Allocation of seats in the European Parliament*

	EU-15				EU-25			
	1999–2004		Interim period		2004–2009			
	Actual		Actual		Envisaged		Actual	
	No.	%	No.	%	No.	%	No.	%
Belgium	25	3.99	25	3.17	22	3.01	24	3.28
Denmark	16	2.56	16	2.03	13	1.78	14	1.91
Germany	99	15.81	99	12.56	99	13.52	99	13.52
Greece	25	3.99	25	3.17	22	3.01	24	3.28
Spain	64	10.22	64	8.12	50	6.83	54	7.38
France	87	13.9	87	11.04	72	9.84	78	10.66
Ireland	15	2.40	15	1.90	12	1.64	13	1.78
Italy	87	13.9	87	11.04	72	9.84	78	10.66
Luxembourg	6	0.96	6	0.76	6	0.82	6	0.82
Netherlands	31	4.95	31	3.93	25	3.42	27	3.69
Austria	21	3.35	21	2.66	17	2.32	18	2.46
Portugal	25	3.99	25	3.17	22	3.01	24	3.28
Finland	16	2.56	16	2.03	13	1.78	14	1.91
Sweden	22	3.51	22	2.79	18	2.46	19	2.60
United Kingdom	87	13.9	87	11.04	72	9.84	78	10.66
Czech Republic	–	–	24	3.05	20	2.73	24	3.28
Estonia	–	–	6	0.76	6	0.82	6	0.82
Cyprus	–	–	6	0.76	6	0.82	6	0.82
Latvia	–	–	9	1.14	8	1.09	9	1.23
Lithuania	–	–	13	1.65	12	1.64	13	1.78
Hungary	–	–	24	3.05	20	2.73	24	3.28
Malta	–	–	5	0.63	5	0.68	5	0.68
Poland	–	–	54	6.85	50	6.83	54	7.38
Slovenia	–	–	7	0.89	7	0.96	7	0.96
Slovakia	–	–	14	1.78	13	1.78	14	1.91
Bulgaria	–	–	–	–	17	2.32	–	–
Romania	–	–	–	–	33	4.51	–	–
Total	626	99.99	788	99.97	732	100.03	732	100.03

fewer MEPs (20) than Portugal (22), despite having larger populations. One consequence of the new allocations is that the new member states see a slight increase in their share of seats compared with the interim period.

The Council of Ministers

For the Council of Ministers, enlargement normally entails three notable changes: an increase in the number of participants; an adjustment of the QMV threshold; and a rescheduling of the rotation of the Presidency. In the case of the 2004 enlargement, changes only occur in the case of the first two, at least initially. As far as participation is concerned, the number of member states represented in the Council increases to 25. This is a two-thirds increase and is unprecedented in the history of the EU. Needless to say, it creates an enormous Council. Based on pre-enlargement practice (see Nugent, 2003: 175), it means more than 150 attending full Council meetings. Further logistical challenges arising from the increased number of Council participants include reducing the range of languages to be used in meetings, limiting the time taken up by *tours de table*, and obtaining consensus and unanimity.

The task of ensuring the Council continues to function effectively post-enlargement is extremely challenging. It was partly addressed by the June 2002 Seville European Council which agreed reform 'in the direction of enhancing the efficiency of the institution on the eve of an unprecedented increase in the number of Member States of the Union' (European Council, 2002a: point 4). Of the reforms agreed at Seville, three in particular merit being noted. First, there was a reduction in the number of Council formations – to nine – and a streamlining of responsibilities. The former included a new General Affairs and External Relations Council replacing the previous General Affairs Council. Second, provisions were made for the activities of the Council to be guided by an annual operating programme of Council activities designed to implement the new multi-annual strategic programme adopted every three years by the European Council. Third, the Presidency's role as chair of the Council was strengthened (European Council, 2002a: annex II).

Adjusting to these structural and procedural changes and accommodating the new member states in the activities of the Council are significant challenges for the enlarged EU. Equally challenging, especially in the first year of EU-25, is the mastering of new rules for qualified majority voting. These come in two stages and comprise two elements: the allocation of votes and the threshold for a decision to be adopted. During the first stage or 'interim period' from 1 May 2004 until the arrangements agreed at Nice and subsequently adjusted enter into force on 1 November 2004, each of the new member states is allocated a number of votes in accordance with the distribution among the EU-15. As a consequence, the relative voting strengths of the EU-15 naturally fall. As for the total number of votes available in the Council, this rises to 124 (see Table 8.2). In order to obtain a qualified majority, 88 votes are required (see Table 8.3). This threshold represents 70.96 per cent of the total votes available, a level slightly lower than that required in EU-15–71.26 per cent or 62 votes out of a total of 87.

From 1 November 2004, the allocation of votes changes to create a Council with 321 votes. Larger member states see their number of the votes roughly treble and their relative voting strengths increase compared to the interim period. Spain and Poland gain disproportionately, enjoying almost the same number of votes (27) as Germany (29) despite having populations less than half the size. In all, the largest member states – France, Germany, Italy, Poland, Spain and the United Kingdom – still

Table 8.2 *Vote allocations in an enlarging Council of Ministers*

	EU-15		*EU-25*			
			Interim period		*From 01 11 2004*	
	No.	%	No.	%	No.	%
Belgium	5	5.75	5	4.03	12	3.74
Denmark	3	3.45	3	2.42	7	2.18
Germany	10	11.49	10	8.06	29	9.03
Greece	5	5.75	5	4.03	12	3.74
Spain	8	9.20	8	6.45	27	8.41
France	10	11.49	10	8.06	29	9.03
Ireland	3	3.45	3	2.42	7	2.18
Italy	10	11.49	10	8.06	29	9.03
Luxembourg	2	2.30	2	1.61	4	1.25
Netherlands	5	5.75	5	4.03	13	4.05
Austria	4	4.60	4	3.23	10	3.12
Portugal	5	5.75	5	4.03	12	3.74
Finland	3	3.45	3	2.42	7	2.18
Sweden	4	4.60	4	3.23	10	3.12
United Kingdom	10	11.49	10	8.06	29	9.03
Czech Republic	–	–	5	4.03	12	3.74
Estonia	–	–	3	2.42	4	1.25
Cyprus	–	–	2	1.61	4	1.25
Latvia	–	–	3	2.42	4	1.25
Lithuania	–	–	3	2.42	7	2.18
Hungary	–	–	5	4.03	12	3.74
Malta	–	–	2	1.61	3	0.93
Poland	–	–	8	6.45	27	8.41
Slovenia	–	–	3	2.42	4	1.25
Slovakia	–	–	3	2.42	7	2.18
Total	87	100.01	124	99.97	321	100.01

Table 8.3   *Qualified majority voting thresholds in the Council of Ministers*

	EU-15	EU-25	
		Interim period	*From 01 11 2004*
Votes available	87	124	321
Votes required	62	88	232
Per cent	71.26	70.96	72.27
On a Commission proposal	–	–	Absolute majority
No Commission proposal	10	2/3 majority	2/3 majority
Verification	–	–	62% of EU population

control a majority (52.94 per cent) of the votes in the Council, although this is marginally lower than in EU-15 (55.16 per cent). In the case of the other member states, albeit with a number of exceptions (Estonia, Latvia, Malta and Slovenia), all witness at least a doubling of their votes (see Table 8.2). Yet in all cases, their relative share of votes decreases compared to the interim period. In the case of the smallest of the new member states it almost halves.

Under the arrangements for EU-25, a qualified majority requires 232 votes. In percentage terms, the new threshold (72.27 per cent) represents an increase on that for the interim period (see Table 8.3). It is lower, however, than that envisaged (74.78 per cent) and the maximum agreed (73.40 per cent) at the time of the Treaty of Nice (see Church and Phinnemore, 2002: 384–385). In addition to the Council requiring the number of votes indicated for a decision to be adopted, where it acts on the basis of a proposal from the Commission the 232 votes must be cast by a majority of the member states. In other cases, a two-thirds majority is required. Moreover, from 1 November 2004, member states will be able to request verification that the member states constituting the qualified majority represent 62 per cent of the total population of the EU. If this new threshold is not cleared, then the measure in question cannot be adopted. Seemingly, another hurdle to decision-making needs to be overcome. That said, with the new arrangements in place from 1 November 2004, the Ioannina compromise of 1994 (which requires the Council, where member states representing 23–27 votes oppose a measure, to prolong discussion to see if agreement can be reached) will cease to have effect (Official Journal, 2001b: 48).

The effect of the changes is a slightly more equitable distribution of voting power among the member states, although it clearly disadvantages some of the smaller countries as their vote relative to population size has decreased. By contrast, Spain and the larger member states have gained. As for the population criterion, views differ on its impact. It certainly increases Germany's blocking power and allows it, along with two other large member states, to prevent a decision being adopted (Moberg, 2002). Yet there are some who argue that it does not significantly influence the voting power of any individual state (Plechanovova, 2003). Equally, although decision-making using QMV becomes more complex, insiders argue that there is little likelihood of serious deadlock ensuing. This reflects the fact that consensus is the norm within the Council. Changes in relative voting weights may affect the relative bargaining power of each member state, but they do not undermine the decision-making capacity of the EU (Moberg, 2002). While a fair reflection of the *status quo ante*, this view arguably underestimates the impact that an unprecedented increase in the size of the Council will have.

Finally, as far as the Council is concerned, there is the matter of the rotation of the Presidency. Since 1995, this has been governed by a Council decision, the most recent of which envisages the rotation set out in Table 8.4 with the exception, however, that Germany was originally scheduled to hold the Presidency in the second half of 2006. So as to avoid holding the Presidency at the time of the Bundestag elections in autumn 2006, Germany negotiated a swap with Finland which was due to hold the Presidency in the first half of 2007 (Official Journal, 1995: 220; Official Journal, 2002: 17). At the Brussels European Council in October 2002, it was agreed that the scheduled rotation would last until the end of 2006 so as to give the new member states 'the time to prepare for their Presidency'. The order of the Presidency from 2007 onwards would be decided 'as soon as possible and at least one year after accession of the first new Member State' (European Council: 2002b: 14). To date, the Council has not acted, and in all likelihood any decision will only be taken once the outcome of the IGC on the 'constitutional Treaty' is known.

However, the IGC may well provide for a thorough overhall of the Council presidency system. The European Convention proposed replacing the rotating six-month presidency. In the case of a new Foreign Affairs Council, a permanent Union Minister for Foreign Affairs (who

Table 8.4   *Rotation of the Council Presidency*

	January–June	*July–December*
2004	Ireland	Netherlands
2005	Luxembourg	United Kingdom
2006	Austria	Finland

would also be a member of the Commission) would chair meetings. As for other Council formations, they would have one-year presidencies shared out among member states on a rotating basis. The European Convention also proposed adopting a simpler QMV system based on one vote per member state with an absolute majority of votes representing 60 per cent of the EU's population being sufficient for a decision to be adopted. A clear majority of member states were willing to accept this proposal. Yet it was resolutely opposed by the Spanish and Polish governments – the major beneficiaries of the re-weighting of votes in the Treaty of Nice – and led to the failure of the Italian Presidency to conclude the IGC at the Brussels European Council in December 2003.

The European Council

For the European Council, enlargement brings with it changes similar to those affecting the Council of Ministers. Where voting by a qualified majority is concerned, the new allocations and thresholds apply from 1 May and 1 November 2004 (see Tables 8.2 and 8.3). Similarly, the European Council is affected by changes in the operation of the Presidency. Of note here is that each end-of-presidency European Council is scheduled to be held, in line with the *Declaration on the Venue for European Councils* adopted at Nice in 2000, in Brussels (Official Journal, 2001a: 85). In fact, the practice was introduced prior to enlargement, with the Italian Presidency in the second half of 2003 foregoing the 'privilege' of hosting a European Council.

Also in advance of enlargement, the European Council adopted new rules for its own organization and proceedings designed, in part, to ensure its effective functioning in EU-25. These limit the duration of the meetings to effectively two days, enhance the preparatory role of the new General Affairs and External Relations Council, limit the size of each meeting and, as with Council formations, strengthen the role of the Presidency as chair (European Council, 2002a: annex I). Whether these reforms will ensure that the European Council can operate effectively in EU-25 remains to be seen. Further reform is, however, on the agenda. Much support existed in the European Convention and in the 2003 IGC for a full-time President of the European Council who would chair and 'drive forward' its work as well as represent the EU externally.

The Court of Justice and the Court of First Instance

As on previous occasions, enlargement in 2004 brings about an increase in the number of judges in the Court of Justice and the Court of First Instance. The increase follows the number of member states, so is from 15 to 25. It does not, however, entail any major reforms to the functioning of

the Court as these were already in place following the entry into force of
the Treaty of Nice. Hence, the Court will continue to meet in chambers
of three or five judges and the size of the Grand Chamber will remain at
11 judges. Rather surprisingly, given the anticipated increase in the work-
load of the Court, the number of Advocates-General remains at eight. A
Joint Declaration on the Court of Justice of the European Communities
formally adopted when the Treaty of Accession was signed recalls,
however, that the Council may, acting unanimously, increase the number
of Advocates-General on a request from the Court of Justice (European
Commission, 2003u: 3). To date no request has been made.

The European Central Bank and European System of Central Banks

Although none of the acceding states will become part of the eurozone
until two years after they have joined the EU at the earliest, the European
Central Bank (ECB) is affected by enlargement in that the membership of
its General Council increases to include the governors of the national
central banks of the new member states. However, with membership of
the eurozone remaining unchanged at 12 member states, the number of
members of the far more important Governing Council stays at 18. The
size of the Executive Board, which comprises six independent bankers,
also remains unchanged. Concerns over the impact of enlargement on the
decision-making capacity of the Governing Council have, however, led to
the adoption of changes in decision-making rules. Hence, once membership of the eurozone reaches more than 15 members, voting will no
longer be on the basis of one vote for each national central bank governor. Instead, voting rights will rotate among national central bank governors through a complex series of member state groupings based on gross
domestic product rather than population size (Official Journal, 2003:
66–68). The new system will mean that there would be a maximum of 21
votes available: one each for the six members of the Executive Council
and 15 rotating among national central bank governors (see Chapter 13
for details).

The European Investment Bank

The 2004 enlargement also results in some complex changes to decision-
making in the European Investment Bank (EIB). In EU-25, the number of
directors and alternates on the Board of Directors increases from 25 and
13 to 26 and 16 respectively and is accompanied by a redistribution of
directors so that one is nominated by each member state and one by the
Commission. This contrasts with the situation in EU-15, where the larger
member states nominated three directors each, Spain two and the

remainder one each. The distribution of alternates in EU-25, however, remains one based on differentiation between member states according to population size: the four larger member states nominate two each, and regional groupings of member states nominate between one and three alternates. The Commission nominates one alternate too. A new provision is also made for co-opting six 'non-voting experts' (three members and three alternates) to the Board. Accompanying these changes is a shift in decision-making requirements. Instead of decisions requiring a straight simple majority of the Board, in EU-25 decisions can be adopted by one-third of the Board representing at least 50 per cent of the EIB's subscribed capital, thus giving the larger member states a greater say in decision-making. Where qualified majorities are concerned, the existing requirement of 17 votes is replaced by 18 votes representing at least 68 per cent of the subscribed capital. Finally, enlargement sees the number of vice-presidents on the EIB's Management Committee increase from six to eight.

Advisory Committees and Bodies

By contrast to the complex changes enlargement brings to the ECB and the EIB, those affecting the Union's advisory committees and other bodies are relatively straightforward. In the cases of the Committee of the Regions and the Economic and Social Committee, the membership is simply increased in line with what was envisaged in the *Declaration on the Enlargement of the European Union* noted earlier. Both committees comprise 317 members, with members being allocated as follows: Germany, France, Italy and the United Kingdom (24), Spain and Poland (21), Austria, Belgium, Czech Republic, Greece, Hungary, the Netherlands, Portugal and Sweden (12), Denmark, Finland, Ireland, Lithuania and Slovakia (9), Estonia, Latvia and Slovenia (7), Cyprus and Luxembourg (6) and Malta (5). What is striking is that not all of the new member states are allocated a number of members that is divisible by three, as has traditionally been the case. Such an allocation enabled equal representation on the Economic and Social Committee of three broad groups: employers, workers and other interests. Also, and in contrast to what happened in the case of the EP, no re-allocation of the 'spare' seats allocated to Bulgaria (12) and Romania (15) was agreed during the accession negotiations. As for the third advisory body mentioned in the European Treaties – Euratom's Scientific and Technical Committee – enlargement brings with it only a small increase in the membership. It now comprises 39 as opposed to 38 members. Other committees and bodies are enlarged in accordance with the existing applicable rules on composition.

Governance in a More Diverse Union

The impact of enlargement on the EU's institutions, at least in terms of membership and size, is felt as soon as the new member states accede. The impact elsewhere on the EU as a system of governance is likely to be less immediately obvious. It is widely accepted, however, that the introduction of an increased diversity of interests poses challenges for existing approaches to policy-making. This raises two key questions. The first is whether the EU should adopt more flexible forms of integration that allow some member states to press ahead with closer cooperation while others either opt-out of, or only assume over time, the same obligations The introduction, through the Treaty of Amsterdam, of mechanisms for 'enhanced cooperation' has certainly created the option of doing so (Usher, 2002; Warleigh, 2002). Whether the provisions, which were further revised by the Treaty of Nice, will be used, however, is much debated. Within EU-25 there may be a greater temptation to do so where a clear majority of member states wishes to proceed on an issue which does not enjoy unanimous support. Frustration with the failure of the Brussels European Council in December 2003 to conclude the IGC certainly rekindled ideas of France and Germany leading a pioneer group of those member states willing to pursue closer integration. There is the danger, however, that 'enhanced cooperation' could create a more obviously two-tier EU, something that the new members have cautioned against, fearing that they might be relegated to a second-class membership status. The second question is whether the EU should adopt policy-making modes more appropriate to the increased diversity of interests and capacities among its enlarged membership. Enlargement raises the possibility that newer modes, such as the 'open method of coordination' based on peer review, bench marking and best practice may be used more, rather than the traditional 'Community-method' involving regulation and the possibility of judicial review. This may facilitate policy making, but it raises questions about the capacity of the EU to ensure policy coherence and uniform application of rules and laws.

Enlargement also creates challenges for the EU with regard to ensuring its own legitimacy. At one level, it is imperative that the nationals and representatives from the new member states are given the opportunity to participate as equals in the EU's institutions and bodies. Any sense of an 'old' versus 'new' division must be avoided if enlargement is to proceed smoothly and the EU is to retain the support of the new member states. Expansion of the transnational party groupings in the EP to include parties from the new member states has already been taking place and observers from the new member states attended EP plenaries and committee meetings for a year prior to accession. Representatives from the new member states also attended Council meetings as observers during the same period. So a process of socialization has been taking place since before enlargement. But familiarization with practices needs to be translated into full participation. The new member states, for so long recipients of EU requirements as part of the pre-accession and accession processes, need to feel that they are having a notable impact on policy-making, whether through their ministers, MEPs, representatives in the advisory bodies, or through the lobbying that influences the Commission and the other institutions. This will not only be important for their own self-esteem, but also as evidence for their populations that membership means being treated as an equal, not some second-class latecomer to the EU club.

This leads to the need for the EU to ensure that its democratic deficit does not widen further as a consequence of enlargement. The EU must 'connect' with its citizens (European Commission, 2001b). Good governance demands this. The outcomes of the national referenda on EU membership that were held during 2003 in nine of the acceding states show high levels of support for the EU within the new member states (see the Chronology (pp. 278–9) for the results of the referendums). Only in Malta did less than two-thirds of voters vote 'yes'. Precedent suggests, however, that such high levels of public support will decline. Public support for the EU has traditionally fallen in the years after a state has joined. In 2003, there were less voters in Austria (34 per cent), Finland (42 per cent) and Sweden (41 per cent) than in any other of the EU-15 member states except the United Kingdom (30 per cent) who believed EU membership to be 'a good thing' (Eurobarometer, Spring 2003: B.45). If voters in the new member states believe that membership fails to provide benefits and that they and their governments are not having their voices heard in the policy-making processes, support levels may fall. Equally, electorates in the EU-15 may feel that enlargement makes the EU even more remote, particularly as the process leads to either a decrease in the direct financial benefits of membership, increased immigration at a time when populist politicians and newspapers are stirring anti-immigrant feelings, or a sense that their voices too are not being heard.

That the EU needs to close its democratic deficit, enhance its legitimacy and promote participation has been a semi-permanent item of the EU's political agenda for more than a decade. In 2002–2003 it was a key concern of the European Convention, which proposed a number of measures to help remedy the shortcomings affecting governance in the EU. Prominent among these measures were clearer implementation of the subsidiarity principle and an increased role for national parliaments in the monitoring of legislative proposals. Such proposals found considerable support in the IGC that opened in October 2003 and, if implemented, may well make the EU appear more accountable and less meddlesome. Equally, plans to increase openness and transparency, notably in the Council, may contribute to a decrease in popular scepticism toward the

EU and enhance the EU's legitimacy, particularly among the electorate of the EU-15 states. (The issue of the EU's legitimacy post-enlargement is explored at length in Chapter 7.)

Conclusion

The 2004 enlargement of the EU, as with all previous enlargements, brings with it institutional adjustments to accommodate the new member states. None of these have proved too contentious. Enlargement at the institutional level should therefore be a relatively smooth affair, even if some of the rules and procedures change only six months after the accession of the new member states takes place. And with the period between the signing of the Treaty of Accession and actual accession seeing representatives of the new member states observing practice in most of the EU institutions, the institutional upheaval that enlargement entails should be kept to a minimum. This is not to underestimate either the changes that enlargement involves or the need for all involved institutionally in the move from EU-15 to EU-25 to adapt as part of the process, but it is to suggest a manageable scenario.

A key point to recall is that enlargement takes place at a time of ongoing constitutional change and institutional reform. Arrangements in place for EU-25 at the time of enlargement may be short-lived if the outcome of the 2003–2004 IGC is successfully ratified, for this most likely would involve further institutional change in 2006. But even without such change, the EU's institutions will continue to develop. An important reason why they will do so is that, as Chapter 19 shows, enlargement is not scheduled to stop at EU-25 However, the scale of future enlargements will no doubt be much smaller than in 2004, so the accompanying adjustments and institutional changes should be neither so great nor so complex.

Chapter 9

Intergovernmental Politics

MICHAEL BAUN

Among the most important questions posed by enlargement is whether a larger and more diverse EU will be able to function effectively. The answer to this question will partly depend upon whether the institutional reforms agreed to by the 2003–2004 IGC prove adequate for decision-making in an EU of 25 or more member states. It will also depend, however, on the nature and pattern of political cleavages in an enlarged EU and their impact on EU intergovernmental politics. What will be the major political cleavages in the enlarged EU, and will these give rise to rigid new divisions that inhibit compromise and threaten the EU with decision-making paralysis?

These are the central questions that this chapter addresses. One much-discussed possibility is that enlargement will lead to a rigid new division between 'East' and 'West' or old and new member states. It is argued in the chapter that the complexity and cross-cutting nature of political cleavages in an enlarged EU should prevent such rigid or simplified divisions from emerging. Instead, enlargement should reinforce the present trend in EU intergovernmental politics towards a system of flexible and shifting coalitions. At the same time, frustration with the loss of cohesion and increased complexity of EU decision-making after enlargement may spur increased interest among some member states in the idea of a 'core Europe.'

Political Cleavages in an Enlarged EU

The growing importance of political cleavages has been a key feature of EU intergovernmental politics over the past two decades. A major reason for this is enlargement. Successive enlargements, by adding new member states and increasing the diversity of member state interests, have created the potential for new cleavages or reinforced existing divisions within the EU. The accession of Ireland in 1973, for instance, introduced for the first time a significant gap in the economic development levels of the member states. This gap was then further accentuated by the accession of three poor Mediterranean countries in the 1980s (Greece, Spain, and

Portugal). Successive enlargements have also added member states not sharing the integrationist goals of the founding members, and thus intensified the conflict between 'federalists' and 'intergovernmentalists.' The accession of mostly smaller countries over the years has worsened the institutional imbalance between large and small member states, and created the potential for conflict over the issue of institutional reform.

The emergence of these cleavages has not necessarily been debilitating, but it has made the EU's intergovernmental politics more complex, and the achievement of consensus more difficult. Because of the cross-cutting nature of these cleavages, bargaining and compromise has generally been possible, and by the late 1990s EU decision-making could be characterized as a system of shifting and flexible coalitions. This has allowed the formation of variable issue-based alliances among national governments and prevented the emergence of more permanent or rigid divisions between member states.

What will be the impact of the 10 + 2 enlargement round on the EU's political cleavages and intergovernmental politics? In many ways, this enlargement is the most challenging and difficult expansion that the EU has ever undertaken, because of the number of acceding states, their relatively low level of economic development, and the fact that most of them are small or even very small countries. The divergent historical experiences of the EU-15 states and the acceding states also create important cultural and social differences that could impede the integration of the latter. As a result, the 10 + 2 enlargement could have a tremendous impact on the nature and pattern of the EU's political cleavages, intensifying existing divisions or creating new ones, with significant implications for its intergovernmental politics.

One possibility is that the enlarged EU will be rigidly divided along East–West or old versus new member state lines. This scenario is grounded in the belief that the CEECs possess a sufficiently distinctive set of common interests, based on economic position, historical experience, and institutional status, to establish them as a cohesive bloc *vis-à-vis* the interests of EU-15 states. For some Europeans, the prospect of such a cleavage was underscored by the 'old' versus 'new' Europe division that appeared over the Iraq crisis in early 2003, even though this division also split the EU-15 states (Grabbe, 2003a).

Will the division between old and new member states define the intergovernmental politics of an enlarged EU? The remainder of this chapter considers this question, as it examines some of the major political cleavages that will characterize the EU in the future.

Wealthy vs. poor member states

The EU's rich–poor divide is not new, but has been a major factor in EU politics since at least the mid-1980s. This cleavage mainly affects EU policies with budgetary and distributional consequences, notably the Structural and Cohesion Funds and the CAP. The main conflict is over who benefits from EU spending and subsidies, relative to what they pay into the EU budget. The struggle, therefore, is often between relatively wealthy member states that are net contributors to the budget and seek limitations on EU spending or a re-balancing of national contributions in their favour, and relatively poor member states seeking to preserve their share of EU subsidies and net recipient status. This cleavage assumed increased importance in the late 1990s, when the combination of slow economic growth, budgetary and fiscal restrictions imposed by EMU, and growing concern about the potential cost of eastward enlargement, led wealthier net contributors – in particular Germany, the Netherlands, and Sweden – to demand limitations on EU spending. This was strongly opposed by poorer member states, especially Spain, Portugal, and Greece. Because it is the main item in the EU budget, accounting for nearly 45 per cent of all spending, reform of the CAP also featured strongly in this debate. This intergovernmental struggle came to a head at the March 1999 Berlin summit, which decided upon the 'Agenda 2000' budgetary package for 2000–2006.

As a result of enlargement, this important cleavage will become even more severe, but also more complex. The 10 countries acceding in 2004 have an average per capita GDP that is barely half of the EU average. The future accession states of Bulgaria and Romania are even poorer. Among the 10, the wealthiest, Cyprus, which is also one of the smallest, has a per capita GDP that is only 80 per cent of the EU average. The next three 'wealthiest' applicants are Slovenia (69 per cent), the Czech Republic (57 per cent), Malta (55 per cent), and Hungary (51 per cent). By comparison, the three poorest EU-15 states, Greece, Portugal and Spain, have per capita GDPs at 69 per cent, 73 per cent, and 82 per cent of the EU average respectively (European Commission, 2002b: A18). In other words, only two of the applicants (Cyprus and Slovenia) are at an economic level comparable to the poorest current member states; the others are far below this level. Thus, enlargement greatly accentuates the gap between rich and poor member states, with this gap becoming even larger in an EU of 27.

Enlargement will also make the EU's economic division more complex. There is already a considerable amount of economic differentiation among the accession states, and this is only likely to increase. Most economic forecasts predict highly differentiated growth rates for the new member states, with some expected to make rapid progress towards catching up with, or even passing, the poorest EU-15 states. For instance, the Austrian Institute for International Economic Studies forecasts that in 2013 Cyprus will have achieved a per capita GDP that is 108 per cent of the EU-15 average, Slovenia 86 per cent, the Czech Republic 73 per cent, Malta 68 per cent, Hungary 64 per cent, and Slovakia 63 per cent.

The next highest figure among the new member states is Estonia, at 55 per cent. These percentages are even higher when calculated for an EU of 25 or 27 (Landesmann and Richter, 2003: 12–13).

In the medium term, such trends could result in a three-tier economic division of the EU: 1) a top tier consisting of the majority of EU-15 states; 2) a middle tier consisting of the poorest EU-15 states – Greece, Portugal, Spain – plus the wealthiest new member states – Cyprus, Slovenia, Malta, the Czech Republic, Hungary, and perhaps Slovakia; and 3) a bottom tier consisting of the very poorest new member states – Poland, the three Baltic states, and eventually Romania and Bulgaria. In fact the Commission, in its *Second Progress Report on Economic and Social Cohesion*, has already begun utilizing a tripartite classification, although this study, which is based on current rather than projected economic position, places only Cyprus and Slovenia in the middle group along with Spain, Portugal and Greece. The remaining eight accession countries are lumped together in the poorest category (European Commission, 2003i). This three-tier economic division will both complicate and attenuate an otherwise severe rich–poor divide, which generally runs along the EU's north–south and east–west geographical axes.

Among the key issues that will be affected by this more complex economic division will be the future of EU structural and cohesion policy. Here the debate will be not only between poor and wealthy member states, with the former trying to maintain high levels of structural and cohesion assistance and the latter trying to reduce their payments into the EU budget, but also between second tier (medium–poor) and third tier (the poorest) member states over the mechanisms and criteria for allocating regional aid. Medium–poor member states, especially the current cohesion countries – Spain, Portugal, Greece, Ireland – will no doubt oppose proposals to concentrate structural assistance on the poorest member states, which would mean a reduction or elimination of their own receipts. Instead, they will likely argue for raising the threshold criteria for receiving structural and cohesion aid above current per capita GDP levels, since enlargement will otherwise disqualify them because of a statistical effect, or press for adequate compensatory mechanisms to offset the potential loss of assistance. In other words, the EU-15 cohesion countries will fight hard to maintain their share of EU subsidies, even after enlargement boosts their relative economic status. In the struggle over Structural Funds reform these countries could be joined by wealthier member states with large poor regions, such as Italy and the UK. Rapidly developing new member states – notably Slovenia, the Czech Republic and Hungary – might also support efforts to raise the per capita GDP thresholds for structural and cohesion aid, in anticipation of quickly reaching the current thresholds themselves.

The EU's new economic divisions also affect the issue of budgetary contributions and the related issue of CAP reform. The main net contributors – Germany, the Netherlands, the UK, Sweden, France, and Austria – will continue arguing for a reduction in their net payments, but will be opposed by poor member states seeking to maximize net receipts from the EU budget. In the middle will be the net recipients among the EU-15 states – Spain, Greece, Portugal, Ireland, Ireland, Belgium, and Luxembourg – which will seek to prevent a slide to net contributor status. More prosperous new member states, which will be in danger of quickly moving from net recipient to net contributor status after accession, might increasingly align themselves with this group. Together, these countries could push for the revision of EU agricultural and structural policies so that they can retain their current shares of EU subsidies. France, as both a net contributor and a major beneficiary of EU spending, mainly via the CAP, occupies a uniquely conflicted position on budgetary issues. In its defence of CAP spending, France is likely to gain a major ally in Poland, which will seek increased subsidies for its bloated and inefficient farm sector.

In an enlarged EU, therefore, the distributional conflict over budgetary and spending issues will not take place along a simple rich–poor divide. Instead, it will be complicated by the divergent interests produced by the EU's more differentiated economic structure. As a result the EU's distributional cleavage, at least beyond the initial struggle, over the 2007–2013 budgetary package, will not necessarily be a new versus old member state divide.

Large vs. small states

Another major political cleavage in the EU is the division between small and large member states on the issue of institutional reform. This cleavage stems from the growing number of smaller member states, further distorting an EU institutional and decision-making system that was designed to give disproportionate weight to smaller countries. Larger member states have lost relative influence and voting weight as a result. By the mid-1990s, with additional enlargement promising to further expand the number of small member states, the reform of decision-making institutions and procedures became an important issue on the EU agenda. Two successive efforts at reform, the 1996–1997 and 2000 IGCs, achieved inadequate results, however, leading to a third attempt with the Convention on the Future of Europe and 2003–2004 IGC. Throughout this process, the key factor impeding institutional reform has been the growing division between small and large member states. Generally speaking, while small states have sought to preserve their full representation on the Commission and a strong role for the Commission in EU decision-making, the large states have demanded a greater voting weight in the Council and the concentration of executive authority in the European Council (Král, Brinar, and Almer, 2003; Magnette and Nicolaïdis, 2003).

This cleavage is both accentuated and complicated by enlargement. With the exception of Poland (39 million) and Romania (22 million), all of the 10 + 2 states are small countries, with populations of 10 million or less. Some, though not quite micro-states, are very small states indeed – most notably the Mediterranean island countries of Malta (400 000) and Cyprus (800 000). Enlargement thus swells the number of member states with an interest in preserving an EU institutional and decision-making system that is biased towards smaller countries and ensures that their interests are represented against the potential domination of larger member states. This consequence of enlargement has been evident in the Convention and IGC, where the new member states have generally sided with other small states on institutional reform issues (Král, Brinar, and Almer, 2003; Magnette and Nicolaïdis, 2003).

While at the time of writing the outcome of the IGC remains uncertain, the enhanced size of the small-state lobby will make it even more difficult for large member states to push through reforms that favour their institutional interests. Enlargement, therefore, could favour an institutional outcome in which balance is preserved between the Commission and Council, and between small and large state interests, yet at the cost of strong (concentrated) executive leadership. This result could spur greater interest in multi-speed or differentiated integration models, in which the relative dominance of large countries within smaller sub-groupings would be restored. Such initiatives could build on existing mechanisms for enhanced cooperation, or, more radically, attempt to create a narrower and more exclusive 'core Europe.'

The large–small cleavage in an enlarged EU is not quite so simple or its effects so clear-cut, however. One major complicating factor is Germany, which despite being a large member state (the largest) also traditionally favours federalized structures and a strong Commission, thus giving the small member states and supporters of the Commission a powerful ally. In the Convention and IGC, the Schröder government has attempted to straddle the institutional fence, endorsing the French–British–Spanish idea of a full-time Council President, while also supporting a stronger Commission and European Parliament election of the Commission President. The big-state pretensions of middle- (or medium-large) sized member countries such as Spain and Poland (and later Romania) could add another complicating factor to this institutional divide. Indeed, it may be more accurate to speak of a tripartite division in an enlarged EU, because of the divergent institutional interests of large, medium, and small member states (Wessels, 2001: 206).

Federalists vs. intergovernmentalists

The federalist–intergovernmentalist division in the EU dates back to the very beginnings of the European integration process. It has grown deeper over the years through the accession of member states that have not shared the political union goals of most of the EU's founding members. For many late-joiners, EU membership has been a matter of economic necessity rather than an affair of the heart. As a consequence, some of these states – most particularly the UK, Denmark, and Sweden – have tended to support only as much integration as necessary, while seeking to retain as much national sovereignty and control as possible.

On the surface, enlargement should strengthen the intergovernmentalist camp. The new member states are generally highly sovereignty conscious. Most have only recently regained their political independence, and have little desire to be submerged into a centralized supranational framework, especially one that is dominated by larger countries. However, the new member states also tend to support federalist positions in the institutional reform debate, such as a stronger and more democratically legitimate Commission and retention of the Community method of decision making. They also wish to be included in all integration arrangements, in order to avoid second-class membership in a multi-tier Europe. They are therefore highly sceptical of proposals for enhanced cooperation and generally oppose the creation of a 'core Europe' (Smith M., 2003; Villa Faber, 2001).

This apparent paradox indicates the extent to which the traditional federalist–intergovernmentalist debate has been fundamentally transformed, as a consequence both of deepening and enlargement. With the EU now discussing seriously such issues as common defence and economic policies, it is no longer so much a question of how far integration should go, but how decisions in an enlarged EU should be made. It is here that the federalist–intergovernmentalist debate intersects with the large—small state divide. For the new member states, as for smaller countries among the old member states, the issue is not so much loss of national sovereignty, but ensuring that they have an equal voice in the making of policy decisions. The real danger for these governments is the loss of control in a supranational system that is dominated by larger countries. In an enlarged EU, therefore, the traditional federalist–intergovernmentalist debate will be increasingly usurped by debate about the representativeness and inclusiveness of decision-making institutions.

Atlanticists vs. Europeanists

The conflict between Atlanticists and Europeanists is another old one, dating back at least as far as the early 1960s and the battles between French President de Gaulle and Atlanticists in the German and Dutch governments over European cooperation on foreign and security policy. This cleavage generally concerns the extent to which Europe should develop its own foreign policy and defence identity, separate from that of the US and US-dominated institutions such as NATO. The cleavage gained a new centrality with the fierce transatlantic and intra-European debate over the Iraq war in 2003, where a key issue was the split between 'old' and 'new' Europe over US policy towards Iraq, with most of the candidate states joining several EU-15 states in supporting the US, in contrast to the anti-war positions of France, Germany and other member states.

The Iraq episode hints that, in the near term at least, enlargement could deepen the gap between Atlanticists and Europeanists and strengthen the Atlanticist camp. The CEECs generally have strong emotional and political ties to the US, with many in these countries crediting US steadfastness during the Cold War for their independence from Soviet domination. The CEECs also rely on NATO and the US for their hard security, in the absence of any effective or credible European defence alternative. It is not surprising, therefore, that these countries have strong Atlanticist leanings, and that they favour continued close security and defence ties between the EU and the US. The CEECs generally oppose EU moves to strengthen common security and defence policies in a manner that would alienate the US or undermine NATO. Most were opposed to the April 2003 four-country initiative, led by France and Germany, to create a European defence headquarters that might duplicate NATO structures. In the Convention and IGC most of the new member states have also opposed 'core Europe' initiatives on foreign and defence policy, fearing that these could exacerbate transatlantic tensions while also being exclusionary (Cameron and Primatarova, 2003; Grabbe, 2003b).

This does not mean that the new member states are opposed to the creation of a common European defence identity and capability. Indeed, most view this as necessary for their own long-term security. However, they do not want this to be at the expense of transatlantic security ties and NATO. In the near term, the CEECs hope to act as a 'bridge' between the US and the EU, and as a catalyst for stronger transatlantic relations. The worst situation, from their perspective, would be one in which they were pressured to choose between Washington and Brussels (or Paris/Berlin), either by the US or by their fellow member states. In the longer run, given their geographical location and the socialization effects of integration, it is likely that these countries will adopt a more 'European' perspective on questions of foreign and defence policy, thus greatly alleviating this internal EU cleavage (Grabbe, 2003b).

Conflict over transatlantic relations and NATO will not be the only foreign and security policy debate in an enlarged EU. The end of the Cold War opened up new possibilities for the EU to exert influence and shape developments in neighbouring countries and regions, as well as creating new security threats and responsibilities. In response, the EU has sought to develop a new 'neighbourhood' or 'proximity' policy for a wider Europe (European Commission, 2003m). However, these new external threats and opportunities have also created new potential for conflict within the EU over which neighbouring regions should receive the greatest share of attention and resources. In the mid-1990s, France and other southern member states pushed for greater attention to the EU's unstable Mediterranean rim, seeking to balance the dominant focus on Central and Eastern Europe favoured by Germany and other northern member states. In an enlarged EU, different member states have divergent foreign policy interests and priorities, based upon their geographical situation and neighbours.

Among the new member states, Poland has already stated its desire to play a leadership role in the EU's new 'Eastern policy.' A key goal of this policy would be stability and security in the countries on the EU's eastern borders (Ukraine, Belarus, Russia – including Kaliningrad, and Moldova), and preventing new divisions from opening up in Europe (Polish Ministry of Foreign Affairs, 2003). Hungary and Slovenia, along with eventual members Bulgaria and Romania and EU-15 states Greece and Italy, have a keen interest in further stabilization and integration of the Balkans. This group of countries, along with Cyprus, also has a strong interest in EU relations with Turkey. Looking further to the east, the south-eastern member states could become proponents of a 'Black Sea initiative' that would seek to stabilize the Black Sea basin and the Caucasus region (Adams *et al.*, 2002; Emerson, 2001). Meanwhile, southern member states (Spain, Portugal, France, Italy, and Malta especially) will continue pressing for greater attention to northern Africa. In an enlarged EU, conflict could also occur over the relative priority of external and internal security goals. For the new member states, a major goal of proximity policy is to ensure that the EU's new borders to do not become a permanent 'iron curtain' dividing peaceful and prosperous Europe from neighbouring zones of poverty and instability. This could put them at odds with more internal security-conscious old member states.

Liberals vs. statists

Another potentially important cleavage in an enlarged EU is the division between economic liberalizers and 'statists.' This cleavage has gained in importance with EMU and the 'Lisbon agenda' for economic liberalization that was agreed at the March 2000 Lisbon European Council meeting. The Lisbon initiative, which aims at making the European economy the most competitive and knowledge-based economy in the world by 2010, was promoted particularly by the 'middle way' centre-left governments in the UK and Germany. More traditionally statist–protectionist or socialist-governed member states – including France, Belgium, and Greece – remained sceptical of the new liberalization emphasis. By 2002, the Lisbon agenda had largely stalled, however, indicating a stalemate – amid conditions of slow economic growth and a growing backlash against American-led globalization – between liberalizers and statists within the EU.

The EU's economic policy divide is also manifested in the debate over the future of EMU's 'Stability and Growth Pact' (see Chapter 13 for an explanation of the Pact). Since 2001 there has been a mounting backlash against the rigid monetarist orthodoxy represented by the Pact's fiscal and budgetary straightjacket. Gaining strength are the views of those – such as the French government – who favour a more flexible system of economic governance within the Eurozone that allows for growth-oriented policies and counter-cyclical fiscal measures. This debate reflects, to some extent, a long-running division within the EU between member states favouring a market-oriented, monetarist EMU regime (notably Germany and the Netherlands) and those favouring a more politically controlled and growth-oriented system of EU economic governance (notably France and Italy). However, many of the member states that have opposed efforts to loosen the Stability Pact are traditionally weak-economy countries that do not want to forfeit the hard-won monetary credibility they have gained through membership in the eurozone. Small member states also resent the ability of large countries like France to flaunt the Stability Pact's rules and not be punished. The economic policy cleavage is also reflected in the debate within the Convention and IGC on the issue of EU economic governance.

Enlargement is unlikely to break this stalemate on economic liberalization. In many of the post-communist states there was initial enthusiasm for markets and economic liberalism. However, this had receded considerably by the end of the 1990s in the face of more difficult-than-anticipated transitions, severe structural problems and high unemployment. Economic difficulties and insecurity even led to a revived popularity for former communist or socialist parties in some candidate countries, accompanied by nostalgia for former levels of economic and social security. A return to communism and state-controlled economies is impossible, and in any case is not desired by most people in these countries. Instead, a stabilization of domestic party competition between moderate liberals and moderate social democrats, on a left–right pattern familiar to Western European democracies, is the most probable scenario for these countries.

Rather than an energizing shot of liberalism into the rigidified EU economic system, therefore, enlargement is likely to have a less predictable impact on the economic policy cleavage between liberalizers and statists. In the short run, it could make achievement of the Lisbon agenda goals more difficult because of the economic problems of the new member states. Enlargement could also expand the group of member states opposing the Lisbon agenda: once they are 'in the club', further internal and external liberalization may have little appeal for the governments of these relatively poor countries. In the longer run, however, liberalizing governments in the more prosperous accession states could join with their counterparts in EU-15 states to push forward these goals.

On the question of EU economic governance, once inside the eurozone many of the relatively poor new member states will probably support a more growth-oriented regime. However, economic differentiation among the new member states and the varied ideological persuasions and views of individual national governments could lead to divergent positions on this issue as well.

Conclusions: Flexible Coalitions or Rigid Divisions?

Having examined the political cleavages in an enlarged EU, several important conclusions can be drawn. First, most of these cleavages are not simple or clear-cut. Both the rich–poor and large–small state divides, for example, are more likely to be three-dimensional cleavages rather than simple dichotomies. A similar or greater differentiation of interests and views should occur along the integration (federalist–intergovernmentalist), foreign policy (Atlanticist–Europeanist) and economic policy (liberalizer–statist) cleavages. Thus, while enlargement may intensify existing cleavages, it will also make them more complex.

Second, these cleavages are generally cross-cutting rather than mutually reinforcing. The rich–poor state cleavage, for example, does not coincide with the large–small state divide. There are both rich and poor countries among the large states (Germany and Poland), and large and small states among the poor countries (Poland and Lithuania), for example. The intersection of these cleavages becomes even more complicated when one considers each from a more differentiated three-dimensional perspective – for example, large–medium–small for member state size, and high–middle–low for levels of economic development. Both the rich–poor and large–small state cleavages, in turn, are dissected by the divisions on foreign policy, integration and economic liberalization. Most of these cleavages are also fluid. With the exception of the large–small divide, the position of member states on the various cleavages is subject to change, depending on altered circumstances (such as economic growth and the external security environment), domestic politics and the ideological preferences of particular governments.

A third conclusion is that there will be no post-communist bloc of new member states. All of the accession states are relatively poor and generally small, and they are entering the EU at the same time and under similar conditions. However, a closer examination reveals a number of potential divisions within this group of countries that are likely to prevent such a bloc from emerging. One of these divisions is economic, separating relatively prosperous and fast-growing new member states – Slovenia, the Czech Republic, Hungary, Slovakia, Cyprus, and Malta – from those which are much poorer and have somewhat dimmer medium-term economic prospects. Rapid economic growth in the former group of countries could make them into net contributors to the EU budget in a relatively short period of time. This would place them in the same economic category as Spain, Portugal, and Greece (in fact, some of the applicant countries are already comparable to the latter), with interests to match on distributional questions such as budgetary contributions, the CAP, and structural and cohesion policy. The economic interests of these middle-tier countries could thus increasingly diverge from those of the poorest new member states, especially after the accession of Bulgaria and Romania. The new member states are all likely to bargain hard to improve their budgetary situation immediately after joining – especially in view of the perceived 'unfair' financial deals they were forced to accept in order to conclude the accession negotiations – and this common interest could provide some incentive for cooperation. Such solidarity is unlikely to last beyond bargaining on the budgetary package in 2006, however, as national economic and financial interests increasingly diverge. Even in the 2006 budgetary negotiations, divergent economic interests could lead to new and interesting coalitions among old and new member states.

There are other potential divisions among the new member states. One is on institutional questions, where Poland might increasingly find common cause with other large or medium-large member states against the institutional interests of the smaller countries. The new member states share a common scepticism or suspicion of enhanced cooperation, fearing that such arrangements could lead to a multi-tier Europe in which they would be relegated to a second-class status. Nevertheless, distinctive national interests on particular issues, as well as the emergence of close links (or 'special partnerships') with certain EU-15 states – for instance Poland with Germany, Hungary with Austria – could lead some of these countries to support the use of enhanced cooperation in certain instances. Divergent foreign policy interests could also split the new member states. For example, the focus of Poland and the Baltic states on the 'Eastern dimension' of EU foreign policy could conflict with the orientation of Hungary and Slovenia (and eventually Bulgaria and Romania) towards the Balkans and south-eastern Europe.

Also arguing against the potential for a post-communist bloc is the experience of the accession process. In the accession negotiations the applicant countries generally eschewed a cooperative approach that could have given them more bargaining leverage *vis-à-vis* the EU, each seeking instead to achieve the best possible deal for itself. There was admittedly greater cooperation in the final months and weeks of the negotiations, especially among the 'Visegrad four' – Poland, Hungary, the Czech Republic, Slovakia – as the applicant states perceived the advantages to be gained from a more unified approach on the CAP and financial matters. Nonetheless, the overall picture from the accession process was one of individualistic and competitive behaviour by the applicant countries, which does not augur well for unity among the new member states.

Both the cross-cutting nature of EU cleavages and the limited potential for a post-communist bloc indicate that the enlarged EU will not be characterized by a deep or rigid division between East and West, or old and new member states. Instead, enlargement probably reinforces the present tendency in EU intergovernmental politics towards a system of flexible and shifting coalitions. In intergovernmental bargaining, coalition alignments among member states will vary depending on the issue under discussion. In many cases, these coalitions will reflect the structural cleavages discussed above, for instance on distributional and institutional questions. In others they will follow a much less predictable pattern. Making coalition alignments even more difficult to predict will be the enhanced potential for tradeoffs, linkages and package deals among governments and across issues after enlargement, of the sort that are already common in the EU. However, while permanent, cross-issue alliances among large groups of member states may be unlikely in an enlarged EU, smaller and more cohesive groupings that seek to coordinate national positions on a wide variety of issues may become increasingly important. Sub-regional blocs such as the Benelux group and the 'Visegrad four' are possible examples of smaller groups that may seek to maximize their bargaining and voting power through closer cooperation.

In the final analysis, therefore, enlargement is unlikely to alter significantly or transform EU intergovernmental politics; instead it probably reinforces the status quo (Moravcsik and Vachudova, 2002). A different scenario must also be considered, however. For it is possible that enlargement will give rise to a new central cleavage in the EU between 'core' and 'periphery,' the former consisting of more economically advanced member states that favour closer integration in certain areas, and the latter consisting of member states that either prefer or are required to remain behind. The concept of core Europe is not new, but it has generally remained in the background of formal debates and negotiations on institutional reform. It is qualitatively different from the concepts of flexibility and enhanced cooperation that are currently part of the EU's treaty framework, since these mechanisms are heavily restricted by safeguard provisions and the requirement that they remain open to all member states. The idea of core Europe, by contrast, suggests an exclusive club that would not be open to all EU members. The most likely focus of such an arrangement would be common foreign and defence policies, and possibly more integrated economic governance.

Because it would be a radical break from the EU's current constitutional trajectory and the many problems that would have to be surmounted for it to become reality (including substantial differences of interest and views between France and Germany, the necessary 'core of the core'), the idea of core Europe remains on the backburner for now. However, it is said to be 'high on the hidden agenda' or part of the contingency planning for most of the core's prospective member states, in the event that an enlarged EU proves too unwieldy or is unable to function effectively (Wessels, 2003: 13). External factors, such as increased unhappiness with US unilateralism, could also promote core Europe as a vehicle for greater foreign and security policy independence. For some Franco–German elites, core Europe would also provide a means for reasserting the leadership and influence of these two countries in an enlarged EU. Ironically, then, enlargement could lead some to look 'forward to the past.'

Whether core Europe is a realistic alternative or likely long-term outcome of enlargement remains to be seen. Many of the cleavages discussed in this paper divide the Franco–German tandem and other prospective members of the core, while the enhanced variety and number of alternative coalition possibilities in an enlarged EU also argues against this scenario. The future may not be the past, but instead a messier and more complex EU that is also immensely more unpredictable. Some undoubtedly view this prospect with trepidation, agreeing perhaps with Portuguese Prime Minister José Manuel Durao Barroso that Europe is like 'a Boeing 747 without a pilot,' as the 'struggle for power and money' within an enlarged EU begins (White, 2002: 3). Others, however, may view it more complacently, as the normal state of affairs in a larger, more diverse and complex democratic polity.

Chapter 10

The Economy of the European Union

NICKOS BALTAS

Introduction

The purpose of this chapter is to consider some of the key economic dimensions of EU enlargement, focusing on the characteristics of the new member states and on the economic implications of enlargement for the EU. The chapter should be read in conjunction with the other chapters of the book that cover economic dimensions of enlargement – in particular, chapters 5, 11, 12, 13, and 15.

Enlargement promises gains for both the EU-15 and the new member states. However, though economic projections have varied considerably, most empirical analyses have suggested that the expected gains will be relatively small for the EU-15 and may not be as significant for the acceding states as has been commonly supposed. For example, Baldwin *et al.* (1997) have indicated a total real income gain of only 1.5 per cent for CEECs and even less for the EU-15. Better results are reported by Brown *et al.* (1997) and Breuss (2001): Brown estimates overall welfare gains for the CEECs between 3.8 and 7.3 per cent, though only around 0.1 per cent for the EU; Breuss anticipates total effects on real GDP between 4 and 9 per cent for the CEECs and about one-tenth of that for the EU. Lejour *et al.* (2002) explore the economic implications of enlargement with respect to three dimensions: the move towards a customs union, the enlargement of the internal market, and free movement of labour. Overall, they project that the GDP of accession states will increase by more than 8 per cent on average in the long run, but for EU-15 states increases will be much more modest. For example, the Dutch GDP per capita is projected to increase by a mere 0.15 per cent, whilst in Germany, where the economic effects tend to be dominated by migration, a slight reduction in GDP per capita is anticipated. Lejour *et al.*'s estimates are comparable with those produced by the European Commission (see Chapter 1, pp. 5–6).

As well as bringing economic benefits, enlargement also brings economic costs for both EU-15 and acceding states. CEECs still have fragile economies that will be exposed to fierce competition in the Single European Market (SEM). However, they will receive only limited EU financial assistance, it having been decided at the 1999 Berlin summit to limit spending for all EU activities, including enlargement, for the 2000–06 period to a 1.27 per cent limit of total EU GDP. The December 2002 European Council meeting in Copenhagen 2002 confirmed that the Berlin decision must be respected. This means that, whilst enlargement is relatively cheap for the EU in financial terms, the weaknesses of new member states may be over-exposed and not sufficiently supported.

The extent and nature of these weaknesses varies. An important reason why they do so is the uneven macroeconomic performances of CEECs since the collapse of communism. This unevenness can to some extent be attributed to the differing situations of CEECs at the start of the post-communist transformation. However, it also reflects the varying extent to which institutional reform programmes have been implemented in these countries. Legal systems, public administrations, and markets for capital products and services in CEECs are still under-developed, which will make it very difficult for them to perform effectively in the SEM.

Other economic concerns arising from enlargement include implications for immigration, jobs and wages. Heijdra *et al.* (2002) found that the labour market effects of trade integration are rather modest compared to those of immigration. Their analysis reveals, amongst other things, that low-skilled workers in the EU-15 will find their wages and employment prospects directly impaired by an inflow of low-skilled immigrants, while the high-skilled are likely to gain on both wage and employment counts.

The Economic Structures of the New Member States

GDP

The eventual accession of all 10 + 2 states will increase the EU's population by 28 per cent but its GDP only by 7 per cent at 2001 prices and by 15 per cent in terms of purchasing power standard (PPS) (Eurostat, 2002). In absolute terms, the new member states with the largest GDPs are, in descending order, Poland (€197 billion), the Czech Republic (€63 billion), and Hungary (€58 billion). Those with the smallest GDPs are, in ascending order, Malta (€4 billion), Estonia (€6 billion), and Latvia (€8 billion). See Appendix 1 for a complete list of the GDPs of all EU-15 and 10 + 2 states.

Measured by GDP per capita in PPS, the 10 + 2 countries are at a significantly lower level of development than the EU-15 average. However, as Appendix 1 shows, there are significant differences between them. Broadly speaking, the 10 + 2 states can be set in four groupings:

- GDPs of over 60 per cent the EU-15 average: Cyprus and Slovenia;
- GDPs of around half the EU-15 average: the Czech Republic, Malta, Hungary and Slovakia;
- GDPs of around of one-third of the EU-15 average: Estonia, Poland, Lithuania, and Latvia;
- GDPs of around one-quarter of the EU-15 average: Bulgaria and Romania.

Economic sectors

The economic structure of the 10 + 2 states shows that, as in the EU-15, services constitute the predominant economic sector, accounting for over 60 per cent of GDP in all states other than Romania (see Table 10.1). As GDP has grown, the demand for services has increased due to higher income elasticities. However, despite a substantial fall in output in the early 1990s, industrial production still accounts for between 20 and 30 per cent of GDP in most CEECs, which is significantly higher than in most EU-15 countries. This implies the important role of the manufacturing sector in the economies of the CEECs. The long-standing tradition in manufacturing along with the relatively low costs of labour and raw materials helps to explain why there has been a rapid inflow of foreign direct investment (FDI) in the CEECs (on FDI, see below).

Table 10.1   *Structure of GDP in the 10+2 states and the EU-15*

Country	Agriculture[1]	Manufacturing[2]	Services
Bulgaria[3]	13.8	23.0	63.2
Cyprus[4]	4.2	13.3	82.5
Czech Republic	4.2	32.8	63.0
Estonia	5.8	22.7	71.5
Hungary[3]	4.2	28.3	67.5
Latvia	4.7	18.7	76.6
Lithuania	7.0	28.3	64.7
Malta	2.4	24.5	73.1
Poland	3.4	25.4	71.2
Romania	14.6	28.5	56.9
Slovakia	4.6	27.5	67.9
Slovenia	3.1	31.0	65.9
EU-15	2.1	22.3	75.6

Source: Eurostat (2002); figures are for 2001.
[1]Agriculture, hunting, forestry and fishing; [2]Excluding construction; [3]2000; [4]1999.

The agriculture sector is a major concern, because of its proportionately large size and its relative inefficiency. Indications of how important agriculture is in many of the 10 + 2 states, and the consequent policy challenges this poses for the EU, are seen in the following:

- The share of agriculture in the GDP of the new member states ranges from 2.4 per cent (Malta) and 3.1 per cent (Slovenia) to 13.8 per cent (Bulgaria) and 14.6 per cent (Romania) (see Table 10.1). These figures compare with an average of 2.1 per cent for the EU-15, where Greece has the highest percentage with over 6 per cent.
- Labour markets are discussed in the next section, but it merits being noted here that all of the 10 + 2 states apart from Malta have a higher proportion of people engaged in agriculture than the EU average of 4.2 per cent (see Appendix 1 for a complete list). In three of the new member states – Poland, Lithuania and Latvia – the figures are significantly higher than the EU-15 average, whilst in the candidate states of Romania and Bulgaria they are very markedly so – at 44.4 per cent and 26.7 per cent respectively.
- When all 10 + 2 states have become members, the Union's agricultural area will increase by 60 million hectares to make a total close to 200 million hectares. Of these 60 millions hectares, two-thirds are arable land, adding 55 per cent to the EU-15's arable area of 77 million hectares.

These figures serve to demonstrate why debates on agricultural reform have featured prominently in the 10 + 2 round and why agriculture will continue to be a key policy issue in the enlarged EU. The fact is that there is a pressing need for structural improvement in the agricultural sectors of most of the 10 + 2 states – most obviously on the farms themselves, but also in the up- and down-stream sectors (Mergos, 1998).

Labour markets

With the exceptions of Cyprus and Malta, unemployment levels in the new member states present at least as pressing a problem as they do in most EU-15 states. In 2001, the average unemployment rate in the EU-15 was 7.6 per cent. Similar levels were recorded in the Czech Republic, Estonia, Hungary, Latvia, and Romania, but the level was 18.6 per cent in Slovakia, 17.4 per cent in Poland, 17.3 per cent in Bulgaria, 12. 9 per cent in Lithuania, and 11.8 per cent in Slovenia (Eurostat, 2002).

Labour productivity (real gross value added per worker) in manufacturing has been rising in all CEECs (Podkaminer, 2001). The reasons for productivity growth are, however, quite different across countries. Only in Poland and Slovakia have productivity gains been due to increased output produced by a practically unchanged workforce. In Hungary,

Slovenia and the Czech Republic, employment cuts and output increases have contributed positively to productivity improvement, while in Bulgaria and Romania productivity gains have been due to falling employment levels outpacing falling (or stagnant) output.

Significantly, there is no obvious link between changes in unit labour costs and other sets of indicators. Rising labour productivity, for example, is differently 'rewarded' in terms of real wages. Strong gains in Hungarian productivity (average annual growth was 11.1 per cent between 1992 and the end of the 1990s) was not rewarded at all (real wage growth was about zero). On the other hand, equally strong gains in Poland (11.5 per cent) were rewarded (relatively ungenerously) with a 4.3 per cent real wage growth. Weaker gains in the Czech Republic (4.8 per cent), Slovenia (6.7 per cent) and Slovakia (3.7 per cent) were rewarded more generously (with real wages rising by 4, 3.5 and 3.1 per cent respectively). Gains in Romania (7.3 per cent) and Bulgaria (0.2 per cent) were 'punished' with falling real wages (−3.3 and −2.4 per cent respectively).

Differences in employment patterns are particularly pronounced in respect of agriculture. As was noted above, Romania 'heads' the list, with 44 per cent of the labour force employed in agriculture, which is more than ten times the EU-15 average (see Appendix 1). In Bulgaria around one-quarter of the labour force is employed in agriculture and in Poland just under one-fifth. An indication of the challenge this poses not only for the new member states but also for the enlarged EU is seen in the fact that the near 20 per cent of the Polish population engaged in agriculture contribute little more than 3 per cent to Poland's GDP. This compares with figures of 4.2 and 2 per cent, respectively, for the EU-15. Labour migration to the cities should increase agricultural productivity in Poland and other CEECs, but if there are no new jobs in the manufacturing and services sectors to absorb such an inflow there may be a significant rise in social tensions (Jovanovic, 2002).

Macroeconomic Developments in the New Member States

Growth rates

As indicated by the evolution of key macroeconomic indicators, stabilization policies have been implemented in most of the CEECs since the mid-1990s and most of them have been experiencing satisfactory growth rates (see Table 10.2). Some of the CEECs had particular problems in the mid-to-late 1990s, but these have been largely overcome. For example, the Bulgarian and Romanian economies experienced major crises in 1996, which had a negative impact for some time. The Baltic states were affected

Table 10.2   *Annual growth rate of GDP in the 10+2 states and the
EU-15: 1997–2002*

Country	1997	1998	1999	2000	2001	2002*
Bulgaria	−5.6	4.0	2.3	5.4	4.0	4.0
Cyprus	2.4	5.0	4.5	5.1	4.0	2.5
Czech Republic	−0.8	−1.0	0.5	3.2	3.6	3.6
Estonia	9.8	4.6	−0.6	7.1	5.0	3.5
Hungary	4.6	4.9	4.1	5.2	3.8	3.5
Latvia	8.4	4.8	2.8	6.8	7.7	5.0
Lithuania	7.3	5.1	−3.9	3.8	5.9	4.0
Malta	4.8	3.4	4.0	5.5	−0.8	−0.3
Poland	6.8	4.8	4.0	4.0	1.1	1.4
Romania	−6.0	−4.8	−1.1	1.8	5.2	4.5
Slovakia	5.6	4.0	1.3	2.2	3.3	3.6
Slovenia	4.6	3.8	5.2	4.6	3.0	3.0
EU-15	2.5	2.9	2.8	3.4	1.5	1.5

Source: Economic Commission for Europe (2002); Eurostat (2002). All figures are percentages.
*Estimate

by the Russian economic crisis of the late 1990s, which damaged their growth rates at the end of the decade. However, with the exception of Malta, there has been consistent economic growth in all of the 10 + 2 states since 2000. The challenge is to maintain this positive differential growth rate over and (well) above the EU rate for a long period of time in order to catch up with the EU level of development. Long-run growth projections predict that it may take around 30 years (one generation) for many of the CEECs to catch up with the income levels in 'low income' EU countries (Fisher *et al.*, 1998: 28; European Commission, 2002c: 183).

The stabilization policies in many of the new member states started with tight monetary and fiscal policies in the mid-1990s. But as their economies went into recession and political pressures rose, fiscal and monetary discipline could not in many cases be maintained. Inflation rates in most CEECs have been brought down sharply from their peaks in 1991 to 1993, the first years of price liberalization, but as compared to the average EU-15 level (of 2.6 per cent in 2001) they remain very high (see Table 10.3).

In most CEECs, monetary policy is seemingly one of the more success-ful areas in the reform process. However, the conduct of fiscal policies has not been as successful, not least because in most CEECs large-scale tax evasion and corruption are very common. The dilemma is that stricter

152

Table 10.3 *Annual rate of inflation in the 10 + 2 states and the
EU-15: 1997–2001*

Country	1997	1998	1999	2000	2001
Bulgaria	1,082.6	18.7	2.6	10.3	7.4
Cyprus	3.3	2.3	1.1	4.9	2.0
Czech Republic	8.0	9.7	1.8	3.9	4.5
Estonia	9.3	8.8	3.1	3.9	5.6
Hungary	18.5	14.2	10.0	10.0	9.1
Latvia	8.1	4.3	2.1	2.6	2.5
Lithuania	8.8	5.0	0.7	0.9	1.3
Malta	2.6	2.3	2.3	3.1	3.0
Poland	15.0	11.8	7.2	10.1	5.3
Romania	154.9	59.1	45.8	45.7	34.5
Slovakia	6.1	6.7	10.5	12.0	7.3
Slovenia	8.3	7.9	6.1	8.9	8.6
EU-15	2.1	1.8	1.3	2.5	2.6

Source: Economic Commission for Europe (2002); Eurostat (2002). All figures are percentages.

Table 10.4 *National debt in the 10 + 2 states and
the EU-15: 1997–2001*

Country	1997	1998	1999	2000	2001
Bulgaria	105.1	79.6	79.3	73.6	66.3
Cyprus	57.7	60.1	62.1	63.0	..
Czech Republic	13.0	13.7	14.5	17.0	23.7
Estonia	6.9	6.0	6.5	5.1	4.8
Hungary	64.2	61.9	61.0	55.4	53.1
Latvia	12.0	10.6	13.7	13.9	16.0
Lithuania	15.7	17.1	23.0	24.0	23.1
Malta	51.5	64.9	59.9	60.7	65.7
Poland	46.9	41.6	42.7	38.7	39.3
Romania	16.5	18.0	24.0	24.0	23.3
Slovakia	28.8	28.9	40.2	45.2	44.1
Slovenia	23.2	25.1	26.4	27.6	27.5
EU-15	71.0	68.8	67.7	63.8	63.1

Source: Eurostat (2002). All figures are percentages of GDP.

enforcement of tax collection and punishment of tax evasion would push many of the chronically financially weak enterprises in these countries over the edge to bankruptcy, while at the same time low tax revenues make the financing of public expenditure even more difficult and further accentuate the fiscal imbalances observed in most of the CEECs. This in turn transforms into deficits in the balance of payments and thus to increasing foreign debt. As a result, many transition countries have to pay high amounts of interest on debt. Nevertheless, the burden of public debt in all of the new member states apart from Bulgaria and Malta is lower than the EU-15 average (Table 10.4). This is largely because vigorous efforts have been made in most CEECs to sustain and stabilize public finances by reducing general government spending (Table 10.5).

Trade

Trade issues are considered in Chapters 11 and 15, so only brief observations will be made here.

Following the collapse of the communist trading block – the Council for Mutual Economic Assistance – and then the establishment in the early 1990s of the Europe Agreements between the EU and the CEECs, trade between CEECs and the EU-15 increased significantly. EU tariffs on

Table 10.5   *Government deficit/surplus in the 10 + 2 states and the EU-15: 1997–2001*

Country	1997	1998	1999	2000	2001
Bulgaria	−0.3	1.3	0.2	−0.6	1.7
Cyprus	−5.3	−5.6	−5.0	−2.7	−3.0
Czech Republic	−2.7	−4.5	−3.2	−3.3	−5.5
Estonia	2.0	−0.4	−4.0	−0.4	0.2
Hungary	−6.8	−8.0	−5.3	−3.0	−4.1
Latvia	−0.2	−0.7	−5.3	−2.7	−1.6
Lithuania	−1.1	−3.1	−5.6	−2.7	−1.9
Malta	−10.7	−10.8	−8.3	−7.0	−7.0
Poland	−4.3	−2.3	−1.5	−1.8	−3.9
Romania	−4.5	−3.2	−4.5	−4.5	−3.4
Slovakia	−5.5	−4.7	−6.4	−12.8	−5.6
Slovenia	−1.9	−2.3	−2.2	−3.2	−2.5
EU–15	−2.4	−1.6	−0.7	1.0	−0.8

Source: Eurostat (2002)*Estimate. All figures are percentages of GDP.

industrial goods were removed and there was a progressive reduction of quantitative restrictions, though some trade quotas remained on agricultural products. Between 1993 and 2001, the total value of trade increased almost threefold. As can be seen from Table 10.6, by 2001 virtually all 10 + 2 states were sending at least 50 per cent of their exports to the EU. In the cases of the Czech Republic, Estonia, Hungary, Poland and Romania, the figure exceeded or was close to 70 per cent.

The new member states were, before their accession in 2004, the EU's second largest trading partner after the USA, with 14.0 per cent of total trade. However, as Table 10.6 shows, most of them were running trading deficits – and in some case very large deficits – with the EU. In 2001, the EU's total trade surplus with the candidate countries was €11.4 billion, which though much reduced from the €25.8 billion of 1999 was still very large.

Table 10.6   *External trade balances of, and foreign direct investment in, the 10 + 2 states, 2001*

Country	External trade				Foreign Direct Investment	
	Trade balance exports/ imports (%)	Exports to EU (%)	Imports From EU (%)	Balance of EU with the accession countries (million euro)	Stock (euro per capita)	Net inflows (As % GDP)
Bulgaria	76.3	54.8	49.4	380	272	5.1
Cyprus	13.0	49.0	55.5	1,670	na	1.8
Czech Rep.	91.6	68.9	61.8	2,376	2,284	8.7
Estonia	77.0	69.4	56.5	19	2,084	9.7
Hungary	90.5	74.3	57.8	–481	1,790	4.7
Latvia	57.1	61.2	52.6	466	970	2.3
Lithuania	72.1	47.8	44.0	773	720	3.7
Malta	71.8	41.3	63.6	1,304	na	8.8
Poland	71.8	69.2	61.4	83,976	952	3.2
Romania	73.0	67.8	57.3	967	245	2.8
Slovakia	85.5	59.9	49.8	–264	521	6.3
Slovenia	91.2	62.2	67.7	1,819	1,527	1.9

Source: Eurostat, 2003.
na: non-available.

Foreign direct investment

FDI in the CEECs has increased as their attraction to EU companies has grown as a result of their geographical proximity, the availability of skilled labour, and the ease of access to EU markets through the Europe Agreements. The inflow of investment has served to transfer technology, introduce new management techniques and create jobs. Net inflows were higher that 3 per cent of GDP in most CEECs in 2001 (see Table 10.6). The Czech Republic, Estonia and Hungary are the biggest recipients.

Between 1992 and 2001, the volume of FDI going to the CEECs relative to the volume received by the southern EU members (defined here as Greece, Spain and Portugal) increased by a factor of six (for more details, see www.source.oecd.org). This implies that in the long-run an intensification of the ongoing process of reorientation of FDI away from the southern EU members toward the new entrants is to be expected.

The financial sector

The financial sectors of CEECs are in need of considerable development. Under the communist regimes, money had only a minor function to play and banking and finance were of little importance. In consequence, the organizational settings and the capacity of financial institutions in the CEECs were quite different from those in market economies. They also varied among CEECs: Hungary, Poland and former Yugoslavia started to reform their banking systems in the second half of the 1980s, whilst Bulgaria, Czechoslovakia and the Baltic States had rather underdeveloped financial structures with a central bank also engaged in financial transfers among firms, a foreign trade bank, savings institutions and a few other specialized banks.

After 1990, a number of new state-owned commercial banks were created through the transfer of existing loans from the portfolio of the central bank. In addition, governments had to re-establish capital markets and their respective institutions (stock exchanges, investment houses, supervisory agencies, etc). Nevertheless, after years of slow and hesitant action, significant progress in the implementation of the EU *acquis* began to occur from 2000 with the adoption of the relevant banking regulations and directives. Moreover, foreign banks were finally allowed to take over troubled CEEC banks as majority shareholders. As a result, the financial sector is more advanced in countries like Hungary and Estonia (and to a lesser extent Poland), which were the first to allow a strong foreign equity involvement in the banking sector. The critical element, however, is not the selling of relative majority stakes to a foreign bank but is rather the transfer of real management control and responsibility to prudent strategic partners that intend to run the banks as financial intermediaries and not to strip assets like a portfolio manager (Baltas, 2001).

In addition to largely immature governance structures, the financial sectors in the CEECs are also plagued by other weaknesses. Most notably, financial markets in most of the CEECs are small in relative and absolute terms. They are so for several reasons: a relatively small extent of financial intermediation; a low level of GDP per capita; successive waves of excessive lending followed by credit crunches; and distrust of the financial system after the experience of repeated bank failures. In addition to the small size of the CEECs' financial markets, poor asset quality and serious under-capitalization continue to be a major problem, with problematic assets in the range of 15–30 per cent of total assets and with estimated contingent liabilities of 4–10 per cent of GDP, even in the best performing group of Estonia, Hungary and Poland (Fink and Haiss, 2000:1–3; European Commission, 2000a).

Implications of the 10 + 2 Round for the EU Economy

The traditional model of EU enlargement is based on certain principles linked to the rights and duties of both applicant countries and current members. These principles have been applied successfully in previous enlargement rounds and may yet serve as a sound model for some applicants in the future. At the heart of the traditional model is a requirement that acceding states align with Union laws, practices and guidelines and participate fully in Union policies unless exemptions are granted in the form of derogations or transition periods. This procedure for accession was very much like joining a club with pre-established membership rules (Jovanovic, 2000).

However, as was shown in Chapters 1, 3 and 4, the 10 + 2 enlargement round has been different to previous rounds in that it has posed unprecedented challenges for the EU. In economic terms, the challenges arise largely from the fact that the new member states are relatively poor and are still in the process of making the transition to the establishment of efficient and competitive market economies. This raises many questions, not only about how the new member states will cope in the EU's integrated markets for goods and factors, but also about how the EU itself will cope. For enlargement raises many complex issues about virtually all aspects of international market integration and international transfer payments. Established theory of trade integration holds a presumption of gains from trade and thus implies that enlargement will 'work' in economic terms, but this does not mean there are not concerns and dangers. For example, will producers in EU-15 states be 'under-cut' by cheaper competitors in CEECs; will budgetary transfers between member states be sufficient to promote necessary economic regeneration and acceptable levels of social cohesion; will workers in low-wage CEECs seek to move on a large scale to higher-wage EU-15 states, and will this impose intolerable strains in those countries which receive the largest inflows; and could currency problems arise because the expanded internal market is seen to be not functioning satisfactorily?

These and related questions are explored in other chapters where, in essence, it is argued that whilst enlargement certainly will impose severe strains, most of the challenges are ultimately likely to prove to be, in the customary EU manner, 'manageable'.

Conclusions

Uneven macroeconomic developments in the new member states can to some extent be attributed to their individual situation at the start of the transformation. However, they also reflect the varying extent to which institutional reform programmes have been implemented in these countries. Their economies are not yet fully adjusted to the efficient functioning of the market economy. To establish the necessary institutions, radical reforms of their financial sectors and their fiscal and financial policies are necessary. Their manufacturing and services sectors still remain fragile. Economic set-backs can easily occur, as was the case in the Balkan countries in 1996 and 1997. Entering the EU without a full macroeconomic stabilization and a modernization of output structures may produce considerable pain. Countries passing through 'transition' may have particular difficulties withstanding the EU's strict competition rules.

Most CEECs have yet to put in place an efficient legal system, public administration has yet to be fully reorganized, and markets for products and services are still for the most part in a trial phase. A particular problem is the agricultural sector, which in most CEECs is very significant in terms of both the size of the employed workforce and of the arable surface but is backward in terms of productivity.

The overall economic effects of the 10 + 2 enlargement are positive. They are so particularly for the acceding countries, which have the prospect of clear gains, even if the costs are greater and many of the benefits are slower to arrive than they anticipated. For the EU-15, the direct economic gains are relatively modest, with enlargement not expected to bring much extra efficiency or growth, nor to create many new jobs. However, the final operational adhesion conditions set by the December 2002 Copenhagen European Council mean that the costs for the EU-15 are relatively cheap in budgetary terms. But beyond the 'narrow' costs, the EU-15 have achieved their main economic objective in the enlargement process, which was never enlargement for its own sake but was rather to give support to friendly countries undertaking fundamental programmes of economic transformation and stabilization.

Chapter 11

The Operation of the Internal Market

GERHARD MICHAEL AMBROSI

Introduction

The 10 + 2 enlargement round would not have been possible without the collapse of the Soviet Union (USSR) and of the economic system it imposed on the countries in its sphere of influence. But at the time of that collapse, the former UK Prime Minister Edward Heath (1991) warned against hasty enlargement of the European Community (EC): 'If they [the former Soviet block countries] enter the EC now, they will be wiped off the face of Europe . . . There is nothing we want to buy from them. They want our products.' That assessment now appears to have been badly misguided. Indeed, it looked to be so soon after it was made, for by the mid-1990s all CEECs had established free-trade agreements with the EU. After these agreements were established, protecting the CEECs' national markets – seemingly Heath's main concern – was no longer an issue. In this sense, in terms of economics, eastward enlargement is largely 'yesterday's news' (Barysch, 2003: 1).

Nevertheless, in spite of their seeming obsolescence, Heath's comments do convey a relevant and lasting concern over the ability of the new member states to participate fully in the economic exchanges of the EU. For example, looking at the years 1989 to 2001, Landesmann (2003: 32) has observed that all eight Central and Eastern European accession countries, with the exception of Slovenia, experienced at times dramatic – and unsustainable – deficits in their current accounts (see also Task Force Enlargement, 2002).

Concern about the sustainability of the balance of trade deficits of the CEECs emphasizes the great importance of the working of the European internal market for the cohesion of the Union and the well being of its citizens. It is quite clear that great challenges lie before the enlarged Union in this regard. The pre-accession process did establish that the legal, economic and societal prerequisites for membership by the applicant states were met. But that not withstanding, it is important to be conscious of the type of economic expectations which were implied by

158

attesting that the new members would be able to participate in the economic life of the EU on an equal footing. This chapter will examine this matter by looking at the challenges and promises offered by the workings of the EU's internal market for the new member states.

The European integration of the formerly socialist CEECs is, of course, without any precedent. Since socialism means by definition that society and not individual 'capitalists' should own a country's means of production, there were no major private firms in the former socialist countries. The internal economic exchanges were not left to the 'chaos of the market'. Instead, they were predominantly dictated by central planning authorities. In the absence of private capital, there were no capital markets, no commercial banks and no credit markets. Trade was predominantly pre-planned in the context of the Soviet-dominated 'Council of Mutual Economic Assistance' (COMECON). Thus, the CEECs enter the Single European Market (SEM) with an economic and administrative background that is very much at odds with the market-oriented institutions and traditions built up in the EU. The CEECs will thus very much add to the heterogeneity of the EU in economic terms (see Sapir *et al.*, 2003). But what does this imply for the progress of European integration and for the operation of the internal market?

'Completing' the Internal Market

Those who are responsible for 'running' the EU are often criticized for using jargon so unintelligible that most people have difficulties in understanding issues (see in particular Charlemagne, 2003). The term 'internal market' is a good case in point. Its specific meaning in the context of the EU is defined in Article 14 (2) of the Treaty Establishing the European Community (TEC). The Treaty is not a document that makes for light reading, but it is the contractual basis for European integration. According to the Treaty, the 'internal market' is meant to comprise 'an area without internal frontiers in which the free movement of goods, persons, services and capital is ensured'. At the heart of the internal market, there are thus 'four freedoms'. Their significance is such that they took a position of paramount importance in the enlargement negotiations – constituting the first four of the 31 negotiating chapters (see Appendix 2), and with many of the other chapters being elaborations of these.

But 'internal market' is not just a descriptive term but is also an aim. This follows from the beginning of the said Article 14 TEC, where the first sentence states that the EC should adopt 'measures with the aim of progressively establishing the internal market over a period expiring on 31 December 1992'. This statement is likely to appear as rather strange to the uninitiated reader. Is establishing the internal market a project which ended in 1992? If so, why is this passage still in a treaty which has been three times re-negotiated since that provision was incorporated in the EC Treaty via the 1986 Single European Act (SEA)? The answer is that the EU is still working at the 'completion of the internal market'.

The successful undertaking of this task involves not only actors on the supranational EU level but also the individual EU member states, their firms and citizens. To try and ensure compliance with requirements, the Treaty provides for 'sticks and carrots', in the form of disciplinary measures and incentives. The administrative organ which is charged with applying the sticks and carrots is the European Commission, which is the driving force and the guardian of the EU's treaties. In respect of the internal market it keeps a 'scoreboard' in which it monitors and quantifies the extent to which in practice the market is being completed and realized (European Commission, 2002f). Somewhat remarkably, in May 2003 it reported that in recent years the completion had not been progressing but rather had been regressing among the EU-15; regressing in the sense that the incorporation of internal market legislation into national law was increasingly lagging behind agreed targets (European Commission, 2003p). In September 2003, the Commissioner charged with internal market affairs – Frits Bolkestein – put this matter in dramatic terms:

> The growth of intra-EU trade has slowed to a crawl. Intra-EU trade in services as a share of GDP is less today than it was 10 years ago. Foreign direct investment has taken an even bigger dip. Member States seem to be turning increasingly to their domestic economies. Price convergence, which was rapid immediately after the launch of the Internal Market in 1993, has – like trade integration – come to a halt . . . This is all bad news for our competitiveness. We should not forget that the Internal Market Strategy is all about competitiveness. (European Commission, 2003t: 1)

If the EU-15 have had such difficulties in completing the internal market, it can be anticipated that the difficulties are likely to be even greater in the EU-25. What are these difficulties? They fall under three headings: implementation, infringement, and standardization.

Implementation difficulties concern the translation, or transposition to use the correct 'jargon', of EU directives (essentially framework laws) that are passed by the Council of Ministers and the EP into national laws. Such laws are supposed to be transposed according to a fixed timetable, but in practice transposition is often slow and delayed, with the consequence that EU laws do not always come into force in all member states on schedule. Problems in this field are sometimes related to the mechanisms of national legislation which are, for example, quite different in federal systems such as Germany, where there are several levels of legislation, as compared with centralist governments like France. However, legislative processes are not always the decisive factor when it comes to explaining problems of implementation. Indeed, according to the Commission, implementation hinges most of all on the political will behind it (European Commission, 2002f: 10). Reasons why political will is lacking in some cases are explored later in the chapter.

Infringement difficulties relate to member states' non-conformity with or misapplication of internal market laws. Such cases of alleged 'infringement' have increased from 700 in 1992 to over 1500 cases in 2002 (see European Commission, 2002f: 11). Again, there are several factors at work. Amongst them are: the large number of internal market related laws increases the number of potential misapplications of such laws; some laws are formulated in such a way that they are too difficult for those who are responsible for administering them to fully understand; and there are instances of a lack of determination to apply laws in the sense they were intended. The Commission has devised a consultative mechanism, known as SOLVIT, to address these type of problems. It brings together the parties concerned so that no formal measures are required for dealing with the infringement complaint. No doubt this approach is to be commended as being conducive to the promotion of integration in a transnational context. The approach seems to be particularly appropriate for the new EU members in view of their lack of appropriate administrative experience. However, the approach is at odds with the normal procedure in cases of unwarranted infringement of internal market law, which involves the Commission filing a case with the European Court of Justice (ECJ) against the uncooperative state. There is an apprehension that in the EU-25 the normal procedure will put too much strain on the EU's judicial system. The SOLVIT approach might therefore be a promising alternative, but the danger is that its negotiation orientation might give the wrong impression to inexperienced administrators that the internal market *acquis* itself is flexible and open for negotiation.

Apprehensions and suggestions in this field are well expressed in the 2003 Internal Market Strategy paper where the Commission declared:

> In the end, success in an Internal Market of 25 countries will depend on mutual trust and confidence. The key is administrative cooperation and understanding between officials in competent authorities leading to ways of finding practical solutions to problems. This can only develop over time – there is no magic solution. (European Commission, 2003r: 33)

The third difficulty, standardization, involves the existence of many national technical standards and operating norms, in areas ranging from pharmaceutical products to environmental protection. These can and do constitute severe barriers to trade, in the form of non tariff-barriers.

Originally, the founding fathers of the EC thought that this problem could be solved by EC legislation, but this proved to be too clumsy and so other approaches have also been used, most notably the use of European-wide standardization bodies. However, by no means all differences in national standards have been removed or agreed and they do still constitute a significant barrier to trade and a major obstacle in the way of the smooth running of the internal market.

The 'Market Bias' of European Integration

The preoccupation with the internal market and its 'completion', as documented in the preceding section, might appear to express an unsound overemphasis on the economic aspects of European integration. The rich and varied cultural heritage of Europe, the traditional intellectual communication of European thinkers across many political, administrative and even cultural borders, and the yearning for peace in Europe which found such a fruitful expression in Robert Schuman's famous May 1950 declaration – all these elements of a pan-Europeanism seem to find far too little consideration in contemporary debates. Even when non-economic aspects of European integration do find expression at the level of official European activities, they seem to be rather nebulous, like the many appeals to common European values, or they are somewhat inconsequential, like the frequent invocations that a more integrated European foreign policy should be created.

Seen in an historical context, and in particular the relative failure of the EU to develop integrated 'political' policies, the market-oriented preoccupation of European integration emerges not as the *cause* but rather as the *consequence* of the lack of military and political integration. The force that has really driven European integration forwards has been predominantly *economic* integration. The creation of European market exchange has been at the very heart of the European integration process since its outset. There has increasingly been seen to be no sensible economic alternative to European integration, and experience suggests that there is no viable basis for European integration but economics. Perhaps, therefore, the heading of this section should have referred not to the market *bias* of European integration but rather to its market-*centred* approach.

In principle, economic integration can be approached in two alternative ways: *via* creating a free trade area or *via* a customs union. Under both regimes, the partners abolish trade restrictions between themselves, in particular tariffs on goods imported from the partner countries. The scope of this liberalization of trade can be narrow or wide in both cases, embracing, for example, only manufactured goods or including also agricultural produce and services. The crucial difference is the treatment of non-partner countries. In a free trade area this is left up to each member, thus leaving national sovereignty to be largely preserved for the members of the free trade area. A customs union is different in that it is based on having a common external trade policy. Thus national sovereignty is abandoned, or rather one should say that it is pooled amongst equal partners and exerted collectively in trade matters. Both types of integration have been and are being tried in Europe: via EFTA and the Europe Agreements (see Chapter 3) in the case of free trade areas and via the EU in the case of the customs union.

A case can be made in terms of economic theory that welfare, efficiency and volume of trade are better promoted in a free trade area than in a comparable custom union. A central plank of this case is that free trade areas leave scope for member states to be more liberal in external trade policy than other partners. However, free trade areas do not remove what can be costly transaction costs on internal trade, and of course they do not permit the degree of market integration that is possible in customs unions. The next section considers a key aspect of the EU's internal market integration.

The Four Freedoms and Enlargement

The scope of any cooperation and integration between sovereign states can only be as wide as the partners agree upon. Since the EEC Treaty of 1957, there has been a generally accepted understanding between the member states that the Common Market/internal market/Single European Market (the preferred name has changed over the years) should be at the core of the Community/Union.

The main foundations of the market are the so-called 'four freedoms' – of goods, persons, services and capital. The particular treaty wording referring to the freedoms entered the EEC Treaty (now TEC) only with the SEA, but a commitment to their substance always had treaty status and moves to further liberalize the market by extending the reach of the four freedoms have constantly featured on the Community's/Union's policy agenda.

Free movement of goods

This freedom follows immediately from the 'basis' of European integration, namely the customs union and Articles 23 and 24 TEC which stipulate that no internal barriers can be imposed on the circulation of goods, including products coming from a third country once they have passed the common external border.

In the context of enlargement, it might be suspected that this freedom would be of limited importance since all the new members had free trade agreements for most products with the EU before their accession and hence there were few tariffs to remove. However, 'non-tariff' barriers, which are equally inadmissable in the SEM, have been and are a problem. These barriers require that there be common ground between all member states on such matter as technical standards and certification of goods, which, in turn, requires wide-ranging administrative changes in the new member states. Adjustment difficulties are being partly overcome by temporary transitional arrangements, which several entrants – including Cyprus, Poland and Slovenia – have obtained for sensitive products such as medical supplies.

Free movement of persons

Article 39 (1) TEC states that 'Freedom of movement for workers shall be secured within the Community'. This freedom has not created any serious problems for the EU-15 in the sense that any country has been 'flooded' by workers from another country. On the contrary, indeed, the internal movement of workers in the EU-15 has been stagnant.

There has, however, been considerable apprehension that the domestic labour market will suffer in some of the EU-15 if this freedom is used too extensively in the enlarged EU. Although the 'threat' of large migrations of peoples from CEECs to EU-15 states is almost certainly exaggerated (see Chapter 5) some EU-15 states, including Germany and Austria, have been extremely concerned that it could happen. In consequence, during the accession negotiations the EU-15 sought and secured long transition periods in which the citizens of new member states would not automatically be granted full access to their labour markets.

In addition to a perceived possibility of direct threats to jobs, enlargement has been seen as also creating other problems related to this freedom. For example, from the viewpoint of employers, free movement of workers creates difficulties regarding monitoring the quality and qualifications of their employees. Just as consumers need to be protected against the marketing of goods unfit for consumption, so also there needs to minimum standards for specific job qualifications. The new member states will, of course, be subject to EU laws on the mutual recognition of diplomas and certificates, but there have been some concerns about how comparable many CEEC qualifications really are. As a result, in the accession negotiations the EU-15 put considerable stress on the qualifications of workers and required in particular that new member states reform their public educational institutions in such a way as to guarantee a competence of workers in compliance with Union norms.

Freedom to provide services

Article 49 TEC states that 'restrictions on freedom to provide services within the Community shall be prohibited' in the sense that suppliers of services do not necessarily have to reside in the same EU country as their recipients.

As with the free movement of goods and people, problems of quality control apply to the free movement of services, though even more so because of the often intangible character of services. But the problem of prohibitive requirements concerning extra-territorial suppliers of services is also a consequence of fending-off competitors through administrative measures. This is a key reason why trans-border markets in services have been relatively under-developed in the EU.

In developing legislation designed to promote the free movement of services the EU has had to find a difficult balance between legitimate protection of regional interests on the one hand and chicaning protectionism against external competitors on the other. Such a balance had also to be sought in the accession negotiations. It seems likely, as result of positions adopted by some EU-15 states in those negotiations, that the new member states will encounter considerable protectionism in the service area – a protectionism that was exemplified by Germany and Austria securing temporary protection in the construction and hygiene sectors from their new competitors.

Free movement of capital

During the 10 + 2 accession negotiations, the chapter dealing with free movement of capital was particularly sensitive and was given an absolute priority.

A central reason for this was that the CEECs were still adjusting to the private ownership of capital. This absence of private ownership was *the* most important element of their former economic and societal systems. The absence meant, amongst other things, that the service infrastructure associated with capitalism – of banking, financial services, legal protection and the like – was either poorly developed or even absent for decades until the collapse of the communist regimes. However, even in those cases where there has been no need for fundamental systemic reform – Malta and Cyprus – there was seen to be ample scope for reform of the services industries, especially in Cyprus, which has a large 'off shore' banking sector.

This need for reform in the pre-accession period was because services are no different from other goods in needing a shared regulatory framework if there is to be free movement. Aspects of investor protection, for example, and matters relating to economic criminality must be regulated on a common footing lest regional suppliers of services and of capital experience an unfair bias.

Another reason why issues associated with the free movement of capital have been, and continue to be, both sensitive and highly important in the context of enlargement is that they have long been sensitive and important issues for established EU members. There was an article in the 1957 EEC Treaty on capital and payments which had liberalizing intentions, but there was little policy development in the area until the 1992 programme was developed. A considerable volume of legislation is now in place, but many problems still remain. Amongst these problems are ones arising from the fact that the opening of capital markets is based on the principle of home country surveillance. This is analogous to practices on the goods market in that it holds that a supplier of financial services accredited in one country should be admitted to the markets of other member countries. However, because financial and insurance services are so sensitive, and often personal, this principle is extremely problematic. To be given full effect it requires, arguably all the more so with the different economic backgrounds and traditions of the new member states, more EU-wide standards for the purpose of consumer protection.

Competition and Competitiveness

The expression 'completing the internal market' often seems to mean at the national level almost the opposite of what it means at the European level. This is not just a problem of words but is also one of substance. At the national level, fostering the internal market might be taken to mean two types of activities: (i) stimulating market exchange – that is strengthening market *competition* by restraining monopolies and abolishing administrative obstacles; and (ii) improving national *competitiveness* – that is, enhancing the ability of national suppliers to penetrate outside markets or to protect national producers from 'unfair' outside producers. These two activities go together – there can be no fair competition without competitiveness of the participants. There are, in other words, no honourable laurels to be won in a race in which the winner competes only against handicapped competitors. However, politicians are often tempted to try and strengthen national competitiveness by 'helping' – that is, subsidizing – national firms or by boosting them in other ways (such as with Margaret Thatcher's 'Buy British' campaign of the 1980s). But, like doping sportsmen, although the provision of such assistance gives an artificial advantage, in the end it ruins the health of the recipient.

There is, thus, a fundamental problem in the relation between competition and competitiveness. It is a problem that creates considerable difficulties in the EU, with a danger that fostering national competitiveness involves ever-mounting national subsidies as governments follow suit, but without producing any overall change in competitive outcomes. Rather, it shifts the cost of production from producers to taxpayers without returning to the latter appropriate benefits of such transfers. But once a situation of pervasive subsidization is established, no government can easily opt out of such a situation because that would make national companies less competitive than subsidized foreign companies. Sectors in the EU where this is a particular problem include shipbuilding and agriculture, where there is a general bemoaning of the detrimental and wasteful effects of subsidies but where all countries keep paying them in an attempt to maintain domestic activity.

Tackling these sort of problems have long been on the EU's agenda and have been at the heart of its competition policy. National governments are forbidden to pay subsidies, or, as Article 87 TEC puts it, 'any aid granted by a Member State or through State resources in any form whatsoever which distorts or threatens to distort competition by favouring certain undertakings [or firms] or the production of certain goods shall, in so far as it affects trade between Member States, be incompatible with the common market'. In other words, state aid is strictly forbidden 'in any form whatsoever' – *in principle*. A key task for the Commission is to ensure that this principle is upheld. It is a task that has created many difficulties for it and will do so even more so in the EU-25 with the accession of states with many firms that will not be competitive without 'assistance' and with national politicians and administrators coming from cultures and traditions where local 'intervention' has long been common. Aware of the challenges facing it in this regard, even in the pre-accession period the Commission monitored state aid in the applicant countries and published detailed investigations into the subject.

But though it is forbidden 'in principle', in practice state aid in the form of transfers to individuals and firms amounts to approximately one-third of national budgets in many member states. Indeed, the EU's budget itself is mostly concerned with state aid in some form, with about half of the budget going to agricultural aid and one-third going to the financing of structural and regional policy measures which are mostly justified on the grounds of boosting the competitiveness of regions and sectors in the EU. Thus about 80 per cent of the EU's budget is state aid, loosely defined: it is granted because of a lack of competitiveness, as is the case with much of CAP funding, or in an attempt to remove the lack of competitiveness, as is the case with cohesion policy. There is thus the irony that in parallel to monitoring the granting of state aid by national authorities, the Commission finds itself in the position of overseeing the granting of aid in the framework of competitiveness policy.

It can be questioned whether this EU spending is really warranted by the aim of competitiveness. These doubts have been repeatedly addressed at meetings of the European Council. Thus, the March 2001 Stockholm summit concluded that 'the level of state aids in the European Union must be reduced and the system made more transparent' (European Council, 2001: 52). One year later, the March 2002 Barcelona summit renewed this appeal and called for a change in the rationale of giving state aid so that in future it would be directed more to 'horizontal' objectives like environmental and social policy (European Council, 2002d: 52). Since the European Council has the statutory role of giving the guideline for the general development of European integration, some fundamental reorientations may therefore be expected. Thus, coincidental with enlargement, there is an increased awareness of the problematic aspects of promoting competitiveness policy *via* state aid. It is an awareness that will feed into future debates on EU spending just as the new member states formally become part of the debate. It can be anticipated that they will press to be allocated considerable funding for their still transitional economies.

The 'Lisbon Strategy' and Enlargement

On the occasion of the Lisbon European Council in March 2000, the Heads of Government of the EU-15 stated that a central aim for the coming decade would be EU competitiveness. They declared: 'The Union has today set itself a new strategic goal for the next decade: to become the most competitive and dynamic knowledge-based economy in the world' (European Council 2000: 5). Based on this declaration, a 'Lisbon Strategy' was developed which aimed at – among other things – 'stepping up the process of structural reform for competitiveness and innovation' and at 'completing the internal market' (*ibid.*). The Lisbon Strategy does, of course, involve all the new members of the EU. This raises the question as to whether the ambitious aims of the Lisbon Declaration are suitable for them, given their particular situations and problems.

One of the reasons for concern about competitiveness in the EU in general stems from the observation that for decades the EU-15 have long been, on average, about 30 per cent below the USA as far as GDP per capita is concerned (Sapir *et al.*, 2003: 21–3). A central reason for this superiority of the US economy seems to be a better integration of its goods and factor markets and a more dynamic research and development sector. Therefore, the EU's aim to insist on finalizing the completion of the internal market and on speeding up structural economic reforms seems sensible. But with economic performance being an important concern in the EU, what contribution towards these aims comes from enlargement? None of the new members reaches the EU-15 average GDP per capita, and only Cyprus and Slovenia are comparable with even the economically weakest EU-15 members, Greece and Portugal (see Appendix 1). Thus, the social aspect of economic cohesion in an integrated market economy becomes far more important than it was in previous rounds of enlargement. This might have an impact on future economic policy measures, which could be ruled more by redistributive concerns than by questions of targeting a more dynamic European economic structure.

In addition, there is the problem of infrastructure and regional cohesion.

As Sapir *et al.* (2003: 38) have put it in an assessment of the Lisbon Strategy:

> From the point of view of the Single Market, the most serious current deficiency lies in the fact that infrastructure has been built around national economic priorities. As a result, an integrated transport network for Europe is largely lacking, a weakness that will become much more evident after enlargement when east–west connections are likely to become as important as the currently dominant north–south routes.

Overcoming these problems of infrastructure will bind large amounts of finances which then are not available for more progressive tasks of supporting developments in the field of more advanced technologies.

Other dimensions of the competitiveness challenge include those arising from attitudes in CEECs. For decades under communism a quite different model of economic governance was practised to that which now applies. This naturally fostered ways of thinking and acting that are not all wholly appropriate in competitive market systems. This 'cultural problem' is one of the least discussed, but arguably is one of the most important, ways in which enlargement has increased the challenge for the EU in making a success of the Lisbon Strategy.

Many proposals have been advanced as to how to deal with these various challenges. For example, it has been suggested that there should be a stronger role of the Commission in the 'processes of benchmarking, targeting and coordination with partners from the member countries' (Sapir *et al.*, 2003: 158). But such proposals hinge on there being sufficient political will to give them effect – and this is by no means certain to exist.

Concluding Remarks

In the introduction it was stated that in terms of economics, the problematic eastward enlargement of the EU has come to be seen as rather 'yesterday's news'. This chapter has sought to establish that this is most likely too optimistic a view. For even the founding members of the Common Market still have problems with fulfilling their self-imposed aim of market integration. Certainly great progress had been made toward establishing the free movement of goods, people, services and capital, but further advances need to be made and there is a considerable apprehension among economic commentators that many of the problems identified in this chapter will be even more difficult to overcome in the EU-25. The Lisbon Process is supposed to address many of the problems in a renewed spirit of dynamism and innovation, but it must be doubted whether its aim of Europe becoming the most dynamic economy in the world by 2010 can be realized.

The ambitions associated with the enlargement of the EU do, of course, range beyond the confines of the market. As the Commission stated in a 2000 strategy paper on enlargement, 'enlargement can only succeed if it is a social project involving all citizens and not just an elite' (European Commission, 2000f: 5). So embracing an aim cannot just be based on market considerations, for these by themselves will not lead to the equitable results an impartial union must offer to its citizens. The situation of most of the new member states will require for some years that a special effort, involving good neighbourly intentions and actions, must be made by all sides. As part of this, the efficient and fair functioning of the internal market will be a factor in determining the extent to which and the speed at which the new member states are integrated. This, in turn, will require a persistent commitment to the aim of completing the market by *all* the members of the EU-25 'club'.

Chapter 12

The Budget and 'the Spending Policies'

ELEANOR E. ZEFF*

Introduction

EU financing has long been controversial. Enlargement rounds have usually added to the controversy by increasing disputes over spending and revenue policies, not least in respect of the distribution of EU funds.

The 10 + 2 round is no exception to this pattern. Indeed, it has focused attention on budgetary matters in a particularly intense manner. A key reason for this is that the new member states are relatively poor, with an average income per head of less than half of that in the EU-15. There is a doubling of regional disparities in the EU-25 as compared with the EU-15, and a drop of overall per capita income of 18 per cent.

The relatively under-developed nature of the new member states, especially the CEECs, has raised considerable budgetary challenges for the EU and has led to serious thinking about its spending policies and financial priorities (European Policy Center and Notre Europe, 2003: 3). Indeed, a central debate during the 10 + 2 pre-accession process was whether enlargement would be possible at all without either substantially increasing budgetary resources or restricting new members' access to funding. Many had their doubts. However, Michaele Schreyer, the EU Budget Commissioner, emphasized that the EU budget was an 'appropriate instrument' to meet expectations in the EU-25 (Schreyer, 2003:1).

This chapter examines the procedures and philosophies of the EU's 'spending policies' and describes the EU's budgetary process and financial frameworks within the context of the 2004 enlargement. It asks how the challenges and opportunities of enlargement are influencing these policies and how funding can be applied to effectively manage the impact of the additional members. The chapter explores how EU funding mechanisms are adjusting to accommodate new members and whether these will help them to reach parity with earlier members, which is a stated

* The author would like to thank Marie Manil and Marketa Dvorakova for their research help with this chapter.

political goal of the EU's cohesion policies. The chapter also contains an examination of the Common Agricultural Policy (CAP) and the Structural Funds – the EU's main areas of expenditure – and their place in the overall budget. Throughout the chapter consideration is given to the budget's likely influence on the new member states and, conversely, the pressures these states have put on the budget and on EU-15 members to develop spending policies.

The Budget and 'Spending Policies' in Context

The EU budget is small relative to national budgets, constituting only slightly over 1 per cent of the combined GNP of the member states. More than half of the budget is assigned to what is known as compulsory expenditure, of which by far the largest component is the CAP. The other major area of expenditure, accounting for over one-third of the budget, are funds directed to promoting cohesion across the EU. The funds, of which the so-called Structural Funds are the main component parts, are directed primarily towards supporting regional and social projects that are designed to further such political goals as promoting equity among the member states and forging a closer union.

A combination of reasons account for the relatively small size of the budget. The most important reason is that control of such heavy spending areas as health, education and social welfare remains firmly at member state level. A second reason is that the budget is grounded on the principle that the cost of regulatory policies is also funded at member state level rather than by the Union. A third reason is that the budget must be financed entirely from its own resources, and member states are reluctant to increase these resources. And a fourth reason is that the budget must always be balanced.

Whereas in the member states the budget has considerable political significance, the small size and dedicated nature of the EU budget inevitably limit its influence as a policy tool. However, this has not prevented the budget becoming the focus of considerable political debate and attention. Who gets what from the budget has always been a highly controversial political issue (Hancock *et al.*, 2003: 514), and has become even more so with the 10 + 2 enlargement. Arguments about equality and fairness revolve very much around national issues, as was demonstrated in the 10 + 2 accession negotiations when there were fierce debates about how to direct the EU's funds: toward the newer members or stretched throughout EU-25?

The other side of the coin to how the money should be spent is, of course, how it should be raised and who should pay. Deciding which countries should shoulder the costs of the budget has also promoted political disputes over the years, most notably in the 1980s when the then UK Prime Minister, Margaret Thatcher, campaigned vigorously, and ultimately reasonably successfully, for the UK's large net budgetary contributions to be reduced. In more recent years, other net contributors to the EU budget, notably Germany and the Netherlands, have pressed for rebates of the sort given to the UK.

The nature of the EU's budgetary situation is clearly such that without a fundamental reform of payments and/or resources, the budget's political potential for achieving greater parity and more effective integration among the member states will remain limited. However, the prospect for being able to bring about such reform is not bright. This is largely because there is no great drive for reform amongst the member states, but partly also because of the nature of budgetary decision-making. Whereas in most democratic countries, the government and legislature work closely together to establish and control the budget, budgetary processes are much more complex in the EU, with the European Commission, the Council of Ministers, the European Council and the EP all playing important roles in establishing the annual budgets and the multi-annual financial frameworks within which the annual budgets are tightly framed. Furthermore, responsibility for implementing the budget is shared by the member states and the Commission – both of which are monitored by the EP and the Court of Auditors.

The Costs of Enlargement

The 10 states joining the EU in 2004 may have met the requirements for accession into the Union, but they lag behind the EU-15 economically and politically. This means reaching parity, or at least reaching a level of development that will enable them to be 'comfortable' EU members, will be costly. But the EU-15 have recognized that costs do have to be paid, and the acceding states themselves have pressed hard for more equality. Because of this, the 10 + 2 round is the most expensive enlargement round to date.

Financial preparations for enlargement may be said to have been ongoing almost since the collapse of communism in CEECs in 1989–90. Although the first membership applications by CEECs were not made until 1994, the financial assistance the EU was providing to CEECs from the very early 1990s (see Chapter 3) was made at least partly with a view to their eventual membership. As part of the preparations for enlargement, the EU has used several financial and legal instruments to help candidate states during the pre-accession period. From first being launched, these instruments became progressively more attuned to the needs of applicant states. So, for example, in 2000, pre-accession aid was both doubled in size and two new instruments for providing support and financial aid were added to the existing Programme of Community Aid for Central and Eastern European Countries (PHARE), which was being used primarily for targeting institution building and investment support. The first new instrument was the Instrument for Structural Policies for Pre-Accession (ISPA), which was to support infrastructure investments, and the second was the Standard Accession Programme (SAPARD), which was to help agriculture and rural development. In the EU-25, rural development programmes will replace SAPARD for 2004–2006.

The bases of the main financial framework for enlargement were laid down in the Commission's 1997 *Agenda 2000* document (European Commission, 1997), the thrust of which was adopted, with some revisions, at the March 1999 Berlin European Council meeting. This Berlin financial framework for 2000–2006, which was based on the assumption that six new members would accede in 2002, allocated €21.84 billion to help these countries prepare for accession, and €58.07 billion in payment appropriations for five years starting in 2002 to help meet the costs of enlargement after accession (European Commission, 2002d: 20–21). These sums represent between 16 and 22 per cent of the EU's annual budget (depending on the year). The allocations were subsequently revised and updated at the 2002 Copenhagen summit, both to take account of inflation and, more importantly, the now known fact that 10 states would be joining the EU in 2004 and Bulgaria and Romania would probably be joining in 2007. Table 12.1 places 2004–2006 enlargement costs in the context of the whole financial perspective. Particular points to note in Table 12.1 are:

- CAP expenditures for the period do not significantly increase, despite the addition of 10 less-developed countries, some of which have relatively large agricultural sectors. This is because payments to CEEC farmers are to be phased-in only gradually (see below). Despite extensive debates and negotiations on the matter in the early 2000s, a fundamental reform of the CAP was avoided in the years prior to the 2004 enlargement. However, in June 2003 farm ministers did approve significant reforms, including allocating increased funding for rural development (see below).
- The greater amounts designated for structural actions. These are composed of the Structural Funds – of which the most important are the European Regional Development Fund and the European Social Fund – and the Cohesion Fund. These funds have as their main purpose the promotion of economic activity and social cohesion in less-favoured areas of the EU. They are considered later in the chapter.
- The increased spending on internal policies. These include research, the environment, and energy.
- The category Pre-Accession Strategy designates aid for Romania and Bulgaria, and also for Turkey if it becomes a candidate country during the 2004–2006 period.

Table 12.1   *Financial perspective (EU-25): 2003–06*

Commitment Appropriations	2003	2004	2005	2006
Agriculture	47,378	49,305	50,431	50,575
CAP	42,680	42,769	43,724	43,735
Rural Development	4,698	6,536	6,707	6,840
Structural actions	33,968	41,035	41,685	42,932
Structural Funds	31,129	35,353	36,517	37,028
Cohesion Fund	2,839	5,682	5,168	5,904
Internal policies	6,796	8,722	8,967	9,093
External actions	4,972	5,082	5,093	5,104
Administration	5,211	5,983	6,154	6,325
Reserves	434	442	442	442
Monetary Reserve	0	0	0	0
Emergency Aid Reserve	217	221	221	221
Guarantee Reserve	217	221	221	221
Pre-accession strategy	3,386	3,455	3,455	3,455
Agriculture	564			
Pre-Accession Structural	1,129			
PHARE (applicants)	1,693			
Compensation		1,410	1,299	1,041
Total appropriations for Commitments	102,145	115,434	117,526	118,967
Total appropriations for payments	102,767	111,380	112,260	114,740
Ceiling as % of Gross National Income	1.09%	1.08%	1.06%	1.06%
Margin unforeseen expenditure	0.15%	0.16%	0.18%	0.18%
Own Resources Ceiling	1.24%	1.24%	1.24%	1.24%

Source: The European Commission (2003l).
Note: Figures are in € millions and are at 2004 prices.

Table 12.2 shows the total commitment appropriations for 2004–2006 agreed at the December 2002 Copenhagen Summit for each individual new member state. The appropriations do not include upward adjustments made in April 2003 for internal policies and in the Schengen and nuclear safety categories to tackle specific problems.

Table 12.2 *EU financial assistance for the new member states – total commitment appropriations 2004-2006*

	Cyprus	Czech Republic	Estonia	Hungary	Poland	Slovenia	Lithuania	Latvia	Slovakia	Malta	Totals
Agriculture											
The CAP											4,682
Rural development	66	482	134	534	2543	250	434	291	352	24	5,110
Structural actions	101	2328	618	2847	11369	405	1366	1036	1560	79	21,746*
Internal policies											4,256
Of which:											
Existing								:			2,642
Institution building											380
Schengen	0	0	69	148	280	107	136	71	48	0	858
Nuclear safety	0	0	0	0	0	0	285	0	90	0	375
Administration											1,673
Special cash flow	38	358	22	211	1443	101	47	26	86	66	2,398
Temporary budget compensation	300	389	0	0	0	131	0	0	0	166	987
Total commitments											40,852

Source: European Council (2002c).

Notes: Figures are in €millions at 1999 prices. The amounts are fixed for the Schengen facility, nuclear safety, the special cash-flow facility and temporary budgetary compensation. The amounts for structural actions and rural development are indicative. The allocations by country cannot be definitely fixed in advance for the CAP, existing internal policies, and institution building.

* Includes €38m of non-allocated technical assistance.

Setting the Union's Budget: Process, Philosophy and Problems

Following a series of budget crises in the 1980s, EU member states and institutions agreed that improved budgetary planning and discipline were essential if political priorities were effectively to be pursued and implemented. In consequence, the EU began using multi-annual, inter-institutional frameworks for expenditures in the shape of financial perspectives. These perspectives, of which three have been agreed and applied up to the time of writing – 1988–1992, 1993–1999, and 2000–2006 – specify binding income and expenditure ceilings and divide expenditures into headings reflecting policy options and political priorities. In the 2000–2006 perspective, the main headings are agriculture, structural operations, internal policies, external action, administration, reserves and pre-accession aid. The EU's annual budgets, which are tightly framed within the perspectives, then determine the actual level of spending within and among the headings and under the ceilings. The multi-annual financial perspectives have been crucial in facilitating medium-term financial planning, and have also helped to smooth relations between the Council of Ministers (formerly Budget Ministers, now Ecofin Ministers) and the EP during the annual budgetary cycle.

Although it was not originally, and is still not legally, part of the budgetary process, the European Council has established a key budgetary role for itself: it lays down – but does not legally adopt – the key multi-annual financial perspectives, on the basis of preparatory work undertaken by the Commission and Ecofin (Dinan, 2000: 189). The European Council also agrees on any major revisions or updates to financial perspectives. So, for example, in December 2002, the Copenhagen summit updated the financial consequences of enlargement in an annex on budgetary and financial issues. In April 2003, the EP, the Council and the Commission formally amended and approved this three-year financing framework for an enlarged union with 2004 price adjustments, so that enlargement could become a reality.

The annual budgetary process begins with the Commission producing a preliminary draft (PDB) each spring for the following year. This draft is debated in Ecofin, amended, and approved by July. Because of the restrictions imposed by the financial perspectives, the amendments necessarily involve relatively small financial changes. The draft as approved by the Council then proceeds to the EP for a first reading where modifications to compulsory expenditure and amendments to non-compulsory expenditure are proposed. As in the Council, changes are necessarily relatively minor. There is then at least one more reading of the budget in both Ecofin and the EP before the annual budget is approved. Both the Council and the EP must approve the budget before it can enter into force. Since the

EU's budgetary year runs from January until December, the aim is to reach a final agreement by the time of the EP's December plenary meeting.

Over the years the EP has gained budgetary powers similar to many European legislatures. Within the restrictions imposed by the financial perspective and certain other limitations, the Council retains the last word on compulsory spending, whereas the EP is more influential on non-compulsory expenditure. The existence of the distinction between compulsory and non-compulsory spending is a constant source of irritation in the EP and a source of friction for budget planners.

The Commission is responsible for the overall implementation of the budget and for protecting EU money from waste or theft. However, in practice, the member states actually manage about 80 to 85 per cent of the 'front line' implementation of the budget, which inevitably makes it very difficult for the Commission to monitor all financial activities. Certainly, it is just not possible for it to eliminate all fraud when so much administrative power is devolved to the individual members

In August 2003, the Commission's, chief accountant, Marta Andreasen, and its chief internal auditor, Jules Muis, resigned, citing problems with the Commission's financial controls (Economist, 9 August, 2003: 44). One serious consequence of enlargement is that with more members, fraud will be harder to detect. Even in the EU-15, working through local implementation and law-enforcement agencies involved 'fragile controls' and, according to Muis, the EU was actually 'ripe' for scandals. It is a concern that the new member states have even less resources than the EU-15 to combat fraud and much weaker administrative and legal control systems and traditions to try and prevent it.

It must, however, be emphasized that notwithstanding control difficulties, the EU functions with considerable budgetary restraint. In the context of enlargement, this was demonstrated by the EU-15's insistence that many payments to the new member states be phased-in only gradually. This was partly for the purpose of easing the financial demands on the EU-15 themselves, but partly also to give the new members time to adjust their administrative systems to meet the demands of managing new funds. In this latter context, a major concern for enlargement is how well the political and administrative institutions of the new members will handle their co-management budgetary responsibilities.

Sources of Revenue for the Budget

The EU has four main sources of revenue, which are considered its 'own resources' (European Commission, 2002p). These are funds that belong to the Union but originate in the member states. The funds are: tariffs on industrial imports imported from outside the EU; levies on agricultural products imported from outside the EU; 1.4 per cent of the base used for calculating value added tax (VAT) in each member state; and a percent-age of the combined GNP of the member states. This last resource, which is the largest in volume terms, gives the EU some budgetary manoever-abilty since it does not depend on international trade or other uncontrol-lable economic revenue. The total size of the EU budget has been capped in the 1993–1999 and 2000–2006 financial perspectives at 1.27 per cent of the EU's GNP. A few spending areas – most notably the European Development Fund (EDF) – are not financed from the budget but rather from direct national contributions.

The accession of new member states increases the importance of the EU's own sources of revenue, both politically and economically. Though the new members are relatively poor, they must contribute to the financ-ing of EU expenditures from the first day of their membership (European Council, 2002c: 7). They have, however, been assured that they will not initially be net contributors to the budget. Their contributions can, of course, like those of EU-15 states, be offset by the receipt of funds received from the spending policies, though some new members appear to have unrealistic expectations concerning the financial benefits this will produce. One reason they are likely to be unrealistic is that taking full advantage of the budget requires national administrative structures that can meet rigid EU financial and budgetary requirements. In 2001 and 2002 there were EU budgetary surpluses of €15 billion and €7 billion respectively, brought about because EU-15 states were unable to use all their allocated money as designated and had to return leftover funds to the EU (European Parliament, 2003b: 4). Such surpluses are expected to grow as new members with less-developed administrative structures join the Union.

Expenditure Commitments: Realities and Goals

EU spending is, as was noted above, divided into compulsory and non-compulsory expenditure, each of which accounts for around 50 per cent of total expenditure. Compulsory spending is spending that is designated in the Treaties and is dominated by the CAP. Non-compulsory spending is dominated by cohesion policy. Issues associated with these two main areas of spending – agriculture and cohesion – are considered in the two sub-sections below.

Another spending area meriting comment here is the administrative costs of the EU, which is part of compulsory expenditure and which accounted for 5.2 per cent of the 2002 budget. In the preliminary budget for 2004 provision was made by the Commission for an additional 244 posts for the language service (the acceding states will increase the number of official EU languages by nine), plus 536 posts to help imple-ment the *acquis* and manage structural programmes in the acceding states. These proposals became the subject of considerable attention and debate, even though the absolute costs involved were small in relative terms. That they did attract such attention and debate is indicative both of how niggardly the EU-15 have been in respect of overall EU spending and how politically sensitive budgetary matters can be.

The Common Agricultural Policy

The EU's largest and most controversial expenditure is the CAP. It is sometimes presented as having been unchanged over the years and as being rooted in an era when circumstances were quite different – with large numbers of almost self-sufficient farmers across Europe and with production surpluses largely unknown. This picture is, in fact, misleading, for the CAP has been much reformed, not least because of pressures from the EU's trading partners in GATT and now the WTO. Following reforms initiated in 1992, CAP spending declined from over 60 per cent of the budget to the 48.55 per cent approved for 2003 (Gower, 2002:168). However, in the context of the 10 + 2 round, concern about the EU's ability to finance the costs of supporting the many underdeveloped farms of the candidate countries led Franz Fischler, the Agricultural Commissioner, to propose additional CAP reforms in July 2002, designed to move the CAP away from subsidies and towards a system less focused on increasing output levels and more focused on supporting objectives of concern to European citizens such as the protection of the environment and food quality standards (Poole, 2003:110). The proposed reforms included three key modifications: 'decoupling' direct subsidies from production levels; reducing direct price support for farmers; and orienting to the market by lowering the intervention price to support farmers (*Le Soir*, Brussels, 23 January, 2003).

In October 2002, France and Germany, the two most important countries in respect of CAP reform in the EU-15, negotiated an agreement to keep the CAP relatively unchanged until 2006 and for support to the new members then to be phased-in over 10 years. This phase-in period would reduce the amount of support the candidate countries would receive, but it would mean there would be less demands on the EU budget and it would also pressurize the new member states to modernize their agricultural sectors. Before signing the December 2002 Accession Accords, the applicant states, particularly Poland, sought to improve the agricultural terms they were being offered following the Franco–German 'deal', which led to a compromise in which the phase-in timetable was advanced and additional resources were made available. Direct aid would now be phased-in more rapidly with, in the initial period, new members receiving 25 per cent of the full EU rate in 2004, rising to 30 per cent in 2005 and 35 per cent in 2006. This level could also be 'topped up' domestically by between 30 per cent and 55 per cent in 2004, 60 per cent in 2005 and 65 per cent in 2006.

Following extensive discussions and negotiations throughout the spring of 2003 involving the Commission and Agriculture Ministers, the Agriculture Council agreed in June to further, and more fundamental, CAP reforms. These were based on the Commission's earlier 2002 ideas (EU News Release, 26 June 2003: 1–2). Key elements of the reforms include: a single farm payment for EU farmers, independent of production; a reduction in direct payments for bigger farms to help finance rural development policy; and a much higher priority than hitherto to be given to such issues as food safety, the environment, rural development, and animal welfare. The reforms will alter the CAP system significantly, most especially because the majority of subsidies will not be tied to the volume of production. Coupled with earlier reforms and ceilings, the CAP should look quite different in a few years. Furthermore, the proportion of the budget directed toward agriculture should decrease, which in turn should allow the budget's role as a political instrument and policy tool to increase.

Cohesion policy and the Structural and Cohesion Funds

Cohesion policy seeks to reduce social and economic disparities between the richest and poorest regions by redistributing financial resources. It is at the core of the EU's aim for equitable development and is the next highest spending category after agriculture. Although the idea of members' parity was envisioned by the foundation members of the EC, and policies and funds designed to promote greater parity were developed over the years, the term 'cohesion' was first formally used in the 1986 Single European Act (SEA). It was so particularly with reference to assisting the poorest member states to 'catch up' with the others, but it has come to be also used in a more general sense to refer to the wide range of not only national but also regional and social inequalities that exist in the EU.

To encourage cohesion in the growing Community, four re-distributive funds, known as the Structural Funds, exist for the purpose of furthering cohesion. These are the European Regional Development Fund (ERDF), the European Social Fund (ESF), the European Agricultural Guidance and Guarantee Fund (EAGGF) and the Financial Instrument for Fisheries Guidance (FIFG). There is also a Cohesion Fund, which was created for the development of infrastructure in the EU-15's four poorest member states – Greece, Ireland, Portugal and Spain. While the Cohesion Fund is used for structural programmes, it is not one of the EU's Structural Funds.

Structural Funds are funneled into three objective areas. Most of the

EU's structural operations are spent on Objective One, which is designed to help regions whose development is lagging behind other EU regions. Objective 2 supports economic and social conversion of urban and rural areas facing structural problems. Objective 3 helps modernize training systems and promotes employment (European Commission, 2002q).

In advance of the 2004 enlargement, there was considerable debate amongst the EU-15 about the future of the cohesion funds – a debate that was fuelled not only by the expense of the funds and different views on their future distribution, but also growing evidence that they do not sufficiently reduce the economic differences among EU countries (Dinan, 2000: 50). Certain decisions were made, including that Structural Fund allocations to new member states would be capped at 4 per cent of national GDP, but major policy reform was postponed until after enlargement occurred. When the reform debate does get underway, fierce political battles can be anticipated, not least because major decisions about the size and distribution of the Structural Funds can be made only by the member states acting on the basis of unanimity.

Conclusions

Enlargement has created both problems and opportunities for the EU's budget and spending policies. The main problem has been that the addition of new member states has placed greater strains on the budget. Each of the new member states has its own distinct funding needs – needs that each has sought, and will continue to seek, to have at least partially alleviated by financial assistance from the EU. These needs have produced considerable pressures both for the overall size of the budgetary cake to be increased and also for many individual slices to be larger than resources permit.

Budgetary problems have been exacerbated by attitudes amongst the EU-15 which, whilst recognizing the needs of the new member states, have wished to continue to receive themselves at least a constant level of EU funding from projects from which they benefit. But, at the same time, they have not wanted enlargement to increase their contributions to the budget, especially at a time when their own finances are strained.

The interplay between national and supranational interests and the strength of strong and entrenched groups in the EU-25 will continue to limit the amount of movement that can be realized in an already constrained budget. However, the new members will need aid for many years if they are to be successful, effective and efficient EU members. The scale of the challenge is exemplified by the case of Greece, which though a 1981 entrant was still receiving aid to the amount of 3.5 per cent of its GNP in the early 2000s (European Commission, 2002r: 1).

As for the budgetary-related opportunities presented by enlargement, the principal one has been to use enlargement to make overdue reforms. As yet, this opportunity has been only partly utilized, but there have been some developments, the most important of which has been the CAP reforms. The reforms to the CAP are, of course, also a consequence of international pressures, but the prospect of the number of EU farmers greatly increasing has also played a part in the reform programme that has at its heart the unlinking of direct subsidies from production levels.

In conclusion, it is clear there are many budgetary challenges ahead. Some are relatively routine, including ensuring that, with pressures on the budget increasing, budgetary ceilings continue to be respected. Others challenges, however, will be more demanding, not least ensuring that budgetary resources are sufficient to finance the full and proper integration of the new member states into the EU.

Chapter 13

Economic and Monetary Union

MICHELE CHANG*

Introduction

Enlargement brings the prospect of important changes to the economic
and political priorities of Economic and Monetary Union (EMU) and to
its decision-making structures. Countries that prefer price stability even
at the expense of growth dominated the construction of EU monetary
integration and their preferences formed the basis for the principles,
institutions and rules of EMU that were laid down in the 1990s.
However, political pressures have made the founding arrangement difficult to enforce strictly, and since the early 2000s there has been something of a political battle over the importance of price stability relative to
growth. The inclusion of the accession countries impacts on this battle,
on the institutional structure of EMU, and on the alliances that can be
formed to promote or block certain policies. Such alliances will be
formed based on the extent to which governments believe on the one
hand that national economies will benefit most from an emphasis on
stability and on the other believe a more flexible arrangement is necessary that will promote faster growth but that also might lead to higher
inflation levels. Decisions on these potentially competing preferences will
affect the efficiency of EMU, the credibility of its institutions, and the
ability of Europe to play a more active role in international monetary
relations.

This chapter covers key aspects of EMU, especially as they relate to
enlargement. A central focus of the chapter is the ways in which accession countries may alter the economic priorities, institutional design and
policy outcomes within an expanded monetary union. In this context, it
is emphasized that acceding states, especially CEEC's, may tip the
balance within EMU in favour of prioritizing growth even at the expense
of higher inflation.

* I would like to thank Neill Nugent and William Paterson for their support with
this project. Venelin Saltirov provided excellent research assistance.

Why Monetary Union? The Political Economy of Monetary Integration

European monetary integration initially was seen primarily as providing an opportunity for participating states to increase their influence both within the EU and internationally by creating a stable monetary environment in which trade and investment could thrive. It later took on the function of promoting price stability, which came to be viewed as the key to stable, long-term economic growth (Cukierman, 1992). EMU would build on the European Monetary System (EMS), while changing the focus of monetary policy towards European developments rather than German ones (Grieco, 1995).

In 1999, 11 states became founding members of monetary union, and Greece joined them to become the twelfth EMU member in 2001. Three states, however, did not become EMU members at the first opportunity, and have continued to remain outside. The UK government has chosen not to recommend EMU membership to the British people until five economic tests indicate that the British economy has converged sufficiently with the eurozone. In June 2003, the government announced that two of the tests, on sustainable convergence and on flexibility, had still not been met. Denmark held a referendum on EMU in September 2000, when 53 per cent of voters rejected membership. Sweden held a referendum in September 2003, when 56 per cent of voters said 'No'.

The accession countries were given no option in the accession negotiations but to accept that in due course, though not immediately on accession, they would enter EMU. This presented them with no great difficulties, for they are mostly eager to join. EMU membership is seen as providing substantial benefits, including reduced exchange rate risk, lower transaction costs and lower interest rates. They anticipate that EMU membership could boost trade, investment and growth, could make their economies less vulnerable to shocks, and will increase their influence in that they will be helping to decide European monetary policy via their participation in EMU bodies. The ratings agency Moodys already has increased the foreign currency ratings of the accession countries on the basis of the inevitability of EU expansion and monetary union (*Prague Business Journal*, 18 November 2002). (Ratings agencies predict the risk associated with investing in countries, and an improved rating can substantially increase investment flows into the country.)

But though new member states are required to join the eurozone, there is no agreement between eurozone countries, EU institutions and the accession countries over when that should be. The Maastricht Treaty established five criteria countries must meet to be eligible for EMU membership:

- A budget deficit of less than 3 per cent of GDP;
- Public debt to be under 60 per cent of GDP;
- The inflation rate to be within 1.5 per cent of the three EU countries with the lowest rate;
- Long-term interest rates to be within 2 per cent of the three lowest interest rates in the EU;
- The exchange rate to have been within 'normal' fluctuation margins of the ERM.

Despite their rapid progress in fulfilling the Maastricht convergence criteria, a debate has developed over the degree to which the accession countries have achieved 'nominal' versus 'real', convergence. Nominal convergence refers to formally achieving the convergence criteria, while real convergence refers to the institutional and legal restructuring of the economy in order to make it market-oriented and competitive, and the need to catch up with the more developed economies of the EU in regard to productivity and per capita levels (Eden *et al.*, 1999).

There is an apparent contradiction in the position of the EU-15 in that they have emphasized the importance of the convergence criteria yet have cautioned against rapid membership for new member states regardless of whether or not they have met the Maastricht criteria. However, the caution is understandable in that enlargement could have a potentially destabilizing impact on monetary union. The Euro-12 states became a part of monetary union because they believed that they could reap greater political and economic gains within an institutionalized EMU. But just a few years into EMU the system was already showing signs of strain due to dissent among the eurozone members regarding the extent to which price stability should be prioritized. Enlargement could exacerbate this trend further by bringing in a large number of countries that, once they are voting members of the EU and EMU, have the potential to disrupt the system further by tipping the balance of EU preferences away from those oriented towards stability and towards those that would prefer a more vigorous pursuit of economic growth.

The Political Structure of EMU

Three main bodies dominate the decision-making processes of EMU and monetary integration:

- *The European Council*, comprised of the Heads of State and Government of the EU, determines which countries may become members of monetary union. This is not a mechanistic process, as a considerable amount of discretion can be used given the wording of the Maastricht Treaty's convergence criteria that allow a country to become a member if the European Council determines that it has met or is approaching the economic criteria. For example, in 1999 both Italy and Belgium failed to fulfill all of the criteria but nevertheless gained admittance to EMU.

* *The European System of Central Banks* (ESCB), which consists of the European Central Bank (ECB) and the national central banks (NCBs) of the EU-15 states, manages monetary policy for the EMU. Decision-making is centralized in the Executive Board and the Governing Council of the ECB. The Executive Board comprises the President, Vice-President, and four other members who are appointed by the member states. The Governing Council comprises the Executive Board and the Euro-12 central bank governors and is the body that formulates monetary policy for the eurozone, including the setting of interest rates. There is also a General Council comprised of the Governing Council plus the non-eurozone central bank governors. The Council operates on a system of 'one country, one vote', though the President may cast two votes in the event of a tie. As is explained later in the chapter, new arrangements were agreed in 2003 for the composition of ESCB structures post-enlargement.

* *The Economic and Financial Council* (Ecofin), which is comprised of the Finance Ministers of all member states, monitors economic and financial developments in the EU and reports its findings to the European Council and the European Commission. In accordance with Articles 99 and 101 of the Treaty on European Union, it also issues recommendations to the European Council as part of multilateral surveillance of the member states and makes decisions according to the excessive deficits procedures (outlined below in the section on the Stability and Growth Pact).

In addition to these three bodies, two other groupings are also important in the EMU management structure. First, there is the Euro Group of EMU Finance Ministers. This was formed in 1999 in order to provide a political counterweight to the ECB, which it charged with lacking democratic accountability. Second, there is the Economic and Monetary Affairs Committee of the European Parliament. This also has tried to improve the ECB's democratic credentials – in its case by subjecting the President of the ECB to regular questioning and providing EP reports and recommendations to the ECB. Neither institution has, as yet, impinged on the independence of the ECB, nor have they made great headway in establishing themselves as alternative centres of authority. However, most EMU-12 states would like to see a greater role for the Euro Group and the Commission also supports a Eurozone Finance Council (*European Report*, 17 September 2003). It is quite possible that the 2003–2004 IGC will make such provision.

The Principles of EMU and the Effect of Enlargement: Price Stability and Monetary Influence

The two primary rationales for monetary union focus on price stability and increased influence in monetary policy-making. The second of these rationales is examined later in the chapter. This section of the chapter considers how the emphasis on controlling inflation has been codified in the independence of NCBs and the ECB, in the Maastricht Treaty's convergence criteria, and in the Stability and Growth Pact (SGP). It also considers how the member states have dealt with the price stability goal in the context of enlargement.

Central Bank independence

The Maastricht Treaty prioritized the pursuit of price stability, reflecting the interests of Germany and other stability-oriented states that had learned the importance of low inflation as an economic goal. This desire for price stability converged with the preference of most EU states for independent central banks – preferred because they were seen to provide governments with greater credibility and to make price stability easier to achieve. Thus, one of the conditions for EMU entry is making national central banks independent, which many of the accession countries have done (see Table 13.1).

Despite its formal independence, the ECB is not considered to be so independent and technocratic that the nationality of the central bankers is seen to be irrelevant. The nationality of the central bankers could be highly relevant if they have different policy preferences for the level of interest rates within their respective countries or within the eurozone. Enlargement threatens to bring just this situation about due to the Balassa–Samuelson effect – wherein rapidly growing countries experience higher structural inflation and therefore have a different optimal interest rate than more developed economies (Balassa, 1964; Samuelson, 1964, 1994).

Aware of the possibility that this could create major difficulties post-enlargement, the EU-15 used the Treaty of Nice to insert an enabling clause, Article 10.6, into the Statute of the ESCB/ECB, allowing the European Council to amend Article 10.2 of the Statute on voting rules within the ECB Governing Council. The following principles guided the original rotation system of the Governing Council: 'one member, one vote'; *ad personam* participation, in which all Governing Council members attended meetings and all votes cast by NCB Governors with voting rights were weighted equally; representativeness; transparency; and consistency (European Central Bank, 2003). This system was threatened to be overburdened and its decision-making character was seen to be under risk with the addition of new states. This was because increasing the

Table 13.1 *Exchange rate regimes and central bank*
independence of new member states

Country	Currency Exchange rate regime
Bulgaria	Lev Currency board (EUR)
Cyprus	Cyprus Pound Target zone (EUR), 15% fluctuation margin
Czech Republic	Koruna Managed float
Estonia	Kroon Currency board (EUR)
Hungary	Forint Target zone (EUR), 15% fluctuation margin
Latvia	Lats Peg (SDR), 1% fluctuation margin
Malta	Lira Peg (EUR, GBP, USD)
Lithuania	Litas Currency board (EUR)
Poland	Zloty Float
Romania	Leu Managed float
Slovakia	Koruna Managed float
Slovenia	Tolar Managed float

Source: National central banks.

number of participating NCBs could make it more difficult to reach a consensus and could, due to the one member, one vote principle, disproportionately increase the power of states with smaller economies.

In consequence, reform proposals were considered, in much the same way as they were for the composition and operation of the College of Commissioners. The ECB proposed a governing structure in which the number of NCB governors with voting rights is capped at 15. The system groups states according to economic size, progressively reducing the voting frequency of the NCB governors of the smaller states over time (all of the members of the group with the smallest voting frequency are enlargement countries, see Table 13.2). The stages of the reform process are conceived as follows:

Table 13.2 *Possible distributions of countries into ECB voting groups*

	Euro-28	Euro-25 (without, Bulgaria Romania and Turkey)	Euro-22 (Without UK, Sweden and Denmark))
Group 1	Germany UK France Italy Spain	Germany UK France Italy Spain	Germany France Italy Spain The Netherlands
Group 2	The Netherlands Belgium Sweden Austria Denmark Ireland Poland Portugal Turkey Greece Luxembourg Finland Czech Republic Hungary	The Netherlands Belgium Sweden Austria Denmark Ireland Poland Portugal Greece Luxembourg Finland Czech Republic Hungary	Belgium Austria Ireland Poland Portugal Greece Luxembourg Finland Czech Republic Hungary Slovak Republic
Group 3	Romania Slovak Republic Slovenia Bulgaria Lithuania Cyprus Latvia Estonia Malta	Slovak Republic Slovenia Lithuania Cyprus Latvia Estonia Malta	Slovenia Lithuania Cyprus Latvia Estonia Malta

Source: Gros 2003: 3.
*Based on 2002 data.

- *Stage 1*: Once the number of NCBs rises to between 15–18 members (at the discretion of the Governing Council), the governors will be allocated into two groups (based on the country's GDP and the size of its financial sector). Members of each group share voting rights; each NCB governor from the first group will have a voting frequency of 80 per cent, and the second group 85 per cent, assuming 13 members in this group (the 5 governors of the first group will share 4 voting rights, and the remaining governors will share 11).

- *Stage 2*: Once the number of governors reaches 22, the governors will be divided into 3 groups: the first group's NCB governors will have an 80 per cent voting frequency (sharing 4 voting rights); the second group (comprising half of the total number of governors) will have a voting frequency of 73 per cent (11 governors sharing 8 voting rights, assuming 22 total members); and the third group will have a voting frequency of 50 per cent (6 governors sharing 3 voting rights).

Table 13.2 forecasts the expected groups in each round. The composition of the groups will be adjusted over time according to changes in GDP, changes in financial sector size, and increases in the number of national central bank governors due to enlargement (European Central Bank, 2003). While the voting frequency of the NCB governors from larger countries remains stable at 80 per cent, those from the smaller economies will see their voting frequency diminish with enlargement. Once the number of governors reaches 27, for example, according to the ECB's recommendation the voting frequency of the first group will be 80 per cent, of the second group will be 57 per cent and of the third group will be 38 per cent.

The Commission issued a positive opinion of the ECB's revised rotation solution, though it criticized the lack of a population measure (European Commission, 2003d). The EP, however, issued a non-binding rejection, citing confusion over the rotation's frequency, the allocation of voting rights to governors within each group, the clarity and transparency *vis-à-vis* markets and the general public, and uncertainty over when the rotation system will begin (European Parliament, 2003a). Others have criticized the lack of appropriate regional representation and the failure to improve the efficiency of the ECB's decision-making process (Gros, 2003; Horn, 2003).

But the ECB defended the rotation system and its economic criteria. Bank of Luxembourg President and ECB Governing Council member Yves Mersch argued: 'The ECB is an economic and not a political body, [therefore] the use of the population criterion appeared . . . inappropriate . . . moreover, the financial criterion, in contrast to GDP or population, is not purely national, but reflects the effective contribution of the various central banks to the Eurosystem' (Mersch, 2003). A similar calculation hierarchy exists in the US Federal Reserve System: the Presidents of the New York and Chicago Federal Reserve Banks have permanent voting rights and a 50 per cent voting right in the Federal Open Market Committee (FOMC), recognizing their role as financial centres, compared to the 33 per cent voting rights for other regional governors. Nevertheless, while the rotation system may preserve the principle of 'one person, one vote', it clearly damages its spirit and will make it more difficult for smaller countries to voice national and regional concerns at the European and international level. Though a system based on 'one country, one vote' may be inefficient, changing it alters one of the central interests that many original eurozone states had in joining EMU: a seat at the bargaining table.

The Council accepted the ECB's proposal in March 2003, and it will come into effect in May 2004.

*　　*　　*

Before the accession countries earn their seat at the ECB bargaining table, they must first be accepted into EMU. This will not happen until they fulfill the convergence criteria and convince their European partners that they are ready for monetary union. The following section considers the Maastricht criteria and the extent to which they are appropriate measures of monetary integration. Although the accession countries fulfill many of the criteria even better than existing eurozone countries did at similar stages, monetary union may still be a fundamentally different enterprise for them than it was for the Euro-12, due to different levels of economic and financial development.

The Maastricht convergence criteria

During EMU negotiations in the 1990s, a major concern – especially in Germany – was how to guard against inflation creeping into the European economy by allowing less inflation-averse countries to enter EMU. Accordingly, the Maastricht Treaty specified stringent economic criteria for entry into EMU, designed to ensure exchange rate stability and the convergence of inflation rates, interest rates, debt levels and deficit levels. Flexible interpretation of these criteria meant that although Belgium, Italy and Greece failed to meet the criterion on debt, they gained admission to EMU.

Much has been made of the economic differences between the economies of the accession countries versus the EU-15. But some have argued that the differences are either short-term or relatively insignificant in regard to the functioning of EMU. The accession countries are well positioned for meeting the convergence criteria (see Table 13.3), and some have even argued that several of them satisfy the criteria for an optimum currency area at least as well as most EMU participants. Moreover, the economic impact of the accession countries would be so small as to make it difficult in theory for them to affect monetary conditions in the eurozone: the GDP of the 10 accession countries will be one-fifteenth of the euro area, their financial sectors are small, and their combined monetary aggregates amount to just slightly more than 8 per cent of the euro

Table 13.3   *EMU convergences of acceding CEECs**

	Inflation %	Interest rates 10 year	Fiscal deficit as % of GDP	Public debt as % of GDP
Reference value	3.0	5.5	−3.0	60.0
Czech Republic	1.8	3.8	−6.8	29.9
Estonia	3.6	2.8	1.2	5.2
Hungary	5.3	8.0	−9.3	49.2
Latvia	1.8	7.4	−2.5	14.6
Lithuania	0.3	6.4	−1.2	27.0
Poland	1.9	6.6	−5.1	46.1
Slovakia	3.3	5.0	−1.5	44.3
Slovenia	7.5	5.1	−1.0	30.5

Source: Deutsche Bank, *EU Monitor*: 11 (6 January 2004: 25).
* Based on 2002 data.

aggregate. In any event the accession countries will be affected by monetary policy decisions over which they may not have much control, even post-EMU, thus forcing a large number of citizens to live under inappropriate monetary conditions, which in turn might threaten public support for EMU (Maier and Hendrikx, 2003).

The European Banking Federation is amongst those voicing concern over a too-rapid integration of the accession countries into monetary union, pointing to the still-divergent business cycles between accession and eurozone countries, and noting that the transitional nature of the accession countries' economies makes the relinquishing of the exchange rate as an adjustment tool costly. It could force countries to endure a 'more painful and longer adjustment process . . . nominal convergence 'a la Maastricht' may not be the best way to achieve real growth and real convergence' (*European Report*, February 6, 2002). Enlargement Commissioner, Günter Verheugen, has also warned that 'the future member states are well advised to take the time necessary and not rush the process . . . joining prematurely risks being negative both for the new member states and for monetary union.' (*Enlargement Weekly*, March 11, 2003). Bundesbank Council member Franz-Christoph Zeitler has taken this position even further and argued that the accession countries should be subject to additional criteria before admission to EMU (*Wall Street Journal*, July 31, 2000). Such warnings run counter to the preferences expressed by representatives of some of the accession countries for a rapid transition: Estonia, Latvia and Slovenia were amongst those expressing an interest in EMU membership well before the conclusion of the accession negotiations.

Pursuit of the convergence criteria could actually damage the economies of acceding states and be politically difficult. The accession countries not only need to deal with structural problems in social security, health care and education, they also need to invest in infrastructure and the environment. Governments may be tempted to delay or minimize these costly but necessary investments so as to keep down government expenditures and thus achieve the convergence criteria, which ultimately would harm their economies. Such pursuit of the criteria could lead to social unrest and decreased public support for European integration (Backé, 1999). The relatively under-developed and fragile financial sectors of the accession countries' economies also could become more vulnerable, due to the large capital inflows expected after accession.

Despite the precedent of the flexible interpretation of meeting the convergence criteria on the part of EU-12 EMU members, the debate over the importance of nominal versus real convergence indicates that rapid membership for the accession countries should not be a priority. Additional reform, including on the fiscal front, is necessary, not least to ensure the countries fulfill the Maastricht criteria and also that, post-EMU membership, they do not infringe the SGP – which was designed to ensure that countries' commitment to price stability does not falter after they enter the eurozone.

The Stability and Growth Pact

The Stability and Growth Pact was devised to ensure that once monetary union was established, states would not lose their fiscal discipline and threaten price stability. Under the terms of the Pact, if a country's budget deficit exceeds 3 per cent of GDP for three consecutive years it can be subject to heavy fines. A majority vote of Finance Ministers determines whether or not such fines are levied.

The demands of the SGP soon created difficulties for some eurozone states. In early 2002, Germany successfully lobbied to avoid a Council warning, though Portugal was not so lucky. Such differential treatment led to accusations by the Netherlands, Spain and Finland that different rules existed for larger members (*Financial Times*, 8 October 2002). This criticism intensified when the French Finance Minister, François Mer, responded to criticisms of his government's growing deficit by noting that the French government had 'other priorities than abiding by the Pact' (*Financial Times*, 10 October 2002). In January 2003, the Finance Ministers issued a formal warning to France that it was in danger of breaching the SGP, and in May 2003 the Commission advised that the Council should conclude that France had excessive deficits and should be required to end this situation by 2004 at the latest, with necessary measures to be taken before 3 October 2003. The issue 'tore apart' the Euro Group, which was divided on how stringently the SGP rules should be applied (*Financial Times*, 16 July 2003). Despite their breaches of the SGP for 2003, both Chancellor Schröder and French President Chirac assured their long-term commitment to the Pact, though Schröder noted 'a temporarily higher deficit' would be preferable to following rules 'that cripple any recovery tendencies' (*Irish Times*, 19 September 2003). But tension continued, and in January 2004 the Commission initiated legal proceedings against the EU's Finance Ministers for failing to sanction France and Germany's violations of the Pact (*Financial Times*, 15 January 2004).

Though the EU has been criticized for both flexible interpretations of the Maastricht criteria and for the reluctance of Finance Ministers to punish large state transgressors of the Pact, efforts have been made towards rectifying some of the unnecessary rigidities of the SGP. In 2002, the Commission announced plans to reform the Pact by allowing countries with sound finances greater flexibility in running modest deficits (thus emphasizing debt as well as deficits) (*Financial Times*, 28 November 2002). However, shortly after the Commission proposal was announced, several countries – including Belgium, Denmark, Spain, the Netherlands, Italy, Finland and Greece – expressed reservations with the plan, mainly on the grounds that it could have inflationary consequences and erode market credibility. As a result, the Finance Ministers watered down the proposal, only agreeing to take into account a country's circumstances and its long-term economic health when determining whether or not to impose fines (*AFX European Focus*, 7 March 2003).

Given this background, the new member states are likely to find allies among EMU-12 states in any effort to loosen restrictions that hinder growth. Important EU actors have openly criticized the Pact and attempted reform. In late 2002 alone: European Commission President, Romano Prodi, derided the Pact as 'stupid' (*Le Monde*, 17 October 2002); Portuguese President, Jorge Sampaio, declared it should be changed (*The Economist*, 22 October 2002); Italy's Deputy Prime Minister, Gianfranco Fini, characterized Prodi's criticism of the Pact as 'courageous' (*ibid.*); and the chief economist of the OECD, Jean-Philippe Cotis, remarked that the rules of the Stability Pact 'haven't worked' (*EUobserver*, 11 November 2002).

However, despite economic difficulties, important policy practitioners have remained steadfast in their support of the SGP: Belgian Prime Minister, Guy Verhofstadt, has called the Pact 'our bible' (*The Economist*, 26 October 2002); Spanish Prime Minister, Jose Maria Aznar, has argued against reform of the SGP: 'Economic cycles will always exist, and it is up to governments to take responsibility and prepare for economic downturns when times are good' (*El Pais*, 25 October 2002); Austrian Chancellor, Wolfgang Schuessel, has reasoned that 'it would be crazy to break the promise that we gave when we introduced the euro' (*BBC Monitoring*, 20 October 2002); and Danish Prime

Minister, Anders Fogh Rasmussen, has announced that he 'stand(s) by the Pact, and [has] no intention to change anything.' (*ibid.*)

Recent attempts at making the SGP more growth oriented may have failed, but the inclusion of Finance Ministers from faster-growing economies among those eligible to vote on such matters could alter this in the future. The Pact was designed with mature, high-income economies in mind. The expected growth of the accession economies could also result in inflationary pressure that would threaten compliance with the SGP. As noted above, the Balassa–Samuelson effect posits that poor but rapidly growing economies experience higher structural inflation, creating a tension between the simultaneous pursuit of inflation and exchange rate stability (De Grauwe and Lavrac 1999; Natalucci and Ravenna, 2002). The growth in the accession countries would not be due to monetary or fiscal laxity, the kind that the Pact was intended to punish, but would stem from the 'natural' rapid growth of less mature economies, which is likely to intensify as a result of EU and EMU membership. More generally, inflation resulting from increased productivity and a high growth rate can be viewed as a sign of success and not something to be reprimanded, as the Irish government complained in 2001 when it found itself the object of Council recommendations to change its fiscal policy in order to dampen its inflation. The wisdom of this reprimand was widely questioned, and served to promote debate on the reform of the SGP and on the economic priorities of the Euro-12 – which have diverged since the inception of EMU.

The SGP Pact is unquestionably poorly adapted for CEECs given that they have debt levels considerably lower than the eurozone average and, like Ireland, will likely experience higher growth and more inflationary pressure. These factors, combined with their rising GDP and need to keep interest rates aligned with the eurozone while maintaining a balanced budget and reducing debt, make the SGP ill-suited for an expanded EMU (*Banque Paribas Conjoncture,* 30 April 2003). While the CEECs themselves will comprise just a fraction of the EU's total output, and their economies can be expected to have a minimal impact on policy-making for the eurozone as a whole, they could conceivably ally not only with other faster-growing economies in the EU, like Ireland, Spain and Greece, but also with countries like France and Italy that may also prefer a looser interpretation of the terms of the SGP. Accession countries have already complained about the stringency of the SGP and even offered their own solutions. For example, Gyorgy Surany, former governor of Hungary's Central Bank, has insisted that Hungary would experience higher growth within a less rigid fiscal structure. (*The Economist,* 7 December 2002). Polish Finance Minister, Grzegorz Kolodko, has proposed loosening the fiscal rules by applying the budgetary rules to the aggregate deficit in the eurozone, rather than to each country (*The Economist,* 7 December 2002).

European monetary integration needs built-in flexibility in order to deal with both expected and unexpected occurrences. The remarkably smooth beginning of one of the biggest monetary experiments in history should not be discounted as EMU faces criticism from those who would prefer greater certainty and clarity in the application of rules. The flexibility of interpretation should be viewed as a source of strength rather than a weakness, for flexibility has been crucial in allowing national economies to come together under a single currency and cement European cooperation. Just as economic circumstances and priorities have shifted since the early 1990s, so will they continue to do so; a durable EMU needs to be able to accommodate such developments. The tweaking of the interpretation of both the convergence criteria and the SGP indicate the resilience of EMU, a trait that is likely to continue as it expands to incorporate countries even more diverse than its current members.

Prospects for European and International Influence and Leadership

In addition to monetary stability and economic growth, EMU promised most participants the chance to exercise a greater amount of influence on the European and the international monetary stage. Whether this will occur post-enlargement is questionable given the aforementioned reforms of voting in the ECB which will result in the accession countries facing an increasingly hierarchical environment within EMU. Nonetheless, most acceding states do want early EMU membership, in order both to promote economic stability and growth and to avoid losing influence within the EU and becoming peripheral members.

Moves have already been made to further separate Euro-12 from the EU-15 countries. In May 2003, the Euro Group submitted a proposal to the Convention on the Future of Europe that would formally recognize the Group and give it sole voting rights over a larger list of areas (*Financial Times*, 13 May 2003). The Convention's resulting draft constitution proposed that the Euro Group become a legal entity with the sole authority to enforce fiscal rules (Article III-88). EMU could thus easily turn into a formal two-tiered system of those in the eurozone and those outside. The latter would include all of the accession countries (as well as larger economies like the UK) and would be greatly affected by decisions made within the eurozone, but would lack a voice in deliberations.

In addition to greater influence within Europe, EMU promised countries the prospect of having more control over international monetary matters. This has not yet materialized. The US continues to act as the focal point for international economic coordination, and Europe has been too preoccupied with internal developments to assume some of the burdens of leadership *(The Economist,* 26 November 2002). This was especially true during economic crises in emerging markets in Asia, Latin America and Russia during the late 1990s when the European countries played a marginal role in the crisis management. Though these crises occurred prior to monetary union, the long-term nature of European monetary cooperation and the certainty of monetary union beginning in 1999 at the latest could have enabled the EU to act more cohesively. Instead, however, the US took the lead in most international negotiations, and larger EU states such as Britain and Germany represented national rather than EU interests.

Will a larger eurozone area necessarily translate into greater international power and influence for the euro? This will depend largely on the extent to which the member states can act as a unit and not be divided by diverging preferences. Enlargement clearly will have a major impact on this, with new competing interests added to those already existing amongst the EMU-12. Delay of necessary reforms, public acrimony and the inevitable efforts to woo market and public opinion in favour of one solution versus another could undermine the ECB's credibility at a time when the euro system already faces criticism for not speaking with one voice (McNamara and Meunier, 2002).

Conclusions

Enlargement has many important implications for the future of EMU. On the one hand, most, if not all, of the new member states are likely to quickly meet the convergence criteria set out by the Maastricht Treaty. As such, it will be politically difficult to refuse them membership, even if they have not yet achieved real economic convergence. On the other hand, the lack of real convergence could become problematic if it means that the new member states have different economic interests than the EMU-12. They could alter existing tendencies towards price stability by aligning with other countries experiencing stronger growth. Their admission could also lead to gridlock and impede the development of the eurozone as a leader in international monetary affairs.

The successful incorporation of new members into EMU will determine not only the success of EMU itself, but also will impact greatly on the future of European integration as a whole and the extent to which it can continue to serve as an instrument of economic growth, democratic development and international cooperation.

Chapter 14

Justice and Home Affairs

JOHN D. OCCHIPINTI

The 10 + 2 enlargement round has had, and for the foreseeable future will continue to have, a very considerable impact on the policy sphere of justice and home affairs (JHA). This chapter examines this impact. After introducing JHA, the chapter demonstrates how enlargement has influenced JHA since its creation by the Maastricht Treaty as the third pillar of the European Union. This is followed by an examination of the implications of enlargement for the Union's emerging institutional and legal infrastructure of crime fighting. The chapter concludes with a brief consideration of how the 2003–2004 Intergovernmental Conference will shape JHA in an enlarged EU.

The Challenge of Enlargement to JHA

The addition of the 10 + 2 states has always threatened the internal security of the EU. This is because of the nature of transnational organized crime in Europe, the prospect of an enlarged free-travel area, the status of several former and current candidate states as sources of, or transit-countries for, transnational crime, and the planned shift of responsibility for the EU's external border security to many of these countries. It has also resulted from the challenge of coordinating and sharing information among a greater variety of crime-fighting agencies, as well as the need to overcome differences among contending criminal codes in more states.

The member countries of the EU have tried to deal collectively with the problem of transnational organized crime since the 1970s. Initially, this was attempted wholly intergovernmentally and outside the framework of the Community treaties – principally via the so-called Trevi Group, which was formed in 1975. At the time, the main concerns focused on terrorism and drug trafficking – both crimes with significant cross-border dimensions and with sources based inside and outside EC countries.

But despite their concerns about transnational crime, a number of EC members established the objective of a Europe without borders. The goal of removing the *physical* checks at international boundaries stemmed from growing concerns that increased commercial trade in Europe was both clogging many border crossings but was also being hindered by that clogging. The agreement signed at Schengen, in Luxembourg, in 1985 by the Benelux states, France, and Germany was followed by a detailed Implementation Convention in 1990 (ultimately adopted by Norway, Iceland and all EU states aside from Ireland and the UK), aimed not only at removing inspections at borders, but also providing police with greater means to fight cross-border crime and helping the contracting states to create a common external border to better deal with the growing problem of illegal immigration in its various forms. At the same time that this idea for the Schengen free- travel zone was developed, the EC formally embraced the notion of 'free movement,' which was embodied in the 1986 Single European Act (SEA) and set the Community on a course to remove *technical* barriers to the free movement of goods, services, people and capital.

Of course, it was recognized that opening the borders among EC members would exacerbate the problem of transnational crime. Thus, the Schengen agreement and the SEA helped provide the impetus for the creation of the third – JHA – pillar in the new European Union that was created by the Maastricht Treaty. Among the Treaty's provisions on fighting crime was a prescription to establish a European Police Office, known as 'Europol', which was intended to be a kind of liaison network for national law enforcement authorities. However, as the original third pillar limited the role of the Commission and largely restricted authority to the intergovernmental Council in which individual member states had a potential veto over decisions, progress on JHA was quite slow.

Meanwhile, in the immediate aftermath of the Cold War, illegal immigration and the related problem of the trafficking of human beings joined terrorism and drug trafficking as major cross-border crimes impacting on the internal security of member states. These and other forms of transnational crime have become problematic for the EU mainly because organized crime groups find it much easier than national law enforcement authorities to operate across national boundaries.

For example, the provisions of the Single European Market (SEM) for the free movement of capital have facilitated the transfer and laundering of criminal revenues. Along with this, the implementation and gradual expansion of the Schengen free-travel area after 1995 allowed people and goods to cross national borders without any physical barriers to impede them, further easing the ability of organized crime groups to operate transnationally. In contrast, law enforcement authorities have faced many barriers preventing their ability to do the same. Schengen rules allow hot pursuit or maintaining surveillance by police across national boundaries by land, but not by sea, air, or rail. In practice, police operating on foreign soil under Schengen rules must obtain assistance from local authorities as they may detain, but not arrest, suspects. Another limitation has been the existence of different criminal codes across the EU, inhibiting the ability of policing agencies to agree on when and how to cooperate. Consequently, with criminal organizations operating in several countries simultaneously, the Union has explored ways to help national law enforcement authorities to coordinate investigations and share best practices for crime fighting.

In this context, it became clear that several prospective EU members had become important source- or transit-countries for a wide variety of transnational crimes, involving criminal organizations. These organizations would more easily be able to extend their activities into the rest of the EU post-enlargement. This was especially disturbing given that the criminal justice institutions in many of the candidate states were relatively weak, which inhibited their ability to fight crime and control their borders effectively. This was particularly problematic given the likelihood that these countries would one day join the Schengen zone, when they would then share responsibility for the EU's external border security.

Thus, as enlargement to CEECs increasingly loomed from the mid-1990s, it was assumed that their membership would only add to the EU's existing problem of dealing with shared borders. In addition, the admission of new member states promised to exacerbate the difficulty of coordinating the activities of policing, intelligence and border security agencies. Likewise, enlargement was expected to complicate the Union's efforts to resolve differences among its members' criminal codes.

The Impact of the Amsterdam Treaty

The challenges of EU enlargement for its internal security helped shape the 1997 Treaty of Amsterdam's modifications to JHA. The prospect of adding new members and expanding the Schengen free-travel area contributed to new resolve among the EU-15 to cooperate more effectively on JHA. This was necessary not just to strengthen the EU's internal security mechanisms, but also to make as much progress as possible before the addition of new member states made decision-making more problematic. Although this was true of virtually every area of EU policy, the need to make progress ahead of EU widening was especially true for the third pillar given that it remained relatively underdeveloped, especially before 1999.

The increasingly evident crime problem in Western Europe was exacerbated by concerns over the post-Cold War refugee problem in the EU and came at a time of economic recession for most member states. For European leaders, strengthening cooperation on JHA offered a new way to fight crime, as well as a means of placating publics that demanded that something should be done. By the mid-1990s, the CEECs seemed on the path to eventual EU accession, but their criminal justice institutions had proved unable to deal with rising crime which was, by then, impacting on Western Europe as well. During this time, the EU also experienced a refugee crisis stemming from the ethnic conflict in the Western Balkans, followed, in 1995, by the creation of the Schengen free-travel zone for the original five signatories, plus Spain and Portugal. In sum, the external phenomena of enlargement pressure and crime stemming from the CEECs, combined with the functional spillover from cooperation on free movement, provided added impetus for the EU to increase its cooperative efforts on JHA (Occhipinti 2003).

By the time of the 1996–9797 IGC, these pressures had contributed to a desire to reform the third pillar. Although the modifications contained in the Amsterdam Treaty fell short of expectations, the changes made were nonetheless significant. The new treaty established the goal of a creating an 'Area of Freedom, Security, and Justice' (AFSJ) and entailed a number of amendments to the TEU to bring this about. First, the entire Schengen *acquis* was brought into the TEU, with the provision that it would not apply to the UK or Ireland unless they chose to opt-in at a later date. Given that a free-travel area already existed among the five Nordic states, special provisions were also included to allow the participation of the two non-EU members in the Schengen zone, namely Iceland and Norway.

Second, the Amsterdam Treaty established the goal of transferring all free movement-related aspects of the third pillar to the first pillar by mid-2004, including the Schengen *acquis*, visas, immigration and asylum policy. This eventual 'communautarization' of policy-making on these matters would entail the power of co-decision for the EP, qualified majority voting (QMV) in the Council of Ministers, and the sole right to initiate legislative proposals for the Commission. In addition, the EU's JHA pillar – Title VI of the TEU – was renamed, 'Provisions on Police and Judicial Cooperation in Criminal Matters', having been stripped of its articles relating to free movement. Title VI bestowed the right of initiative on the Commission, but it was obliged to share these powers with individual member states. The Council continued to vote by unanimity on Police and Judicial Cooperation but was permitted to decide upon implementation measures for this using QMV. The EP was granted the right of consultation, meaning that the Council must at least wait for Parliament's opinion on a proposal before deciding definitively on the item.

An important innovation of the Treaty of Amsterdam for the third pillar was the mechanism of the framework decision, which was intended to facilitate the approximation of criminal laws in the member states regarding definition of crimes, and lengths of criminal sentences. Similar to the directives of the first pillar, framework decisions are binding on the member states but do not entail direct effect, meaning that national authorities are left to decide the particular form of legislation to achieve the intended results. Just as the EU created its Common Market mainly through the use of directives, it was hoped that framework decisions would enable the EU to achieve the prescribed AFSJ.

In the months following the Amsterdam Treaty's entry into force in May 1999, a new College of Commissioners was assembled under Romano Prodi, with Portugal's António Vitorino as the new Commissioner for JHA. From the beginning, Vitorino enjoyed three distinct advantages over his predecessor, Anita Gradin: he was more experienced on JHA matters and surrounded himself with a more competent *cabinet* (Uçarer, 2001); the Amsterdam Treaty gave the Commission the ability to be pro-active in shaping JHA policy; and a JHA Directorate-General (DG) was finally created within the Commission's bureaucracy to facilitate its legislative new role. All of this increased the overall influence of the Commission on JHA, helping to expedite progress on the AFSJ before the impending enlargement both exacerbated transnational crime and complicated decision-making in a larger and more diverse EU.

After the Tampere European Council

Soon after the Amsterdam Treaty took effect, and with 12 countries officially recognized as candidate states for accession, the Finnish Presidency hosted a special meeting of the European Council at Tampere in October 1999. The conclusions of this summit laid down 10 general 'milestones' for progress toward the AFSJ, which included some items already proposed in previous action plans and new goals, such as the creation of Eurojust, a kind of liaison network for criminal prosecutors. The Tampere milestones also emphasized that the AFSJ should be established on the principle of 'mutual recognition' in criminal matters, just as the SEM has been built on the same notion regarding national health and safety standards that could otherwise impede free trade. In this regard, for example, the Tampere European Council called for the virtual elimination of traditional criminal extradition and its replacement by an arrest and surrender warrant that would be mutually recognized throughout the EU – the so-called 'Euro-warrant'.

As with the SEM however, mutual recognition on criminal matters would have to be supplemented by some approximation, or harmonization, of criminal law among the member states, and for this, the new mechanism of the framework decision would be used. The resulting legal infrastructure of crime fighting in EU would work in tandem with newly created JHA institutions to help the EU realize the AFSJ, which was supposed to be in place before the next enlargement. In addition, progress on developing the JHA *acquis* would serve as a legislative target for the candidate states as they made their final preparations for accession.

The Tampere European Council was also significant for *how* it suggested that the EU implement its objectives on internal security, endorsing the creation of a so-called JHA 'Scoreboard' that encompassed the new milestones. The Commission was charged with creating and biannually updating the Scoreboard, which took the form of a grid detailing some 50 distinct objectives, specific actions needed to achieve these, the actors responsible for taking these measures, the timetable for doing so, and the current 'state of play' regarding progress. With enlargement approaching, it was hoped that the JHA Scoreboard would foster steady progress toward the AFSJ, just as the '1992 clock' promoted the timely development of the SEM following the entry into force of the SEA. However, as in other policy areas, the mere agreement on ambitious goals by the Heads of State and Government did not automatically, or even easily, translate into the implementation of actual policies, although the EU was moving ever closer to accepting new members. Consequently, the new institutional and legal infrastructure for JHA cooperation was gradually established, but not without frequent disagreement among member states and a lack of progress in some areas – especially immigration and asylum policy.

Throughout 2000, work on the Tampere milestones continued simultaneously with the IGC on institutional reform. The resulting Treaty of Nice contained little in the way of significant change for JHA. The most important amendment to the TEU was the elimination of individual member states' right to block 'enhanced cooperation'. Other JHA matters covered by the Nice Treaty include the nature and role of Eurojust and the partial and deferred switch to QMV regarding some minor aspects of refugee and asylum policy.

Of course, the broader importance of the Treaty of Nice was that it prepared the EU for enlargement by resolving many thorny institutional issues. In addition, by approving the Commission's roadmap for negotiating with the candidate states and declaring that the EU would be ready for new members by June 2004, the Nice European Council consolidated the likelihood of enlargement in the near term, thereby adding to the pressure for timely progress on JHA. This came all at a time when the EU was continuing to develop its institutional and legal infrastructure for JHA and was thus presenting the applicant states with a constantly moving target regarding the JHA *acquis* they would have to meet.

In this endeavour, the applicant states were guided by their accession partnerships with the EU (see Chapter 3). Concerning JHA, these partnerships identified the need to reinforce external border facilities in the short-term, as well as several longer-term goals, including institution-building and the strengthening of administrative capacity for a range of JHA entities, including ensuring sufficient and properly trained police and judicial personnel. The applicant states were also reminded of the need to reform their asylum procedures, fight organized crime, and, eventually, to adopt and effectively implement the Schengen *acquis*.

The CEECs took advantage of the PHARE programme (see Chapter 3), which was re-oriented in 1998 to encompass JHA and began to fund horizontal programmes and 'twinning' projects involving personnel exchanges. These efforts entailed direct collaboration between EU-15 and applicant states, as well the transfer to the latter of technical and administrative know-how to help improve the performance of new criminal justice institutions. In addition, the applicant states also participated in a number of so-called 'structured dialogue' sessions with the member states on JHA, resulting, for example, in an important pre-accession pact on organized crime in 1998. This identified a number of common objectives and priorities regarding candidate states, such as the need for them to forge formal ties with Europol prior to their accession.

Justice and home affairs was amongst the most difficult and time-consuming issues in the accession negotiations. The six candidate states of the so-called Luxembourg group opened accession deliberations with the EU in March 1998, but it was not until late in the Portuguese Presidency of 2000 that the EU could even produce a draft common position on JHA for negotiations with these countries, thus allowing talks on the JHA chapter of the accession treaties – Chapter 24 – to be opened with these states that May. By June 2001, accession negotiations on JHA were under way with all of the candidate states aside from Romania, which did not start talks on Chapter 24 until April 2002.

JHA and Enlargement After September 11

Just as the Treaty of Amsterdam brought the Commission 'from the sidelines to the center stage' in JHA policy-making (Uçarer, 2001), the shocking images of death and destruction at the World Trade Center and Pentagon propelled internal security to the forefront of the EU and created a new political will among the member states to hasten their progress toward the AFSJ. Nevertheless, aside from the freezing of assets of groups and individuals suspected of being involved in the attacks, nearly every action taken by the EU to fight terrorism after September 11 had already been noted on the JHA Scoreboard, including the new Euro-warrant, a framework decision on terrorism and stronger relations with third countries. In other words, the impact of the terrorist attacks on the US was the acceleration of policy-making on JHA, rather than the inspiration for totally new endeavours (Occhipinti 2003).

Following September 11, the capacity of the candidate states to adopt the *acquis* on JHA and reform their criminal justice institutions became more important than ever – and not just because these measures were needed to allow the timely enlargement of the EU and the eventual extension of the Schengen free-travel zone. Rather, after the attacks on the US, greater significance was attached to the ability of the candidate states to strengthen their external borders, monitor the travel of third-country nationals through their territory, and cooperate directly with national police authorities in the EU-15 in the overall fight against terrorism as well as at the EU-level via Europol and Eurojust. Thus, in the EU and candidate countries, the implications of EU enlargement for JHA became all the more significant after September 11, helping to expedite progress on a variety of internal security initiatives.

In this context, the ongoing accession negotiations with the candidate states took on greater importance. Hungary became the first candidate state to provisionally close negotiations on Chapter 24 in November 2001, followed within a month by Cyprus, Slovenia and the Czech Republic. The remaining candidate states set to join the EU in 2004 closed their chapters of accession on JHA during 2002, with Poland becoming the last do so in July of that year. Meanwhile, accession negotiations on JHA were concluded with Bulgaria during the Italian Presidency of 2003, while deliberations with Romania continued into 2004.

At least temporarily, the fight against terrorism overshadowed progress on accession talks, as well as illegal immigration, which, until September 11, had emerged as Europe's most prominent transnational crime problem. However, as several candidate states continued to be major source- or transit-countries regarding the flow of illegal immigrants, this problem remained high on the EU's internal security agenda even in the immediate aftermath of the terrorist attacks. For example, the regularly scheduled JHA Council session on 27–28 September 2001 featured a televised debate with the candidate countries on the trafficking of human beings and served as the occasion for the signing of a 10-point document of mutual commitment to enhance cooperation to fight this crime.

With enlargement drawing nearer during the Spanish Presidency of 2002, internal security issues continued to top the EU's overall policy agenda. As the memory of September 11 began to fade, however, attention in the EU began to shift away from terrorism and back to the problem of illegal immigration. The first signal of this change came in February when the JHA Council approved a new global action plan to combat illegal immigration and the trafficking of human beings. This served as the start of a series of activities on border control issues that culminated in the Seville European Council in June 2002, which was virtually dedicated to this topic in the wake of a series of immigration crises and rising support for anti-immigrant political parties throughout the EU. These forces, along with pressure from the Spanish Presidency and the UK, contributed to the nature and outcome of the Seville summit, which helped expedite cooperation throughout 2002–2003 on issues related to border control, human trafficking and asylum.

All of this took place as the accession negotiations with 12 of the candidate states neared their conclusions and the prospect of a 'big-bang' enlargement of the EU in 2004 increased. Although it was recognized that the future EU members would not immediately become part of the Schengen zone upon their accession to the EU, this eventuality contributed to the sense of urgency to develop common policies under the framework of the AFSJ. Some illegal immigrants found their way into the EU directly by air or sea, but many candidate states remained important source- or transit-countries for much of this illicit traffic of human beings. As in the past, it was widely recognized that these states would soon share in the responsibility of maintaining the EU's external borders and protecting its internal security, and that their ability to do so effectively would require having many common EU policies already in place. Moreover, adopting the outstanding legislative items on the JHA Scoreboard in this regard would only become more difficult with the addition of new member states to the EU, meaning progress had to be made sooner rather than later.

Crime-Fighting and Border Management in the Enlarged EU

In its efforts to ensure internal security in an expanding Union, the EU has gradually established a new institutional and legal infrastructure of crime-fighting (Occhipinti, 2003, 2004). The most important components of the infrastructure are identified and described in Box 14.1. The new member states established partnerships with many of the EU's new law enforcement bodies in preparations for their accession, as well as working at implementing the *acquis* of the evolving legal infrastructure on JHA.

Along with the bodies identified in Box 14.1, cooperation in the area of crime-fighting in the EU is supported by a number of shared databases aside from those managed by Europol, including a few still in their infancy. The oldest of these is the Schengen Information System (SIS), which gives police officials in participating states rapid access to criminal data and warnings about suspects who may attempt to cross the external border of the free-travel area. In 2003, the EU implemented the Eurodac system for the storage of asylum seekers' fingerprints to combat both 'asylum shopping' and illegitimate claims, as well as the Customs Information System (CIS), which allows national authorities to share data in the prevention of smuggling. By the end of the Greek Presidency in the first half of 2003, the EU was also considering a new biometric database for visas that would allow national officials to track the movements of third-country nationals in and out of the Union. Each of these databases must be extended to the new member states, entailing a number of financial, technological and legal challenges to overcome. In fact, the new member states will not be able to join the free-travel area until after the

Box 14.1 New institutional infrastructure of EU crime-fighting

• **Europol** is based in The Hague and has been fully operational since July 1999. It is responsible for helping member states to fight a recently expanded list of transnational crimes, but it lacks such executive policing powers as the authority to make arrests or use coercive measures. Europol's staff create analytical work files on specific crimes and may request the launching of investigations by member states. Europol utilises its in-house liaison officers supplied by the member states, as well as their national contact points, to facilitate international information exchanges and to coordinate multi-national police operations through simultaneous operations or joint investigation teams. Europol's staff and budget has increased steadily as its crime-fighting mandate has expanded, but more growth is needed if it is to demonstrate its effectiveness in an EU that is not only larger, but entails more source- and transit-states for transitional organized crime. Europol also faces the challenge of incorporating the new member states into its governing Management Board, which operates via unanimity, as well as fully integrating their liaison officers into its work and extending the long-delayed rapid information exchange computer network, known as the European Information System (EIS) (www.europol.eu.int).

• **Eurojust** was prescribed in the Tampere milestone and is also based in The Hague. It began its official operations in 2002. Eurojust entails a liaison network of national criminal prosecutors, which it uses to facilitate and coordinate criminal investigations by encouraging better contacts among national investigators, advising Europol, and helping to simplify the execution of 'letters of rogatory' – international court-to-court requests for assistance or information. Eurojust works in conjunction with the European Judicial Network (EJN), which is a decentralized network of legal contact points in the EU created in 1998. It is also charged with cooperating closely with the anti-fraud office, OLAF (*Organisation pour la Lutte Anti-Fraude*), in cases affecting the

→

successful deployment of the planned second generation of the SIS, and this is not expected until late 2005 at the earliest.

Along with these crime-fighting bodies and databases, the EU promotes horizontal cooperation among law enforcement authorities through co-financing programmes which were open to candidates states before their accession. The Agis programme, for example, has combined and replaced a number of smaller, defunct programmes – Grotius, Oisin, Stop, Hippocrates and Falcone – to provide collaboration, personnel exchanges and training for judicial and law enforcement officials in the areas of organized crime, human trafficking, sexual exploitation of children, drug trafficking, firearms offences, computer crime, financial crime, corruption,

→

Union's financial interests. Like Europol, Eurojust is challenged by enlargement to demonstrate its effectiveness in the larger, and likely more crime-ridden, EU. Amongst the tasks that are likely to increase in importance post-enlargement is helping national authorities to overcome any legal barrier to international cooperation posed by enduring differences in substantive and procedural criminal law (www.eurojust.eu.int).

- **The Police Chiefs' Task Force** was also prescribed in the Tampere milestones and is intended to help high-level national police officials to share best practices and information on current trends in cross-border crime and contribute to the planning of joint operations. It has convened at least every six months since the Portuguese presidency of 2001, outlining common priority areas on each occasion. It can be useful in promoting the Europeanization of crime-fighting priorities and strategies in the new member states.

- **The European Police College** (often known by its French acronym, CEPOL) acts as a virtual training academy for high level police officers. It began operation in 2001, provisionally based in Copenhagen-Brøndby, with the explicit intention of building a common police culture among law enforcement agencies in the EU. With its permanent secretariat to be located in London, CEPOL helps organize and fund training programmes run by police academies of the member states. All of its programmes were open to the new member states prior to their accession. (www.cepol.net).

- **Common Unit for External Border Practitioners.** This was created late in the Danish Presidency of 2002 under a mandate by the Seville European Council and oversees a larger liaison network of national immigration officers. This unit helps plan and coordinate joint operations and pilot projects in the fight against illegal immigration. It is also developing a common training curriculum for immigration personnel, which can be helpful for the new member states as they take steps to implement the Schengen *acquis*. In December 2003, the European Council decided to replace this unit by the end of 2004 with a European Border Management Agency which will have its headquarters in Brussels.

counterfeiting, environmentally threatening activities, illegal immigration, and illegal trade in cultural goods and stolen works of art. Similarly, the Argo programme has taken over from the Odysseus programme to cofinance cooperative projects for the administration of asylum, immigration and border control. Although these programmes were open to the new member states prior to their accession, post-enlargement they will require much more funding to maintain their effectiveness.

Just as the EU's institutional infrastructure of crime fighting must prove able to meet the needs of enlargement, so too must its burgeoning legal infrastructure for internal security. Intended to supplement the principle of mutual recognition, the EU has approved several framework decisions defining transnational crimes and sanctions for these. This has resulted in the approximation of penal codes for several offences, including counterfeiting of the euro, money laundering, terrorism, the trafficking of human beings, child sexual exploitation, fraud, counterfeiting of non-cash payments, drug trafficking, environmental crime and 'cyber-crime' (that is, attacks on information systems). By early 2004 some of these items were still awaiting formal passage pending the expected lifting of parliamentary scrutiny reservations, and some were still being transposed into national law in some states. There were also problems in the Council, with enduring dissent inhibiting agreement on proposals for framework decisions covering racism and xenophobia and the trafficking of human organs. In contrast, significant progress had (finally) been made on several components of the Commission's legislative package on asylum policy, including, for example, defining national responsibility for applicants, minimum conditions for their reception and a common definition of 'refugees' (Giraudon, 2004).

The gradual approximation of substantive criminal law and asylum policies illustrates the Europeanization of JHA in the EU, which can be at least partly attributed to concerns for enlargement's expected impact on internal security in the EU. Europeanization is evident not only in this legal harmonization, but also in the sharing of best practices and strategies for law enforcement, which has been promoted by, for example, seminars administered and funded by the European Police College (CEPOL) (see Box 14.1) and the development of a common training curriculum for border-patrol personnel. Europeanization of this kind is also fostered through the efforts of the other newly created crime-fighting bodies identified above, along with the projects sponsored by the Agis and Argo co-financing programmes.

As part of their effort to conform to the EU's emerging legal structure of crime fighting, the new member states must also fully implement the Schengen *acquis* and demonstrate their ability to control their part of the free-travel area's external boundaries. Only when this is accomplished will the EU allow them to participate in the Schengen zone, and for this the Council's decision must be unanimous. This is not expected until some time in 2006, after the SIS II is operating. Once this is achieved, it might be hard for the EU to resist the likely political pressure to include the new members in the Schengen zone, even if several outstanding internal security issues in these states remain unresolved.

With the aim of avoiding this scenario, the April 2003 Accession Treaty offered the new member states two forms of financial assistance. With the exception of the three countries lacking land borders with non-EU states – Cyprus, Malta and the Czech Republic – the new EU member states collectively receive approximately €285 million annually from a newly created 'Schengen Facility', allocated until the end of 2006. These funds are earmarked for the renovation or construction of border-crossing infrastructure, training for border guards, support for logistics and operations, and investment in equipment, such as hardware and software for the SIS II. During this same time period, the Accession Treaty also provides for a 'Transition Facility' that allocates a total of €380 million spread among all new EU members for tasks not covered by the Structural Funds nor the lump-sum cash-flow payments provided elsewhere in the Treaty. These additional funds are aimed at fostering the exchange of best practices and developing and strengthening new members' administrative capacity to implement and enforce EU legislation. Concerning JHA, this money can be allocated for improving judicial systems, external border controls, anti-corruption strategy and law enforcement capacities. Clearly, the enhancement of internal security in new member states and a response to calls from CEECs for more burden-sharing in external border control must be addressed in the EU's next financial perspective for 2007–2013.

Conclusions: JHA in an Enlarged European Union

The widening of the EU presents several challenges to its new infrastructure of crime fighting. In particular, enlargement will test the capacity of the newly created law enforcement institutions to absorb the new member states and contribute to the fight against transnational crime over a wider area. Related to this, the EU must also ensure that new member states can fully participate in the exchange of best practices, approaches and strategies through the new JHA institutions, and by doing so share in the creation of any emergent common culture of law enforcement regarding the fight against transnational crime. As the EU grows, it must also continue to promote the approximation of criminal codes for transnational crimes, which is even more vital in a larger and more diverse Union. In short, if the expanded EU is to combat transnational crime most effectively, then it must not allow enlargement to detract from the Europeanization of JHA and the gradual shift in the direction of a more supranational approach to crime fighting

The ability of the EU to meet the internal security challenges posed by EU enlargement rests, at least to some degree, on the outcome of the 2003–2004 IGC. Regarding JHA, the fundamental issue is the extent to which the constitutional treaty will implement QMV in the Council and legislative co-decision with the EP. At the time of writing, the resolution of this question remained in doubt, but it seemed clear that a substantial portion of the third pillar would be retained. That is, the Commission will continue to share legislative initiative with the member states on police and judicial cooperation in criminal matters, and unanimous voting in the Council and mere power of consultation for the EP will be the norms for legislation impinging on the operational powers of law enforcement authorities.

Nevertheless, the new constitution will likely bring a stronger role for the European Court of Justice on JHA and open the possibility of creating a European Public Prosecutor to be established within Eurojust, provided the EU-25 can agree unanimously to do so. However, by the time of the breakdown of the IGC in December 2003 it was clear that some of the 25 were uncomfortable with such a prosecutor having crime-fighting authority beyond the financial interests of the EU. In addition, it was also clear that the new constitution will neither transform Europol into a 'European FBI', prescribe a true European Border patrol, nor strip member states of the right to set their own immigration quotas.

In contrast, the constitution is likely to include a clear legal basis for the approximation of not only substantive, but also procedural, criminal law. But some countries in the IGC, notably the UK, were unwilling to allow the communautarisation of these matters without the possibility of retaining a veto to block measures that infringe upon fundamental principles of their legal systems. If a veto is retained, decision-making in these areas will be all the more difficult and member states' ability to collaborate in the fight against transnational organised crime in an enlarged EU will be inhibited.

Overall, it is still too early to evaluate the impact of the EU's efforts in the fight against transnational crime. Europol has yet to play a major operational role, the other EU-level crime-fighting bodies are only cutting their teeth, and several of the recently approved framework decisions have only just been transposed into national law. Moreover, the effect of enlargement on internal security will only be felt once the Schengen free-travel area is widened. Consequently, more time is needed to determine whether the new institutional and legal infrastructure of crime-fighting will make a positive impact in practice, particularly in the new member states. In the interim, the Union must continue to make progress on implementing and strengthening its new infrastructure of crime-fighting. Otherwise, the enlargement of the Union might serve to worsen the problem of transnational crime and cast a dark shadow over the planned accession of Bulgaria and Romania, not to mention the aspirations of Turkey and the countries of the Western Balkans.

Chapter 15

The European Union as an International Economic Actor

ADRIAN VAN DEN HOVEN[*]

Introduction

This chapter analyzes the impact of enlargement on the EU's trade policy. Enlargement affects both the internal and external aspects of EU trade policy (Preston, 1997: 157). From an internal perspective, the EU needs to internalize the trade interests of new members and to reorder its priorities. Enlargement also affects the patterns of trade of the acceding countries and could require the EU to compensate World Trade Organization (WTO) members that suffer from trade diversion. Each enlargement is equivalent to creating a new EU customs union. From an external perspective, enlargement makes the EU market bigger and hence more important in the multilateral trading system. If, as is sometimes suggested could happen, enlargement results in a more protectionist EU on the world stage, this could threaten the global multilateral trading system.

Internalizing the Priorities of Acceding States into EU Trade Policy

Previous enlargements

Historically, the EU has integrated the interests of acceding countries into its trade policy priorities. In some cases this has been done almost immediately and in other cases has been gradually phased-in. For example, following the accession of the UK in 1973, the EC moved quickly to avoid a severance of the UK's special trade relations with undeveloped Commonwealth countries by negotiating the Lomé Agreement which was centred on a preferential trading arrangement with the African,

---

[*] The views expressed in this chapter are solely those of the author and should not be taken as representing the views of his employer, the Union of Industrial and Employers' Confederations of Europe (UNICE).

Caribbean and Pacific (ACP) countries (Preston, 1997: 160). Since its accession, the UK, and Denmark, which also joined in 1973, has had an important liberal influence on trade policy. At the sectoral level, the UK has contributed, especially since the early 1990s, to shifting the focus of trade policy away from industrial and agricultural products so as to better reflect its comparative advantage in services.

When Greece, Spain and Portugal joined the EC in the 1980s, trade relations with the rest of the Mediterranean and with Latin America were affected. To offset the trade diversion that might be produced, new trading relationship with Mediterranean and Latin American countries were devised. The main objective of what became EuroMed policy was, and still is, to negotiate free-trade agreements with all of the Mediterranean countries by 2010. By mid-2003 the EU had signed cooperation agreements with Tunisia, Morocco, Jordan, Israel, the Palestinian Authority, Egypt, Lebanon and Algeria. With Latin America, the EU had negotiated free trade agreements with Mexico (2000) and Chile (2002) and was engaged in free trade negotiations with Mercosur (the 'Common Market of the South', which includes Argentina, Brazil, Uruguay and Paraguay amongst its members). At the sectoral level, Greece's accession influenced the EU's priorities over shipping liberalization both internally and externally (Aspinwall, 1995), whilst the Iberian enlargement strengthened the group of countries opposed to CAP reform. Surprisingly, the Iberian enlargement did not lead to a significant rise in protectionism in the textiles sector despite the vulnerability of the Spanish and Portuguese industry. This suggests that enlargement to countries with less competitive industries does not necessarily lead to more protectionism in the EU.

The accession of Sweden, Finland and Austria shifted the EU's geographic priorities eastward because these three countries support improving economic relations with Eastern Europe and the countries of the former Soviet Union (Valtasaari, 1999; European Commission, 2001h). At the sectoral level, Finland and Sweden have supported the EU's strong position on services liberalization so as to promote their comparative advantage in telecommunications services.

For a summary of the trading effects of previous enlargement rounds, see Box 15.1.

The 10 + 2 enlargement

Geographical focus

The 10 + 2 enlargement round pushes the EU's trade policy focus further eastward still. For example, in anticipation of its eastward expansion, the EU negotiated economic cooperation agreements with Russia (1994), Ukraine (1994) and Kazakhstan (1995) and called in 2003 for the negotiation of a Common Economic Space with Russia. Only Belarus has

Box 15.1 How enlargement has changed EU trade policy

Acceding countries	Shift in geographic focus	Shift in sector focus
1973 UK, Denmark, Ireland	Lomé/Cotonou Preferential Agreements	Services trade
1981/1986 Greece, Spain, Portugal	EuroMed Agreements, trade agreements with Latin American countries	Shipping liberalization Agricultural protectionism
1995 Sweden, Finland, Austria	Europe Agreements, economic cooperation with Russia	Services trade, notably telecommunications.
2004 Czech Republic, Estonia, Hungary, Poland, Slovenia, Latvia, Lithuania, Slovakia, Malta and Cyprus	Europe Agreements with Romania and Bulgaria, Common Economic Space with Russia, economic cooperation with Ukraine, Balkan Stability Programme	Industrial liberalization Agricultural protectionism? Services protectionism?

been excluded from this eastward shift in EU trade policy because of its poor record on human rights issues.

This movement eastward has been reinforced by the heavy dependence of some CEECs on trade with former Soviet states, which in some instances has been underpinned by special bi-lateral trading arrangements. This close relationship between CEECs and former Soviet states, and in some instances with former Yugoslav states too, created difficulties in the accession negotiations. Hungary, for instance, requested special terms attached to its accession protocol to maintain economic and trade ties with its former eastern trading partners, while Slovenia sought a 15-year transition for the phasing-out of its free trade agreements with Croatia and the Former Yugoslav Republic of Macedonia (Johnson and Rollo, 2001: 18). In the negotiations, the EU did not accept any transitional measures for the phasing-out of bilateral trade. Consequently, the new members are obliged to withdraw from any free trade agreements and to adapt or terminate any bilateral agreements that are not in conformity with EU trade legislation (European Commission, 2003f: 52).

The heavy trade reliance of many CEECs with countries to their east and also in south-east Europe has been an important factor in driving the EU to improve trade relations with its new neighbours. It wishes to avoid generating large-scale trade diversion that could have a negative impact on the economies of CEECs and on countries with which they are closely linked and which, in several cases, are themselves possible future EU members. This is in keeping with the precedent of previous enlargement rounds in which the most obvious impact of enlargement on trade policy was linked to geographic focus. As Box 15.1 thus indicates, an important consequence of enlargements has been to redirect the geographical focus of trade policy – partly in order so as to prevent the EU from become a trade 'fortress'.

Sectoral interests

With regard to sectoral interests, the new member states probably will support trade liberalization for industrial goods, with the exception perhaps of Poland. Once they open to industrial imports from the EU, the newcomers will have little incentive to oppose imports from third countries. However, some trade scholars are concerned that the acceding states will be strong supporters of anti-dumping measures for basic industrial goods such as steel, chemicals and textiles (Messerlin, 2001: 246). This concern may be exaggerated, for whilst countries with inefficient basic industries like Poland or Slovakia could show some interest in anti-dumping, most of the smaller acceding states – including Malta, Cyprus and Estonia – are not likely to support anti-dumping measures because they are primarily consumers of industrial goods. In addition, the acceding states may harbour ill-will towards the trade defence instrument because they were the targets of EU anti-dumping measures during the period of their to accession to the EU.

There are also concerns that the new member states will oppose agricultural liberalization once they gain access to CAP subsidies (Francois and Rombout, 2001; Messerlin, 2001: 246). However, as is the case with anti-dumping, it is impossible to generalize. National positions will depend on the competitiveness of the agricultural sectors of each acceding state. For instance, agriculture accounts for a very small share of Czech Republic and Hungarian exports, while it accounts for a slightly higher share for the Slovak Republic and Poland than it does for the EU-15 (see Table 15.1). Based on these raw figures, Hungary and the Czech Republic can be expected to promote agricultural liberalization, while Poland and the Slovak Republic can be expected to support the status quo.

However, this situation could change over time, as the acceding states will not receive their full share of CAP funds until 2013. Direct support payments to farmers will be phased-in over a 10-year period: 25 per cent in 2004, 30 per cent in 2005, 35 per cent in 2006, and 100 per cent by 2013. The Commission claims that this phasing-in is necessary to allow the acceding states time to restructure their agricultural sectors because immediate and full access to the CAP would freeze existing, inefficient structures, notably in Poland (European Commission, 2002k). However, the acceding states feel like 'second-class members' and they are

Table 15.1   *Agricultural and industrial exports of the EU-15 and of*
selected new member states

	EU-15	Czech Rep.	Slovakia	Hungary	Poland
Agricultural exports (% of total exports of goods)	9.2	4.7	10.1	4.0	9.9
Industrial exports (% of total exports of goods)	80.9	89.1	83.7	86.5	80.6

Source: World Trade Organization, 2002: 64, 75.

concerned that subsidized EU farm products will flood their national markets. This staged approach to funding could also inadvertently block CAP reform, which has been partly put off until the new member states benefit from full CAP subsidies. The new member states will not have much incentive to support CAP reform if it means they will lose funding. Should this reluctance to reform the CAP combine with large EU surpluses of such exported products as wheat, milk and beef, then a crisis in WTO agriculture negotiations would ensue (Francois and Rombout 2001). This risk is compounded by the fact that the acceding countries produce similar agricultural products to the EU-15 – including cereals, meat, sugar and milk (Ardy, 2000). A crisis would be aggravated if WTO members began opposing 'blue' and 'green' box subsidy authorization arrangements that allow the EU to provide direct payments to farmers.

In addition to problems associated with CAP funding, the Commission has demanded that the *acquis communautaire* health and safety standards be adopted in agriculture before accession (Ardy, 2000). However, the costs of applying EU regulations are very high. For instance, Poland will need to spend between 4 and 8 per cent of its GDP annually for the next 20 years to implement all of the EU's environmental directives (Messerlin, 2001: 223). Consequently, most acceding states have had difficulty meeting EU product safety and sanitation standards for many agricultural products. This situation could potentially undermine the EU position in the WTO on the precautionary principle, which the EU justifies by claiming that European consumers will not accept the import of potentially unsafe foods (Lamy, 2001). Yet, if the EU were to accept lower-quality food safety standards in the new member states, even for a transition period, it could undermine its position on food safety in the WTO.

Overall, however, the impact of enlargement on the CAP reform process and the associated trade policies is likely to be small. After all, enlargement to the UK, Denmark, Ireland and the Nordic countries did not have much effect on the CAP, despite the vocal support of these countries for agriculture liberalization. Similarly, the Iberian enlargement did not lead to a significant reduction in CAP spending or to an increase in agricultural protectionism in the EU.

Since the acceding states have relatively underdeveloped service sectors, with the possible exception of Hungary (World Trade Organization, 2002: 20), there may be a weakening of support in the Union for services liberalization in the WTO. However, given that this is the EU's major offensive interest in the WTO and that the EU-15 states overwhelmingly support services liberalization, it is unlikely that the new member states will be able to exercise much influence over the Doha Development Agenda on this issue.

The Trade Diversion Effects of Enlargement

The non-discrimination and most-favoured nation (MFN) principles are the fundamental pillars of the multilateral trading system because they ensure that trade liberalization measures benefit all WTO members. The WTO authorizes an exception to these principles for the creation of regional trading arrangements (RTA) and customs unions as long as they liberalize a significant amount of trade, they are trade creating, and they do not increase trade barriers against third countries under Article XXIV of the General Agreement on Tariffs and Trade (GATT). The application of WTO RTA rules can be problematic because it is difficult to assess the extent of trade diversion and trade creation. In principle, the EU will have to compensate WTO members affected by enlargement through negotiations at the multilateral level.

Previous enlargements were followed by negotiations, mainly between the EU and the US, over compensation for trade diversion effects. As concerns the 10 + 2 enlargement, the EU agreed, 'to enter into an Article XXIV: 6 compensation process' with any WTO partners affected by the enlargement (World Trade Organization, 2000b: 150–157). However, while Spanish and Portuguese accession led to several years of compensation negotiations between the EU and the US (Johnson and Rollo, 2001: 19), the EU refuses to offer large compensatory measures for the 10 + 2 enlargement in the WTO because the overall level of trade affected will be very small. Altogether, the acceding states represent around 3 per cent of world trade (World Trade Organization, 2002: 26), whilst over 70 per cent of their trade is already with the EU (World Trade Organization, 2002: 73). The case for compensation in the WTO is therefore weak (Abbott, 2001).

The adoption of the EU's common external tariff will lead to a significant reduction in tariff barriers in the new member states, because it is lower than the average level of tariffs in the acceding countries for most

Table 15.2   *Comparison of average tariff levels in six new member states and the EU-15**

Product	Poland	Hungary	Czech Republic	Estonia	Slovenia	Cyprus	EU-15
All	15.1	11.7	6.2	3.2	9	9.9	6.3
Agriculture	34	31	13.4	15.2	13.7	13.4	16.2
Fisheries	18.3	15.1	0.1	3.2	5.9	10.2	12.4
Industrial	9.9	7.1	4.6	0	8.1	4.1	3.6

Source: European Commission 2001j.
*Note: all figures are percentages.

industrial goods. Based on EU tariff calculations (see Table 15.2), accession will lower average tariff levels in all of the acceding states except Estonia. However, when agricultural tariffs on specific products (see Table 15.3) are compared, accession will increase tariff levels in the new member states for wheat, sugar, beef, milk and dairy products, which account for over half of the EU's agricultural exports and a third of its imports (Eurostat, 2002: 56–57). Therefore, although the impact of enlargement on world agriculture markets will be rather limited, agricultural exporters will likely demand compensation in the WTO for trade diversion effects in these specific sectors (Messerlin, 2001: 225; Francois and Rombout, 2001; Government of the United States of America, 2000; Wayne, 2001).

With enlargement on the horizon, the US adopted a policy in the 1990s of trying to gain concessions from CEECs in the WTO or in bilateral relations that it hoped to use against the EU in negotiations over compensation. For instance, the US delayed the accession to the WTO of certain acceding states to force them to adopt weak versions of the EU's 'Television Without Borders' directive – a directive that discriminates

Table 15.3   *Comparison of Polish, Hungarian and EU-15 tariffs on specific agricultural products**

Product	Poland	Hungary	EU-15
Wheat	20.3	0.0	49
Beet and cane sugar	0.0	0.0	45.5
Bovine animals	3.5	4.1	63.8
Raw milk	50.0	33.3	93.6
Bovine meat	3.5	3.4	63.8
Dairy	10.1	58.8	93.1

Source: Francois and Rombout, 2001: 10.
*Note: all figures are percentages.

against American programming (Abbott, 2001). The US also negotiated bilateral investment treaties with the acceding countries that liberalized investment in the audiovisual sector and which were incompatible with the EU's restrictive audiovisual policy. Johnson and Rollo, (2001: 8) have argued that this policy's objective was clearly designed to give the US some leverage over the EU in WTO negotiations over audiovisual market liberalization.

To prevent third countries from using strategies to undermine the EU's trade policy through the acceding states, the EU encouraged cooperation on trade policy matters with its prospective members. From 1995, the acceding states supported the EU's position on a 'comprehensive trade round' in multilateral trade negotiations (Pietras, 1998: 360) and they were faithful allies during the EU's trade policy review process (World Trade Organization, 2000b: 47–48, 52–53). However, the coordination of bilateral trade policies was problematic until the acceding states became official observers in EU institutions in May 2003. Prior to 2003, the Commission had difficulty monitoring the bilateral trade negotiations of acceding states with third countries, even though they were required to abrogate bilateral trade agreements that were not in conformity with EU trade law (European Commission, 2003f).

Trade policy coordination was especially problematic with Poland. In its 2001 Regular Report, the Commission criticized Poland for negotiating a preferential trading arrangement with the US 'without any prior consultation or information of the EU' (European Commission, 2001j). Poland also negotiated a bilateral investment treaty with the US, which the Commission demanded be abrogated because it included clauses that could undermine the EU's audiovisual policy. Poland's openness to US trade and investment offers is linked to its growing trade deficit, which is not being offset by large inflows of foreign direct investment (International Monetary Fund, 2002). In fact, EU foreign direct investment (FDI) in the accession countries only amounts to €57.7 billion (5 per cent of the total stock of EU FDI) which is about half of the €110.4 billion the EU has invested in Latin America (Eurostat, 2001; Eurostat, 2003). In September 2003, the Commission was able to reach a compromise with the US over the bilateral investment treaty issue by signing a Memorandum of Understanding with the US and the acceding countries that effectively rescinded the acceding country obligations to give national treatment to American investors in 'sensitive' sectors such as the audiovisual sector.

In all probability, the trade diverting effects of enlargement will prove to be no more controversial than the bilateral investment issue. The diversion of Russian and Ukrainian trade away from the EU is, for example, not a serious legal problem because they are not WTO members (Francois and Rombout, 2001: 21). Moreover, the trade diverting effects of enlargement are likely to be much lower than the EU's trading partners in the WTO claim (World Trade Organization, 2000b: 27 and 125). Overall, the EU's trading partners will be more concerned about the manner in which an enlarged EU will affect the balance of power in the multilateral trading system.

Securing Preferential Access to the World's Largest and Expanding Market

The EU-15 is the world's largest market and exporter (17.5 per cent of world exports) although it is only the second largest import market after the United States (18 per cent of world imports for the EU vs. 23.5 per cent for the US) (Eurostat, 2001). By expanding eastward, the EU's population rises from 380 million to over 450 million. This will have two effects on the world trading system: more countries will seek preferential access to the EU's ever-expanding market, and the EU's trading partners will pay more attention to the internal trade policy debate of the EU.

The EU's vast system of preferential trading arrangements (PTAs) is unique because it is the source of over half of the PTAs in the world (Messerlin, 2001: 197). All WTO members with the exception of Australia, Canada, Hong Kong, China, Japan, the Republic of Korea, New Zealand, Singapore and the United States benefit from some kind of EU PTA, be it the Generalized System of Preferences (GSP), the ACP Agreements, or bilateral arrangements (World Trade Organization, 2000b: 39). Many of these PTAs are the indirect consequence of successive EU enlargements or are linked to political events that have pushed the EU to stabilize relations with countries on its periphery. Messerlin (2001:1) argues that EU trade policy is heavily influenced by such political considerations 'because the EC has no other way (foreign policy or army) to express its political views'.

This myriad of PTAs is not necessarily a panacea for the countries that gain preferential access to the EU market because they can produce negative side effects. For instance, developing countries often raise tariffs against third countries after signing trade agreements with the EU to make up for lost tariff revenues or to protect national industries that have to face competition from EU industries. This provides EU industries with captive markets. A second problem associated with the EU PTAs is that they transform the EU into a 'hub and spoke' system in which the hub market gains access to the markets of all the spoke countries through separate trading arrangements. Meanwhile, the spokes only gain access to the hub market which becomes increasingly competitive as new spokes are added (Hill and Wonnacott, 1991; Wonnacott, 1990). In addition, investors prefer to invest in the hub market rather than its spokes because it ensures them access to a much larger market (Messerlin, 2001: 199).

This may explain why inflows of FDI in the new member states were not very high prior to accession.

Liberal economists are highly critical of the EU's numerous PTAs because they question their economic value for the EU and the countries that gain preferential access. In addition, the EU's 'addiction' to PTAs (Messerlin, 2001: ch.6) is perceived to be a threat to the multilateral trading system. However, while PTAs can be justifiably criticized from an economic perspective, they may have some value for the multilateral trading system in political terms.

Some EU PTAs are transitory agreements for countries that are expected to join the Union in the future. These agreements have prevented the EU from isolating its European neighbours economically. In addition, the eagerness with which countries are willing to negotiate PTAs with the EU or to apply for GSP benefits seems to show that these agreements provide access to the EU market. Finally, and most importantly, PTAs can be used to build up political support for the EU's policy in the WTO because they are a means of offering concessions that the EU would be unable to make at the multilateral level.

The EU's penchant for PTAs can be understood within the context of a power struggle between the US and the EU for leadership in the multilateral system. The EU's drive for leadership in the WTO revolves around trying to isolate the US by gaining the support of developing countries through concessions in the WTO and in EU PTAs. The most obvious place to look for support in the WTO is situated on the EU's periphery. These states have an interest in supporting the EU position because they need EU support in the WTO to defend their own positions. Although the EU lost 10 of its 'allies' in the WTO due to enlargement, it will continue to pursue this strategy by establishing good relations with countries on its eastern border, such as Russia and Ukraine, which wish to become members of the WTO.

An Enlarged 'Fortress Europe'?

Enlargement of the EU will highlight the impact that the internal EU trade debate has on the global trading system. If the EU continues to open its market to trade then enlargement will be beneficial to the world trading system. However, enlargement could also generate protectionism for two reasons: the EU decision-making process may be unable to cope with 25 members and/or the new members may shift the balance of power within the Council in favour of protectionism.

The impact of enlargement on decision-making processes

There are fears that EU decision-making processes will be unable to function properly with 25 member states. If there was to be institutional paralysis, the EU would be prevented from being able to negotiate common positions in the WTO and to offer concessions to WTO partners. The impact of enlargement on the delegation of trade authority is expected to weaken the EU's ability to promote a liberal multilateral trading system. The US is concerned that the enlargement process will divert EU energies away from the multilateral system (Wayne, 2001) and that the institutional system will be unable to go beyond a lowest common denominator approach to trade policy. The complex system of legal competences granted to the EU for trade policy could also grant the acceding states a right of veto over important trading issues, such as agriculture or services trade.

Under the TEC, the Commission has exclusive competence for the negotiation of treaties on trade in goods, but some trade in services and intellectual property rights measures – the so-called 'new trade agenda' at the WTO – fall under a mixed competence rule. Under exclusive competence, the Commission negotiates on behalf of the member states, which ratify decisions based on qualified majority voting, while under mixed competence, the Commission negotiates with the assistance of the member states, which ratify decisions based on unanimity. Despite this legal confusion, Young *et al.* write that 'the member governments are, as they did in the Uruguay Round, negotiating [in the WTO] *as if* all of the issues fell within the EU's exclusive competence'(Young *et al.*, 2000: 5).

Given that GATT/WTO agreements are the result of cross-sector bargaining between trading partners, the EU delegation of authority for trade negotiations is very confusing to the EU's trading partners because they are never really sure who is in charge. Meunier and Nicolaïdis (1999: 498) argue that this confusion is a source of weakness because it makes the EU an unreliable negotiator and because the EU's trading partners may try to divide the member states. They warn that '[fragmented] actors facing each other in complex multilateral negotiations are less likely to be able to come up with packages of linked deals and are more likely to take heed of internal protectionist forces from within' (*ibid.*). Therefore, the addition of 10 new member states to the EU's already complex system of delegating trade authority could lead to a protectionist EU in multilateral trade negotiations (Messerlin, 2001: 14–17).

However, although the fears of institutional paralysis should not be dismissed, history suggests that enlargement does not strengthen protectionism. There have only been 'limited formal changes' to the treaty articles regulating trade policy and yet, 'the EC's foreign economic policy has adapted substantially and has largely coped with challenges for which its treaty base is not technically equipped' (Young, 1998: 1–3). Moreover, enlargement could make the institutional structure of the EU even less protectionist because negotiations in the Council of Ministers will be more difficult to control for national trade ministers (Johnson and Rollo,

2001: 12). This confusion could concentrate power over trade policy in the hands of the Commission, which has an interest in promoting multilateral trade liberalization. In addition, the 2002–2003 Convention on the Future of Europe proposed to simplify trade policy-making by granting the EU exclusive competence for trade in goods, services, investment and intellectual property rights (IPR) trade-related issues. If adopted, this reform should alleviate fears of an institutional breakdown in trade policy-making.

The trade preferences of the new member states

Institutional paralysis in the EU is not the only threat to the trading system because enlargement could shift the balance of power in the Council from countries that are in favour of trade liberalization to those that are opposed. It is generally assumed that the new member states will be committed to free trade because they enacted radical market-oriented reforms and unilateral trade liberalization in the 1990s. For instance, Estonia had to raise tariffs and even to introduce them on industrial goods in order to approach the common EU tariff level. Similarly, Hungary was a member of the CAIRNS group of agricultural exporters during the Uruguay Round, which pressed the EU to dismantle protectionist barriers in the CAP (Johnson and Rollo, 2001: 7). However, joining the EU may change their incentives. Johnson and Rollo (2001: 12) argue that the CAP may convert Hungary, Bulgaria and Romania, which are currently exporters of agriculture, into protectionists because they will be able to increase their productive capacities with CAP subsidies. Moreover, once the acceding countries gain full access to the EU market, where prices for agricultural products are maintained at artificially higher prices than on the world market, they will have little incentive to liberalize because this would lower EU agricultural market prices.

An assessment

Possible protectionist pressures arising from enlargement thus certainly exist, but they should not be exaggerated. Moreover, such pressures as do exist will be at least partly held in check by WTO pressures, not least in the context of the Doha Development Agenda negotiations, which were launched in 2001 and which are scheduled to be concluded by 1 January 2005 (though whether in practice they will be is doubtful). The Doha Round will lead to substantial reductions in EU industrial and agricultural tariff levels, will liberalize EU services markets and will encourage further reform of CAP. This should offset any increase in protectionist pressures arising from enlargement.

Historically, multilateral trade rounds have reduced average EU tariff levels in parallel with the creation of the EC customs union and with each successive enlargement. The Kennedy Round (1964–1967) prevented the Common External Tariff, which officially came into force in 1969, from increasing the level of protection in the EC (Preston, 1997: 168). The Tokyo Round (1973–1979) ensured that EC tariffs were reduced following the UK, Denmark and Ireland's accession in 1973. The Uruguay Round (1986–1994) did the same for the Iberian enlargement of the 1980s. In the Doha negotiations, the EU has proposed a compression formula that will lower EU tariffs by an average of 50 per cent. Thus, the Doha Development Agenda will limit any increase in protection resulting from eastern enlargement.

Conclusions

As in other policy areas, enlargement is modifying EU trade policy. It has contributed to shifting the geographic focus of trade policy eastward through the negotiation of pre-accession trade agreements with the candidate countries and trade arrangements with countries on the EU's eastern border. The latter agreements should reduce the amount of trade diversion caused by expanding the EU customs union eastward. The EU may need to compensate WTO members whose trade will be diverted as a result of the new member states adopting higher EU tariffs for some goods. However, such higher tariffs will be restricted largely to agriculture trade, so the amount of trade diversion is likely to be small.

Enlargement will also make the EU a bigger and more important trading bloc. Thus, third countries will continue to seek preferential access to the European market through the EU's myriad of preferential trading arrangements. In turn, this will strengthen the EU in the WTO because many countries will become dependent on preferential access to its market.

There are fears that an enlarged EU could shift its energies away from the global multilateral system and that it could become a kind of 'fortress Europe'. However, if previous enlargements are any indication, then the eastern enlargement should not transform the EU into a protectionist bloc. As it expanded from six to 15 member states, the EU strengthened its commitment to multilateral trade liberalization. Although the current enlargement may make it more difficult to reform the CAP in the future, the protectionist impact of the accessions even in this area is unlikely to be great. Enlargement will not transform the EU into a 'fortress Europe'.

Chapter 16

The European Union as an International Political Actor

CLIVE ARCHER

Introduction

The enlargement of the European Union could provide an opportunity to develop the EU as an international political actor – as has happened after previous enlargements – or may just dash such hopes. In reality, the role of the EU on the world stage will depend not just on internal developments in the Union and on its increased membership but more on the configuration of power in the world and the agenda of issues that will confront richer states in the coming decades. This dominance of outside forces has been felt by the Union since its creation, but it is particularly relevant at a time when the United States has been prepared to demonstrate its strength in wars in Afghanistan in 2002 and in Iraq in 2003.

Seeing the EU as an international political actor raises certain questions. From the start of the European integration process, the EU's predecessors – the ECSC, Euratom and the EEC – were players on the world stage, but mainly in the limited area of trade. Even in some commercial areas, the Commission has had to share with member states the competence to negotiate and sign agreements. The creation of the EU broadened external policy areas that could be dealt with collectively, but did not change the bicephalous nature of the EU in the world. As a result, it often becomes difficult to identify the extent to which the EU as an organization – as opposed to some or all of its members – is involved internationally. The balance between the role of member states and that of the Union-based institutions has changed over time and continues to change. The EU's international involvement takes many forms, including through its external economic policies (see Chapter 15), its development policy (see Chapter 17), and its 'political' policies in the form of the Common Foreign and Security Policy (CFSP) and indeed the European Security and Defence Policy (ESDP) aspect of CFSP. The ESDP represents the recognition that the EU needs to tackle security policy, including military defence questions, if it is to have a complete external policy. As will be seen, this has proved to be a controversial issue.

226

How the EU will develop as an international actor through the CFSP thus depends on the world in which it is acting, on the institutions it has to hand, and on the part of the EU machinery being used. A final complicating element is whether the new EU members will add little to the external face of the EU or whether they will re-shape it. Is a Europe of 25 going to find it even more difficult than a Europe of 15 states to agree on a common diplomacy and defence?

This chapter will examine the rise of the EU as an international political actor and will consider how its position and behaviour as such an actor has been affected by previous enlargements and is likely to be affected by the 10 + 2 enlargement.

The EU as an International Political Actor

The construction of the CFSP

EU foreign policy has its origins in the 1970s, when the governments of the European Community began to exchange ideas and information and to cooperate with each other on foreign policy matters of shared interest and concern. Known then as European Political Cooperation (EPC), the policy was wholly intergovernmental in nature. It formed a 'pillar' of cooperation between EC member states. EPC had some modest successes. For example: it led to the creation of the 'Gymnich Formula' for EPC–US consultations in 1974, which allowed the US to be informed of key EPC and EC activities; it promoted cooperation with regional groups such as the Association of South East Asian Nations (ASEAN); and it resulted in the Venice Declaration on the Arab–Israeli dispute in 1980 (which, in the event, satisfied neither side). However, overall, by the early 1990s, EPC was seen to be failing, as was exemplified by the inability to coordinate member states' actions during the 1991 Gulf War – an occurrence that was described as 'an object lesson . . . on the limitations of the European Communities' by Jacques Delors, President of the Commission (1991:99). The inability of the EC to deal effectively with the collapse of Yugoslavia further displayed the weakness of EPC.

The pillar structure was formally developed under the 1992 Maastricht Treaty, when EPC was re-named CFSP and was constituted as the second of three pillars of the newly created EU (see Cameron, 1999; Hill and Smith, 2000). Four particular points arise from the 1992 Treaty and its provisions for the CFSP. First, the EU was to have a *common* foreign and security policy, not just greater co-ordination of national policies as in the EPC. Second, it was recognized that the CFSP was only part of the external policies of the Union and that a different institutional mix was needed in the various sections of external policy.

Third, whereas the commercial policy was part of the Community system, the CFSP was to remain outside and to be essentially intergovernmental in character. Finally, defence as well as security was included in the scope of CFSP.

The 1997 Amsterdam Treaty attempted to strengthen the CFSP, notably by providing the EU with more instruments to face some of the post-Cold War turbulence. Membership of the EU in 1995 by three non-NATO states – Austria, Sweden and Finland – could have undermined the promise of developing the defence aspect of the CFSP at Amsterdam. However, these countries supported the transmission to the EU of tasks adopted by the West European Union (WEU) at its 1992 Petersberg meeting, namely those of humanitarian and rescue tasks, peacekeeping, and tasks of combat forces in crisis management, including peacemaking. This gained the support of the other member states, as did a number of other developments that resulted in the Amsterdam Treaty laying foundations for what later became the ESDP. Maastricht had cautiously introduced defence onto the agenda by specifying that the CFSP included 'all questions related to the security of the Union, including the eventual framing of a common defence policy, which might in time lead to a common defence' (Article J.4.1, TEU) The WEU – in effect, the intergovernmentalist European wing of NATO – was tasked 'to elaborate and implement' decisions with defence implications, with policy being compatible with NATO obligations and not interfering with closer NATO and WEU cooperation. The Amsterdam Treaty changed J.4.1 to now read that the CFSP included 'the progressive framing of a common defence policy . . . which might lead to a common defence, should the European Council so decide' (Article 17 under the new numbering system). The Amsterdam Treaty also made provision for the possible integration of the WEU into the Union.

The 2001 Treaty of Nice made a few further changes to the CFSP structure. The main change concerned enhanced cooperation, which was to be allowed for joint actions and common positions (two of the main CFSP policy instruments – see Box 16.1) but was to be excluded from anything with a defence or military implication (Galloway, 2001: 135).

*   *   *

Events in the latter half of the 1990s fully challenged the CFSP. In 1999, EU states saw the necessity to counter the Serb ethnic cleansing of Kosovo but it was a US-led NATO operation that took the province out of Serb hands and led to the downfall of President Milosevic. The events of 11 September 2001 produced a united response to al Qaeda's attack on New York and the Pentagon, but sympathy for the US did not bring EU agreement on the US-led attack on Afghanistan in 2002 to rid it of the Taliban regime. The main EU states were even more divided in their response to the US-led invasion of Iraq in early 2003, with the UK, Denmark, Italy and Spain being prominent supporters of the US, while France and Germany led the opposition to the use of force.

More positively, the EU continued, as it had since the TEU established the instrument, to adopt joint actions under the CFSP; the WEU identified members' armed forces answerable to the WEU and most of the WEU's tasks were absorbed by the EU after the enactment of the Amsterdam Treaty; and the 1998 Franco–British St Malo summit recognized that the Union needed to have 'the capacity for autonomous action, backed up by credible military forces, the means to decide to use them, and a readiness to do so, in order to respond to international crises' (Embassy of France, 1998).

The June 1999 Cologne European Council decided that the General Affairs Council (that is, the Foreign Ministers) could be held with Defence Ministers present and later in 1999 the Secretary-General of the EU Council (and of the WEU) was designated the CFSP High Representative. The December 1999 Helsinki European Council set a 'headline goal' by which member states would make available forces of up to 60 000 personnel within 60 days for the Petersberg tasks. Later, plans were added for the availability of up to 5 000 police officers by 2003 for international civilian crisis management. By early 2003, the Council was able to declare that this force would be capable of undertaking peacekeeping activities. An EU police force was deployed in Bosnia-Herzegovina and a military force in Macedonia (see below). These deployments were part of a wider involvement of the EU in the region through its West Balkans Common Strategy and its Stability Pact for South Eastern Europe.

The instruments and institutions

As is shown in Box 16.1, several instruments are available for giving effect to the CFSP. However, useful and important though they are, they need to be placed in the context of two key facts. First, most of the EU's 'foreign affairs' are still conducted by the member states, either on a bilateral basis with other countries or in international organizations. These activities feed into the EU process, but they are still nation-bound. The new members will add their perspectives to those of the older ones. Second, most of the EU's *external* relations are economic and involve trade matters, aid and development.

As for the institutions of the CFSP, there are four main Commissioners who deal with external relations: the Commissioners for External Relations (called 'Relex'), for Development and Humanitarian Aid, for Enlargement, and for Trade. The Council Presidency represents the EU in CFSP matters, but then so does the

---

Box 16.1   CFSP instruments

- European Council defines the *principles* of and *general guidelines* for CFSP.
- European Council adopts *common strategies* for areas where members have important common interest, and may also cover Pillar I and III matters.
- The Council takes *common positions* to clarify the EU position about a situation and these are legally binding acts.
- *Joint actions* are decided by the Council and are legally binding operational actions with financial means attached to them.
- *International agreements* are negotiated by the Presidency, assisted by the Commission, on Council authorization in CFSP matters.
- *Declarations* express a position, request or expectation of the EU regarding an international issue or a third country.
- *Contacts with third countries* may take place by the EU holding a 'political dialogue' with a group of countries on an issue. A *démarche* is usually a diplomatic complaint by the EU to a third country.
- *Systematic cooperation* includes information exchange, co-ordination and convergence of national action.

Source: 'CFSP – Common Foreign & Security Policy' at Commission's External Relations' web site, http://europa.eu.int/comm/external_relations/cfsp/intro/index.htm, and 'The Council of the European Union and the Common Foreign and Security Policy' at http://ue.eu.int/pesc/pres.asp?lang=en)

High Representative. These two and the Commissioner for External Relations make up what is known as the CFSP 'troika'. Within CFSP, security and defence matters have special institutions that include an EU military staff with a Situation Centre, and a Political and Security Committee (COPS) which is advised by a Military Committee made up of military representatives. There are thus ample grounds for confusion for those dealing with the EU (see Figure 16.1).

CFSP decision-making does not follow the Community method. The intergovernmental European Council sets the 'principles and general guidelines' and sets common strategies (Article 13, TEU), and the Council is the principal institution with responsibility for giving effect to the general framework so laid down. Unlike under the Community method, the Commission does not have the virtual monopoly of initiation. Unanimity is the dominant form of decision-making in the Council, although the Amsterdam Treaty did increase the opportunities for qualified majority voting (QMV). The Treaty also included the possibility of a 'constructive abstention' under Article 23.1 TEU, whereby a state is not obliged to apply a decision

Figure 16.1   *CFSP decision-making institutions*

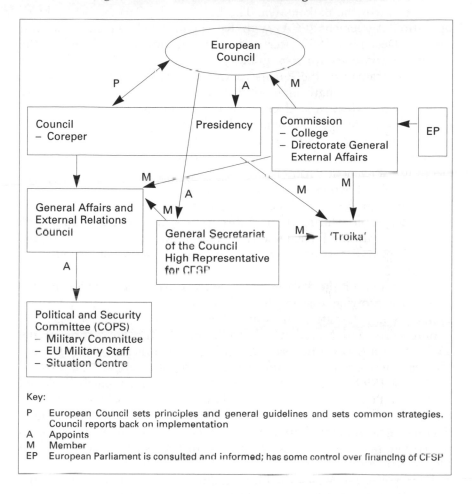

Key:

P   European Council sets principles and general guidelines and sets common strategies.
    Council reports back on implementation
A   Appoints
M   Member
EP European Parliament is consulted and informed; has some control over financing of CFSP

but must not impede consequent EU action. The role of the EP has been one of consultation and information (Article 21 TEU), though it has an important voice in the financing of the CFSP.

Pre-enlargement policies

The new EU members must deal with an existing corpus of CFSP activity covering a number of important areas and issues, including policies towards and agreements with other states. This section of the chapter will identify aspects of the corpus that are likely to particularly attract the attention of the new member states.

Of greatest interest to the CEECs are relations with Russia and the policy towards the Balkan area. The EU signed a Partnership and Co-operation Agreement (PCA) with Russia in 1994, which came into force in December 1997 after its implementation was delayed by the EU in response to Russian military action in Chechnya. The first common strategy of the European Council was on Russia, in 1999, which aimed at strengthening political dialogue on foreign and security matters with Moscow and encouraging economic reform (European Commission, 2003j). Environmental and crime questions were also to be tackled. In late 1999, relations with Russia were again under scrutiny by the EU after heavy-handed action in Chechnya, though the election of President Putin placed the links back on an even keel. After the events of 11 September 2001, Russian action in Chechnya was seen increasingly in the light of the war against terrorism, and thus became more acceptable. During the UN discussions in early 2003 leading to the war in Iraq, the French and the Germans were careful to bring the Russians into discussions – not least because Moscow supported their viewpoint.

As a result of the Balkans turbulence during the 1990s, the EU adopted a growing role in South-Eastern Europe – Albania, Bosnia-Herzegovina, Croatia, the Yugoslav republic (now Serbia and Montenegro) and Macedonia. It took on the implementation of the 1995 Dayton Accords that saw the end of the conflict involving Bosnia-Herzegovina, Croatia and the Yugoslav republic. Also, the Kosovo conflict of 1999 was brought to an end by an agreement partly brokered by former President Ahtisaari of Finland, acting on behalf of the EU, and involved an EU-led reconstruction plan. The EU Balkans Stability Pact has included Stabilisation and Association Agreements for states in the region, preparing them for future EU membership (Cameron, 1999: 88; European Commission, 2003o).

For Cyprus and Malta, the EU's Mediterranean initiative is of particular relevance. Since 1990, EU relations with countries on the southern shores of the Mediterranean have been based on its New Mediterranean Policy, which aims at increasing trade links with and supporting economic and social reform in the region. The 1995 Barcelona Declaration dealt with: the political and security aspects of the relationship; economic and financial matters – a free trade area is scheduled for 2010; and social, cultural and human issues (European Commission, 2003q).

Another area of importance for all EU members is the Middle East. The EC initiated a Euro–Arab dialogue in 1974 and has since striven to broker peace (Dosenrode and Stubkjær, 2002: 97–9). Since the 1993 Oslo Accords, the EU has contributed finance to help build the infrastructure of the Palestinian authority, but this has alienated it from Israel which sees the US as the principal external power in the area.

Enlargement and the EU as an International Political Actor

How will the EU of 25 members look as an international political actor? Any answer involves the concept of the EU as an international actor. What does it mean and how is it constructed? If the enlarged EU is to act on the world stage, what new impetus will it receive from the new members?

Acting and being there

The notion of the EC having international 'actorness' was introduced by Cosgrove and Twitchett (1970) and then developed by Sjöstedt, who considered that an international actor should possess autonomy and actor capability (1977:15–16). Sjöstedt estimated that the EC had the necessary minimum of 'internal cohesion' and that it was 'discernible from its environment', which meant it had autonomy. In regard to capability, he asserted that the EC had:

- the ability to identify policy priorities and create coherent policies;
- the ability to negotiate with other actors in the international system;
- the use of policy instruments;
- domestic legitimization of the external policy-making process.

Writing in 1990, Allen and Smith attempted to downplay the implicit comparison with states that the notion of being an international actor suggests and, instead, claimed the EC had 'presence', which was defined by factors such as 'credentials and legitimacy, the capacity to act and mobilize resources, the place it occupies in the perceptions and expectations of policy makers' (Allen and Smith, 1990:21). Bretherton and Vogler have remarked on the closeness of this definition to the capability aspect of actorness; they prefer a subtler concept of presence, one that is a function of '*being* rather than action' (Bretherton and Vogler, 1999: 33, italics in original) and can cause a response just by being there (as did the EU's Single Market). In relation to enlargement, it may be that the EU-25 will find it harder to be an effective actor on the world stage, not least because of internal dissension and institutional deadlock, but its *presence* will be weightier, purely because its size and borders have expanded.

What an enlarged EU will do with its greater presence internationally is partly dependent on the opportunities set for the EU-25 by the international environment. Nevertheless, there are some broad considerations that also reflect choices from within the Union, including the extent to which the EU should have a military presence. In 1972, Duchêne (1972: 43–4) saw the EC as a 'civilian power' that could nevertheless play 'a very important and potentially constructive role' in the world. The notion of 'civilian power Europe' has since been rejected by Bull (1983) and Hill (1993), among others, partly on the grounds of the weakness of the EC/EU as an actor, and partly because some military capability was seen as being necessary for effective action. With the adoption of an ESDP, it could be argued that the EU has at least given itself the option of becoming more than a civilian power. Will the institutional processes and the addition of new interests allow effective action?

New members, new input

Previous enlargement showed new members feeding in their external concerns to the EC/EU system fairly rapidly. While negotiations for membership have mostly been conducted on a 'take it or leave it' basis by the EC/EU, new members have always wanted to re-arrange the furniture in their new home. The UK, with its Commonwealth experience, pushed to change the EC's links with the Third World from the colonial-style Yaoundé Convention to the more seemingly respectable Lomé Conventions that had the African, Caribbean and Pacific states as 'equal partners' with the EC. The British presence also helped lead to the Gymnich Formula for consultation with the US. The Mediterranean enlargement actually resulted in a cooling of relations between the EU and North African states, which were seen as trade rivals by the new members. After some time, however, the EC developed closer relations with the North African countries in the 1990 New Mediterranean Policy. Spanish and Portuguese membership also saw the EC take a more active approach to Latin America, dominated as it is by Spanish- and Portuguese-speaking countries. Likewise, the membership of two Nordic states in 1995 led to the Northern Dimension Initiative that, especially, reflected Finnish interests and involvement (Ojanen, 1999). The new neutral states, especially Finland and Sweden, were also largely responsible for the inclusion of the Petersberg tasks in the Amsterdam Treaty.

Will the 10 + 2 states be acquiescent in their acceptance of the CFSP as it was at the time of their accession, or will they try to alter its contents?

Purely by enlarging eastwards, the subjects of the CFSP will change. The new members will have new concerns and perspectives that are bound to feed into the CFSP. Some of these may well bolster aspects of policy that have not been developed; others will underscore existing policies. In some cases, the new states may be faced with pre-existing divisions within the EU and may have to 'choose sides'. What are the likely concerns of the new members?

Further enlargement

First, a number of the new states – like many of the 15 they joined – will want to continue the process of enlargement. How far this should go will be a matter for contention, even among the new members. There is little disagreement that Bulgaria and Romania should become members once they are fully prepared. There are more reservations about some of the other Balkan states. The Slovenian Foreign Minister's 2002 overview of foreign relations did not mention any support for EU membership by the Yugoslavia republic, Bosnia-Herzegovina and, above all, Croatia (Rupel, 2002) and later only mentioned 'the gradual integration of the countries of South-Eastern Europe into European structures' (Rupel, 2003). There was no reflection here of the Commission President's message to the South-East European states that 'We want you to become members of the Union – with no "ifs" and "buts" ' (Prodi, 2003: 2). Meanwhile, engaging the countries of this region through the Stability Pact for South-Eastern Europe finds favour, especially with Hungary, which itself suffered as a result of the Yugoslav conflicts (Ministry of Foreign Affairs Hungary, 2003).

Turkey is a particular problem for future enlargement. It is not, however a new problem, because differing views of the desirability of welcoming Turkey have long existed among the EU-15. Greece, because of its historical enmity with Turkey, has been portrayed as the EU-15 state most wanting to keep Turkey on the doorstep, but it has not been alone. France is one of a number of EU-15 states with concerns about a country rooted in Asia being an EU member, and even Commissioners have shown some ambiguity about this issue (Sjursen, 2002: 504). These doubts notwithstanding, the European Council has promised Turkey that if it continues to meet the political goals of the Copenhagen conditions for membership (see Chapter 3), then a decision will be taken at the December 2004 summit to open accession negotiations with it without delay. What the European Council has not formally said, though clearly it is a *de facto* condition, is that the Cyprus Problem must also be resolved, if for no other reason than Cyprus itself is hardly likely to support accession negotiations with Turkey when Turkish troops occupy one-third of the island.

The 'new neighbours'

A second concern of the new members is over the 'new neighbours', some of whom are not so new. The line between these countries and future enlargement states may be a moveable one, depending on how soon Turkey and the South-Eastern European states are brought within the fold. A not-so-new neighbour that does not aspire to EU membership is Russia, but new neighbours that have such hopes are Ukraine,

Belarus and, after Romanian membership, Moldova (White, McAllister and Light, 2002).

Russia already had a pre-2004 frontier with the EU (with Finland) but enlargement has brought it into greater contact with the Union. The new input will come especially from the Baltic states – Estonia, Latvia and Lithuania – and from Poland. As early as 1998 the then Polish Foreign Minister advanced the notion of an Eastern Dimension of the EU, based on the Northern Dimension, and this idea was taken up in a Polish 'non-paper' to the European Commission at the end of 2002. The aim was to prevent new divisions in Europe appearing along the eastern border of the EU and to encourage the EU 'to have a coherent, comprehensive framework of its Eastern policy' (Cimoszewicz, 2003a: 4). This was an implicit criticism of the pre-enlargement policies towards Russia and other Eastern European countries, though the Polish Foreign Minister was less circumspect in his remarks in March 2003 about the EU preferring to go ahead with 'its concept of "neighbourhood" initiative without adequate participation of new member states' (Cimoszewicz, 2003b: 8). Broadly, the Eastern Initiative would encourage cooperation in a wide range of policies and would also include a non-governmental input. However, it would not replace the EU's central instrument for relationships with Russia, the Partnership and Cooperation Agreement.

For Poland and Lithuania, there is another important point of contact with the Russian Federation, the region of Kaliningrad which forms a Russian enclave in the EU-25. The land route from Russia to Kaliningrad crosses Lithuania, which resulted in the issue of whether Russians travelling from one part of the Russian federation to another would need visas being a difficult part of the negotiations between Russia, the EU and Lithuania in the lead-up to Lithuanian accession. The European Commission (2001c) had identified the Kaliningrad issue as one where problems might arise, not just because of the visa issue but also because of issues such as energy supplies, fisheries, transport and the environment. Indeed, the presence of Kaliningrad in the Baltic Sea – which is now an 'EU-dominated' sea – has been tackled by the EU's Northern Dimension, but with only limited success. The three Baltic states and Poland will join the Nordic countries and Germany in trying to find ways of managing the externalities of Kaliningrad within the EU's midst – emigration, drug smuggling, prostitution, disease, the size of the military presence – without seeming to threaten Russian sovereignty over the enclave. Perhaps a more imaginative solution could be to use Kaliningrad as what its former governor, Vladimir Yegorov, has described as 'a laboratory for working out new forms of cooperation between Russia and the European Union' (cited in Sergounin, 2001: 175) rather than a bone of contention between the two.

The 'new neighbours' of Belarus, Moldova and the Ukraine are also of 'particular interest to Poland' (Cimoszewicz, 2003b: 6), which is another reason why for some time before its accession to the EU, Poland was already actively contributing to the EU's new neighbours' policy. However, the Poles were recommending a differentiated approach to these three countries based on their good behaviour. The Polish Foreign Minister considered that 'Ukraine, Moldova and even Belarus – provided it enters the path towards democracy – should be given an opportunity of integration with the EU' (Cimoszewicz 2003b: 7). This would involve political dialogue, free trade, streamlined assistance programmes and cooperation in justice and home affairs. For Poland there is a difference between the sort of leverage that can be exercised by the EU on Ukraine and Moldova 'which aspire to the European structures' and where a 'prospect, not a promise of EU membership, should be conditional on reforms and meeting strict criteria' and Russia – 'which does not aspire to the membership of the Union' – and Belarus, where democratic reforms are first needed (Cimoszewicz 2003a: 5).

The Mediterranean

The accession of Cyprus and Malta brings considerable experience of the Mediterranean to the EU and their membership will strengthen the Union's sensitivity to the Mediterranean region. Both countries, indeed, were involved in the Euro–Mediterranean Partnership as Mediterranean Partners previous to their accession, so they are well positioned to exercise facilitating and bridging roles between the two 'sides'. In the words of an expert on Malta, 'Malta's participation in the EU and in the Mediterranean regional politics thus become mutually reinforcing not diametrically opposed' (Pace, 2001: 406). As for Cyprus, the Ministry of Foreign Affairs of the Republic of Cyprus (2002) is clear that the EU will be able to benefit from 'Cyprus' close and excellent relations with the region'.

ESDP

An area of policy to which the new members have been eager to contribute is that of the ESDP. However, the outbreak of the US-led war with Iraq called into question that policy and faced the new members with some difficult decisions. As long as the ESDP remains based around the Petersberg tasks, the new member states, like the EU-15, can busy themselves in deciding on the best form of contribution they can make for peace-support operations and the like. Indeed, a number have already made such contributions in UN and NATO contexts. For example, Estonian forces participated in UN operations as part of a Danish battalion in UNPROFOR in Croatia and in NATO-led operations such as SFOR in Bosnia-Herzegovina (Estonian Ministry of Defence, 2001: 10). Mannik (2002: 86) makes the point about Estonia – which seems to cover other small states joining both the EU and NATO – that while forces for NATO and ESDP can be 'double-hatted' (that is, serve both), the 'preliminary commitment [to ESDP] is likely to be too extensive to be sustainable'. Furthermore, ESDP, unlike NATO, does not easily allow for 'the contribution of valuable capabilities in the form of small units'. EU membership by the CEECs is thus unlikely to help bridge the gap between expectations raised by the ESDP and the capabilities available to fulfil them (Hill, 1993; Schuwirth, 2002).

Because the ESDP currently deals with the Petersberg tasks and 'soft security' issues (Archer, 2001: 189–92), the involvement of the Baltic states and Poland is unlikely to concern Russia. However, should the ESDP develop a hard collective defence capability, then Russia may consider it to be an EU-based NATO and wonder against which states it is aimed.

The ESDP has brought to the fore the nature of the EU's relationship with the US. A common theme running through commentary by CEECs is the need to keep close to the US on security matters. This reflects a number of factors: the general dominance of US military and diplomatic power; the cautious concern that, should the security situation in Europe turn sour – as it did in the Balkans throughout the 1990s – it will be the US and not the EU that can and will act militarily; and the close connection of a number of CEEC leaders to the US, forged by NATO links. The 2003 Iraq war tested the then members-to-be, with the EU-15 divided between the UK, Spain, Italy, Denmark and Portugal, all of which supported the US policy, and France, Germany and Belgium which vocally criticized US action. The CEECs supported the US, allowing the Bush administration to contrast the attitude of 'Old Europe' (France and Germany) with that of 'New Europe'. This stance of CEECs confirms that they will want to avoid any choice between NATO and the ESDP (Cameron and Primatarova, 2003). By thus adding support to the EU's Atlanticist wing, enlargement might be seen as widening the split on defence issues, but it may also help Paris and Berlin realize that a sizeable majority of the EU-25 are not interested in building an ESDP *against* the US, and that some compromise must be reached.

In 2003, the EU mounted its first police and military operations when the EU Police Mission took over operations in Bosnia-Herzegovina and a EU Military Mission replaced a NATO force in Macedonia. Practically all the new member states were willing to make some contribution to these operations. This seemed to show the limits of ESDP: it is able to undertake modest Petersberg tasks, but when troops are placed 'in harm's way' operations remain either with NATO (as in Afghanistan) or based on coalitions of the willing (as in Iraq), both led by the US.

The EU's Ability to Act After Enlargement

The previous section examined what extra contribution the new EU members may make to the CFSP. But what about the machinery itself? Will it be able to digest the new input or will it suffer from overload?

The EU-15 were aware that the 10 + 2 enlargement round could put a strain – 'an institutional drag' – on the already precarious institutional balance of the Union. They attempted to address the most obvious aspects of potential gridlock in the Treaty of Nice but this had little to say about the CFSP (see above). The European Convention provided another opportunity for addressing CFSP reform. Proposals in the Constitutional Treaty that was agreed by the Convention that particularly affected CFSP included the creation of a 'European President' rather than a rotating presidency of the European Council and the appointment of a 'European Foreign Minister' to be appointed by the Council but to be located in the Commission. Furthermore, Article I-15 of the Convention's Constitution obliged member states to 'actively and unreservedly support the Union's foreign and security in a spirit of loyalty and mutual solidarity' and to comply 'with the acts adopted by the Union in this area' (European Convention, 2003: 10). These proposals created a certain amount of discord among the governments of the EU-25, not least because they touch on areas still regarded as the sovereign prerogative of the nation state. The subsequent debate, however, has only rarely been between the EU-15 and acceding states. Rather, it has been between the larger countries and the smaller states and also between supporters of the retention of as much national independence as possible, led by the UK and France, and states such as Belgium, Germany and the Netherlands that want a more Union-based approach (Cameron and Primatarova, 2003).

Assuming the post-Convention IGC adopts reforms that are at least not unlike those proposed by the Convention, the possibility of 'institutional drag' clearly will be lessened. Two other factors should also help in this repect. First, as noted by the former Estonian Foreign Minister, Toomas Ilves (1999), 'for a number of years our Foreign Service has been part of a dense web of foreign policy cooperation and co-ordination'. As part of this, even before their accession the new members were associating themselves with many EU declarations. Second, the EU has long been developing its diplomatic 'presence' in the world. By 2001, the EU, via Commission representations, had a presence in 123 countries and five international organizations, making it 'the fourth largest 'diplomatic service' in the world' (Duke, 2002: 858). This presence will doubtless increase further after enlargement.

How does the EU-25 measure up as an international actor according to Sjöstedt's criteria (see above)? The autonomy of the Commission to act on the world stage is clear in economic matters, but, the 'internal cohesion' of the CFSP and its relationship with the EU's Common Commercial Policy is by no means so clear. Nevertheless, the EU is as 'discernible from its environment' as many states. Concerning its capability, the EU has the structures to identify policy priorities – for example in its common strategies – and to create coherent policies, though this coherence is often muddied by contrasting state interests, a factor likely to be increased by the move to EU-25. The ability to negotiate with other actors has been there even with the troika and should improve if a 'European Foreign Minister' is appointed. However, such a minister could well find himself/herself engaged in 'turf wars' with both member state Foreign Ministers and also with members of the Commission and the Council.

The CFSP has developed a number of policy instruments over the years – common strategies, common positions, joint actions, international agreements among them – and these will be bolstered by the operationalization of the ESDP. However precarious the fulfilment of the headline goals may be, an ability to carry out at least some of the Petersberg tasks will mean that the EU will become a 'Civilian-Plus Power'. The new members have made modest contributions to this new capability.

Finally, the domestic legitimization of external policy-making processes comes with a question-mark. However, doubts here do not so much concern the acceding states, all of which except Cyprus held referendums on membership, but some of the EU-15. Politicians and the public in France and the UK in particular, but also to some extent in countries such as Denmark and Sweden, are used to their Foreign Ministers acting on the world stage and have not always taken kindly to the EU taking their place.

Conclusions

The new member states do not themselves create major problems for the future development of the CFSP. They may have added new emphases – for example with Polish pleas for an Eastern Dimension – but they have not in themselves led to difficulties. The very nature of the CFSP is the cause of its shortcomings. By definition it is *the* policy of the EU that is most dependent on external factors, many of which are out of the control of the EU and its members.

EU foreign policy is a policy that takes much of its input from the foreign ministries of the member states and their diplomatic services. An effort has been made to create an infrastructure for EU diplomacy. This is limited, but the new members can add to its size and, with their special interest, even its range.

The CFSP is still a common, not a 'single', foreign policy and it is still in the intergovernmentalist domain rather than that of the Union's Community institutions. Even with the changes suggested by the Convention, the EU cannot become an actor on the foreign policy stage (as opposed to the international commercial and economic stage) until the larger members are willing to give up their national control of foreign policy. This would mean a perception of a single EU foreign policy, albeit one with many contributing views. That this seems some way off is scarcely the fault of the new members.

Chapter 17

Development Policy

MAURIZIO CARBONE

Introduction

Development policy is one of the central elements in the EU's external affairs, together with trade policy and foreign and security policy. The foundations for a development policy were laid down in the Treaty of Rome (EEC), which contained provisions on the relations between the six members of the Economic Community and their colonies in the developing world. Since then, the activities and responsibilities of the EC/EU in respect of development policy have gradually progressed, with a major role in this evolution having been played by successive enlargements, which have been instrumental in helping to transform a policy that originally was directed only to Africa into a more global policy covering almost all countries in the developing world. Development cooperation was formally included in the objectives of the EU in the Treaty of Maastricht in 1992, which provide the policy with a secure legal foundation and framework.

The EU is unique in that it combines characteristics of a bilateral donor, by providing direct assistance to developing countries, and of a multilateral institution, by coordinating the efforts of the EU member states. As for its financial contributions, the EU is the major source of foreign assistance to developing countries, providing more than half of global official development assistance (ODA). Most of this aid is still channelled bilaterally by member states, but the amount of resources managed by the European Commission has increased over the years, from 7 per cent of total EU aid in 1970 to 23 per cent in 2001 (Development Assistance Committee, 2003).

Despite this long tradition and the large amounts of resources disbursed, development cooperation received scarce attention in the debate that preceded the 10 + 2 enlargement round. It was not included as a separate item in the list of 31 topics covered in the accession negotiations, but rather was subsumed in Chapter 26, which dealt with 'external relations'. This was perhaps unfortunate, because though it may be understandable that the need to transform the economies of the acceding countries was the main concern of EU policy-makers dealing with enlargement, the fact is that the *acquis communautaire* obliges the new member states to shift from being recipients of large amounts of development assistance to becoming donors committed to international development.

Against this background, this chapter investigates the impact of the development *acquis* on the new member states and assesses how enlargement may affect the future of EU development cooperation policy and practice. In particular it focuses on the quantity of aid, the quality of aid, and the geographical focus and scope of aid.

The Impact of Previous Enlargements

EU development cooperation is very much a product of history, and in particular of the history of enlargement. When the EEC was established, France sought to share with other member states the burden of providing assistance to its African colonies. Belgium and Italy supported the French proposal, whereas Germany and the Netherlands opposed any form of privileged status with any developing country and called rather for a global development cooperation policy that would not necessarily be confined to former colonies. The EEC Treaty had a specific section on the 'Association of Overseas Countries and Territories', which included many sub-Saharan African countries and some possessions in the Caribbean and the Pacific. Following the de-colonization process of the 1960s, the ties with former colonies were formalized via the Yaoundé Conventions of 1963 and in 1969 (Grilli, 1993).

The 1973 enlargement considerably changed EC development policy. A key reason for this was that the UK asked for special treatment for the African members of the British Commonwealth. This led to the first Lomé Convention in 1975, in which French colonies no longer held a dominant position in the distribution of EC aid: Britain's accession resulted in a shift of portions of aid to its former colonies. Another consequence of the 1973 enlargement was to increase the scope of cooperation not only with associated countries, but also with non-associated countries: a small budget line for development cooperation was created in 1976 for non-associated countries in Asia and Latin America (Van Reisen, 2002).

The Southern enlargement of the 1980s resulted in a further expansion of EC aid, with an intensification of the relationship with countries in Latin America and the Mediterranean. The new Mediterranean policy, which was launched in 1991 following some small disbursements in the 1980s, tripled the financial commitments of the EC to this region. The accession of Spain and Portugal also put a stronger emphasis on the political and cultural aspects of the relationship between the EC and Latin America.

The Nordic enlargement in 1995 had a less direct, but nevertheless still important, effect on EU development policy. The accession of Finland and Sweden strengthened the already dominant northern European lobby towards a more global approach of EU development policy and the partial weakening of the preferential treatment of the former European colonies in sub-Saharan Africa. The Nordic countries also played a significant role in expanding the 'ideological' scope of EU development policy, by concentrating more on poverty alleviation, debt relief, women's rights, partnership with developing countries, and multilateral aid (Lister, 1998, 1999).

Donors, Recipients, and Donors Again

The 10 new member states have different experiences in dealing with development cooperation policy. Slovenia was part of the former Republic of Yugoslavia, which, within its non-aligned foreign policy framework, provided considerable resources to developing countries. Cyprus and Malta, which were under direct British administration for much of their history, have little experience with development assistance. The other seven were, until the collapse of communism, members of the Soviet dominated block, the Council of Mutual Economic Assistance (CMEA). Estonia, Latvia, and Lithuania were members of the CMEA as part of the former Soviet Union; the Czech Republic and Slovakia were so as part of the former Czechoslovakia; Hungary and Poland were so in their own capacity.

Among the CMEA members, the former Soviet Union was by far the largest donor. Most of its aid was characterized by a strong and strategic orientation, concentrating on political allies and friendly countries which were pursuing socialist goals. Most of this assistance consisted of concessional loans for capital goods and equipment, especially in the energy and industry sectors, tied to Soviet procurement and technical personnel, and implemented only by government agencies (Burnell, 1997). Although some 60 countries received Soviet bilateral aid, about three-quarters of it was provided to three countries within the CMEA: Cuba, Mongolia, and Vietnam (Browne, 1990).

The CEECs that provided the most significant amounts of aid were East Germany, Czechoslovakia and Bulgaria. The recipients of this aid were mostly the same as those of the Soviet Union: Cuba, Vietnam, Afghanistan, Cambodia, Laos and Mongolia. All CEECs, however, offered scholarships to students of developing countries for educational opportunities in the host country (Browne, 1990).

Measuring CMEA aid was very difficult due to the unwillingness of communist countries to disclose verifiable data. But statistics were also used for political purposes: on the one hand, communist official information tried to convey the impression of generosity (claiming that aid from the Soviet Union reached 1.3 per cent of GNP in the 1980s); on the other hand, the Development Assistance Committee of the OECD manipulated data to provide a basis for attacks on communist countries (Raffer and Singer, 1996).

With the collapse of communism, Poland, Hungary, Romania, and Bulgaria retained their state identity, while Czechoslovakia, Yugoslavia and the Soviet Union disintegrated and were replaced by new independent states. Due to the severe decline in their GNPs and the disappearance of Cold War objectives, most of these states discontinued their aid programmes (Dauderstadt, 2002). However, by the mid-1990s, as they looked towards EU accession and began to make progress with transitional issues, CEECs launched, or re-launched, their own development policies. In so doing, they thus faced the unique situation of being recipients of aid from the EU while simultaneously preparing to become donors.

The institutional arrangements of CEECs that have provided the most significant amounts of development funding since the mid-1990s are similar to those that existed during the socialist period. The responsibility for the aid programme generally lies with the Ministry of Foreign Affairs, which also plays a role in coordinating the projects funded by other ministries. Levels of aid are small, with the major part of the funds being directed to fund humanitarian programmes and to a limited number of strategic and neighbouring countries. A significant part of ODA of the Czech Republic, Slovakia, and Slovenia is committed to a programme administered and implemented by the EU Stability Pact for South Eastern Europe. Established in 1999, the Stability Pact aims to strengthen the countries of South Eastern Europe in their efforts to foster peace, democracy, respect for human rights and economic prosperity in order to achieve stability in the region (Giffen and Press, 2002).

The Acquis in Development Policy

The primary legal bases for EU development policy lie in the provisions of the TEU and in secondary legislation. An entire chapter of the TEU sets out specific principles for development policy: the sustainable economic and social development of the developing countries, and more particularly the most disadvantaged among them; their smooth and gradual integration into the world economy; the campaign against poverty in the developing countries; and the promotion of democracy, the rule of law and respect for fundamental rights and freedoms.

The TEU also spelled out the key principles of development policy coordination: the EU should coordinate and consult with member states, especially in international organizations and during international conferences;

complementarity – EU development policy should complement the bilateral policies of the member states; coherence – the EU should take development objectives into account in any of its policies likely to affect developing countries. The Treaty of Amsterdam added the principle of consistency – development policy should be consistent with the other EU external activities.

In contrast to trade policy, where the EU mostly enjoys exclusive competence, development is a policy area where the Union and the member states hold mixed competences. Member states are entitled to enter into agreements with non-member countries, either collectively or individually. However, once the Union has adopted a decision in the field of development aid, member states cannot undertake actions that could have adverse consequences on the policies pursued by the Union (McMahon, 1998).

In addition to the primary development cooperation law in the TEU, a significant amount of secondary legislation has been adopted over the years, with more that 30 Council regulations. Regulations are always binding in their entirety and directly applicable in all member states. There also are a series of soft laws, which include decisions on contributions to international programmes – for example, the Global Fund to fight HIV/AIDS, the Global Health Fund, and food aid programmes.

Many policy documents have been adopted by the EU over the years, many of them in the form of Commission and Council, or just Council, decisions, statements and common positions (Cox and Chapman, 1999). A particularly important document is *The European Community's Development Policy: Statement by the Council and the Commission*, which was adopted in November 2000 and which defines the scope and priorities of EU development policy (European Commission, 2000b). The statement declares that in order to increase efficiency and ensure that its activities provide an added value to those of the member states, the EU will concentrate its development assistance efforts on a limited number of priorities where it has comparative advantages. Six priority areas are identified: the link between trade and development; support for regional integration and cooperation; support for macroeconomic policies and the promotion of equal access to social services (especially education and health); transport; food security and sustainable rural development; and institutional capacity-building, particularly in the area of good governance and the rule of law. It is also specified in the statement that cross-cutting issues, such as gender equality, environmental sustainability and respect for human rights, must be systematically incorporated into all EU development programmes.

All these changes are reflected in the Partnership Agreement between the African, Caribbean, and Pacific (ACP) group of countries and the EU, which was signed in Cotonou in June 2000. The relationship between the EU and the ACP Group, regulated for 25 years by the Lomé Convention

(1975–2000), is considered the hallmark of the EU's policy towards the Third World, but under Lomé it was widely seen as having failed to meet the needs and expectations of the developing world. In view of the expiration of Lomé IV (1990–2000), the European Commission launched a comprehensive and radical review of its relations with the ACP Group, which resulted in the Cotonou Agreement heralding a radical departure from the past. One major innovation is a stronger political foundation for the EU–ACP partnership: dialogue is used to discuss political issues such as peace and security, prevention and resolution of conflicts, progress in human rights and democratization, institutional reforms and capacity building to ensure good governance. A second major feature is an active role for non-state actors in the planning of national development strategies: as post-independence strategies gave a leading role to central government agencies in promoting development, civil society, NGOs, private sector and local government were not involved in the policy-making process. A third change is in the area of trade policy, which will undergo a profound transformation: the overall preferential regime of Lomé will most likely be split into several trade and economic agreements, where different ACP countries and regions receive different treatment from the EU. A fourth innovative feature is related to performance-based aid management: aid allocations will be based on an assessment of each country's needs and performance, with the possibility of adjusting the financial resources allocated through a system of rolling programming (Holland, 2002).

The Implications of Enlargement

Accession negotiations in the 10 + 2 enlargement process gave little attention to development policy. The Commission's key 1997 document on enlargement, *Agenda 2000*, did not include any reference to the implications of enlargement for development policy. The European Parliament, in a resolution adopted in December 1997: regretted that there was 'no reference to development policy in Agenda 2000, which means that the intentions of the Commission in this policy field will remain unclear and ill-defined'; stressed that 'an enlarged European Union has an even greater role to play at the global level and an even greater responsibility to the Third World, and that the image of a European Union that only protects its own interests cannot be justified'; and pointed out that 'budgetary constraints must not lead to this commitment to third countries being abandoned' (European Parliament, 1997).

Despite being a separate policy, development policy fell, as was noted above, under the chapter on external relations in the accession negotiations. This chapter was primarily concerned with the Union's economic and trade relations with third countries and international organizations.

The chapter was provisionally closed with all of the applicant states apart from Bulgaria and Romania between the first half of 1999 and the first half of 2000 and was definitively closed, along with all other chapters, at the Helsinki December 2002 summit.

Regarding compliance with the *acquis*, the Commission's 2002 Regular Report (see Chapter 3) highlighted that the acceding states accepted the *acquis* in the field of external relations and stated that there was a good level of alignment between the candidate countries external policies and those of the EU. However, this should not be taken as implying that there are not still challenges to meet. These challenges are reviewed in the following sections.

Quantity of aid

The most difficult challenge that new member states will have to tackle relates to volume of aid and their compliance with EU requirements concerning bilateral policies. At the International Conference on Financing for Development, which was held in March 2002 in Monterrey (Mexico), EU-15 states committed to boosting substantially their volume of aid. This decision involved two separate commitments: one was collective – to 0.39 per cent of Gross National Income (GNI); the other was individual – to not less than 0.33 per cent of GNI for each member state.

These commitments represent an important part of the political *acquis* that the new member states are expected to implement. Almost all the new member states have expressly signalled an intention to increase their aid expenditures, but given their low levels of pre-accession aid and the economic pressures that they will face following accession, 'it would be unreasonable to expect the new members to go to 0.39 per cent by 2006' (Nielson, 2003).

The new members must first contribute to the general EU budget, part of which is devoted to external relations activities. This budget allocation comprises: (i) activities in the Mediterranean (MEDA programme), Asia and Latin America (ALA programme), Central and Eastern Europe (PHARE programme), the Independent States of the former Soviet Union (TACIS programme), and the Balkans (CARDS programme); (ii) horizontal activities such as humanitarian aid, food aid, NGO co-financing activities, initiatives in the field of democracy and human rights, health, environment and other areas. It is already established that 4.68 per cent of the new member states' contribution to the EU budget will automatically take the form of development aid. This will inevitably increase their level of aid. For instance, in the case of Slovenia, Cyprus and Malta, their overall ODA budget should automatically increase from the 0.01 per cent of GNI in 2001 to about 0.07 per cent of GNI in 2004. For Poland, Hungary and the Baltic states, which spend between 0.01 and 0.02 per cent, the aid volume will automatically reach 0.06–0.08 per cent of their GNI. The Czech Republic and Slovakia, which spend more on ODA, will reach at least 0.12 per cent of GNI without any additional effort (European Commission, 2003g).

In addition to the EU general budget, the new member states are required to contribute to the next European Development Fund (EDF). The EDF, which is used to finance development in ACP countries, is replenished by voluntary contributions from member states every five years. The ninth EDF was signed for the first five years of the new ACP–EU Partnership Agreement (2002–2007); however, the new member states are required to pay only into the tenth EDF, which will be negotiated in 2007. As the GNP of most of the new members is small, their contribution to the EDF will not result in a substantial increase in resources. Actually, past experience shows that, in previous enlargements, some EU member states even cut their contribution to the EDF, with the consequence that the total did not rise (Granell, 2002).

Quality of aid

Increasing resources does not have the desired effects if aid is not delivered efficiently. For some years the EU has been trying to work towards a better coordination and complementarity between the bilateral policies of member states and the policies pursued at the EU level. Moreover, in response to major criticisms, in 2000 the EU launched a fundamental reform of its external assistance, aiming at improving aid quality, cutting implementation time, and harmonizing and simplifying aid management. The project cycle is shared between the geographical directorates – DG Development for the ACP countries, DG RELEX for the rest of the developing world – which are responsible for the programming stage, and an implementing body – EuropeAid – which is in charge of the other stages (Dearden, 2003).

The accession of the new member states, which lack experience in providing development assistance, may complicate these recent efforts to improve aid effectiveness. Indeed, only a small number of acceding states, having recently revised their development cooperation policies and programmes in line with OECD guidelines, are close to EU practices (Michaux, 2002). For most of the new member states: there is an insufficient familiarity with concepts such as implementation of sector-wide approaches, budget support, and policy dialogue; ODA is still seen as a series of projects; an excessive role is played by line ministries in aid policy execution; and evaluations of projects are not carried out (European Commission, 2003g).

A major problem may arise with the issue of the untying of aid, which implies that aid should be freely available to buy goods and services from all countries, not necessarily from the one that provides that aid. The

European Commission has recommended several times not only a full untying of all EU aid, but has also has called for the further untying of member states' bilateral aid. Such proposals, which have already met resistance from some EU-15 states, will probably also meet resistance in some of the acceding states.

Nevertheless, despite these difficulties, having been recipients of substantial amounts of development assistance since the early 1990s, CEECs should certainly play a unique role in fostering a better understanding of the problems faced by developing countries and in supporting efforts towards a more efficient delivery of aid (Richelle, 2002). Enlargement may also represent an incentive towards better coordination during international conferences and in international organizations. Moreover, if intra-EU coordination works, the additional weight coming from the new member states could provide the EU with an opportunity to make its presence stronger in the international arena. Some observers, though, have noted that enlargement may make coordination more difficult due to the strong influence that the US has on some of the new member states, such as Poland and the Baltic states (European Commission, 2003g).

Geographical focus and scope of aid

The geographical focus of EU development policy partly reflects the different perspectives brought by each of the new entrants to the EU, and partly the changing role of international development policy and practice. From an aid relationship limited to former colonies in Africa, the EU has developed a global policy which includes all the developing countries in Asia, Latin America, and the Mediterranean. In addition, the main objective of EU development, introduced by the November 2000 joint statement adopted by the Commission and the Council (see above), changed from assistance to poverty reduction.

The new member states, and in particular the CEECs, have ties with countries that, traditionally, have not been among the major receivers of EU development assistance. Most of them concentrate their development efforts on small projects in the former Soviet Union and in the Balkans, although a modest amount of financing still shows some traces of the communist past, in the form, for example, of aid to Angola, Vietnam and Yemen. For instance, between 1999 and 2001, only 5 per cent of Czech aid (excluding scholarships) was directed to Africa and only 10 per cent went to low-income countries. In 2001, only 0.5 per cent of Slovak ODA (excluding scholarships) was directed to Africa. Poland is the only country whose direction of aid is close to that of EU-15 states, as it cooperates with developing countries in Africa and Asia, in addition to countries in Eastern Europe. Overall, poverty reduction is not the main focus of the aid programmes of CEECs: it is sometimes included in policy documents and statements, but is not reflected in practice (Krichewsky, 2003).

Such clear differences may have implications on the future direction of EU aid, with the new member states calling for a new focus on the Balkans and Central Asia, thus strengthening the existing tendency to link aid to issues of regional security and stability. Indeed, in January 2003, Poland called for the establishment of an 'Eastern Dimension of the EU', whose objective would be to enhance political dialogue with countries in the Caucasus and Central Asia.

Even though most of the new member states do not have strong interests in the ACP region, the financial resources channelled through the EDF should remain stable in real terms, although their relative importance will decrease. However, countries in Asia and Latin America are likely to lose from enlargement as their geopolitical importance for the new Europe is much less than that of Balkan and Mediterranean countries (European Commission, 2003g).

Conclusions

Enlargement rounds prior to the 10 + 2 round have significantly affected EU development policy, most obviously by stretching the EU's activities to regions and areas of cooperation linked to new entrants. Although development policy did not feature prominently in the 10 + 2 enlargement round accession negotiations, significant consequences for enlargement policy can nonetheless, as before, be anticipated to occur as a result of the enlargement.

However, the implications are unlikely to be too significant in the short-term. At the time of accession, the new member states must accept EU development policy as it stands. Thus, they are required to boost their volume of aid and participate in the common efforts to improve the quality of aid. In the long-term, the implications of enlargement may be more relevant: having ties with countries that share their communist past or are their neighbours, the new member states may influence the regional focus of EU development policy, calling for a re-direction of aid towards countries that have not traditionally been significant recipients of EU development assistance.

A major implication of enlargement relates to the role of the EU in the global arena. The EU provides more than half of all official international development assistance and is also the largest provider of humanitarian assistance. Even though the size and timing of the contributions of the new states to international development is still to be negotiated, the overall trend is clear: the future EU will become an even more significant actor in international development.

But notwithstanding the EU's importance as a global actor in respect of development policy, institutional changes are threatening the status of development policy within the EU. The June 2002 Seville European Council, as part of a wide-ranging rationalization of the Council of Ministers' machinery, dissolved the Development Council. Moreover, the debates within the Convention on the Future of Europe raised serious concerns, above all among the NGO community, about a possible subordination of development to foreign policy. However, a positive sign is that in its recommendations to the 2003–2004 IGC, the Convention kept development policy as an independent policy. Doubtless the discussion will continue in the years to come. In this discussion, the new member states will have a key role in influencing whether the EU pursues a policy driven by self-interests or a policy where poverty eradication is the overarching goal.

Chapter 18

Theoretical Considerations

LEE MILES

Introduction

One of the great conundrums facing EU scholars searching for coherent theoretical explanations of all or at least part of the enlargement process relates to the fact that the most obvious point of departure – the 'classical' integration theories, such as neofunctionalism and intergovernmentalism – were not primarily designed to analyse the enlargement process. Schimmelfennig and Sedelmeier (2002: 501) comment, for instance, how 'it is striking that EU enlargement has been a largely neglected issue in the theory of regional integration'.

Of course, this is not the fault of those advocating such theories as explanations of European integration. It should not be forgotten that these were developed in the 1960s before even the first enlargement had taken place. As Schmitter (1996: 13), has commented, neither neofunctionalism 'nor any other theory of integration can explain why the Community began with six – rather than seven or nine – subsequently expanded to twelve, and may even reach twenty-five or thirty before exhausting itself somewhere on the Asian steppes'.

The deficiencies with 'classical' theories in explaining the process of European integration – let alone the sub process of EU enlargement – are well-documented. At best, classical theories can only explain parts or some of the dynamics of the EC/EU, as integration theory in Europe has tended to live a sort of 'shadow existence' as a supplier of ad hoc explanations. It can be argued quite convincingly that no one 'grand theory' has, so far, described adequately the complex intricacies of the EU 'in one go' (see Peterson, 1995).

The EU has, at least officially since the 1997 Amsterdam Treaty (and informally for many years before this), entered into an era of 'differentiated integration' with the new vocabulary of 'flexibility' appearing in discourses on the future of the EU. This development is part of a process whereby the 'elephant' of the EU has evolved over the years into a highly complex animal. The more sophisticated policy options now open to EU decision-makers, as well as the ambitious enlargement agenda since the early 1990s, have been accompanied by a general movement amongst EU scholars away from the search for any single 'meta-theory' that can claim to effectively explain all aspects of the integration process and nature of the Union. In practice, the contemporary preference has been to advocate the usage of 'middle-range' theoretical approaches that focus on *some* of the dynamics associated with the Union.

These twin developments in European integration theorizing – on the one hand towards a more diverse discourse incorporating notions of 'flexibility', and on the other a more selective and modest concentration of effort amongst EU scholars – has advantages and disadvantages for those contemplating EU enlargement. Of course, the central challenge in seeking coherent explanations of EU expansion is related to the fact that the impact of enlargement is comprehensive and not confined to one or a series of EU policy fields. In effect, enlargement, past and future, is closer to being a *phenomenon*. Moreover, its impact is also not confined to the existing member states. Thus, any theorizing pertaining to the EU enlargement process must also pay attention to the interaction between the Union and the respective candidate countries. In short, there must be an explicit recognition that the effects of European integration do not respect the external boundaries of the existing Union. Theoretical considerations apply not only to the Union, but also, albeit to a lesser extent, to the applicant and/or candidate countries. When searching for conceptual and theoretical pointers as regards enlargement, there is thus a need to widen the traditional horizons of European integration theory.

Broadly and ideally, enlargement theory should be focused on three main elements:

- *Conceptualizing the EU accession process* – the enlargement perspectives, conditions and procedures of the Union, and the problems of negotiation and entry for candidate countries.
- *Addressing the transition processes emanating from EU enlargement on existing and new member states as well as for candidate countries* – the complex interrelationship between the EU and the nation-state level. Indeed, we need to recognize within this the distinction between the applicants' enlargement politics and member states' enlargement politics (Schimmelfennig and Sedelmeier, 2002: 502).
- *Analyzing the 'impact' of past and future enlargements on the European* Union – the wider perspective of the pressures and nature of reform of the Union to accommodate past and future accessions. As part of this third aspect of 'EU enlargement politics', we may need to differentiate between macro/polity dimensions and substantive policy impacts (Schimmelfennig and Sedelmeier, 2002: 502) and also the implications for the Union in terms of the relationship between 'deepening' and 'widening' and the growing diversity of the Union (Zielonka and Mair, 2002).

Using these three elements as a 'template', consideration will now be given to what the present array of theories offer in the context of the enlargement research agenda.

Existing Horizons: The 'Grand Theories' of Neofunctionalism and Liberal Intergovernmentalism

Neofunctionalism

It may have become somewhat 'routine to point to [the] obsolescence of classical . . . integration theory' (Matlary, 1993: 64), yet neofunctionalism with its emphasis on being a 'process theory' may offer some insights as regards EU enlargement. In particular, neo functionalism's suggestion that economic and political integration is furthered through the concept of 'spillover' could be of relevance to our enlargement discussions. Indeed, aspects of 'political spillover', whereby 'political actors in distinct national settings are persuaded to shift their loyalties, expectations and political activities towards a new centre, whose institutions possess or demand jurisdiction over pre-existing nation states' (Haas, 1958: 16), may describe not just EU deepening. They may also be pertinent as regards the motives of those outside the Union seeking to get in. In short, if neofunctionalism incorporates a more discernible 'external perspective' of elite interaction (see Miles, Redmond and Schwok, 1995: 181), it can be important as a sub-text explaining why states join the Union.

An interesting exploration of the usefulness of spillover in this context has been undertaken by Peterson and Bomberg (1998), who have argued that the 1995 enlargement can be explained in terms of three different kinds of spillover. First, as 'functional spillover' – through the initial creation of the European Economic Area (EEA). Second, by 'institutional spillover' – such as with the way in which the EEA became politically untenable due to the limited nature of the EFTA countries' influence on Single European Market-related decision-making, and hence provoked the membership applications. Third, through 'political spillover' – as the elites in the new EU member states became acclimatized to operating in the new EU political environment (Peterson and Bomberg, 1998: 44).

A greater emphasis on 'external', rather than 'internal', spillover taking place beyond the Union's boundaries can thus help explain full membership applications and eventual accession (Miles, 1995: 20–3). What can also be helpful is to is to distinguish between 'voluntary' and 'enforced' external spillover (see Miles, 1995: 21) – although the terms are not mutually exclusive and the categories are, in any event, always subjective to a point. With some simplification, voluntary external spillover relates to where the initiation of closer EU ties lies largely with the non-member states and is based upon their recognition of the need for a closer relationship with the Union in some form. Enforced external spillover envisages that third countries are required by the Union to explicitly reform domestic processes in line with EU principles, usually as a precondition of membership. Hence EU principles and policies are being enforced by the Union and are, rather forcefully, spilling over into non-member states. A good example of this is Malta in the 1990s: enforced external spillover was direct since the 1993 Commission opinion required the Maltese economy to restructure (in some sectors necessitating radical reform) before the Union would consent to opening accession negotiations.

Political spillover may also occur from the 'outside in' as new members and their respective political elites bring with them their own preferences for moulding the character of the EU (see Miles, 1995). This may not necessarily all be in the direction of further deepening, as areas of integration may be limited, resisted or even reversed by the presence of new political elites who do not share the premise that further integration is advantageous in itself (see Miles and Redmond, 1996). This 'outside in' effect may begin even before accessions have been completed since the political elites of applicant states interact with EU elites from the time applications are presented, and furthermore they often are given observer status within EU institutions and forums.

Nevertheless, although there are valuable deductive aspects that can be drawn from neofunctionalism, its contribution to theoretical considerations of EU enlargement is restricted to largely background factors. More specifically, neofunctionalism can shed some light on the first (EU accession process) and second (the enlargement politics of the applicants and member states) elements of our research agenda through a more sophisticated interpretation of spillover.

Yet, we are never far away from neofunctionalism's origins in seeking to explain integration between a relatively homogenous EC of six, rather than a diverse Union of 25 plus. Neofunctionalism also has difficulty in accommodating the economic impacts of the accessions of relatively poor members that have widened disparities, undermined the coherence and effectiveness of EU policies, and complicated the search for supranational elite consensus by promoting multi-speed (and even multi-tier) European integration. Enlargements have tended to emphasize the Union's diversity – something neofunctionalism is largely uncomfortable with in its traditional form.

Liberal intergovernmentalism

At the core of liberal intergovernmentalism (LI) (Moravcsik, 1993, 1995, 1998) lie three underlying elements: the assumption of rational state behaviour; a liberal theory of national preference formation (the demand side of European integration); and an intergovernmental analysis of interstate negotiation (the supply side of European integration). These elements largely seek to explain how the costs and benefits of economic interdependence primarily determine national preferences, which governments aggregate and negotiate with during intergovernmental interstate bargaining at flagship 'super-systemic' IGCs. European integration is thus best explained as a series of rational choices by national executives. What are the strengths and weaknesses of Moravcsik's analysis in relation to enlargement?

The initial strength of liberal intergovernmentalism derives from the notion of 'liberal national preference formation', that suggests the importance of state–society relations, economic interests, and the role of 'societal groups' in shaping national preferences. This is of some use when considering national preferences towards EU accession. If groups, for example, 'articulate preferences and governments aggregate them' (Moravcsik, 1993: 483), this provides plausible governmental motivations to support (or oppose) EU membership and why states suffer from varying levels of domestic problems when contemplating accession to the Union. Indeed, the primacy of economic interdependence arguments – an integral part of LI – regularly also drive non-member states to join the Union 'where policy co-ordination increases their control over domestic policy outcomes, permitting them to achieve goals that would not otherwise be possible' (Moravcsik, 1993: 485). LI may therefore have something to say in relation to the first (accession process) and second (the enlargement politics of the applicants and member states) elements of our research agenda.

Moravcsik also identifies that the distributional consequences of EU policies are uneven among and within nations and that those nations and domestic groups that are disadvantaged by policy co-ordination are likely to oppose EU membership. It is only when governments can collectively overcome such opposition that membership is possible. This is especially relevant to applicants using public referendums to legitimize EU accession. Equally, such notions help to explain the arduous nature of EU accession negotiations, since the participating governments are both empowered and constrained by important societal groups, partly because they calculate their interests in terms of expected gains and losses from specific policies. Accession agreements are thus reliant upon the converging of the interests of dominant domestic groups within and between differing countries.

The focus of LI on 'interstate strategic interaction' also has resonance, especially in conceptualizing the accession process (the first element of our research agenda). The strengths of LI are that it helps to elucidate the role of governments during key strategic negotiations in large policy forums dominated by the member state governments, such as IGCs. This seems especially pertinent to EU enlargement, which is littered with such flagship deliberations. The deliberations can occur during key negotiations between existing member states on either EU reforms or treaty changes as preparation for the impact of forthcoming enlargements. Examples include the 2000 Nice Treaty negotiations and the talks between EU-15 governments at the October 2002 Brussels summit on the financial packages to be offered to the new member states.

Flagship deliberations can also occur during head-to-head discussion between the Union (usually via the Council Presidency) and the governments of the respective candidate countries on the actual accession terms. In this context, enlargement questions can reflect Moravcsik's 'co-operative game in which the level of cooperation reflects patterns in the preferences of national governments' (Moravcsik, 1993: 499). LI could possibly explain the reason why the views of large existing member states are also critical in shaping the Union's overall attitude towards specific applicants. Given the complexity of the enlargement negotiations there are, of course, plenty of opportunities for linkages between issues and for 'package deals'.

Nevertheless, LI can only have limited value for our purposes. The main weakness of LI perhaps lies in the almost exclusive positioning of executives as the determiners of EU policy, while cutting them off from rich debates over the character of 'domestic politics', state theory and public policy-making (Wincott, 1995: 599). These are, after all, central features of domestic debates on EU enlargement. LI is also less than comfortable with the important role of the Commission as the Union's chief negotiator in accession negotiations and its influence in shaping the Union's general policy on enlargement – as with the *Agenda 2000* programme. Similarly, the EP's role in the accession ratification process is largely ignored. Finally, LI cannot explain properly why existing member states can be in favour of further enlargement even if their economic interests may be damaged in the short term – as is the case with the opening of the Union to the CEECs, all of which are less economically developed countries that will place great strains on the Union's financial resources. Therefore, as Moravcsik (1995: 611) admits, LI cannot account for all aspects of European integration and the EU enlargement process in particular.

So, neither LI nor neofunctionalism can comment comfortably or fully on all elements of our enlargement research agenda.

Newer Horizons: Multi-Level Governance and New Institutionalism

Dissatisfaction with the limitations of 'grand theorizing' have resulted, especially since the early 1990s, in the application of 'middle-range' theories that 'do not have totalizing ambitions' (Rosamond, 2003: 112). At the forefront of these theoretical investigations are the concepts of 'multi-level governance' and 'new institutionalism'.

Multi-Level Governance

The concept of 'multi-level governance' (MLG) provides a framework for explaining EU decision-making that recognizes 'the existence of overlapping competencies among multiple levels of governments and the interaction of political actors across those levels' (Marks *et al.*, 1996: 341).

Although rather vague and seemingly more promising as a metaphor than a theory (see for example, Aspinwall and Schneider, 1997), MLG amounts to the claim that the EU has become a polity where authority is dispersed (Rosamond, 2000: 110). It does not reject the view that state executives and state arenas are important, nor that these remain the most significant for the European integration puzzle, but does stress that they are not the exclusive link between domestic politics and intergovernmental bargaining in the EU. In short, the MLG concept highlights an 'actor' rather than a 'state centric' approach 'in which authority and policy -making influence are shared across multiple levels of government – sub-national, national and supranational' (Marks *et al.*, 1996: 342). The emerging Euro-polity is reliant upon the outcome of tension between supranational and intergovernmental pressures, evolving into a multi-level polity where control is slipping away from national governments to supranational institutions, and in particular, agenda-setting has become 'a shared and contested competence' (Marks *et al.*, 1996: 359).

What does MLG offer our discussion of EU enlargement? At face value, MLG highlights the importance of contact and cooperation between sub-national actors, such as interest groups, in pushing forward the process of European integration and as part of the general ethos of increased interdependence between states (Marks *et al.*, 1996: 371). For third countries that are considering applying for EU membership and/or are moving further towards full membership, then the links of their respective sub-national actors with those in existing member states are often instrumental in pressing the pro-membership cause and shaping EU accession debates. So, for example, the Europe Agreements that formed the precursor for full membership of CEECs encouraged closer cooperation between such actors and allowed those from non-member states to participate indirectly in the EU policy process. These sub-national bodies can therefore be useful 'actors' in themselves, affecting accession debates and becoming important institutional settings that are, in effect, preconditions for a country's success in joining the Union. There is thus potential for MLG to offer explanations relevant to the first and second elements of the enlargement research agenda.

MLG represents an attempt 'to depict complexity as the principal feature of the EU's policy-making system' (Rosamond, 2000: 111) and, as such, strikes an accord with notions of 'flexibility' and diversity in a post-2004 EU-25. From the perspective of EU enlargement, 'differentiated integration' explains 'horizontal' widths of EU competencies, whilst 'multi-level governance' largely addresses 'vertical' divisions of competencies 'up and down' within the Union's decision-making structure.

Yet, the value of MLG is curtailed since it seems at times to be little more than a description of the EU decision-making system and a rather static model that lacks a means to predict change. This is a worrying commodity since the 1995 enlargement probably represented the last usage of the 'classical method' of EU enlargement (Preston, 1995 and 1997). Certainly, the 10 + 2 round signifies a qualitative change since – as the Nice Treaty testifies – the expansion to EU-25 invokes changes in the rights not just of the new member states but also of the existing EU-15. It would seem that MLG represents largely an account of the status quo.

New institutionalism

Another theoretical avenue lies with new institutionalism, especially since in recent years it has emerged from a quiet back-water of political science into a mainstream approach for those studying European integration. That is not to say that institutional analysis is something new, for organization theory and theories of collective action and corporatism are commonplace. In general, new institutionalism, like MLG, should be regarded as something of 'an umbrella term' (see Armstrong and Bulmer, 1998). It incorporates literature focusing on institutional actors, examinations of the complexities of bargaining between actors from different levels, and evaluations of the role of norms and socialization on the process of European integration (see for example, Bulmer, 1994; Shepsle, 1989; Norgaard, 1996). There has been almost no convergence towards a common understanding of European institutions within the existing new institutionalism literature. It may be correct to call it a 'movement' rather than a clearly delineated theory (see Rosamond, 2000: 113–22), incorporating sociological, historical and rationalist perspectives (see Hall and Taylor, 1996).

However, all new institutionalists argue that 'institutions matter' and that they affect outcomes between 'units' – whether these be individuals, firms, states, or other forms of social organizations such as the EU. In short, institutions contain the bias individual agents have built into their society over time, which in turn leads to important distribution consequences. They structure political outcomes, rather than simply mirroring social activity and rational competition among desegregated units. (March and Olsen, 1984, 1989; Thelen and Steinmo, 1992).

The distinctiveness of new institutionalism lies in its wider interpretation of what constitutes institutions, with a shift away from formal constitutional–legal approaches to broader aspects of government. In particular, historical, rather than rational choice, institutionalism is more popularly (but not exclusively) applied to the EU context (see Armstrong and Bulmer 1998; Pierson, 1996). In general terms, new institutionalism includes broader aspects of government – allowing it to incorporate concepts of 'policy community' and 'policy networks' (see Peterson, 1995: 69–93). Further to this, new institutionalists recognize that EU decision-making is steeped in norms and codes of conduct, which make it 'difficult to isolate formal institutional rules from the normative context' (Armstrong and Bulmer, 1998: 51).

The vagueness surrounding the definitions of 'institutions' seems to be the greatest strength but also the underlying weakness of new institutionalism. This is conceded by its advocates. Some argue that it 'is neither a theory nor a coherent critique' (March and Olsen, 1984: 747) and it is certainly not a 'grand theory' of integration as it makes no predictions of the path ahead. So how can new institutionalism help the anaylsis of EU enlargement?

It is useful – especially in its historical variant – in several ways. First, in helping to explain the structure of the debates on EU accession in both member states and applicant countries. This has resonance for the second element of our enlargement research agenda in particular. According to historical new institutionalism, 'long-term institutional consequences are often the by-products of actions taken for short-term political reasons' (Pierson, 1996: 136). Actors are not fully aware of the complete implications of participating in institutional venues. This is especially appropriate when discussing the motives of countries and is endemic within national accession debates. Information on EU accession is not perfect and the reasons for joining or not joining the Union are often premised on highly speculative assumptions and limited 'time-horizons'. Domestic and even supranational institutional actors often base their policies on EU enlargement on incomplete information and, more broadly, on what the EU may become rather than what it consists of at the time.

Second, political institutions are central to domestic EU accession debates since they structure political life. The views of key institutions, such as labour and employers organizations, feature strongly in accession debates. Furthermore, institutions disseminate information and mobilize their membership either for or against full membership status. It is often the balance between 'pro' and 'anti' EU membership forces within key institutions that influence whether accession is pursued and secured, particularly within corporatist societies.

Third, a central assumption of new institutionalism is that institutions tend to 'lock-in' to place and create 'path dependencies'. Participation in supranational arrangements and further Europeanization locks-in member states and their respective political elites. In the enlargement context, leading institutional actors continue to favour EU membership even when there may be fundamental changes in the very reasons why they joined. Hence, the role of institutions helps explain why, even where anti-EU membership feelings remain high in some quarters after EU accession, governments and leading interest groups are usually able to convince sceptical electorates to remain 'inside the Union'. Moreover, they become 'locked-in' to further integration pathways. Over time, new member states gradually become more 'supranational inclined' as there is a 'rising price of exit' (Pierson, 1996: 144).

There would also seem to be valuable lessons to be drawn from new institutionalism as regards the supranational context, and in particular the Union's reform process spurred on by past and future enlargements. From the enlargement perspective, EU institutions are 'supranational actors' with their own institutional preferences. The European Commission and the EP, for instance, have increasingly made inputs into the enlargement process since the 1970s. The Commission is responsible for defining accession criteria and pre-accession strategies, delivering 'Opinions' on the applications and 'Progress Reports' on the preparations of candidate countries towards accession. It is also the case that the Parliament has been regularly consulted on accessions by the Commission and the Council Presidency, and since the 1986 SEA has had to ratify accession treaties.

The EU institutions also input strongly into agendas of institutional and policy reform that have been largely prompted by the fact that enlargements do affect the *acquis communautaire* and *finalité politique* of the Union (part of the final element of our enlargement research agenda). A good relationship between, say, the Commission and the governments of the new member states is essential if the Union's budgetary, agricultural and structural funds (and their reforms) are to be implemented effectively. Indeed, this is an ongoing process. In short, enlargement affects differing institutional configurations and thus the 'governance capacity' of the Union, which new institutionalism seeks to explore (see Bulmer, 1998: 372).

Nevertheless, new institutionalism is only indirectly useful to concepts of EU enlargement. Although the stress on shifting national preferences as 'an unintended consequence' is interesting, the quest by third countries for full membership status is based more on the recognition of 'the deliberate triumphs of European integration' (Moravcsik, 1998: 491). There are often discernible economic and financial motives driving countries towards EU accession, not least in the case of the CEECs as a means of inducing further economic modernization. New member states accept directly the transfer of sovereignty to supranational institutions as part of the 'price' of full membership – and not, as historical institutionalists may argue, an 'unintended or unforeseen consequence'. Hence, it is difficult to argue that European integration has been happening (almost) in spite of the EU member states (Puchala, 1999: 329).

Following on from this, national preferences and national interests are, for the most part, not as unstable or as unpredictable as new institutionalists would have us believe. Indeed, if the preferences of new member states over the previous enlargements are considered, what is striking is the stability and continuity of national preferences. Taking the post-1995 new members – Austria, Sweden and to a lesser extent, Finland – what is most evident is that all three are, to some extent, still interested in securing EU breakthroughs in those areas left unfulfilled by the accession agreements. In the Swedish case, for example, this includes securing greater transparency in EU decision-making. There are as many 'intended' as 'unintended' 'lock-in' effects arising from EU enlargement.

New institutionalism thus remains, for the most part, too loose to provide an adequate explanation of EU enlargement processes.

Expanding Horizons: Constructivism

It is essential then that further work is done on the construction of an adequate theoretical agenda for examining the EU enlargement process. As Schimmelfennig and Sedelmeier (2002: 502) recognize, any such agenda as regards EU enlargement must address existing shortcomings – not least the insularity in which enlargement questions have been treated in terms of theorizing, an under-theorizing of dependent variables, and, most of all, a neglect of important dimensions of enlargement.

The most contemporary attempt at addressing some of these aspects is the 'theoretical turn' of 'constructivism' (which sometimes, but not always, is regarded as an off-shoot of institutionalism). As was shown in Chapter 1, the constructivist hypothesis suggests that the enlargement process will generally be shaped by ideational and cultural factors (Schimmelfennig and Sedelmeier, 2002: 513), especially notions of community or 'cultural match' where the member states and the candidate countries share a collective identity and fundamental beliefs. Thus, third countries join the Union because they share common values and believe it is best to be part of an 'EU club' of liberal democracies and market economies.

At many levels, the constructivist position is convincing. It provides insights into the enlargement politics of applicant states, such as why the CEECs after the 1989 strategic changes in Europe became so keen to join the Union as part of their new 'democratic credentials'. In addition, it helps to explain why identity factors play such a role in enlargements debates in states like Norway and Iceland that have (so far) resisted joining the Union. Constructivism may therefore provide useful insights into the second element of our research agenda pertaining to the enlargement politics of applicants and/or member states.

However, although it is helpful at the margins, it is less confident in terms of differentiating between groups of candidate countries and indeed, in explaining the nuances of why the expanding Union has differing levels of integration between the member states. As Jachtenfuchs (2002: 656) suggests, influential factors such as the role of state executives, domestic responses to external or structural stimuli, and the relationship between material preferences and ideational influences are hard to explain from a constructivist perspective of enlargement. Furthermore, greater attention needs to be placed on the relationship between ideational factors and the strategic alternatives that both the applicants and the member states face both 'inside' and 'outside' a more flexible Union (Wallace, 2002: 663).

Conclusion: Widening of Our Theoretical Horizons?

Part of the challenge when assessing the usefulness of integration theories in helping to explain EU enlargement is that integration theories and EU enlargement have, to some extent, been moving in opposite directions. There are two aspects to this. First, most of the existing theories have sought to explain what is going on within the Union, rather than the relationships between itself and third countries. There thus is a question of analytical appropriateness. Second, recent trends have seen integration theories become more reserved and less ambitious – at the very time when the EU enlargement agenda has become ever busier. It would seem that just as European integration theorizing is 'down-sizing', the EU's enlargement portfolio has 'ratcheted upwards'. It is thus wise to look outside existing theoretical frameworks in order to provide a resounding theoretical consideration of the EU enlargement process.

Scholarship is far from having developed anything like a comprehensive 'theory' to enable us to understand the all-embracing nature and impact of EU enlargement. If it ever is to do so, scholars must focus not so much as they have done on the 'deepening' of the Union, but must pay more attention to how enlargement fits into the integration picture. Thus, the existing trend towards 'middle-range' theory will, almost by definition, not provide us with any major step forward in understanding how and why the Union has grown in size and what this will mean for the future functioning of the EU. If anything, this chapter represents something of a plea to others. It is time to widen once again our theoretical horizons and make the conceptualizing of further EU enlargement a central focus, rather than a peripheral element on forthcoming research agendas.

One possible avenue may be to explore further notions of a 'flexible' or 'differentiated' EU – although just as with the theories analyzed here, concepts of 'flexibility' (Stubb, 1996, 2002) or of a 'Europe of concentric circles' (Baldwin, 1993) need to be more academically rigorous in handling the specific ramifications of enlargement than at present. Indeed, as I have argued elsewhere, a 'Hub and Spokes Europe' – with the euro area as the central hub, and within that perhaps a smaller inner-core – may provide a suitable framework to begin assessing the post-2004 EU-25 (Miles 2003).

Chapter 19

Conclusions

NEILL NUGENT

The 10 + 2 round is part of an intensification of enlargement, both as an issue and as a process, that began in the late 1980s. Between 1987 and 1996 no fewer than 18 countries applied to join the EU (see Chronology, pp. 275–7). Of these applications only one has been rejected as inadmissable – that of Morocco on the grounds that it is not a European country. All the other applicants have either become members (the EFTAns, apart from Norway, and – in May 2004 – the Czech Republic, Cyprus, Estonia, Hungary, Latvia, Lithuania, Malta, Poland, Slovenia, and Slovakia), are likely to become members in 2007 if they make satisfactory transition progress (Bulgaria and Romania), or have been promised the opening of accession negotiations if they make satisfactory progress towards meeting accession criteria (Turkey).

It can be argued that the EU-15 should have pushed the 10 + 2 round along more quickly and that they should have been more generous in the terms they offered to the applicants, but this should not deflect attention from the importance or momentous significance of the eventual achievement. From the end of World War 2 until 1989/90 most of the states of Western and Eastern Europe were grouped into two blocs: the West with market-based economic systems and liberal democratic political systems and the East with communist planned economies and one-party political systems. The 10 + 2 round marks the culmination of a process of bringing these two 'halves' together within the framework of what can be regarded as a quasi-federal system based on market and democratic principles and values.

Will Enlargement Make the EU Stronger or Weaker?

Enlargement strengthens the EU in some respects and weakens it in others. The most obvious way in which the EU is strengthened is by its growth in size. Of the many features of the EU's growth in size, of particular importance are population, territory and GDP. Allied with the dynamic effects that the extension of liberalization and harmonization

266

should impart to the now wider internal market, this growth in size should help to promote, especially in the new member states, trade, economic development and increased prosperity.

The growth in size also creates the potential for the EU to strengthen its position as a global actor. This is especially so in respect of external trade, where the Common Commercial Policy obliges EU states to act as one in their dealings with trade partners, be they conducted on a bilateral or multilateral basis. But there are possibilities for the EU's voice to also become more influential in other external areas, provided it can manage and/or develop its internal coordinating mechanisms effectively. Amongst such areas are foreign, defence, development, environmental and transport policies.

The principal way in which enlargement weakens the EU is that it creates greater internal diversity. But this is hardly likely to be a paralysing diversity. After all, diversity has long existed in the EU, yet the EU has not only survived but has advanced on both institutional and policy fronts. It has been able to do so for two main sets of reasons.

First, the nature of divergences usually has been such as to allow necessary accommodations. This should prove to again be the case with the 10 + 2 states, which do not bring wholly new and sharply divisive issues to the EU table. They do, of course, have their own particular interests and preferences, but these will feed into debates, and doubtless in some instances exacerbate strains, that have long existed between EU-15 states, rather than result in wholly new debates or create completely new strains. The areas in which the newcomers are most likely to cause 'difficulties' are in the related spheres of the CAP, the Structural Funds and budgetary policy, where the CEECs have very direct interests and where they believe they were harshly treated during the accession negotiations. Released from the somewhat subservient role they were obliged to assume prior to becoming EU members, it can be assumed that CEECs will become more 'aggressive' in negotiations in these areas. Certainly, they will do so if past enlargement experience is a lesson, for this suggests that new members quickly seek to take advantage of their membership and of EU decision-making rules to further their interests. Considerable negotiating aggression from CEECs can therefore be expected in the negotiations on the financial perspective for the post-2007 period.

Second, the EU has strategies for managing diversity. As Philippart and Dhian Ho (2001: 39ff.) show, these strategies involve:

- *Suppressing diversity*. This is achieved by, for example, requiring applicant states to adopt the *acquis* before accession and requiring member states to adopt and apply common policies and laws even though they may be opposed to them and have voted against them in the Council.
- *Diminishing diversity*. This is aimed at attaining gradual convergence

and moving diversity to an unproblematic level. Ways in which this convergence is achieved include the operation of market forces, financial transfers between member states, and 'soft' policy instruments focused on learning and coordination rather than imposing immediate uniformity.

- *Buying off diversity*. Where a small group of states or a single state are creating 'difficulties' on a matter arising from their distinctive nature, other group of states may choose or feel obliged to buy off the diversity without necessarily insisting that the diversity be suppressed. The buying off can take different forms. The best known form involves financial 'side payments', such as the creation of a new Structural Fund budget line to help sparsely populated Arctic regions at the time of the EFTAn enlargement round.

- *Accommodating diversity*. This involves accepting diversity and giving it recognition. At a general policy level, this is seen most obviously with the non-participation of a minority of EU-15 states in the single currency and in aspects of the Schengen System. At more specific policy levels it is seen in the way that many EU laws are not tightly constraining and in the way too member states are often given latitude in the way they apply laws.

The difficulties arising from greater diversity should, therefore, not be exaggerated. Two further points about diversity should also be recognized. First, as Philippart and Dhian Ho (2001: 27) note, 'the point beyond which diversity become problematic is determined by the normative perspective chosen by the evaluator – in other words, by what the EU is supposed to be and to do'. Those who wish for a tightly integrated and highly supranational EU are much more likely to view diversity as a problem than those who want the EU to be a reasonably loose confederal-type of organization. Second, diversity may create difficulties but it also can be a strength. It can be so by adding to the richness of the EU's history, experiences and culture. It can be so too by encouraging, even obliging, EU actors to be more understanding, open, facilitating and cooperative. As Zielonka and Mair, 2002:8) observe, 'Diversity teaches adaptation, bargaining and accommodation. It is a source of competition, self-improvement and innovation.'

Will Enlargement Radically Change the Nature of the EU?

As the previous section and most of this book have made clear, enlargement certainly brings significant changes to the EU. Three ways in which change is likely to be particularly marked stand out.

First, decision-making in areas where unanimity between the member states is still required for decisions to be taken inevitably will become more difficult. Areas that do so require unanimous approval and fall to the European Council for final decisions include treaty reforms, accession applications, and the size and allocations of funding in the EU's multi-annual financial perspectives. Areas requiring unanimity that fall mainly to the Council of Ministers include taxation policy and most aspects of JHA and CFSP.

It is not without significance, even though the issues at stake were especially sensitive, that on the first occasion the $10 + 2$ states participated fully in a major EU decision-making forum where unanimity applies, major problems arose. This forum was the IGC on the European Constitution which, contrary to the hopes of virtually all of the participants, including the (Italian) Council Presidency, failed to be completed at the December 2003 Brussels summit. The summit collapsed for a number of reasons, the most important of which was that Spain and Poland allied to resist pressures from other states – led by Germany – to accept the Constitutional Convention's proposal to abandon the formula that had been laid down in the Nice Treaty for QMV in the Council of Ministers post-enlargement: a formula that, as David Phinnemore showed in Chapter 8, very much favoured Spain and Poland.

Second, there will be some shift in policy debates and probably some shift too in policy priorities. Economic and market-focused policies will continue to be developed, adjusted, refined, and stay at the EU's policy core. However, the relative underdevelopment of the CEEC economies may well produce pressures for the EU's liberal market principles to be applied less stringently to them, and seems certain to produce pressures for new member states to be afforded more generous treatment from the EU's 'spending policies' than the EU-15 would like. Away from 'economic' policies, it may also be that a higher priority will be given to the CFSP and JHA policy areas. Regarding the CFSP, enlargement is certainly not the only factor driving policy advancement. Indeed, the major factor is the ineffectiveness of the CFSP in crisis situations. The divisions between European states over the 2003 war with Iraq displayed in a particularly graphic manner how far the EU is from having anything remotely like a true common foreign policy, let alone a common defence policy. Some states, led by the UK and with Spain, Italy plus the CEECs in the same camp, supported the US position; some states, led by France and Germany, firmly opposed the US stance and the war; and some states stood to the side. So, the CFSP is in need of strengthening in any event. But enlargement gives this need an extra push – partly because it increases the general potential for the EU to be a major global foreign policy actor if it can realize its potential, and partly for the more specific reason that, as is discussed further below, the EU needs to establish good political relations with its potentially unstable new neighbours to its east and south. Regarding JHA, concerns about crime and corruption in the CEECs and in the former communist states with which the EU shares its new borders will intensify efforts for the EU to have in place effective measures to combat organized crime, drug trafficking and movements of peoples.

Third, there is likely to be an increase in enhanced/flexible/differentiated cooperation – that is, initiatives and actions between groups of member states. This type of cooperation within the EU can take three broad forms:

- *Multi-speed EU* – all states are moving in the same policy direction but, for reasons of either capacity or choice, are doing so at different speeds.
- *Concentric circles EU* – all states are full participants in core policies (which is usually taken as meaning internal market policies), but around the core are concentric circles of states. Policy participation declines the further the circle is distanced from the core.
- *À la carte EU* – all states again participate in core policies, but outside the core they pick and choose in which policies they participate.

Characteristics of policies that make them more prone to differentiation include: when they are not, or are only indirectly, related to the internal market; when they are strategically important for some states; when they are of concern to only some states; and when member states favour differing regulatory styles (Junge, 2002).

Enlargement increases the prospects of enhanced cooperation because the more member states there are in the EU the more likely it is that characteristics of the sort listed in the previous paragraph will apply or will be seen to apply. Moreover, the Nice Treaty made enhanced cooperation easier to operationalize by replacing the Amsterdam Treaty stipulation that 'at least a majority' of member states must be involved for enhanced cooperation to be able to make use of EU institutions and mechanisms to 'a minimum of eight' member states must be involved. Policy areas that appear to lend themselves to the possibility of enhanced cooperation include foreign, defence, JHA, monetary, and aspects of environmental and social.

As the agreement to the Nice Treaty provisions for enhanced cooperation demonstrate, EU leaders tend not to be opposed to the principle of differentiation as such. Most leaders lean in the direction of mild versions of the multi-speed and *à la carte* models. However, a few leaders – notably President Chirac in the wake of the failed December 2003 IGC summit – have gone further by floating the notion of some states constituting a core or pioneer group post-enlargement: the concentric circles model. Under this approach, core states would push ahead as a group with integration in areas where other states do not wish or are unable to go.

Doubtless in the future there will be further attempts at integration-building along partial membership lines. Some of this probably will be within the EU framework, as with EMU and Schengen, and some may be outside, as with a number of initiatives and operations in the defence field since the late 1990s. However, there appear to be too many divisions – of both interest and principle – between EU states, including potential core members, to envisage the creation of a semi-fixed division between inner and outer groups.

An important final point to be emphasized about enhanced cooperation is that it is not, as is often supposed, necessarily damaging for the integration process. On the contrary, it can be beneficial if handled carefully and sensitively. At a minimum it can allow integration that otherwise would be blocked to at least proceed between the willing and the able. This can, in turn, draw non-participants in – either because they come to see the merits of integration in the policy area concerned or because they come to feel that remaining outside is producing damaging consequences.

*   *   *

Whether changes such as those just outlined constitute radical changes is questionable. The fact is that the EU, in response to a wide variety of factors, including enlargements, has always been in evolution in terms of what it does and how it does it. The 10 + 2 round is a particularly powerful factor driving change, but there is no reason to think that it will lead, for example, to decision-making sclerosis, to the EU striking out in completely new policy directions, or to the EU breaking up into sub groupings of member states. For, as Moravcsik and Vachudova (2002: 1 and 3) note, the acceding states enter the EU as moderately well-qualified member states, as states that are unlikely to support further great advances in the integration process, and as states that are unlikely to import significantly divergent or destabilizing policy agendas. In short, the 10 + 2 enlargement round is more likely

> to reinforce existing incremental ends in EU politics . . . [the] declining persuasiveness of any grand *projet,* and the dissipation of the goal of 'United States of Europe' as a widely-held ideal for Europe. Fears of gridlock, stagnation or backlash are exaggerated; the more likely result is a strengthening of the *status quo.* (Moravcsik and Vachudova, 2002: 1)

The Future of the Enlargement Process

Article 49 of the TEU states that any European state that respects the principles of the EU may apply for Union membership. 'Europe' is not defined in the Treaty. It is not so because there is not, and cannot be, any definitive answer to the 'what is Europe?' question. Even if just the most obvious criterion is taken – geography – no 'correct' and generally accepted definition is possible because geographical boundaries are not just a matter of physical features such as mountains, seas and rivers but also are a consequence of social construction. This is no more clearly seen than with Cyprus, whose European credentials are virtually never queried, despite it being geographically much closer to the Middle East and North Africa than to 'mainstream' Europe. The 'what is Europe?' question becomes even more complex and contestable when other criteria are added, such as common culture, shared values and common historical experience. The fact is that whatever criterion or combination of criteria are taken, there remains a considerable degree of subjectivity in drawing Europe's borders. The borders are elastic, moving according to whom is doing the defining and also sometimes according to the circumstances in which they are doing the defining.

As for the principles referred to in Article 49 that countries applying to join the EU must respect, these are set out in Article 6(1) of the TEU as being 'the principles of liberty, democracy, respect for human rights and fundamental freedoms, and the rule of law'. These principles certainly have a greater specificity than being a 'European state', but they still allow for debate as to their precise nature and how closely they need to be applied.

This all being so, there remains ample room for the enlargement process to continue well after the 10 + 2 round is completed: that is, after Bulgaria and Romania join the EU, which is scheduled for 2007. Most EU governments are, moreover, desirous that it should continue, with enlargement having increasingly become an unstated goal of EU external policy. It is a goal that has a number of policy instruments attached to it, with various forms of financial assistance, of association and cooperation agreements, and of pre-accession strategies being available for would-be member states.

Turkey's application is, as was shown in Chapter 3, moving forward. The European Council at its December 2002 Copenhagen meeting promised Turkey that the December 2004 European Council meeting will authorize the opening of accession negotiations if by that time Turkey fulfils the 1993 Copenhagen political criteria for membership. It seems probable that the criteria will be met, though whether this does in practice lead to the opening of negotiations is likely to be dependent on Turkey doing something that was not explicitly laid down as a condition at the Copenhagen summit but which was implied strongly by the December 2003 Brussels summit. That is, it must use its influence in northern Cyprus to help bring a resolution to the Cyprus Problem.

Beyond Turkey, there are several other countries that are, or that may become, interested in EU membership. They are located in three groupings.

First, there are the states of the Western Balkans – Albania, Bosnia-Herzegovina, Croatia, Serbia-Montenegro and Macedonia. These countries were offered, albeit in somewhat general terms, the prospect of eventual EU membership as part of the Stability Pact for South Eastern Europe that the EU promoted in 1999 in response to the humanitarian crisis in Kosovo. All have indicated their interest in EU membership, and one of them – Croatia – formally applied in April 2003. At the June 2003 Thessaloniki European Council meeting, EU-15 leaders made clear that they anticipated the eventual membership of this group by explicitly stating their 'determination to fully and effectively support the European perspective of the Western Balkan countries, which will become an integral part of the EU, once they meet the established criteria' (European Council, 2003a: 12). Second, there are the three significant Western European states that remain outside the EU – Iceland, Norway and Switzerland. Of these, Norway is the most likely to apply in the foreseeable future. However, an application even from Iceland, which has not applied in the past primarily because of the Common Fisheries Policy (CFP), cannot be ruled out at some point: Icelandics indicate that their position could change if EU flexibilty was to be extended to the CFP! Third, there are western former Soviet states – notably Belarus, Moldova and the Ukraine – all of which have indicated an interest in eventual membership.

Mention of western former Soviet states emphasizes how important it is that discussions and debates about future enlargement policy are placed within the wider context of the EU's policies towards its neighbours. Not all the neighbouring states of the expanded EU can hope for eventual membership, though most would like it. Clearly, for example, the prospect of western former Soviet states becoming members is distant at best, whilst southern Mediterranean states are, as present enlargement criteria stand, not even remote prospective members. But the EU must develop closer and more supportive relations with these neighbours if it is to avoid being surrounded by mostly poor, politically and administratively weak, and potentially unstable states that threaten its borders and security. This will require the enlarged EU to not over-concentrate on internal matters or to devote too much of its attention to issues associated with accommodating the new member states.

Chronology of EC/EU Enlargement

1957	March	The Treaties of Rome signed, establishing the European Economic Community (EEC) and the European Atomic Energy Community (Euratom).
1958	January	EEC and Euratom come into operation.
1961	July	Signing of Association Agreement between Greece and the EEC. Comes into effect November 1962.
	July–August	Ireland, Denmark and the UK request membership negotiations with the Community.
1962	July	Norway requests negotiations on Community membership.
1963	January	General de Gaulle announces his veto on UK membership.
	September	Signing of Association Agreement between Turkey and the EEC.
1967	May	Denmark, Ireland and the UK re-apply for Community membership.
	July	Norway re-applies for Community membership.
	December	The Council of Ministers fails to reach agreement on the reopening of membership negotiations with the applicant states because of continued French opposition to UK membership.
1969	July	President Pompidou (who succeeded de Gaulle after his resignation in April) announces he does not oppose UK membership in principle.
1970	June	Community opens membership negotiations with Denmark, Ireland, Norway and the UK.
1972	January	Negotiations between the Community and the four applicant countries concluded. Signing of treaties of accession.
	May	Irish approve Community accession in a referendum.
	July	Conclusion of Special Relations Agreement between Community and EFTA countries.
	September	Majority vote against Community accession in a referendum in Norway.
	October	Danes approve Community accession in a referendum.
1973	January	Accession of Denmark, Ireland and the UK to the Community.

1975	June	A majority vote in favour of continued Community membership in UK referendum.
	June	Greece applies for Community membership.
1976	July	Opening of negotiations on Greek accession to the Community.
1977	March	Portugal applies for Community membership.
	July	Spain applies for Community membership.
1978	October	Community opens accession negotiations with Portugal.
1979	February	Community opens accession negotiations with Spain.
	May	Signing of Accession Treaty between Community and Greece.
1981	January	Accession of Greece to Community.
1984	January	Free trade area between Community and EFTA established.
1985	June	Signing of accession treaties between the Community and Spain and Portugal.
1986	January	Accession of Spain and Portugal to Community.
1987	June	Turkey applies for Community membership.
	July	Austria applies for Community membership.
1989	September–December	The collapse of communist governments in Eastern Europe. The process 'begins' with the appointment of a non-communist Prime Minister in Poland in September and 'ends' with the overthrow of the Ceausescu regime in Romania in December.
	December	Commission advises Council of Ministers to reject Turkey's application for Community membership.
1990	July	Cyprus and Malta apply for Community membership.
	October	Unification of Germany. Territory of former East Germany becomes part of the Community.
1991	July	Sweden applies for Community membership.
	August–December	Break-up of the USSR.
	December	Association ('Europe') Agreements signed with Czechoslovakia, Hungary and Poland.
1992	March	Finland applies to join the EC.
	May	Switzerland applies to join the EC.
	November	Norway applies to join the EC.
	December	In a referendum, the Swiss people vote not to ratify the EEA by 50.3 per cent to 49.7 per cent. Amongst other implications this means that Switzerland's application to join the EU is suspended.

	December	Edinburgh European Council meeting agrees on several key issues, including the opening of accession negotiations in early 1993 with Austria, Finland, Sweden and Norway.
1993	February	Accession negotiations open with Austria, Finland and Sweden.
	April	Accession negotiations open with Norway.
	June	Copenhagen European Council. It is agreed that CEECs wishing to become members of the EU shall do so once they meet specified economic and political conditions (the Copenhagen criteria).
1994	January	EEA enters into force.
	March	Austria, Finland, Sweden and Norway agree accession terms with the EU.
	April	Hungary and Poland apply for membership of the EU.
	June	In a referendum on accession to the EU, the Austrian people vote in favour by 66.4 per cent to 33.6 per cent.
	June	The Corfu European Council meeting requests the Commission to prepare a pre-accession strategy for CEECs and declares that 'the next phase of enlargement of the Union will involve Cyprus and Malta'.
	October	Referendum in Finland on EU membership. The people vote in favour by 57 per cent to 43 per cent.
	November	Referendum in Sweden on EU membership. The people vote in favour by 52.2 per cent to 46.9 per cent.
	November	Referendum in Norway on EU membership. The people reject accession by 52.2 per cent to 47.8 per cent.
	December	The Essen European Council meeting agrees on a number of measures as part of a pre-accession strategy for CEECs. It also asks the Commission to prepare a White Paper on integrating CEECs into the internal market.
1995	January	Austria, Finland and Sweden become EU members.
	March	The Council of Ministers states that accession negotiations with Cyprus and Malta will be opened no later than six months after the conclusion of the 1996 IGC.
	June	Romania and Slovakia apply to join the EU.
	June	The Cannes European Council meeting approves the Commission's White Paper that had been requested by the Essen summit. Key features of the Paper are: the identification of core elements of the internal market *acquis* that would need to be adopted by the CEECs; an emphasis on the need for the establishment of stronger administrative and legal structures in the CEECs; and the identification of forms of assistance CEECs would need to enable them to modernize and align their economies. The summit confirms the March Council

		statement on the opening of accession negotiations with Cyprus and Malta.

	October	Latvia applies to join the EU.
	November	Estonia applies to join the EU.
	December	The Madrid European Council meeting requests the Commission to prepare reports on enlargement, including detailed opinions on applications received from CEECs and an assessment of the likely financial implications of enlargement. (This request leads to the Commission's *Agenda 2000* document.) The summit also announces that it hopes the 'preliminary stage' of accession negotiations with CEECs will coincide with the start of the negotiations with Cyprus and Malta.
	December	Lithuania and Bulgaria apply to join the EU.
1996	January	The Czech Republic and Slovenia apply to join the EU.
1997	June	Amsterdam European Council agrees to the Treaty of Amsterdam. The Treaty fails to provide for the institutional change that enlargement will require, but does contain some strengthening of EU institutions and policies.
	July	Commission issues its *Agenda 2000* document. It recommends that accession negotiations should be opened with six of the 13 applicant countries – the Czech Republic, Estonia, Hungary, Poland, Slovenia and Cyprus. It also contains recommendations on how EU policies – especially the CAP and the Structural Funds – should be reformed so as to allow for enlargement to occur without significantly increasing the EU's budget.
	October	Amsterdam Treaty formally signed by EU Foreign Ministers.
1998	March	Accession negotiations formally opened with the Czech Republic, Estonia, Hungary, Poland, Slovenia and Cyprus.
	November	European Commission issues its first regular Reports on the Progress of Candidate Countries Towards Accession.
1999	March	At a special European Council meeting in Berlin, the Heads of Government reach agreement on *Agenda 2000* measures. The measures include a financial perspective for 2000–2006, and CAP and Structural Fund reforms.
	May	Treaty of Amsterdam enters into force.
	December	Helsinki European Council meeting takes key decisions on EU enlargement. These include that negotiations will be opened in early 2000 with six more applicant states, that the principles of differentiation and catching up

will apply, and that Turkey will be viewed as having candidate status.

2000	February	Accession negotiations are opened with Latvia, Lithuania, Bulgaria, Slovakia, Romania and Malta.
	December	Nice European Council agrees to the Treaty of Nice. The Treaty consists mainly of a range of institutional reforms designed to enable enlargement to proceed. The summit also endorses Commission proposals on enlargement, at the centre of which is the 'roadmap' as a framework for ensuring the completion of accession negotiations.
2001	February	Treaty of Nice is formally signed by EU Foreign Ministers.
	December	Laeken European Council decides to convene a Convention on the Future of Europe, which will prepare the ground for an IGC to be convened in 2004.
2002	October	In its Regular Reports on the progress made by the candidate countries, the Commission concludes that the Czech Republic. Cyprus, Estonia, Hungary, Latvia. Hungary, Malta, Poland, Slovenia and Slovakia fulfil the political criteria for membership and that they will also have fulfilled the economic and *acquis* criteria by the beginning of 2004. On this basis, the Commission recommends that accession negotiations with these countries be concluded in December 2002 and that the Treaty of Accession be signed in Spring 2003.
	December	Copenhagen European Council meeting takes key decisions on enlargement. These include: 10 states – Cyprus, the Czech Republic, Estonia, Hungary, Latvia, Lithuania, Poland, Malta, Slovakia and Slovenia – are deemed to have completed accession negotiations and will join the EU on 1 May 2004 subject to ratification procedures having been completed; Bulgaria and Romania will be able to join the EU in 2007 if they make satisfactory progress in complying with the membership criteria; the December 2004 summit will authorize the immediate opening of accession negotiations with Turkey if the Commission makes a recommendation to this effect based on Turkey having continued with its reform process.
2003	February	The Treaty of Nice enters into force. Croatia applies to join the EU.
	March	In the first referendum to be held in the countries scheduled to join the EU in 2004, the Maltese people vote to join the EU by 53.6 per cent to 46.4 per cent, on a 91 per cent turnout.

	In a referendum, the Slovenian people vote to join the EU by 89.6 per cent to 10.4 per cent, on a 60.3 per cent turnout.
April	The Treaty of Accession is signed in Athens by representatives of the EU-15 states and the 10 applicant states with which negotiations have been completed.
	In a referendum, the Hungarian people vote to join the EU by 84 per cent to 16 per cent, on a 45.6 per cent turnout.
May	In a referendum, the Lithuanian people vote to join the EU by 91.0 per cent to 9.0 per cent, on a 63.4 per cent turnout.
	In a referendum, the Slovak people vote to join the EU by 92.4 per cent to 7.6 per cent, on a 52.1 per cent turnout.
	The European Convention on the Future of Europe agrees on the contents of the Draft Treaty Establishing a Constitution for Europe.
June	In a referendum, the Polish people vote to join the EU by 77.5 per cent to 22.5 per cent, on a 58.8 per cent turnout.
	In a referendum, the Czech people vote to join the EU by 77.3 per cent to 23.7 per cent, on a 55.2 per cent turnout.
July	The Cypriot House of Representatives votes unanimously to approve Cyprus's Treaty of Accession to the EU. (Of the 10 states to sign the April 2003 Accession Treaty, Cyprus is the only one not to hold a referendum.)
September	In a referendum, the Estonian people vote to join the EU by 66.8 per cent to 33.2 per cent, on a 64.0 per cent turnout.
	In a referendum, the Latvian people vote to join the EU by 67.0 per cent to 32.3 per cent, on a 72.5 per cent turnout.
October	The IGC charged with negotiating a constitutional treaty is opened.
December	The Brussels European Council meeting fails to agree on the contents of the constitutional treaty and the IGC is suspended.

Appendix 1 Key Statistics on EU-15, New and Candidate States[*]

States	Population (millions)	Area (1000 sq.km)	GDP (billion euro)	GDP per capita in PPS (thousands)[1]	Agriculture as a % of total employment
EU-15					
Austria	8.1	84	210	26.7	5.8
Belgium	10.3	30	257	25.1	1.4
Denmark	5.4	43	180	28.3	3.5
Finland	5.2	338	135	24.6	5.8
France	59.3	544	1,456	23.9	4.1
Germany	82.4	357	2,063	24.8	2.6
Greece	10.6	132	130	16.5	16.0
Ireland	3.9	69	116	28.4	7.0
Italy	58.0	301	1,217	25.0	5.2
Luxembourg	0.4	3	22	45.0	1.5
Netherlands	16.1	41	427	26.6	3.1
Portugal	10.3	92	123	17.3	12.9
Spain	40.4	505	650	19.9	6.5
Sweden	8.9	450	234	24.9	2.6
United Kingdom	60.1	242	1,591	24.2	1.4
EU-15	379.6	3,191	8,811	23.9	4.2
New members					
Cyprus	0.8	9	10	18.5	4.9
Czech Republic	10.3	79	63	14.6	4.9
Estonia	1.4	45	6	10.9	6.9
Hungary	10.2	93	58	12.6	6.1
Latvia	2.4	65	8	7.9	15.1
Lithuania	3.5	65	13	8.8	16.5
Malta	0.4	0.3	4	13.3	1.9
Poland	38.6	313	197	9.0	19.2
Slovakia	5.4	49	23	12.0	6.3
Slovenia	2.0	20	21	17.0	9.9
New member states	75.0	738	403	10.8	13.3
Candidates					
Bulgaria	7.9	111	15	7.7	26.7
Romania	22.4	238	44	6.2	44.4
Turkey	66.3	780	165	6.2	37.0

[*] Population and area figures are for 2003; other figures are for 2001.
[1] PPS – purchasing power standard. This is a unit representing the same volume of goods and services in a country, irrespective of price levels. The value of one PPS is approximately one euro.
Sources: European Commission (2003) website on enlargement at www.europa.eu.int/comm./enlargement/docs/pdf; Eurostat (2003); UK Foreign Office website at www.fco.gov.uk; Weber Shandwick (2003).

Appendix 2 Chapters of the Accession Negotiations

1   Free movement of goods
2   Freedom of movement for persons
3   Freedom to provide services
4   Free movement of capital
5   Company law
6   Competition law
7   Agriculture
8   Fisheries
9   Transport policy
10 Taxation
11 Economic and Monetary Union
12 Statistics
13 Social policy and employment
14 Energy
15 Industrial policy
16 Small- and medium-sized undertakings
17 Science and research
18 Education and training
19 Telecommunications and information technologies
20 Culture and audio-visual policy
21 Regional policy and co-ordination of structural instruments
22 Environment
23 Consumers and health protection
24 Cooperation in the field of justice and home affairs
25 Customs union
26 External relations
27 Common foreign and security policy
28 Financial control
29 Financial and budgetary provisions
30 Institutions
31 Other

Bibliography

Abbott, R. (2001) *EU Enlargement and Transatlantic Economic Relations*, speech delivered by the European Commission's Deputy Director General for Trade at the Conference 'Europe's Continuing Enlargement: Implications for the Transatlantic Partnership', 22 October, Paul H. Nitze School of Advanced International Studies, Johns Hopkins University, Washington, DC.

Adams, T., *et al.* (2002) *Europe's Black Sea Dimension* (Brussels: Centre for European Policy Studies).

AFX European Focus (internet) Brussels: AFX Nexus Limited.

Allen, D. and Smith, M. (1990) 'Western Europe's Presence in the Contemporary International Arena', *Review of International Studies*, 16 (1): 19–37.

Almond, G. and Verba. S. (1963) *Civic Culture: Political Attitudes and Democracy in Five Nations* (Princeton: Princeton University Press).

Anderson, B. (1983) *Imagining Nations,* 4th edn (New York: Verso).

Anderson, C. (1996a) 'Economic Benefits and Support for Membership in the European Union: A Cross-national Analysis', *Journal of Public Policy*, 15: 231–49.

Anderson, C. (1996b) 'The Dynamics of Public Opinion Toward European Integration, 1973–1993', *European Journal of International Relations*, 2 (2): 175–99.

Archer, C. (2001) 'The Northern Dimension as a Soft-Soft Option for the Baltic States' security' in H. Ojanen (ed.) *The Northern Dimension: Fuel for the EU* (Helsinki: UPI and IEP): 188–208.

Archer, C. and Nugent, N (2002) 'Introduction: Small States and the European Union', *Current Politics and Economics of Europe: Special Edition on Small States and the European Union*, 11(1): 1–10.

Ardy, B. (2000) *EU Enlargement and Agriculture: Problems and Prospects*, South Bank European Papers (London: South Bank Institute).

Armstrong, K. and Bulmer, S. (1998) *The Governance of the Single European Market* (Manchester: Manchester University Press).

Ash, T. (1989) *The Uses of Adversity: Essays on the Fate of Central Europe*, (Cambridge: Granta Books): 242–303.

Ash, T. (1998) 'Europe's Endangered Liberal Order', *Foreign Affairs*, 77 (2): 51–66.

Aspinwall, M. (1995) 'International Integration or Internal Politics? Anatomy of a Single Market Measure', *Journal of Common Market Studies*, 33 (4): 475–99.

Aspinwall, M. and Schneider, G. (1997) *Same Menu, Separate Tables: The Institutionalist Turn in Political Science and the Study of European Integration,* paper presented to the European Consortium of Political Research (ECPR), University of Bergen, 12–21 September.

Avery, G. (2004) 'The Enlargement Negotiations', in F. Cameron (ed), *The Future of Europe: Integration and Enlargement* (London: Routledge): 35–62.

Backé, P. (1999) 'Integrating Central and Eastern Europe in the European Union: The Monetary Dimension', in P. De Grauwe and V. Lavrac (eds), *Inclusion of Central European Countries in the European Monetary Union* (Norwell, MA: Kluwer Academic Publishers): 119–40.

Balassa, B. (1964) 'The Purchasing Power Parity Doctrine: A Reappraisal', *Journal of Political Economy*, 72 (6): 584–96.

Baldwin, R. E. (1993) *Towards an Integrated Europe* (London: Centre for European Policy Reform).

Baldwin, R. E., Francois, J. F. and Portes, R. (1997) 'The Costs and Benefits of Eastern Enlargement: The Impact on the EU and Central Europe', *Economic Policy*: 127–176.

Baltas, N. C. (2001) 'European Union Enlargement : An Historic Milestone in the Process of European Integration', *Atlantic Economic Journal*, 29 (3): 254–65.

Banque Paribas Conjuncture (internet), Paris: Janet Mathews Information Services and Quest Information Limited.

Barysch, K. (2003) *Does Enlargement Matter for the EU Economy?* (London: Centre for European Reform).

Barysch, K. and Grabbe, H. (2002) *Who's Ready for EU Enlargement?* (London: Centre for European Reform).

Batt, J. (2001) *"Fuzzy Statehood" and European Integration in Central and Eastern Europe* (Birmingham: Centre for Russian and East European Studies) http://www.crees.bham.ac.uk/research/statehood/index.htm

Baun, M. (2000) *A Wider Europe* (Lanham, Maryland: Rowman & Littlefield).

BBC Monitoring (internet) (London: The Financial Times Information).

BBC News (2002) 'View on Enlargement in Pictures', http://newsvote.bbc.co.uk/

Beetham, D (1992) 'Liberal Democracy and the Limits of Democratization', in D. Held (ed.), *Prospects for Democracy* (Cambridge: Polity Press).

Beetham, D and Lord, C. (1998) *Legitimacy and the European Union* (London: Longman).

Billing, M. (1995) *Banal Nationalism* (London: Sage).

Boeri, T., Brücker H., *et al.* (2002) '*Who's Afraid of the Big Enlargement? Economic and Social Implications of the European Union's Prospective Eastward Expansion*, CEPR Policy Paper No. 7 (London: Centre for European Policy Reform).

Bretherton, C. and Vogler, J. (1999) *The European Union as a Global Actor* (London: Routledge).

Breton, A., Galeotti, G., Salmon, P., and Wintrobe, R. (1995) *Nationalism and Rationality* (Cambridge: Cambridge University Press).

Breuss, F. (2001) 'Macroeconomic Effects of EU Enlargement for Old and New Members', *WIFO Working Paper* No. 143/2001 (Vienna: WIFO).

Brewin, C. (2000) *The European Union and Cyprus* (Huntingdon: Eothen Press).

Brown, D., Deardorff, A. V., Djankov, S. and Stern, R. M. (1997) 'An Economic Assessment of the Integration of Czechoslovakia, Hungary and Poland into the European Union', in S.W. Black (ed.), *Europe's Economy Looks East: Implications for Germany and the European Union* (Cambridge: Cambridge University Press).

Browne S. (1990) *Foreign Aid in Practice* (New York: New York University Press).

Bull, H. (1983) 'Civilian Power Europe: a Contradiction in Terms?', in R. Tsoukalis (ed.) *The European Community: Past, Present and Future* (London: Blackwell): 149–70.

Bulmer, S. (1994) 'The New Governance of the European Union: A Neo-Institutionalist Approach', *Journal of European Public Policy*, 13 (4): 351–80.

Bulmer, S. (1998) 'New Institutionalism and the Governance of the Single European Market', *Journal of European Public Policy*, 5 (3): 365–86.

Burnell P. (1997) *Foreign Aid in a Changing World* (Philadelphia: Open University Press).

Calvert, R. (1995) 'The Rational Choice Theory of Social Institutions: Cooperation, Coordination and Communication', in J. S. Banks and E. A. Hanushek (eds) *Modern Political Economy* (New York: Cambridge University Press).

Cameron, F. (1999) *The Foreign and Security Policy of the European Union. Past, Present and Future* (Sheffield: Sheffield Academic Press).

Cameron, F. and Primatarova, A. (2003) 'Enlargement, CFSP and the Convention: The Role of the Accession States', *European Policy Institute Network (EPIN) Working Paper* No. 5.

Candidate Countries Eurobarometer (annual since 2001, plus special reports) (Brussels: European Commission), www.europa.eu.int/comm/public_opinion

Carbone, M. (2003) 'The Role of Civil Society in the Cotonou Agreement', in O. Babarinde and G. Faber (eds), *The EU-ACP Co-operation at the Crossroads* (Boulder: Lynne Rienner).

Carrubba, C. (1997) 'Net Financial Transfers in the European Union: Who Gets What and Why?', *Journal of Politics*, 59 (2): 469–496.

Cederman, L. E. (2000), 'Nationalism and Bounded Integration: What it Would Take to Construct a European Demos', *EU Working Paper* 2000/34 (Florence: European University Institute).

CEPOL. Website of the European Police College, http://www.cepol.net/intranet/

Charlemagne (2003): 'The Tower of Babble – The Curious Cabbalistic Language of Those Who Run the European Union', *The Economist*, 368 (8335): 32.

Church, C. H. and Phinnemore, D. (2002) *The Penguin Guide to the European Treaties* (London: Penguin).

Cimoszewicz, W. (2003a), *The Eastern Dimension of the European Union. The Polish View*, speech by Wlodzimierz Cimoszewicz, Polish Minister of Foreign Affairs, at the conference 'The EU Enlargement and Neighbourhood Policy', http//:www.msz.gov.pl/start.php

Cimoszewicz, W. (2003b) *Future of the Common Foreign and Security Policy*, speech by Wlodzimierz Cimoszewicz, Polish Minister of Foeign Affairs, at the Friedrich Ebert Foundation, Berlin, 12 March 2003, http//:www.msz.gov.pl/start.php

Cohen, B. (1998) *The Geography of Money* (Ithaca: Cornell University Press).

Cosgrove, C. and Twitchett, K. (eds) (1970) *The New International Actors: The UN and the EEC* (London: Macmillan).

Cox A. and Chapman, J. (1999) *The European Community External Cooperation Programmes: Policies, Management and Distribution* (Brussels: European Commission).

Cremona, M. (2003) 'The Impact of Enlargement: External Policy and External Relations', in M. Cremona (ed.) *The Enlargement of the European Union* (Oxford: Oxford University Press).

Cronin, D. (2003) 'Middle East Foes Should Join Single Market by 2005', *European Voice*, 12–18 June: 5.

Cukierman, A. (1992) *Central Bank Strategy, Credibility and Independence* (Cambridge, MA: MIT Press).

Czerwińska, I. (2002) *Warsaw Voice* 44 (732), 3 November 2002, http://www.warsawvoice.pl/v728/Business07.html

Dahl, R. (1989) *Democracy and its Critics* (New Haven: Yale University Press).

Dalton, R and Elchenberg, R. C. (1993) 'Europeans and the European Community: The Dynamics of Public Support for European Integration', *International Organization*, 47: 507–34.

Danilevsky, N. (1964) 'The Slav Role in World Civilization', in T. Riha (ed.), *Readings in Russian Civilization* (Chicago: Chicago University Press).

Dauderstädt, M. (ed.) (2002) *EU Eastern Enlargement and Development Cooperation* (Bonn: Friedrich Ebert Stiftung).

De Grauwe, P. and Lavrac, V. (1999) 'Fiscal Consolidation in the Central European Countries and European Monetary Union', in P. De Grauwe and V. Lavrac (eds), *Inclusion of Central European Countries in the European Monetary Union* (Norwell, MA: Kluwer Academic Publishers): 53–62.

de Tocqueville, A. (1969) *Democracy in America*, ed. by J. P. Mayer (Garden City: Anchor Books).

de Witte, B. (2003) 'The Impact of Enlargement on the Constitution of the European Union', in M. Cremona (ed.), *The Enlargement of the European Union* (Oxford: Oxford University Press): 209–52.

Dearden, S., (2003). 'The Future Role of the European Union in Europe's Development Assistance', *Cambridge Review of International Affairs*, 16, (1): 105–17.

Deighton, A. (2002) 'The European Security and Defence Policy', *Journal of Common Market Studies*, 40 (4): 719–41.

Delors, J. (1991) 'European Integration and Security', *Survival*, 33(2): 99–109.

Deutsch, K., Burrell, S., and Kann, R. (1957) *Political Community and the North Atlantic Area: International Organization in the Light of Historical Experience* (New York: Greenwood Press).

Development Assistance Committee (2003) *Development Co-operation: 2002 Report* (Paris: OECD).

Dinan, D. (2000) *Encyclopedia of the European Union* (Boulder, CO: Lynne Rienner).

Dosenrode, S. and Stubkjær (2002) *The European Union and the Middle East* (Sheffield: Sheffield Academic Press).

Draft Treaty Establishing a Constitution for Europe (2003) (Brussels: European Convention Secretariat).

Dûchene, F. (1972) 'Europe's Role in World Peace', in R. Mayne (ed.) *Europe Tomorrow: Sixteen Europeans Look Ahead* (London: Fontana): 32–47.

Duchesne, S. and Frognier, A. (1995) 'Is There a European Identity?', in O. Niedermayer and R. Sinnott (eds), *Public Opinion and International Governance: Volume 2* (Oxford: Oxford University Press): 193–226.

Duff. A. (2000): 'The Treaty of Nice: From Left-Overs to Hangovers', briefing note on outcome of Intergovernmental Conference and European Council of Nice 7–11 December 2000.

Duke, S. (2002) ' Preparing for European Diplomacy', *Journal of Common Market Studies*, 40 (5): 849–70.

Dunkerley, D., Hodgson, L., Konopacki, S., Spybey, T. and Thompson, A. (2002) *Changing Europe: Identities, Nations and Citizens* (London: Routledge).

Dvorakova, M. (2003) 'Financial and Budgetary Aspects of the Czech Entry into the EU,' unpublished paper.

Dyker, D. (2000) 'The Dynamic Impact of the Central-East European Economics of Accession to the European Union', *Economic and Social Research Council, 'One Europe or Several'* programme, working paper, June 2000.

Easton, D. (1965) *A Systems Analysis of Political Life* (New York: John Wiley & Sons).

Economic Commission for Europe (2002) *Economic Survey of Europe 2002* (New York: United Nations).

Economist (weekly), London: Economist Group.

Eden, H., De Groot, A., Ledrut, E. and Romijn, G. (1999) 'EMU and Enlargement: A Review of Policy Issues', *Economic Affairs Series* working paper no. 1777 (Brussels: Directorate-General for Research, European Parliament, Economic Affairs Series working paper no. 1777).

Eichengreen, B. and Ghironi, F. (2003) 'EMU and Enlargement', in M. Bucci and A. Sapir (eds), *EMU and Economic Policy in Europe: The Challenge of the First Two Years* (Cheltenham: Edward Elgar): 381–408.

Eisenstadt, S. and Giesen, B. (1995) 'The Construction of Collective Identity', *Archives of European Sociology, 56.*

Eiteljorge, U. and Hartmann, M. (1999) 'Central-Eastern Europe Food Chains Competitiveness', in R. Goldberg (ed.), *The European Agro-Food System and the Challenges of Global Competition* (Rome: ISMEA).

El Pais (daily) (Madrid: Diario El Pais S.L.).

Embassy of France (1998) *Joint Declaration on European Defence, 4 December 1998*, at www.ambafrance.org.uk

Emerson, M. (2001) *The Elephant and the Bear: The European Union, Russia and their Near Abroads* (Brussels: Centre for European Policy Studies).

Enlargement Weekly (internet), Europa website.

Estonian Ministry of Defence (2001), *Estonian Defence Forces 2001* (Tallinn: Estonian Ministry of Defence, Department of Defence Policy and Planning).

EU Monitor (internet) (Frankfurt: Deutsche Bank AG, DB Research).

EU News Releases (issued daily by the European Commission), Europa website.

Eurobarometer (twice a year, plus special editions) (Brussels: European Commission – Directorate-General Press and Communication), http://europa.eu.int/comm/public_opinion

EUobserver (daily) online articles on current EU issues, ww.euobserver.com.

Eurojust, website of the European body responsible for the enhancement of judicial cooperation, http://www.eurojust.eu.int/index.htm.

European Central Bank (2003) *Recommendation, Under Article 10.6 of the Statute of the European System of Central Banks and of the European Central Bank, for a Council Decision on an Amendment to Article 10.2 of the Statute of the European System of Central Banks and of the European Central Bank*, ECB/2003/1, February (Frankfurt: European Central Bank).

European Commission (1985) *A People's Europe: Report from the ad hoc Committe'*, in *Bulletin of the European Communities*, Supplement, July 1985 (Adonnino Report).

European Commission (1996) 'Awareness and Role of European Union Institutions, Treaties and Agreement', *Eurobarometer* 44, Chapter 5, http://europa.eu.int/comm/public_opinion/archives/eb/eb44/chap5_en.htm

European Commission (1997) *Agenda 2000: For a Stronger and Wider Union*, Com. 97 (final), in *Bulletin of the European Union*, Supplement 5.97 (Luxembourg: EUR-OP).

European Commission (1999a) *Financial Framework of the European Union*, Europa website.

European Commission (1999b) *Draft of Commission Information Brochure for the General Public on Agenda 2000*, Priority Publications Programme 1999, X/D/5 Final version 31.8.

European Commission (2000a) *Agenda 2000*, Supplements 3/2000, Europa website.

European Commission (2000b) *The European Community's Development Policy: Statement by the Council and the Commission* (Brussels: European Commission).

European Commission (2000c) *Enlargement and Agriculture: Successfully Integrating the New Member States into the CAP*, issues paper, DG Enlargement, SEC(2002) 95 final, January, http://europa.eu.int/comm/enlargement/docs/financialpackage/sec2002-95_en.pdf.

European Commission (2000d): *Competition Policy in Europe and the Citizen* (Luxembourg: Office for Official Publications of the European Communities).

European Commission (2000e) *Entry Into Force of EU–Mexico Free Trade Agreement Signals Start of New Era in Europe's Relations with Mexico*, European Commission press release, 3 July, http://europa.eu.int/comm/trade/bilateral/mexico/ftapr_en.htm

European Commission (2000f): *Enlargement Strategy Paper* (Brussels: European Commission).

European Commission (2000g) *Multi-Annual Indicative Programme: A Framework for Cooperation Between South Africa and the European Community*, http://europa.eu.int/comm/development/nip/za_en.pdf.

European Commission (2000q) *Key Structural Challenges in the Acceding Countries: The Integration of the Acceding Countries into the Community's Economic Policy Coordination Process*, European Commission DG for Economic and Financial Affairs, Economic Policy Committee, occasional papers No. 4, July.

European Commission (2001a) *The Economic Impact of Enlargement* (Brussels: DG for Economic and Financial Affairs).

European Commission (2001b) *European Governance: A White Paper*, Com (2001) 428 final, 25 July, (Brussels: European Commission).

European Commission (2001c) *Commission Launches Debate on Impact of Enlargement on Kaliningrad*, (Brussels: European Commission, IP/01/66).

European Commission (2001d), *The Economic Impact of Enlargement*, (Brussels: European Commission DG for Economic and Financial Affairs K-AA-01 001-EN-C , No. 4 June).

European Commission (2001e) *Positive Gains Seen For LDCs if QUAD Implements EBA*, DG Trade Press Release, 17 May, Brussels, http://europa.eu.int/comm/trade/miti/devel/ldcunctad.htm

European Commission (2001f) *Food Safety: Note by the European Communities*, (DIVERS/500186 ur), 20 July, http://europa.eu.int/comm/agriculture/external/wto/document/food_en.pdf.

European Commission (2001g) *EU Trade Commissioner Pascal Lamy to Rally Support Among ACP Countries For Launch of New WTO Round*, European Commission, DG Trade Press Release, 27 September, http://europa.eu.int/comm/trade/miti/devel/supp_acp.htm

European Commission (2001h) *EU to Speed up Preparatory Work on Russia's Accession to WTO*, European Commission, press release, 3 October.

European Commission (2001i) *Lamy Welcomes Adoption of New Scheme of Tariff Preferences for Developing Countries*, European Commission DG Trade Press Release, 10 December, http://europa.eu.int/comm/trade/miti/devel/pr20011210.htm

European Commission (2001j) *2001 Regular Reports [Poland, Hungary, the Czech Republic, Estonia, Slovenia and Cyprus] on Progress Towards Accession*, (Brussels: DG Enlargement).

European Commission (2002a) *EU Backs Launch of Geneva-based Office to Help African, Caribbean and Pacific Countries Boost World Trade Organisation Presence'*, European Commission DG Trade Press Release, 16 January.

European Commission (2002b) *First Progress Report on Economic and Social Cohesion* Com (2002) 46 final, 30 January.

European Commission (2002c) *Towards the Enlarged Union: Strategy Paper and Report of the European Commission on the Progress Towards Accession by Each of the Candidate Countries*, COM (2002) 700 final, 9 October.

European Commission (2002d) *The European Union: Still Enlarging* (Luxembourg: Office for Official Publications of the European Union, and Europa website).

European Commission (2002e) *Candidate Countries Eurobarometer*, Report No. *2002:2* (Brussels: European Commission, DG Press and Communication).

European Commission (2002f) *10 Years Internal Market Without Frontiers – Internal Market Scoreboard*, European Commission Internal Market DG, Europa website.

European Commission (2002g) *EU Trade Commissioner Pascal Lamy Travels to Middle East to Strengthen Trading Relationship With the Region (6–10 February)*, European Commision Press Release, 6 February, http://europa.eu.int/comm/trade/bilateral/prpror060202.htm

European Commission (2002h) *Progress Report Concerning the Reduction and Reorientation of State Aid: Communication from the Commission to the Council*. Com (2002) 555 final (Brussels: European Commission.)

European Commission (2002i) *EU Responds Firmly to US Decision to Severely Restrict Steel Imports From Rest of World*, European Commission DG Trade Press Krelease, 5 March, http://europa.eu.int/comm/trade/goods/steel/pr_060302.htm

European Commission (2002j) *Special Edition on the Candidate Countries: State Aid Scoreboard*, Com (2002) 638 final (Brussels: European Commission, Europa website).

European Commission (2002k) *Enlargement – Weekly Newsletter*, 25 March, http://europa.eu.int/comm/enlargement/docs/n/weekly_250302.htm

European Commission (2002l) *Analysis of the Impact on Agricultural Markets and Incomes of EU Enlargement to the ACs*, European Commission DG Agriculture, March, Europa website.

European Commission (2002m) *Guide to the European Union's Scheme of Generalised Tariff Preferences*, European Commission DG Trade, http://europa.eu.int/comm/trade/pdf/guide_tariffpref.pdf.

European Commission (2002n) *EU-MERCOSUR Relations and Negotiations*, European Commission DG Trade, http://europa.eu.int/comm/trade/bilateral/mercosur/mercosur.htm.

European Commission (2002o) *EU Budget 2003: Combining Budgetary Discipline With Meeting New Priorities*, EU Institutions Press Release, Europa website.

European Commission (2002p) *Financing the European Union, Commission Report on the Operation of the Own Resources System*, Europa website.

European Commission 2002q) *Regional Policy, the Three Objectives*, Europa website.

European Commission 2002r) *EU Budget Boosts Cohesion Countries*, EU Institutions Press Release, 26 September, Europa website.

European Commission (2003a) *Internal Market Scoreboard 2003*, Brussels, 5 May, http://europa.eu.int/comm/internal_market/en/update/score/index.htm

European Commission (2003b) *Report on the Results of the Negotiations on the Accession of Cyprus, Malta, Hungary, Poland, the Slovak Republic, Latvia, Estonia, Lithuania, the Czech Republic and Slovenia to the European Union*, report prepared by Commission Departments on the Draft Accession Treaty, Europa website.

European Commission (2003c) *Candidate Countries Eurobarometer*, Report No. 2003.2 (Brussels: European Commission, DG Press and Information).

European Commission (2003d) *Commission Opinion: ECB Recommendation ECB/2003/1 of 3 February 2003 for a Council Decision on an Amendment to Article 10.2 of the Statute of the ESCB/ECB (Based on Article 10.6 of the Statute)*, Com (2003) 81, February.

European Commission (2003e) *State Aid Scoreboard. Spring 2003 Update*, Com (2003) 225 final (Brussels: European Commission).

European Commission (2003f) *Report on the Results of the Negotiations of Cyprus, Malta, Hungary, Poland, the Slovak Republic, Latvia, Estonia, Lithuania, the Czech Republic and Slovenia to the European Union*, Europa website.

European Commission (2003g) *The Implications of Enlargement for Development Policy*, report prepared by European Commission Development DG, September, Europa website.

European Commission (2003h) *Act Concerning the Conditions of Accession of the Czech Republic, the Republic of Estonia, the Republic of Cyprus, the Republic of Latvia, the Republic of Lithuania, the Republic of Hungary, the Republic of Malta, the Republic of Poland, the Republic of Slovenia and the Slovak Republic and the Adjustments to the Treaties on which the European Union is Founded*, Document AA2003/ACT/en, Brussels, 3 March.

European Commission (2003i) *Second Progress Report on Economic and Social Cohesion* Com (2003) 34 final, 30 January (Brussels: European Commission).

European Commission (2003j) *The EU's Relations with Russia*, Europa website.

European Commission (2003k) *Community Rules on State Aid*, Europa website.

European Commission (2003l) *Enlargement Financial Framework Agreed*, EU Institutions Press Releases, April, Europa website.

European Commission (2003m) *Wider Europe-Neighbourhood: A New Framework for Relations with our Eastern and Southern Neighbours: Communication From the Commission to the Council and European Parliament*, Com (2003) 104 final, 11 March (Brussels: European Commission).

European Commission (2003n) *A Constitution for the Union*, COM(2003) 548 final, Brussels, 17 September.

European Commission (2003o) *The EU's Relations With South Eastern Europe*, Europa website.

European Commission (2003p) *Internal Market Scoreboard Shows Worsening National Delays in Implementing EU Laws*, European Commission Press Release, Bd. IP/03/621.

European Commission (2003q) *The EU's Mediterranean and Middle East Policy*, Europa website.

European Commission (2003r): *Internal Market Strategy – Priorities 2003–2006. Communication from the Commission to the Council, the European Parliament, the European Economic and Social Committee and the Committee of the Regions*, Com (2003) 238 final, (Brussels: European Commission).

European Commission (2003s) *The Challenge of Enlargement*, European Commission Press Release, 9 April, Europa website.

European Commission (2003t) *Results of the Competitiveness Council of Ministers, Brussels*, European Commission Press Release, 22 September, MEMO/03/181.

European Commission (2003u) *Treaty of Accession: Final Act – Joint Declarations* Document AA2003/AF/TR/DC/en, Brussels, 7 September.

European Convention (2003) *Draft Treaty Establishing a Constitution for Europe*, adopted by the European Convention on 13 June and 10 July, submitted to the President of the European Council 18 July, Conv 850/03 (Brussels: Secretariat of the European Convention).

European Council (1993) *Conclusions of the Presidency*, Copenhagen, 21–22 June (Brussels: General Secretariat of the Council).

European Council (1994a) *Presidency Conclusions*, Corfu, 24–25 June, (Brussels: General Secretariat of the Council).

European Council (1994b) *Presidency Conclusions*, Essen, 9–10 December (Brussels: General Secretariat of the Council).

European Council (1999a) *Presidency Conclusions*, Berlin, 24–25 March, Europa website.

European Council (1999b) *Common Strategy of the European Union Toward Russia* http://www.eur.ru/eng/neweur/user_eng.php?func=rae_common_strategy

European Council (1999c) *Presidency Conclusions*, Helsinki, 10–11 December, Europa website.

European Council (2000) *Presidency Conclusions*, Lisbon, 23–24 March, Europa website.

European Council (2001) *Presidency Conclusions*, Stockholm, 23–24 March, Europa website.

European Council (2002a) *Presidency Conclusions*, Seville, 21–22 June, Europa website.

European Council (2002b) *Presidency Conclusions*, Brussels, 24–25 October, Europa website.

European Council (2002c) *Presidency Conclusions*, Copenhagen, 12–13 December, Europa website.

European Council 2002d) *Presidency Conclusions*, Barcelona, 15–16 March, Europa website.

European Council (2003a) *Presidency Conclusions*, Thessaloniki, 19–20 June, Europa website.

European Council (2003b) *Presidency Conclusions*, Brussels, 12 December, Europa website.

European Parliament (1997) *Resolution on the Communication from the Commission on Agenda 2000*, C4-0372/97, www.europarl.eu.int

European Parliament (2002) 'Combining Budgetary Discipline With Meeting New Priorities', *Europarl News Report*, 19 December, http://www.europarl.eu.int/omk/sipade2

European Parliament (2003a) *Draft Report on the Proposal for a Council Decision on an Amendment to Article 10.2 of the Statute of the European System of Central Banks and of the European Central Bank*. 2003/0803 (CNS), European Parliament Committee on Economic and Monetary Affairs, February.

European Parliament (2003b) 'Budget Surplus', *Europarl News Report*, Committee on Budgets, 17 July, p. 4, http://www.europarl.eu. int/omk/sipade2

European Parliament (2003b) *Rules of Procedure*, http://www.europa.eu. int/parliament/procedure_en.htm

European Policy Centre and Notre Europe, (2003) *Reform of EU Policies in the Perspective of Enlargement and Their Financial Implications* (Paris: Notre Europe).

European Union Press Releases (2003) *EU Fundamentally Reforms its Farming Policy to Accomplish Sustainable Farming in Europe*, 26 June, http://www.eurunion.org/news/press/2003/2003042.htm

European Voice (2003) 'Berlusconi Gets Rap From Monti Over Russian Accession' 12–18 June: 4.

European Voice (weekly) Brussels: Economist Group.

Europol, website of the European Police Office, http://www.europol.eu. int/

Eurostat (2001) *The EU Figures for the Doha Conference*, news release No. 117/2001, 8 November, http://europa.eu.int/comm/trade/pdf/doha1108_ff.pdf .

Eurostat (2002) *External and Intra-European Union Trade – Statistical Yearbook*, 2002 edition (Brussels: EUR-OP).

Eurostat (2003) 'Fall in FDI in 2001: EU-15 as Main Actor', *Statistics in Focus: Economy and Finance*, Theme 2 – 12/2003: 1–8 (Brussels: EUR-OP).

Eurostat, the European Union's agency for collecting and disseminating statistical information, Europa website.

Faist, T. (2001) 'Social Citizenship in the European Union: Nested Membership', *Journal of Common Market Studies*, 39 (1): 37–58.

Favell, A. and Hansen, R. (2002) 'Markets against Politics: Migration, EU Enlargement, and the Idea of Europe', *Journal of Ethnic and Migration Studies*, 28 (4): 581–601.

Feldman, L. G. (1999): 'Foreign Relations and Enlargement of the EU', in T. Banchoff and M. P. Smith (eds), *Legitimacy and the European Union: The Contested Polity* (Routledge: London).

Fella, S. (2000): 'A Europe of the Peoples? New Labour and Democratizing the EU' in C. Hoskyns and M. Newman (eds), *Democratizing the European Union* (Manchester: Manchester University Press).

Financial Times (daily) (London: The Financial Times Limited).

Finer, S. E. (1988) *Man on Horseback* (Colorado: Westview Press).

Fink, G. and Haiss, P. (2000) 'Major Achievements and Open Issues in Financial Market Transition of Eastern Candidate Countries', paper presented at the Fifth European Community Studies Association Conference on Enlarging the European Union, Brussels, 14–15 December.

Fisher, S., Sahay, R. and Vegh, C. (1998) 'How Far is Eastern Europe from Brussels?', *IMF Working Paper*, WP/98/53.

Flynn, T. (1991) 'Foucault and the Spaces of History', *Monist*, 74 (2): 165–86.

Fossum, J. (2001) 'Identity-Politics in the European Union', *European Integration*, 23: 373–406.

Fowler, B. (2002), 'Fuzzing Citizenship, Nationalizing Political Space: A Framework for Interpreting the Hungarian "Status Law" as a New Form of Kin-state Policy in Central and Eastern Europe', *Economic and Social Research Council*, *'One Europe or Several'* programme, working paper 40/02.

Francois, J. and Rombout, M. (2001) 'Trade Effects From the Integration of The Central and East European Countries Into the European Union', *Sussex European Institute Working Paper*, No. 41, January.

Freud, S. (1985) 'Group Psychology and the Analysis of the Ego', in *Civilization, Society and Religion*, Pelican Freud Library, Volume 12 (Harmondworth: Penguin).

Fukuyama, F. (1992) *The End of History and the Last Man* (New York: Avon).

Fuller, J., Beghin, J., Fabiosa, J., Mohanty, S., Fang, C., and Kaus, P. (2000) 'Accession of the Czech Republic, Hungary, and Poland to the European Union: Impacts on Agricultural Markets', *Working Paper 00-WP 259*, December, (Ames, Iowa: Iowa State University, Center for Agricultural and Rural Development).

Gabel, M. (1998) *Interests and Integration: Market Liberalization, Public Opinion, and European Union* (Ann Arbor, MI: University of Michigan Press).

Gabel, M. and Palmer, H. (1995) 'Understanding Variation in Public Support for European Integration', *European Journal of Political Research*, 27 (3): 3–19.

Galli, P. (2000) 'Mbeki Lashes WTO, Globalisation for Fuelling SA's Woes', *Business Report*, 25 May, http://www.hartford-hwp.com/archives/37a/051.html

Galloway, D. (2001) *The Treaty of Nice and Beyond. Realities and Illusions of Power in the EU*, (Sheffield: Sheffield Academic Press).

Gavin, B. (2001) *The European Union and Globalisation: Towards Global Democratic Governance* (Cheltenham: Edward Elgar).

Geddes, A. (2002) 'Europe's Ageing Workforce', *BBC News*, 20 June, http://news.bbc.co.uk/

Geertz, C. (1973) 'Deep Play: Notes on the Balinese Cockfight', in C. Geertz, (ed.) *The Interpretation of Cultures* (New York: Basic Books).

Gellner, E. (1983) *Nations and Nationalism* (London: Blackwell Press).

George, S. A. (1998) *An Awkward Partner: Britain in the European Community*, 3rd. ed, (Oxford: Oxford University Press).

Gerth, H. and Mills, C. W. (1967): *From Max Weber* (London: Routledge and Kegan Paul).

Giffen J. and Press, M. (2002) *Aid Policy and Cooperation in an Enlarged European Union* (Oxford: INTRAC).

Giraudon, J. (2004) 'Migration and Asylum: Now More Than Ever', in D. Dinan and M. Green-Cowles (eds), *Developments in the European Union 2* (New York: Palgrave).

Glenn, J. K. (2003) *From Nation State to Member State: Europeanization and Enlargement*, paper prepared for the European Union Studies Association Eighth Biennial Conference, Nashville, 27–29 March.

Gottdiener, M. (1995) *Postmodern Semiotics: Material Culture and the Forms of Postmodern Life* (Oxford: Blackwell).

Government of the United States of America (2000) *1999 Country Reports on Economic Policy and Trade Practices: Poland*, released by the Bureau of Economic and Business Affairs, Department of State, March, http://www.state.gov/www/issues/economic/trade_reports/1999/poland.pdf.

Gower, J. (2002) *The European Union Handbook*, 2nd edn (London: Fitzroy, Dearborn).

Gower, J. and Redmond, J. (2000) (eds) *Enlarging the European Union: The Way Forward* (Aldershot: Ashgate).

Grabbe, H. (2001) *Profiting From EU Enlargement* (London: Centre for European Reform).

Grabbe, H. (2002a) *The Governance of the EU: Facing the Challenge of Enlargement* (London: Centre for European Reform).

Grabbe, H. (2002b) *Briefing Note: The Copenhagen Deal for Enlargement* (London: Centre for European Reform).

Grabbe, H. (2003a) 'Is an Old Versus New European Divide Replacing East Against West?', *CER Bulletin*, Issue 28, February-March, http://www.euractiv.com/cgi-bin/cgint.exe/3345684-189?targ=1&204&OIDN=250834&-tt=el>

Grabbe, H. (2003b) 'Shaken to the Core', *Prospect*, May: 12–13.

Grabbe, H. (2003c) 'The Implications of EU Enlargement', in S. White, J. Batt and P.G. Lewis (eds), *Developments in Central and East European Politics 3* (Basingstoke: Palgrave): 253–265.

Granell, F. (2002) *The Official Development Assistance of the EU after the Next Enlargement*, speech delivered in Prague, 13 September, www.europa.eu.int/comm/development

Greenwood, J. (2003) *Interest Representation in the European Union* (Basingstoke: Palgrave).

Grieco, J. M. (1995) 'The Maastricht Treaty, Economic and Monetary Union, and the Neo-Realist Research Programme', *Review of International Studies*, 21 (1): 21–40.

Grilli, E. (1993) *The European Community and the Developing Countries* (Cambridge, New York: Cambridge University Press).

Gros, D. (2002) 'Health not Wealth: Enlarging the EMU', *West European Politics*, 25 (2): 141–53.

Gros, D. (2003) *Reforming the Composition of the ECB Governing Council in View of Enlargement: How Not to Do It!*, briefing paper for the Economic and Monetary Affairs Committee of the European Parliament, February, http://www.europarl.eu.int/comparl/econ/pdf/emu/speeches/20030217/gross.pdf

Guay, T. (1999) *The United States and the European Union. The Political Economy of a Relationship* (Sheffield: Sheffield Academic Press).

Haas, E. (1958) *The Uniting of Europe* (Stanford: Stanford University Press).

Haas, P. M. (1992) 'Epistemic Communities and International Policy Co-ordination', *International Organization*, 46 (1): 1–35.

Habermas, J. (1999) 'The European Nation-State: On the Post and Future of Sovereignty and Citizenship', in C. Cronin and P. De Greiff (eds), *The Inclusion of the Other: Studies in Political Theory* (Cambridge: MIT Press).

Habermas, J. (2001) *The Postnational Constellations: Essays* (Cambridge: MIT Press).

Hall, P. (1986) *Governing the Economy: The Politics of State Intervention in Britain and France* (Cambridge: Polity Press).

Hall, P and Taylor, R. C. R. (1996) 'Political Science and the Three New Institutionalisms', *Political Studies*, 44 (5): 936–57.

Hancock, M. D. *et al.* (2003) *Politics in Europe*, 3rd edn (New York: Chatham House).

Handler, H. (2003) *Structural Reforms in the Candidate Countries and the European Union.* (Vienna: Austrian Ministry for Economic Affairs and Labour, Economic Policy Centre).

Havlik, P (2001) *EU Enlargement: Economic Impacts on Austria, the Czech Republic, Hungary, Poland, Slovakia and Slovenia*, WIIW Research Reports, No. 280 (Vienna: the Vienna Institute for International Economic Studies).

Hay, D. (1968) *Europe, the Emergence of an Idea*, 2nd edn (Edinburgh: Edinburgh Press).

Heath, E. (1991) 'Edward Heath Counter-Attacks the "Lies" of Mrs. Thatcher', *Agence Europe*, 5516: 5.

Heijdra, B., Keuschnigg, C. and Kohler, W. (2002) *Eastern Enlargement of the EU: Jobs Investment and Welfare in Present Member Countries*, paper presented at the CESifo-Delphi Conference, Delphi, Greece, 13–14 September.

Helleiner, E. (1998) 'National Currencies and National Identities', *American Behavioral Scientist*, 41(10): 1409–36.

Hill, C. (1983) *National Foreign Policies and European Political Cooperation* (London: Allen and Unwin).

Hill, C. (1993) 'The Capability-Expectations Gap, or Conceptualizing Europe's International Role', *Journal of Common Market Studies*, 31 (3): 305–28.

Hill, C. and Smith, K. (eds) (2000) *European Foreign Policy: Key Documents* (London: Routledge).

Hill. R. and Wonnacott, R. (1991) 'Free Trade With Mexico: What Form Should it Take?' *Commentary: The NAFTA Papers*, March (Toronto: CD Howe Institute).

Hobsbawn, E. J. (1990) *Nations and Nationalism since 1780: Programme, Myth, Reality* (New York: Cambridge).

Hoffmann, S. (2000) 'Towards a Common European Foreign and Security Policy', *Journal of Common Market Studies*, 38 (2): 189–98.

Hoffmann, S. (2003) 'The European Union Between Regional Enlargement and Global Irrelevance', *EUSA Review*, 16 (2): 1, 3.

Holland, M. (1995) *European Union Common Foreign Policy from EPC to CFSP Joint Action and South Africa* (Basingstoke: Macmillan).

Holland, M. (2002) *The European Union and the Third World* (New York: Palgrave).

Holmes, P. and Young, A. (2001) 'Emerging Regulatory Challenges to the EU's External Economic Relations', *Sussex European Institute Working Paper*, No. 42.

Horn, G. (2003) *Consequences of the Modification of the Governing Council Rules*, briefing paper for the Economic and Monetary Committee of the European Parliament, January, httpk://www.europarl.eu.int/comparl/econ/pdf/emu/speeches/20030217/horn.pdf

Howe, P. (1995) 'A Community of Europeans: The Requisite Underpinnings', *Journal of Common Market Studies*, 33 (1): 28–46.

Hudson, R. (2002) 'Changing Industrial Production Systems and Regional Development in the New Europe', in Economic and Social Research Council's *One Europe or Several* programme, working paper 45/02.

Ilves, T. H. (1999) *EU Enlargement and Estonia's Identity on the International Stage*, remarks at the International Conference 'Estonia and the European Union', 5 November, Tallinn, Estonian Ministry of Foreign Affairs, http://www.vm.ee/eng/index.html

International Monetary Fund (2002) *Poland–2002 Article IV Consultation, Concluding Statement of the IMF Mission*, 14 March, http://www.imf.org/external/np/ms/2002/031402.htm

Irish Times (daily) (Dublin: The Irish Times).

Jachtenfuchs, M. (2002) 'Deepening and Widening Integration Theory', *Journal of European Public Policy*, 9 (4): 650–657.

Jesień, L. (2002) 'Before and Beyond the European Convention: The Future of Europe from a Polish Perspective', *Studies and Analyses*, 1 (4) (Warsaw: 'Polska w Europie' Foundation).

JHA Scoreboard (European Commission website), http://europa.eu.int/comm/justice_home/doc_centre/scoreboard_en.htm

Jileva, E. (2002) 'Visa and Free Movement of Labour: The Uneven Imposition of the EU Acquis on the Accession States', *Journal of Ethnic and Migration Studies*, 28(4): 683–701.

Johnson, M., with Rollo, J. (2001) 'EU Enlargement and Commercial Policy: Enlargement and the Making of Commercial Policy', *Sussex European Institute Working Paper*, No. 43, March.

Jones, R. (2001) *The Politics and Economics of the European Union*, 2nd edn (Cheltenham: Edward Elgar).

Jovanovic, M. N. (2000) 'Eastern Enlargement of the European Union: Sour Grapes or Sweet Lemon?', *Economia Internazionale*, 53: 507–36.

Jovanovic, M. N. (2002) 'Eastern Enlargement of the EU: A Topsy-Turvy Endgame or Permanent Disillusionment', unedited final draft, *Universita degli Studi di Genova*, 15 November.

Junge, K. (1999) *Flexibility, Enhanced Cooperation and the Treaty of Amsterdam*, European Dossier Series (London: Kogan Page).

Junge, K. (2002) *Does Differentiation Work? An Analysis of Alternative Methods of European Integration*, Ph.D thesis, University of Birmingham.

Kiseilowsa-Lipman, M. (2002) 'Poland's Eastern Borderlands: Political Transition and the "Ethnic Question" ', in J. Batt and K. Wolczuk (eds), *Region, State and Identity in Central and Eastern Europe* (London: Frank Cass): 133–54.

Kok, W. (2003) *Enlarging the European Union. Achievements and Challenges. Report by Wim Kok to the European Commission 26 March 2003* (Florence: European University Institute, Robert Schuman Centre for Advanced Studies).

Král, D., Brinar, I. and Almer, J. (2003) 'The Position of Small Countries Towards Institutional Reform: From Tyranny of the Small to Directoire of the Big?' *European Policy Institute Network (EPIN)*, working paper No. 6, June.

Krichewsky, L. (2003) *Development Policy in the Accession Countries* (Vienna: Trialog).

Laffan, B. (1996) 'The Politics of Identity and Political Order in Europe', *Journal of Common Market Studies*, 34 (1): 81–102.

Laffan, B. (1997) *The Finances of the European Union* (Basingstoke: Macmillan).

Lamy, P (2001) *Special Treatment for Agriculture: The Way Ahead*, Oxford Farming Conference, January, http://europa.eu.int/comm/trade/speeches_articles/spla44_en.htm

Landesmann, M. A. (2003) 'The CEECs in an Enlarged Europe: Patterns of Structural Change and Catching-Up, in H. Handler (ed.), *Structural Reforms in the Candidate Countries and the European Union* (Vienna: Austrian Ministry for Economic Affairs and Labour, Economic Policy Centre).

Landesmann, M. and Richter, S. (2003) 'Consequences of EU Accession: Economic Effects on the CEECs', *Austrian Institute for International Economic Studies, WIIW Research Reports*, No. 229, August.

Langeheine, B. and Weinstock, U. (1984) 'Graduate Integration: A Modest Path Towards Progress', *Journal of Common Market Studies*, 23 (4).

Leibich, A (2002) 'Ethnic Minorities and the Implications of EU Enlargement', in J. Zielonka (ed.), *Europe Unbound: Enlarging and Reshaping the Boundaries of the European Union* (London: Routledge).

Lejour, A. M., de Mooij and Nahuis, R. (2002) *EU Enlargement: Economic Implications for Countries and Industries*, paper presented at the CESifo-Delphi Conference, Delphi, Greece, 13–14 September.

Le Monde (daily) (Paris: Le Monde).

Lenin, V. I. (1914, 1964) 'Once More on the Segregation of the Schools According To Nationality', in *Collected Works*, Volume 19, (Moscow: International Publishers), http://www.marxists.org/archive/lenin/works

Lenin, V. I. (1915, 1964) 'On the Slogan for a United States of Europe', in *Collected Works*, Volume 22, (Moscow: International Publishers), http://www.marxists.org/archive/lenin/works

Le Soir (daily) (Brussels: Le Soir).

Lipsmeyer, C. S. and Nordstrom, T. (2003) 'East versus West: Comparing Political Attitudes and Welfare Preferences Across European Societies', *Journal of European Public Policy*, 10 (3): 339–64.

Lister, M. (ed.) (1998) *European Union Development Policy* (Basingstoke: Macmillan).

Lister, M., (ed.) (1999) *New Perspectives on European Union Development Cooperation* (Boulder: Westview Press).

Lloyd, T. (1997) 'Union and Division in Europe', *International Journal*, 12 (4): 546–54.

Magnette, P. and Nicolaïdis, K. (2003) 'Large and Small Member States in the European Union: Reinventing the Balance' (updated version), Notre Europe, *Research and European Issues*, No. 25, 5 June.

Maier, P. Hendrikx, M. (2003) 'Implication of EMU Enlargement for European Monetary Policy: A Political Economy View', *Kredit und Kapital* 36 (2): 137–66.

Mair, P. and Zielonka, J. (2002) *The Enlarged European Union: Diversity and Adaptation* (London: Frank Cass).

Malyarov, N. and Hendrick, R. (2003) *Fostering European Identity in an Enlarged European Union: Analysis and Perspective*, paper presented at European Union Studies Association Biennal Conference, 27–29 March.

Männik, E. (2002) 'EU and the Aspirations of Applicant Small States: Estonia and the Evolving CESDP', *Current Politics and Economics of Europe*, 11(1): 77–90.

March, J. and Olsen, J. (1984) 'The New Institutionalism: Organizational Factors in Political Life', *American Political Science Review*, 78: 734–49.

March, J. and Olsen, J. (1989) *Rediscovering Institutions: The Organizational Basis of Politics* (New York: The Free Press).

Maresceau, M. (2003) 'Pre-accession', in M. Cremona (ed.) *The Enlargement of the European Union* (Oxford: Oxford University Press): 9–42.

Marks, G. (1997) 'A Third Lense: Comparing European Integration and State Building', in J. Klausen and L. Tilly (eds), *European Integration In Social and Historical Perspective 1850 to the Present* (Lanham, MD: Rowman and Littlefield): 23–43.

Marks, G., Hooghe, L. and Blank, K. (1996) 'European Integration from the 1980s: State-Centric vs. Multi-Level Governance', *Journal of Common Market Studies*, 39(3) (September 1996): 341–378.

Marks, G. and Hooghe, L. (2001) *Multi-level Governance and European Integration* (Lanham, MD: Rowman and Littlefield).

Marks, G, Nielsen, F., Ray, L. and Salk, J. (1996) 'Competencies, Cracks and Conflicts: Regional Mobilization in the European Union', in G. Marks, F. W. Scharpf, P. C. Schmitter and W. Streeck (eds), *Governance in the European Union* (London: Sage).

Mather, J (2000): *The European Union and British Democracy: Towards Convergence* (Basingstoke: Macmillan).

Matlary, J. H. (1993) 'Norway and European Integration: A Theoretical Discussion', in B. Nelsen (ed.), *Norway and the European Community* (Westport: Praeger Publishers).

McCormick, J. (1999) *The European Union: Policies and Politics*, 2nd edn (Boulder, CO: Westview Press).

McDonald, M. (2000) 'Identities in the European Commission', in N. Nugent (ed.) *At the Heart of the Union: Studies of the European Commission*, 2nd edn (Basingstoke: Macmillan): 51–72.

McMahon, J. (1998) *The Development Co-operation Policy of the EC* (London: Kluwer Law International).

McNamara, K. R. (1998) *Currency of Ideas* (Ithaca, NY: Cornell University Press).

McNamara, K. R. and Meunier, S. (2002) 'Between National Sovereignty and International Power: What External Voice for the Euro?', *International Affairs*, 78 (4): 849–68.

Meinhof, U. and Galasinksi, D. (2002) 'Reconfiguring East–West Identities: Generational Discourses in German and Polish Border Communities', *Journal of Ethnic and Migration Studies*, 28 (1): 63.

Mergos, G. (1998) 'Agricultural Issues in Integration of CEECs in the EU', in N. Baltas, *et al.* (eds), *Economic Interdependence and Cooperation in Europe*, (Heidelberg: Springer-Verlag): 181–98.

Mersch, Y. (2003) *The Reform of the Governing Council of the ECB*, speech given at the European Banking and Financial Forum in Prague, 25 March, http://www.bcl.lu/html/en/discourse_mersch_20030325/discourse_mersch_20030325.html

Messerlin, P. (2001) *Measuring the Costs of Protection in Europe* (Washington, DC: International Institute for Economics).

Meunier, S. (1998) 'Divided but United: European Trade Policy Integration and EC-US Agricultural Negotiations in the Uruguay Round', in C. Rhodes (ed.) *The European Union in the World Community* (Boulder: Lynne Rienner).

Meunier, S. and Nicolaïdis, K. (1999) 'Who Speaks for Europe? The Delegation of Trade Authority in the EU', *Journal of Common Market Studies*, 37 (3): 477–501.

Michaux, V. (2002) 'EU Enlargement: A Brake on Development Cooperation, *The Courier ACP-EU*, July–August: 18–19.

Miles, L. (1995) *Enlarging the European Union: A Theoretical Perspective*, CEUS Research Paper 1/95 (Hull: Centre for European Union Studies, The University of Hull).

Miles, L. (2003) 'Editorial: Towards a "Hub and Spokes Europe" ' in L. Miles, (ed.) *The European Union: Annual Review 2002/2003, Journal of Common Market Studies*, 41: 1–11.

Miles, L. and Redmond, J. (1996) 'Enlarging the European Union: The Erosion of Federalism?', *Cooperation and Conflict*, 31 (3): 285–309.

Miles, L., Redmond, J. and Schwok, R. (1995) 'Integration Theory and Enlargement of the European Union', in S. Rhodes and S. Mazey (eds) *The State of the European Union, Volume 3: Building a European Polity?* (Boulder, CO: Lynne Rienner).

Milward, A. (1992) *The European Rescue of the Nation-State* (Berkeley: University of California Press).

Ministry of Foreign Affairs Hungary (2003) 'The Stability Pact', http://www.kulugyminiszterium.hu/Kulugyminiszterium/EN/printable (accessed 30 May 2003).

Ministry of Foreign Affairs of the Republic of Cyprus (2002) 'Cyprus and the Common Foreign and Security Policy (CFSP)', www.mfa.gov.cy/mfa/mfa.nsf/EUCFSP_ESDP

Missiroli, A. (ed.) (2002) *Bigger EU, Wider CFSP, Stronger ESDP? The View from Central Europe* (Paris: Institute for Security Studies).

Mitsilegas, V. (2002) 'The Implementation of the EU Acquis on Illegal Immigration by the Candidate Countries of Central and Eastern Europe: Challenges and Contradictions', *Journal of Ethnic and Migration Studies*, 28 (4): 665–82.

Moberg, A. (2002) 'The Nice Treaty and Voting Rules in the Council', *Journal of Common Market Studies*, 40 (2): 259–82.

Moore, M. (1999) *Trade For Development – The Way Ahead*, address to the Group of 77 Ministerial Meeting, Marrakesh, Tuesday 14 September, http://www.wto.org/english/news_e/spmm_e/spmm04_e.htm

Moravcsik, A. (1993) 'Preferences and Power in the European Community: A Liberal Intergovernmentalist Approach', *Journal of Common Market Studies*, 31 (4): 473–524.

Moravcsik, A. (1995) 'Liberal Intergovernmentalism and Integration: A Rejoinder', *Journal of Common Market Studies*, 33(4): 611–28.

Moravcsik, A. (1998) *The Choice for Europe: Social Purpose and State Power From Messina to Maastricht* (London: UCL Press).

Moravcsik, A. (2002) 'In Defence of the "Democratic Deficit": Reassessing Legitimacy in the European Union', *Journal of Common Market Studies*, 40 (4): 603–24.

Moravcsik, A. and Vachudova, A. (2002) 'Bargaining Among Unequals: Enlargement and the Future of European Integration', *EUSA Review*, 15 (4): 1, 3.

Moreira, J. (2000) 'Cohesion and Citizenship in European Union Cultural Policy', *Journal of Common Market Studies*, 38 (3): 449–70.

Murray, A. (2003) *The Lisbon Scorecard III: The Status of Economic Reform in the Enlarging EU* (London: Centre for European Reform).

Natalucci, F. M., and Ravenna, F. (2002) *The Road to Adopting the Euro: Monetary Policy and Exchange Rate Regimes in EU Candidate Countries*, Board of Governors of the Federal Reserve System, International Finance Discussion Paper, No. 741, December.

Nello, S. and Smith, K. (1998) *The European Union and Central and Eastern Europe* (Aldershot: Ashgate).

Newman, M. (1996) *Democracy, Sovereignty and the European Union* (London: Hurst and Company).

Nicolaïdis, K. and Howse, R. (2002) ' "This is My Eutopia . . . ." Narrative as Power', *Journal of Common Market Studies*, 40 (4): 767–92.

Nielson, P. (2003), 'Keynote Address' to the Conference on "The Enlarged European Union – Partner of the Developing World', www.dse.de

Norgaard, A. S. (1996) 'Rediscovering Reasonable Rationality in Institutional Analysis', *European Journal of Political Research*, 29 (January): 31–57.

Nugent, N. (1997) 'Cyprus and the European Union: A Particularly Difficult Membership Application', *Mediterranean Politics*, 2 (3): 53–75.

Nugent, N. (1999) *The Government and Politics of the European Union*, 4th edn (Basingstoke: Macmillan).

Nugent, N. (2000) 'EU Enlargement and the Cyprus Problem', *Journal of Common Market Studies*, 38 (1): 131–50.

Nugent, N. (2003) *The Government and Politics of the European Union*, 5th edn (Basingstoke: Palgrave).

Nuttall, S. (1992) *European Political Co-operation* (Oxford: Clarendon Press).

Occhipinti, J. D. (2003) *The Politics of EU Police Cooperation: Toward a European FBI?* (Boulder: Lynne Rienner).

Occhipinti, J. D. (2004) 'Police and Judicial Cooperation', in D. Dinan and M. Green-Cowles (eds) *Developments in the European Union 2* (New York: Palgrave).

Odell, J. and Eichengreen, B. (1998) 'The United States, the ITO, and the WTO: Exit Options, Agent Slack, and Presidential Leadership', in A. Kruger (ed.) *The WTO as an International Organisation* (Chicago: The University of Chicago Press): 181–209.

Odermatt, P. (1991) 'The Use of Symbols in the Drive for European Integration', in J. Leersen and M. Spiering (eds) *Yearbook of European Studies*, Volume 4 (Amsterdam: Radopi Press).

Official Journal (1995) *Council Decision (95/2/EC, Euratom, ECSC) of 1 January 1995 Determining the Order in Which the Office of President of the Council Shall be Held*, L1, 1 January.

Official Journal (2001a) *Treaty of Nice Amending the Treaty on European Union, the Treaties Establishing the European Communities and Certain Related Acts*, C80, 10 March.

Official Journal (2001b) *Reply of the Council Dated 27 September 2001 to Written Question E-1109/01 by Jens-Peter Bonde (EDD) to the Council (9 April 2001)*, C364, 20 December.

Official Journal (2002) Council Decision (2002/105/EC, ECSC, Euratom) of 28 January 2002 on the Order in Which the Office of President of the Council Shall be Held, L39, 9 February.

Official Journal (2003) Decision (2003/223/EC) of the Council, Meeting in the Composition of Heads of State or Government on 21 March 2003, on an Amendment to Article 10.2 of the Statute of the European System of Central Banks and European Central Bank, L83, 1 April.

Ojanen, H. (1999) 'How to Customise Your Union: Finland and the "Northern Dimension of the EU" ', in T. Forsberg and H. Vogt (eds) *Northern Dimension Yearbook 1999* (Helsinki: Finnish Institute of International Affairs).

Olson, M. (1965) *The Logic of Collective Action* (Cambridge: Harvard University Press).

Open Society Institute EU Accession Monitoring Programme (2002) *Corruption and Anti-Corruption Policy* (Budapest: Open Society Institute, www.eumap.org).

Ostry, S. (2000) *WTO: Institutional Design for Better Governance. Efficiency, Equity and Legitimacy: The Multilateral Trading System at the Millennium,* paper presented at the Kennedy School of Government, Harvard, 2–3 June.

Paarlberg, R. (1997) 'Agricultural Policy Reform and the Uruguay Round: Synergistic Linkage in a Two-Level Game?' *International Organization,* 51 (3): 413–44.

Pace, R. (2001) *Microstate Security in the Global System: EU-Malta Relations* (Valletta: Midsea Books).

Petersen, J. and Sjursen, H. (eds) (1998) *A Common Foreign Policy for Europe? Competing Visions of the CFSP* (London: Routledge).

Peterson, J. (1995) 'Decision-Making in the European Union: Towards a Framework for Analysis', *Journal of European Public Policy,* 2 (1): 61–93.

Peterson, J. and Bomberg, E. (1998) 'Northern Enlargement and EU Decision-Making', in P.-H. Laurent and M. Maresceau (eds) *The State of the European Union, Volume 4: Deepening and Widening* (Boulder, CO.: Lynne Rienner).

Peterson, J. and Bomberg, E. (1999) *Decision-Making in the European Union* (Basingstoke: Macmillan).

Philippart, E. and Dhian Ho, M. S. (2001) *Pedalling Against the Wind. Strategies to Strengthen the EU's Capacity to Act in the Context of Enlargement* (The Hague: Scientific Council for Government Policy, Working Documents – W115).

Phinnemore D. and McGowan, L. (2002) *A Dictionary of the European Union* (London: Europa Publications).

Piening, C. (1997) *Global Europe. The European Union in World Affairs* (Boulder, CO: Lynne Rienner).

Pierson, P. (1996) 'The Path to European Integration: A Historical Institutionalist Analysis', *Comparative Political Studies,* 29 (2): 123–63.

Pietras, J. (1998) 'The Role of the WTO for Economies in Transition', in A. Krueger (ed.) *The WTO as an International Organization* (Chicago: University of Chicago Press): 353–65.

Pindar, J. (1995) *European Community: The Building of a Union,* 2nd edn (Oxford: Oxford University Press).

Plechanovova, B. (2003) 'The Treaty of Nice and the Distribution of Votes in the Council – Voting Power Consequences for the EU after the Oncoming Enlargement', *European Integration On-Line Papers,* 7 (6), http://eiop.or.at/eiop/texte/2003-006a.htm

Podkaminer, L. (2001) 'Wages Prices and Exchange Rates: Competitiveness vs. Convergence', in M. Dauderstädt and L. Witte (eds) *Cohesive Growth in the Enlarging Euroland* (Bonn: Friedrich-Ebert-Stiftung): 117–29.

Polish Ministry of Foreign Affairs (2003) *Non-Paper with Polish Proposals Concerning Policy Towards New Eastern Neighbours after EU Enlargement,* February.

Poole, P. (2003) *Europe's Eastern Enlargement* (Westport, CT: Praeger Publishers).

Prague Business Journal (internet) (Prague: New World Publishing).

Press Releases of the Delegation of the European Commission in Poland (2002) 15 December, http://www.cie.gov.pl/eng.nsf/2/index

Preston, C. (1995) 'Obstacles to EU Enlargement: The Classical Community Method and the Prospects For a Wider Europe', *Journal of Common Market Studies*, 33 (3)): 451–63.

Preston, C. (1997) *Enlargement and Integration in the European Union* (London: Routledge).

Pridham, G (2002) 'EU Enlargement and Consolidating Democracy in Post Communist States', *Journal of Common Market Studies*, 40 (5): 953–73.

Prodi, R. (2003) *South-Eastern Europe's Turn*, speech delivered at the South-Eastern European Cooperation Process Summit, Belgrade, 9 April.

Puchala, D. J. (1999) 'Institutionalism, Intergovernmentalism and European Integration: A Review Article', *Journal of Common Market Studies*, 37 (2): 317–31.

Putnam, R. (1993) *Making Democracy Work* (Princeton: Princeton University Press).

Raffer K. and Singer, H. W. (1996) *The Foreign Aid Business: Economic Assistance and Development Co-operation* (Cheltenham: Edward Elgar).

Redmond, J. (ed.) (1994) *Prospective Europeans* (London: Harvester-Wheatsheaf).

Redmond, J. (ed.) (1997) *The 1995 Enlargement of the European Union* (Aldershot: Ashgate).

Redmond, J. and Rosenthal, G. (1998a) 'Introduction', in J. Redmond and G. Rosenthal (eds), *The Expanding European Union: Past, Present, Future*, (Boulder, CO: Lynne Rienner): 1–14.

Redmond, J. and Rosenthal, G. (eds) (1998b) (eds.) *The Expanding European Union: Past, Present and Future* (Boulder, CO: Lynne Rienner).

Reed, J. (2003) 'Foreign Policy: Bringing "Ostpolitik to the EU Table" ', *Financial Times*, 14 April.

Richelle, K. (2002) *EU Enlargement and European Development Policy for a Changing World*, speech delivered at the EADI Conference, Ljubljana, 19–21 September.

Richter, S (2002) *The EU Enlargement Process: Current State of Play and Stumbling Blocks* (Vienna, The Vienna Institute for International Economic Studies, http://www.wiiw.ac.at/summCA17.html)

Robson, P (1998): *The Economics of International Integration* (London: Routledge).

Rosamond, B. (2000) *Theories of European Integration* (London: Macmillan).

Rosamond, B. (2003) 'New Theories of European Integration', in M. Cini (ed.) *European Union Politics* (Oxford: Oxford University Press).

Rupel, D. (2002) Presentation to the Committee on Foreign Policy of the Slovenian National Assembly, www.sigov.si/mzz/ang/speeches/rupels_presentation.html

Rupel, D. (2003) Address at the University of Nitra, Slovakia, 14 May, http://www.sigov.si/mzz/eng/index.html

Sabatier, P. A. and Jenkins-Smith, H. C. (eds) (1993) *Policy Change and Learning: An Advocacy Coalition Approach* (Boulder, CO and Oxford: Westview Press).

Sabin, R. (2000) 'Mbeki's HIV Stand Angers Delegates/Hundreds Walk Out on His Speech', *San Francisco Chronicle*, 10 July.

Samuelson, P. A. (1964) 'Theoretical Notes on Trade Problems', *Review of Economics and Statistics*, 46 (2): 147–54.

Samuelson, P. A. (1994) 'Faccts of Balassa-Samuelson 30 Years Later', *Review of International Economics*, 2 (3): 201–26.

Sandholtz, W. (1996) 'Membership Matters: Limits of the Functional Approach to European Institutions', *Journal of Common Market Studies*, 34 (3).

Sapir, A. *et al.* (2003) *An Agenda for a Growing Europe: Making the EU Economic System Deliver*, report of an Independent High-Level Study Group established on the initiative of the President of the European Commission (Brussels: Commission of the European Communities).

Scharpf, F. W. (1988) 'The Joint-Decision Trap: Lessons from German Federalism and European Integration', *Public Administration*, 66: 239–278.

Schattschneider, E. (1960) *The Semi-Sovereign People* (New York: Holt, Reinhart, and Winston).

Schifferes, S. (2002) 'Analysis: Who Gains from Immigration?', *BBC News*, http://news.bbc.co.uk.

Schimmelfennig, F. (2001) 'The Community Trap: Liberal Norms, Rhetorical Action, and the Eastern Enlargement of the European Union', *International Organization*, 55 (1): 47–80.

Schimmelfennig, F. (2002) 'Liberal Community and Enlargement: An Event History Analysis', *Journal of European Public Policy*, 9 (4): 598–626.

Schimmelfennig F. and Sedelmeier, U. (2002) 'Theorizing EU Enlargement: Research Focus, Hypotheses, and the State of Research', *Journal of European Public Policy*, 9 (4): 500–28.

Schmitter, P. (1969) 'Three Neo-Functionalist Hypotheses about International Integration', *International Organization*, 23 (1): 161–66.

Schmitter, P. C. (1996) 'Examining the Present Euro-Polity with the Help of Past Theories' in G. Marks, F. W. Scharpf, P. C. Schmitter, W. Streeck (eds) *Governance in the European Union* (London: Sage).

Schmitter, P. (2001) 'What is There to Legitimize in the European Union . . . and How Might This be Accomplished?' *Jean Monnet Working Paper*, No 6/01 www.jeanmonnetprogram.org/papers/01/011401_html

Schreyer, M. (2003) *Making the Enlarged Union a Success*, speech given at the seminar 'The New Financial Framework, the Challenging EU Road for the Future,' at the Finnish Ministry of Finance, March.

Schuwirth, R. (2002) 'Hitting the Helsinki Headline Goal', *NATO Review*, 50: 3, http://www.nato.int/docu/review/2002/issue3/english/art4_pr.html

Schwimmer, W. (2001) 'Statement on the Occasion of the Opening of the Second Part of the Colloquy on the European Identity', Council of Europe, 20 September.

Schwimmer, W. (2002) 'Statement on the Occasion of the Opening of the Third Part of the Colloquy on the European Identity', Council of Europe, 18 April.

Sedelmeier, U. (2000) 'Eastern Enlargement: Risk, Rationality, and Role-Compliance', in M. Green Cowles and M. Smith (eds), *The State of the European Union: Volume 5 – Risks, Reform, Resistance, and Revival*, (Oxford: Oxford University Press): 164–85.

Sergounin, A. (2001) 'EU Enlargement and Kaliningrad: The Russian Perspective', in L. D. Fairlie and A. Sergounin (eds) *Are Borders Barriers? EU Enlargement and the Russian Region of Kaliningrad* (Helsinki: UPI & IEP): 139–90.

Shepsle, K. (1989) 'Studying Institutions: Some Lessons from the Rational Choice Approach', *Journal of Theoretical Politics*, 1(2): 131–47.

Shore, C. (1994) 'Citizens' Europe and the Construction of European Identity', in V. Goddard, J. Llobera, and C. Shore (eds) *The Anthropology of Europe: Identities and Boundaries in Conflict* (Oxford: Bera): 275–98.

Sjöstedt, G. (1977) *The External Role of the European Community* (Farnborough: Gower).

Sjursen, H. (2002) 'Why Expand? The Question of Legitimacy and Justification in the EU's Enlargement Policy', *Journal of Common Market Studies*, 40 (3): 491–513.

Smith, A. (1992) 'National Identity and the Idea of European Unity', *International Affairs*, 68 (1): 55–76.

Smith, K. E. (2003) 'The Evolution and Application of EU Membership Conditionality', in M. Cremona (ed.) *The Enlargement of the European Union* (Oxford: Oxford University Press): 105–39.

Smith, M. (2003) 'Small States or New Democracies? The East European Contribution to the Convention on the Future of Europe', unpublished paper presented at the conference on European Union Enlargement: An Eastern Perspective, University of Oklahoma EU Center, 7 April.

Stubb, A. (2002) *Negotiating Flexibility in the European Union* (Basingstoke: Palgrave).

Stubb, A. C. G. (1996) 'A Categorization of Differentiated Integration', *Journal of Common Market Studies*, 34 (2): 283–295.

Task Force Enlargement (2002) *Statistical Annex: Basic Statistics and Trade* (Luxembourg: Parliamentary Documentation Centre of the European Parliament).

Teasdale, A. (1993) 'The Life and Death of the Luxembourg Compromise', *Journal of Common Market Studies*, 31(4): 567–79.

Theiler, T. (1999) 'The European Union and the "European Dimension" in Schools: Theory and Evidence', *European Integration*, 21: 307–41.

Thelen, K. and Steinmo, S. (1992) 'Historical Institutionalism in Comparative Politics' in S. Steinmo, K. Thelen, and F. Longstreth (eds) *Historical Institutionalism in Comparative Analysis* (Cambridge: Cambridge University Press).

Third World Network (2001) *Developing Countries Say 'No' to Negotiations on 'New Issues'*, extracts of statements by WTO Ambassadors, 2–3 October,http://www.twnside.org.sg/title/twr133e.htm .

Tönnies, F. (1957) *Community and Society: Gemeinschaft und Gesselschaft*, C. Loomis (trans. and ed.) (Lansing: Michigan State Press).

Transparency International (2003) *Global Corruption Report 2003* (Berlin: Transparency International, www.globalcorruptionreport.org).

Treaty of Amsterdam Amending the Treaty on European Union, the Treaties Establishing The European Communities and Related Acts (1997) in *Official Journal of the European Communities*, C340. http://europa.eu.int/eur-lex/en/treaties/dat/amsterdam.html

Treaty Establishing the European Community (2003) (Consolidated Version), in *Official Journal of the European Communities*, C325, http://europa.eu.int/eur-lex/en/treaties/dat/ec_cons_treaty_en.pdf

Treaty on European Union (2003) (Consolidated Version), in *Official Journal of the European Communities*, C325, http://europa.eu.int/eur-lex/en/treaties/dat/nice_treaty_en.pdf

Trialog (2002) *Development Cooperation in the Context of EU Enlargement* (Vienna: Trialog).

Tsinisizelis, J. and Chryssochoou, D. (1998) 'The European Union: Trends in Theory and Reform', in A. Weale and M. Nentwich (eds), *Political Theory and the European Union: Legitimacy, Constitutional Choice and Citizenship* (London: Routledge).

Uçarer, E. M. (2001) 'From the Sidelines to Center Stage: Sidekick No More? The European Commission in Justice and Home Affairs', *European Integration Online Papers*.

United Nations Conference on Trade and Development – UNCTAD (2001) *Positive Gains Seen For LDCs if Quad Implements Full Quota and Duty-Free Market Access*, Press Release, 17 May, http://ldc3.unctad.org/ldc3/interactive/is_quad.pdf .

Usher, J. (2002) 'Enhanced Cooperation or Flexibility in the Post-Nice Era', in A. Arnull and D. Wincott (eds), *Accountability and Legitimacy in the European Union* (Oxford: Oxford University Press): 97–112.

Vahl, R. (1997) *Leadership in Disguise: The Role of the European Commission in EC Decision Making on Agriculture in the Uruguay Round* (Aldershot: Ashgate).

Valtasaari, J. (1999) *The EU's Northern Dimension, Union's Strategy Towards Russia and Our Views on the Forthcoming WTO Millennium Round*, speech to the European Economic and Social Committee, Vaasa, 6 October, http://formin.finland.fi/english/.

Van Ham, P. (2000) 'Identity Beyond the State: The Case of the European Union', *COPRI Paper*, George C. Marshall European Center for Security Studies.

Van Ham, P. (2001) *European Integration and the Postmodern Condition: Governance, Democracy, Identity* (New York: Routledge).

Van Kersbergen, K. (2000) 'Political Allegiance and European Integration', *European Journal of Political Research*, 37 (1): 1–17.

Van Reisen, M. (2002) *The Enlarged European Union and the Developing World: What Future?*, paper presented at the EADI conference, Ljubljana, 19–21 September.

Villa Faber Group on the Future of the European Union (2001) *Thinking Enlarged: The Accession Countries and the Future of the European Union: A Strategy for Reform*, (Bertelesmann Foundation and Center for Applied Policy Research), October.

Wall Street Journal (daily) (New York: Dow Jones and Company).

Wallace, C. (2002) 'Opening and Closing Borders: Migration and Mobility in East-Central Europe', *Journal of Ethnic and Migration Studies*, 28 (4): 603–25.

Wallace, H. (1996) 'The Politics and Policy of the EU: The Challenge of Governance' in H. Wallace and W. Wallace (eds) *Policy-Making in the European Union*, (Oxford: Oxford University Press) 3–39.

Wallace, H. (2002) 'Enlarging the European Union: Reflections on the Challenge of Analysis', *Journal of European Public Policy*, 9 (4): 658–65.

Wallace, W. (2003) *Looking After the Neighbourhood: Responsibilities for the EU-25*, policy paper 4, (Paris: Notre Europe – Groupement D'Etudes et de Recherches).

Walzer, M. (1983) *Spheres of Justice* (New York: Basic Books).

Warleigh, A. (2002) *Flexible Integration: Which Model for the European Union?* (London: Continuum).

Wayne, A. (2001) *EU Enlargement and Transatlantic Economic Relations*, speech delivered at the Conference 'Europe's Continuing Enlargement: Implications for the Transatlantic Partnership', 22 October, John Hopkins University, Washington DC, http://www.useu.be/Categori.../Oct2201StateDeptEUenlargement.htm

Weber Shandwick (2003) *Interactive Guide to the European Union*, www.webershandwick-eu.com

Weiler, J. (1996) *Legitimacy and Democracy of Union Governance: The 1996 Intergovernmental Agenda and Beyond*, Working Paper No. 22. (Oslo: Arena).

Weiler, J. (1998) *To Be a European Citizen – Eros and Civilization*, University of Wisconsin – Madison, Center for European Studies Working Papers Series, Special Edition, Spring 1998, http://uw-madison-ces.org/papers/weiler.pdf

Wessels, W. (2001) 'Nice Results: The Millennium IGC in the EU's Evolution', *Journal of Common Market Studies*, 39 (2): 197–219.

Wessels, W. (2003) 'Germany and the Future of the EU: Vision, Vocation, and Mission', AICGS/German–American Dialogue Working Paper Series (Washington, DC: American Institute for Contemporary German Studies).

White, B. (2001) *Understanding European Foreign Policy* (Basingstoke: Palgrave).

White, P. (2002) 'Portuguese Protest that Eurozone Austerity Will Hit the Poorest Hard', *Financial Times*, 29 July.

White, S., McAllister. I. and Light, M. (2002) 'Enlargement and the New Outsiders', *Journal of Common Market Studies*, 40 (1): 135–53.

Whitman, R. A. (1998) *From Civilian Power to Superpower? The International Identity of the European Union* (Basingstoke: Macmillan).

Wiessala, G. (2002) *The European Union and Asian Countries* (Sheffield: Sheffield Academic Press).

Willis, D. (1996) 'When East Goes West: The Political Economy of European Re-Integration in the Post-Cold War Era' in M. Wintle (ed.) *Culture and Identity in Europe: Perceptions of Divergence and Unity in Past and Present* (Aldershot: Avebury): 146–73.

Wincott, D. (1995) 'Institutional Interaction and European Integration: Towards an Everyday Critique of Liberal Intergovernmentalism', *Journal of Common Market Studies*, 33(4): 597–609.

Wonnacott, R. (1990) 'U.S. Hub-and-Spoke Bilaterals and the Multilateral Trading System', *Commentary: The NAFTA Papers*, No. 23 (Toronto: CD Howe Institute).

World Trade Organization (2000a) *Trade Policy Reviews: First Press Release, Secretariat and Government Summaries*, Press Release, PRESS/TPRB/136, Poland, 26 June, http://www.wto.org/english/tratop_e/tpr_e/tp136_e.htm

World Trade Organization (2000b) *Trade Policy Review: European Union 2001*, Volumes 1 and 2.

World Trade Organization (2002) *International Trade Statistics 2002*.

WRR, The Netherlands Scientific Council for Government Policy (2001) *Towards a Pan-European Union* (The Hague: WRR).

Wyplosz, C. (2002) *The Path to the Euro for Enlargement Countries*, Briefing Paper for the Economic and Monetary Affairs Committee of the European

Parliament, Second Quarter, http://www.europarl.eu.int/comparl/econ/
pdf/emu/speeches/20020521/wyplosz.pdf

Young, A, Holmes, P. and Rollo, J. (2000) 'The European Trade Agenda after
Seattle', *Sussex European Institute Working Papers Series*, No. 37,
November.

Young, A. (1998) 'Interpretation and 'Soft Integration' in the Adaptation of the
European Community's Foreign Economic Policy', *Sussex European
Institute Working Papers Series*, No. 29, October.

Zaborowski, M. and Longhurst, K. (2003) 'America's Protégé in the East? The
Emergence of Poland as a Regional Leader', *International Affairs* 79 (5):
1009–28.

Zielonka, J. (2001) 'How New Enlarged Borders Will Reshape the European
Union', *Journal of Common Market Studies*, 39 (3): 507–36.

Zielonka, J. and Mair, P. (2002) 'Introduction: Diversity and Adaptation in the
Enlarged European Union', in P. Mair and J. Zielonka (eds) *The Enlarged
European Union: Diversity and Adaptation* (London: Frank Cass).

Zielonka, J. and Mair, P. (2002) 'Introduction: Diversity and Adaptation in the
Enlarged European Union', *West European Politics*, 25 (2): 1–18.

Žižek, S. (1998) 'For a Leftist Appropriation of the European Legacy', *Journal
of Political Ideologies*, 3(1) 63–78

Zoellick, R. (2001) *American Trade Leadership: What is at Stake?*, speech
delivered to the Institute for International Economics, Washington, DC, 24
September, www.ustr.gov/speech-test/zoellick/zoellick_9.PDF.

Zweifel, T. (2002) '. . . Who is Without Sin Cast the First Stone: The EU's
Democratic Deficit in Comparison', *Journal of European Public Policy*, 9
(5): 812–840.

Index